Frommer's

Běijīng

3rd Edition

by Graeme Smith, Josh Chin &
Peter Neville-Hadley

Here's what the critics say about Frommer's:

"Amazingly easy to use. Very portable, very complete."

—*Booklist*

"Detailed, accurate, and easy-to-read information for all price ranges."
—*Glamour Magazine*

"Hotel information is close to encyclopedic."

—*Des Moines Sunday Register*

"Frommer's Guides have a way of giving you a real feel for a place."
—*Knight Ridder Newspapers*

WILEY

Wiley Publishing, Inc.

Published by:

Wiley Publishing, Inc.

111 River St.
Hoboken, NJ 07030-5744

ISBN 0-7645-3873-X
ISSN 1520-5568

Editor: Lisa Torrance Duffy
Production Editor: M. Faunette Johnston
Cartographer: John Decamillis, Nicholas Trotter
Photo Editor: Richard Fox
Production by Wiley Indianapolis Composition Services

For information on our other products and services or to obtain technical support, please contact our Customer Care Department within the U.S. at 800/762-2974, outside the U.S. at 317/572-3993 or fax 317/572-4002.

Wiley also publishes its books in a variety of electronic formats. Some content that appears in print may not be available in electronic formats.

Manufactured in the United States of America

5 4 3 2

Contents

5   Where to Dine   78

by Josh Chin

6   Exploring Běijīng   103

by Graeme Smith

7   Běijīng Strolls   150

by Graeme Smith

8   Shopping   163

by Graeme Smith

9 Běijīng After Dark   179

by Josh Chin

10 The Great Wall & Other Side Trips from Běijīng   191

by Graeme Smith

Appendix A: Běijīng in Depth   206

by Peter Neville-Hadley and Josh Chin

Appendix B: The Chinese Language   225

by Peter Neville-Hadley

Index   234

List of Maps

About the Authors

Graeme Smith spent 2 years pacing the corridors of Peking and Tsinghua universities in search of enlightenment. He was lured away from the comforts of academic life to contribute to *Frommer's China,* 1st Edition, and then wrote most of what is a brand-new *Frommer's Běijīng,* 3rd Edition, from his base in a traditional courtyard house. This was bulldozed in mid-production, giving him first-hand experience of Běijīng's rapid redevelopment. He sat out SARS, waiting for the city to reopen so this book could be completed, and has now taken up a research position at the Contemporary China Centre of the Australian National University.

Josh Chin has just left Běijīng after 2½ years spent as a freelance journalist and travel writer, and as copyeditor for the government-run *China Daily,* having earlier studied Mandarin at Peking University. He contributed the Běijīng and Northeast chapters to *Frommer's China,* 1st Edition. Time otherwise ill-spent in bars, clubs, music venues, and cinemas, has led to a particularly well-researched After Dark chapter for *Frommer's Běijīng,* 3rd Edition, as well as appendix entries on film and music, and substantial contributions to the dining and accommodations chapters. He can be contacted through **www.chinfamous.com**.

Peter Neville-Hadley, development editor of *Frommer's China,* 1st Edition, also supervised this book, wrote the practical chapters, half the appendix entries, the language section, and contributed to most of the other chapters. A former resident of Běijīng, he's the author of Cadogan Guides' *China: The Silk Routes* and *Běijīng,* and has written on China for *Time, The Sunday Times* (U.K.), the *National Post* (Canada), and many others. He's now working on an account of travel around China's treaty ports for publication in 2005. He moderates *The Oriental-List,* an Internet discussion list dealing with travel in China (see *www.neville-hadley.com*) and can be reached at **pnhpublic@shaw.ca**.

An Invitation to the Reader

In researching this book, we discovered many wonderful places—hotels, restaurants, shops, and more. We're sure you'll find others. Please tell us about them, so we can share the information with your fellow travelers in upcoming editions. If you were disappointed with a recommendation, we'd love to know that, too. Please write to:

Frommer's Běijīng, 3rd Edition
Wiley Publishing, Inc. • 111 River St. • Hoboken, NJ 07030-5744

An Additional Note

Please be advised that travel information is subject to change at any time—and this is especially true of prices. We therefore suggest that you write or call ahead for confirmation when making your travel plans. The authors, editors, and publisher cannot be held responsible for the experiences of readers while traveling. Your safety is important to us, however, so we encourage you to stay alert and be aware of your surroundings. Keep a close eye on cameras, purses, and wallets, all favorite targets of thieves and pickpockets.

Other Great Guides for Your Trip:

Frommer's China

Frommer's China: The 50 Most Memorable Trips

Frommer's Hong Kong, Beijing & Shanghai

Frommer's Hong Kong

Frommer's Shanghai

Frommer's Star Ratings, Icons & Abbreviations

Every hotel, restaurant, and attraction listing in this guide has been ranked for quality, value, service, amenities, and special features using a **star-rating system.** In country, state, and regional guides, we also rate towns and regions to help you narrow down your choices and budget your time accordingly. Hotels and restaurants are rated on a scale of zero (recommended) to three stars (exceptional). Attractions, shopping, nightlife, towns, and regions are rated according to the following scale: zero stars (recommended), one star (highly recommended), two stars (very highly recommended), and three stars (must-see).

In addition to the star-rating system, we also use **seven feature icons** that point you to the great deals, in-the-know advice, and unique experiences that separate travelers from tourists. Throughout the book, look for:

Finds	Special finds—those places only insiders know about
Fun Fact	Fun facts—details that make travelers more informed and their trips more fun
Kids	Best bets for kids, and advice for the whole family
Moments	Special moments—those experiences that memories are made of
Overrated	Places or experiences not worth your time or money
Tips	Insider tips—great ways to save time and money
Value	Great values—where to get the best deals

The following **abbreviations** are used for credit cards:

AE	American Express	DISC	Discover	V	Visa
DC	Diners Club	MC	MasterCard		

Frommers.com

Now that you have the guidebook to a great trip, visit our website at **www.frommers.com** for travel information on more than 3,000 destinations. With features updated regularly, we give you instant access to the most current trip-planning information available. At Frommers.com, you'll also find the best prices on airfares, accommodations, and car rentals—and you can even book travel online through our travel booking partners. At Frommers.com, you'll also find the following:

- Online updates to our most popular guidebooks
- Vacation sweepstakes and contest giveaways
- Newsletter highlighting the hottest travel trends
- Online travel message boards with featured travel discussions

What's New in Běijīng

by Peter Neville-Hadley, Josh Chin, and Graeme Smith

If there's one thing that remains constant in Běijīng, it's that nothing ever remains the same. Returning visitors cry, "Where am I? And what have you done with the *real* Běijīng?" Blame the imminent Olympics for the current accelerated rate of change, and go as soon as you can.

GETTING TO KNOW BĚIJĪNG Perhaps a better indicator of the state of the economy than unverifiable figures provided by the government, the toll on the **Airport Expressway** has fallen from ¥15 ($1.90) to ¥10 ($1.25) because it was too expensive (according to taxi drivers). The Fourth Ring Road is complete, and taxi drivers taking you to hotels along Dōng Cháng'ān Jiē and Jiànguó Mén Nèi/Wài Dàjiē will now wisely take it south from the Airport Expressway. But don't use it to drive around the city—it runs closer in on the east and west sides than it does on the north or south. An even further-flung Fifth Ring Road is under construction.

The metro system has the new light-rail **Line 13,** which makes a northern arc from Xī Zhí Mén to Dōng Zhí Mén and provides an alternative method of reaching the Summer Palace (with a short taxi ride) and some other rural sights. Fares have risen to ¥3 (35¢) on the original two lines, and a ticket, *huànchéng piào,* allowing you to start from or switch to Line 13, is ¥5 (65¢). Proper machine-readable tickets are on their way, after which it will cost ¥2 (25¢) for the first three stops on any line, and ¥1 (10¢) for every three stops after that. Vast new rail/metro/light-rail/bus interchanges are under construction at Dōng Zhí Mén and Xī Zhí Mén.

On the frontiers of hygiene, the nightmarish old public toilets are closing for good, at least in downtown areas, and are to be replaced by new or portable units with flush or chemical appliances.

WHERE TO STAY Competition is heating up in the **five-star** market with the arrival of several familiar names from the West, and more of the top-rank Asian brands. **Grand Hyatt Běijīng** nabbed Běijīng's best address, in the vast Oriental Plaza complex at the junction of Wángfǔjǐng and Dōng Cháng'ān Jiē. (Hyatt's top brand, Park Hyatt, is also on the way.) **The Marco Polo** in Xī Dān is as comfortable as any other five-star, and as well-placed for public transport, shopping, and major sights. Its intimate, beautifully designed public spaces make it the nearest thing to a boutique hotel in Běijīng, although it remains largely undiscovered. **Renaissance Běijīng,** just off the northeast Third Ring Road and handy for the Airport Expressway, offers small-scale elegance. Guests flying out on Air China can use the lobby check-in.

China World Hotel has just had a substantial top-to-bottom refurbishment. (Several Chinese-run hotels, including the Kūnlún and Prime, not included in this volume, have had such lavish revamps that they might make the next edition.) The **Palace**

Hotel has had a major refurbishment and in September 2003 rebranded itself **The Peninsula Palace Běijīng,** finally revealing its connections to famous properties in Hong Kong, Bangkok, New York, and elsewhere.

Converted *hútòng* courtyards *(sìhéyuàn)* are the most interesting **mid-range options.** The latest addition, **Héjìng Fǔ Bīnguǎn,** is the former residence of a Qiánlóng emperor's daughter in Dōng Chéng.

Budget options in Běijīng were once restricted to a cluster of dire hotels on the South Third Ring Road. The arrival of Youth Hostel International has changed that. Simple but clean lodgings are now ubiquitous. The best choices are **Far East Youth Hostel** and **Fēiyīng Bīnguǎn** in the south, as well as the brand-new **Gōngtǐ Youth Hostel** in Cháoyáng. Several of the old imperial-era brothels in the *hútòng* south of Qián Mén have been reinvented as hotels, and you may feel more of a frisson staying here than in the average budget digs. **Shǎnxī Xiàng Dì'èr Bīnguǎn** and **Qián Mén Chánggōng Jiǔdiàn** are the best restored of these.

See chapter 4 for additional details on Běijīng's accommodations.

WHERE TO DINE The latest trend in Běijīng dining is **minority fare** from the south and southwest, as represented in the hip new **Ānyuán No. 5.** Rare mushrooms from minority-dominated Yúnnán Province are the most fashionable ingredient, particularly at hotpot restaurants like **Tàipó Tiānfǔ Shānzhēn** and **Bǎi Shì Jí Huǒguō.** But the best representatives of the minority craze are a pair of Hakka restaurants—**Old Character Hakka** and **Hàn Kèjiā**—both owned by the same artist-entrepreneur and both justifiably packed nearly every night. As with nightlife (see below), the center of gravity in Běijīng dining has finally begun to shift away from

the tired neon of Cháoyáng's embassy areas. The focus now is on the **Back Lakes area (Shíchà Hǎi),** where stylish decor accompanies—and frequently overshadows—the food. **Kǒng Yǐjǐ Jiǔlóu,** a restaurant devoted to the celebration of Chinese writer Lǔ Xùn, serves some fine dishes in the delicate Huáiyáng style of Lǔ's hometown, Shàoxīng. The beloved string of 24-hour restaurants known as **Ghost Street** has largely been reduced to bite-size pieces by the wrecking ball, although a few establishments on its western end still survive. **Starbucks** has continued its inevitable expansion, including a controversial move to the very center of the Forbidden City. Despite the competition from cafes and bars, traditional teahouses have staged something of a comeback; the new **Teahouse of Family Fù,** in a quiet corner of the Back Lakes, is the most welcoming and offers occasional lectures and other cultural events.

See chapter 5 for information on Běijīng's restaurants.

EXPLORING BĚIJĪNG Several major sites have introduced seasonal pricing with higher prices from April 1 to October 31 and lower prices from November 1 to March 31.

Some newly renovated sections of the **Forbidden City** formerly closed to the public are due to open in 2004. These include the **Wǔyīng Diàn (Hall of Valiance and Heroism)** and the **Cíníng Huāyuán (Garden of Love and Tranquility)** in the western section of the palace. Further sections will open by 2006. Those few ancestral tablets that survived the Cultural Revolution will be on show in **Lìdài Dìwáng Miào (Temple for Emperors of Past Dynasties),** which will reopen to the public after decades in October 2004. A fragment of Běijīng's original rammed-earth **Yuán City Wall** is also due to open soon. We've uncovered a eunuch cemetery, the **Tiányì Mù**, in the far west of town, and a eunuch museum is due to open near the Summer Palace, at the **Lìmǎ Guāndì Miào**. In the name of the Olympics, the automobile, or just naked greed, the destruction of the city's charming *hútòng* has been continuing apace. See what you can, because it probably won't be there next time you visit.

For more on the city's attractions, see chapter 6.

BĚIJĪNG STROLLS The **Back Lakes area (Shíchà Hǎi)**, composed of three idyllic lakes, has long been the most pleasant spot for a stroll in Běijīng. Now (for better or for worse), it rivals Sānlǐtún its range of cafes, bars, restaurants, and teahouses. The popularity of this area means these *hútòng* are likely to escape the wrecker's hammer. Pass up the pedicab tour, start early on a weekday, and explore the area with your two best feet.

SHOPPING The future of Běijīng's largest but money-losing **Friendship Store** looks doubtful, although one announcement of its demise has already proven premature. The current favorite for fake and knockoff designer-label clothing, footwear, and luggage is the recently opened **Sānlǐtún Yǎxiù Fúzhuāng Shìchǎng**, located in the old Kylin Plaza building. You'll also find appealing gifts and souvenirs, competent tailors, and even a manicurist there. The antiques

and "antique" furniture outlets of **Gāobēidiàn** and the tea vendors of **Mǎlián Dào** represent a return to the fine tradition of merchant streets specializing in a single commodity.

BĚIJĪNG AFTER DARK Locals and some visitors now buy tickets to Běijīng performances online at **www.webtix.com.cn**; ticket delivery to your hotel is included.

Despite government attempts to nudge nightlife in the direction of Cháoyáng Park, where it is less likely to disturb residents, Běijīng's bars and clubs have instead proliferated all over the city. The greatest explosion has again been in and around the **Back Lakes**, where bright green beer signs and the thump of dance music increasingly confuse the senses, otherwise lulled into vulnerability by the pleasant scenery and lack of traffic. Once the center of fashionable gyration, dance club Vogue has closed down, but it has a potential replacement in a new club connected to Back Lakes restaurant **Nuage**, likely to open in late 2003. DJ-driven party spots **Club FM** and **The Club @ Sānlǐtún** fill the vacuum in the meantime. **ClubFootball**, next to the Red House, is the city's newest and most authentic sports bar, with cheap beer, good chili, and a relaxed crowd. Finally, Taiwanese import **Cash Box** provides Běijīng with the truly classy karaoke joint it's always lacked.

See chapter 9 for more on the city's nightlife.

1

The Best of Běijīng

by Peter Neville-Hadley, Josh Chin, and Graeme Smith

If you can see only one city in China, it should be Běijīng, because many of the capital's "bests" are also China's "bests." The authors of this book are all former residents of Běijīng, and our choices below reflect our approach to selecting the contents for this entire guide. We've included the obvious, but also the offbeat experiences that reflect the city far better than any list of tourist sites, as impressive as those sites are. We give you the best of the five-star hotels, but also the best bed for under $10—a price far more in keeping with the real Chinese economy—and suggest a night in a former brothel. We give you the best Western restaurants, but concentrate more on the food that is best in Běijīng, which, not surprisingly is Chinese food. We take you to tucked-away coffee bars even Beijingers would have trouble finding. Some of our selections will seem instantly familiar, but others, as far as we know, are featured in no other guide. Not until their next editions, anyway.

1 Frommer's Favorite Běijīng Experiences

- **Dining & Drinking around the Back Lakes:** The combination of peaceful man-made lakes, many of the city's best bars and restaurants, and several pockets of rambling lanes called *hútòng* keep foreign residents coming back to while away their evenings here despite the growing crowds. Dine with a view of the lakes (or arrange to eat on a private traditional boat), take a post-meal stroll through the less explored lanes, then find your way back to the lakes to sip gin-and-tonics as lights from nearby courtyard mansions flicker on the water. See "Back Lakes & Dōng Chéng" in chapter 5 for recommended restaurants, and see chapter 9 for recommended bars.

- **Enjoying a Moment of Quiet at the Museum of Ancient Architecture:** Standing just west of the Temple of Heaven on grounds once nearly as extensive as those of

its neighbor, the Altar of Agriculture is largely overlooked. So is its excellent museum, in halls of a grandeur to match those at the heart of the Forbidden City, but receiving fewer than one ten-thousandth of the visitors. See p. 139.

- **Investigating the Northeast Corner of the Forbidden City:** Away from the main north-south axis on which stand the former palace's grander halls, there's a more human scale similar to that of the rapidly disappearing *hútòng* beyond the palace's walls, although with much greater luxury. Usually, only independent travelers venture so far from the main arteries, but the effort to reach the northeast corner is well worth it for such treasures as an ornate theater building where the Empress Dowager Cíxǐ watched her favorite operas on demand,

and the well in which she ended the life of her nephew's favorite concubine. See "Forbidden City" in chapter 6.

- **Rubbing Shoulders with Monks at Běijīng Temples:** Among the capital's temples that have once again become genuine places of worship as well as tourist attractions, the **Yōnghé Gōng (Lama Temple)** has an active and approachable community of Tibetan monks (although under careful scrutiny by the authorities). The **Báiyún Guǎn** is the Daoist alternative, where the blue-frocked monks wear their hair in the rarely seen traditional manner—long and tied in a bun at the top of the head. See p. 135 and 132, respectively.

- **Bargaining for Fakes:** At **Pānjiāyuán Jiùhuò Shìchǎng,** the first asking prices for foreigners are at least 10 to 15 times those asked of Chinese, but this weekend market has the city's best selection of bric-a-brac, including row upon crowded row of calligraphy, jewelry, ceramics, teapots, ethnic clothing, Buddha statues, paper lanterns, Cultural Revolution memorabilia, army belts, little wooden boxes, Míng- and Qīng-style furniture, old pipes, opium scales, painted human skulls, and more conventional souvenirs. Most of the merchandise is of recent manufacture, whatever the vendor may tell you. Bargaining fun can be had all week long at **Sānlǐtún Yǎxiù Fúzhuāng Shìchǎng,** a hunting ground for souvenirs and gifts including kites, calligraphy materials, army surplus gear, tea sets, and farmer's paintings from Xī'ān. The basement and the first two floors house a predictable but comprehensive collection of imitation and pilfered brand-name clothing, shoes, and luggage. Starting prices are only slightly less imaginative than those at the better-known Silk Market. See p. 164 for both markets.

- **Haggling for Tea at Mǎlián Dào:** If you're serious about tea, this is the only place to go. Mǎlián Dào may not have all the tea in China, but it does have over a mile of shops hawking tea leaves and their paraphernalia. Most shops are run by the extended families of tea growers from Fújiàn and Zhèjiāng provinces, and you may rate this friendly street the highlight of your visit. See p. 177.

- **Attending Běijīng Opera at the Zhèngyǐcí Xìlóu:** The Zhèngyǐcí, last of a handful of theaters that supported Běijīng Opera from its beginnings, only occasionally hosts performances and is under constant threat of permanent closure. But the scarcity of performances only makes the experience of watching the colorful operas in this intimate, traditionally decorated space all the more precious. Get your hotel staff to call and ask. See p. 181.

- **Unwinding at a Traditional Teahouse:** Several quiet teahouses offer you the chance to remove yourself temporarily from the tourist rush. The teahouse in the **Sānwèi Bookstore** (p. 184) offers live traditional music with its bottomless cups of jasmine. For a little extra, the **Purple Vine Tea House** (p. 189) near the Forbidden City and **The Teahouse of Family Fù** (p. 190) in the Back Lakes area brew your Oolong (Wūlóng) in the Chinese version of the tea ceremony. All three teahouses are furnished with replica Míng dynasty tables and chairs and make ideal spots for reading, writing, or doing absolutely nothing.

China

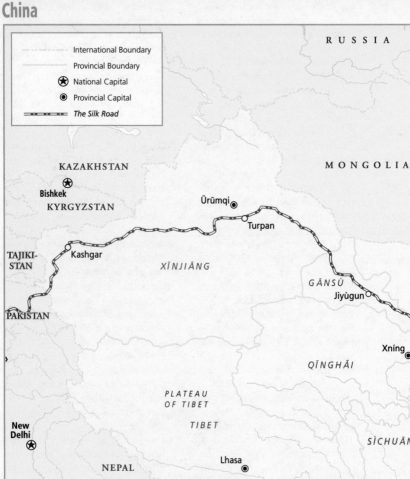

— · — · —	International Boundary
————	Provincial Boundary
✪	National Capital
◉	Provincial Capital
▭▭▭	*The Silk Road*

RUSSIA

KAZAKHSTAN

MONGOLIA

Bishkek ✪
KYRGYZSTAN

Ürümqi ◉

Turpan

TAJIKI-
STAN

Kashgar

XĪNJIĀNG

GĀNSÙ

Jiyùgun

PAKISTAN

Xníng ◉

QĪNGHĂI

PLATEAU
OF TIBET

TIBET

SÌCHUĀN

New
Delhi ✪

NEPAL

Lhasa ◉

▲ *Mt. Everest*

Kathmandu ✪

✪Thimbu
BHUTAN

Lìjing

Dàlǐ   *Ěrhǎi
Lake*

Knmíng ◉

INDIA

Ganges

YÚNNÁN

BANGLADESH

✪
Dhaka

MYANMAR

LAOS

Saluwen

NORTHEAST

Běij̄ıng ★

CENTRAL

SOUTHWEST

MOUNTAIN
CHINA

SOUTHEAST

*Bay
of
Bengal*

Rangoon
✪

Vientiane ✪

THAILAND

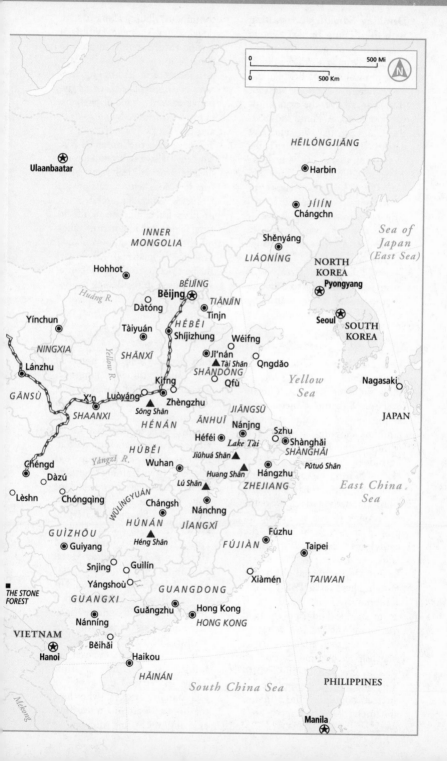

- **Drinking, Smoking, & Sweating with the Bĕijīng Punks:** Despite a flowering of genres in recent years, punk rock is still the dominant musical style of Bĕijīng, and its adherents maintain tattoo-fisted control over the city's musical momentum. Punk shows at the **CD Café** (p. 184) and **Get Lucky Bar** (p. 184) aren't the cleanest of affairs, but you didn't come to China to be clean, did you? They're a good release for frustrations with crooked taxi drivers and relentless souvenir peddlers, at the very least. See Appendix A for more about Bĕijīng music.
- **Hiking along the Great Wall from Jīn Shān Lǐng to Sīmǎtái:** Visitors are few at Jīn Shān Lǐng, although the Wall runs in a continuous ribbon along a high ridge, several kilometers visible at a time. Strike out eastwards to Sīmǎtái and you'll quickly reach unrestored and crumbling sections of considerable charisma giving views across a sea of blossoms in spring, or rich reds and golds in autumn. See p. 197.
- **Taking a Trip to Chuān Dǐ Xià:** This tiny village of around a hundred souls is an ideal 1- or 2-day trip for those with a passion for Chinese vernacular architecture, or keen for a glimpse of life in rural China. Set in a narrow valley off the old trade route to Shānxī Province, Chuān Dǐ Xià boasts the best preserved *sìhéyuàn* (courtyard houses) in the Bĕijīng region. See p. 204.

2 Best Hotel Bets

- **Best Newcomer:** With Bĕijīng's best location—inside the Oriental Plaza shopping complex, directly over the Wángfǔjǐng metro stop, at the foot of the capital's most famous shopping street, and within walking distance of the Forbidden City—the **Grand Hyatt Bĕijīng** does everything else right, too. It has a palatial lobby, modern and comfortable furnishings in the guest rooms, proper shower cubicles in the bathrooms, and excellent restaurants. See p. 65.
- **Best Undiscovered Luxury Hotel:** The **Marco Polo**'s lobby, sumptuously decorated with white marble and rippling gold friezes, and with an art-hung stairwell leading to a restaurant above, is stylish yet of a modest enough scale to give this brand-new 10-story building the atmosphere of a discreet boutique hotel. Rooms are among Bĕijīng's largest, however. See p. 73.
- **Best Service:** The four hotels in the capital under Shangri-La management come closest to providing ideal service—that which anticipates your needs rather then simply reacts to requests, and is creative rather than formulaic in its responses. The group has opened its own training school, so its standards may spread, but for now, if service is important to you, try the **Shangri-La Bĕijīng Hotel** (p. 76), **Kerry Centre Hotel** (p. 70), **China World Hotel** (p. 68), or **Traders Hotel Bĕijīng** (p. 71).
- **Most Relaxed Atmosphere:** The low-rise **Jiànguó Hotel,** the first Sino-foreign joint-venture hotel in Bĕijīng, looks its age from the outside, but has kept itself up-to-date with frequent renovations inside. Its pleasantly bustling lobby has retained the loyalty of long-standing expats, who have meetings over afternoon tea while enjoying the string quartet, or

turn up in droves for the Sunday morning string orchestra concert, a Běijīng institution. Some ground-floor rooms have French windows opening on to small patios alongside goldfish-stocked pools, providing a level of calm quite astonishing in such a hectic city. See p. 71.

- **Best Whiff of Old Běijīng:** The recently refurbished **Lǔsōng Yuán Bīnguǎn,** situated inside a former imperial house in a *hútòng* within walking distance of the Back Lakes, features bright paneled ceilings in the hallways, an inviting teahouse in the lobby, and traditionally furnished rooms that somehow avoid the museum-like feel of rooms in other similar hotels. Certain units have direct access to that most Běijīng of architectural features: the private courtyard. Grander but not yet fully renovated, the **Héjìng Fǔ Bīnguǎn,** originally the home of a Qīng emperor's daughter, will probably eclipse the Lǔsōng Yuán once work on its impressive courtyards finally finishes. See p. 68 and 67, respectively.
- **Best Hotel Garden:** The **Bamboo Garden Hotel**'s three courtyards are filled with rockeries, stands of bamboo, and other green leafiness. A traditional Chinese garden stretches away behind the otherwise modern **Shangri-La Běijīng Hotel** to its tennis courts at the rear. See p. 67 and 76 respectively.
- **Most Luxurious Little Details:** The recently renamed and updated **Peninsula Palace Běijīng** is the only hotel in mainland China which will send a Rolls-Royce to collect you from the airport. It also has a special faucet for drinking water (you otherwise *never* drink tap water in China), and bedside controls for

just about every function in the entire room. Those who've stayed at the legendary Peninsula in Hong Kong will find some of the details familiar. See p. 64.
- **Best Business Hotel:** The **Kempinski Hotel** is part of a vast apartment and shopping complex offering a full-scale business center and a recently refurbished and top-notch executive floor, along with a specialist wine store, endless airline offices and ticket agents, medical and dental clinics with Western staff and equipment, eight restaurants and cafes, a supermarket, a bookshop, and a complete department store. Many who come for business visits never leave the building until they head back to the airport. See p. 69.
- **Most Efficient Hotel:** Four-star **Traders Hotel Běijīng** deliberately markets itself to the "guerrilla traveler," with simple but well-equipped rooms, the city's snappiest service, and a generally straightforward approach as rare in Běijīng as a spring without sandstorms. Room rates are very reasonable, there's a metro stop 5 minutes' walk away, and staff members are genuinely apologetic when there's a delay in service (which there rarely is). See p. 71.
- **Best Health & Fitness Facilities:** The health club and spa at the **St. Regis Běijīng** is brand new and the capital's most luxurious by far, but the most extensive facilities, including a running track and courts for almost everything, can be found at the **Kerry Centre Hotel.** See p. 70 for both.
- **Best Pool:** The pool at the **Grand Hyatt** is very kitsch and out of keeping with the tastefully understated modern but comfortable design of the remainder of the hotel. A small lagoon buried

among mock-tropical decor beneath a ceiling of electric stars, it's worth visiting even if you have no plans to swim, and it has plenty of space if you do. See p. 65.

- **Best for Children:** The **Kerry Centre Hotel** has the largest and best supervised play area for children, handy for a wide range of sports facilities and a pool for the older ones. See p. 70.
- **Best Breakfast:** A close race: The **St. Regis Běijīng** has a comprehensive breakfast buffet stocked well beyond the average, but the **Grand Hyatt's** breakfast service is more comprehensive still, and the freshest—its range of Chinese, Western, and Japanese dishes is only displayed in small portions and constantly topped up from the open kitchen. See p. 70 and 65, respectively.
- **Best Long-Stay Choice:** The **Red House** has spacious apartments, upgraded in late 2002 and now fully equipped with separate bedroom, small kitchen, and generous sitting room. A long stay is only

about ¥300 ($37) per night (after bargaining). See p. 72.

- **Best Value for the Money:** At the **Lǔsōng Yuán Bīnguǎn**, ¥480 to ¥600 ($60–$75) will get you a small but nicely furnished room in a beautifully restored Qīng courtyard house in a quiet part of the city's most charming neighborhood. Rates can be bargained down by 40% in winter. See p. 68.
- **Best Under $30:** The best budget option in Běijīng is the **Far East Youth Hostel,** located at the center of one of the city's most interesting *hútòng* neighborhoods, only a 10-minute walk from both the Hépíng Mén and Qián Mén metro stops. It has clean, nicely renovated three-star rooms at unbeatable rates (¥200/$25 with a little bargaining). See p. 75.
- **Best Under $10:** The recently renovated **Fēiyīng Bīnguǎn** is the most "hotel-like" branch of Youth Hostelling International in Běijīng. Dorms have in-room bathroom and brand-new floors, and beds are only ¥50 ($6).

3 Best Dining Bets

- **Best Chinese Restaurant:** There are fancier places to eat in Běijīng, but none can top the **Hàn Kèjiā** for its Hakka minority food. Literally every item on the menu sings with flavor. The paperwrapped fish is culinary Nirvana. Add a charming location, delightful decor, and reasonable prices. A close runner-up is **Kǒng Yǐjǐ Jiǔlóu,** decorated with the trappings of Chinese scholarship and named for the scholar-bum protagonist of a Lǔ Xùn short story. It specializes in the delicate and delicious Huáiyáng dishes of northern Zhèjiāng, the author's place of origin, as well as the birthplace of

"yellow wine" which impaired his character's career. See p. 86 and 87, respectively.

- **Best Běijīng Duck:** Běijīng's most famous dish is available at dozens of locations, but nowhere is it as crisp and fine as at **Běijīng Dàdǒng Kǎoyā Diàn,** just east of the Sānlǐtún drinking district on the East Third Ring Road. See p. 94.
- **Best Non-Duck Běijīng Food:** Loud as any street market, with service like a hurricane, **Dào Jiā Cháng** offers the most memorable experience of the capital's native cuisine, from shouted welcome to final belch. See p. 99.

- **Best Sìchuān:** Fiery dishes from Sìchuān Province grace most menus in Běijīng regardless of whether the restaurant identifies itself as Sichuanese or not. **Yúxiāng Rénjiā,** a popular chain devoted exclusively to Sichuanese food, offers the most comprehensive and authentic selection. See p. 98.

- **Best Cantonese: Horizon,** inside the Kerry Centre Hotel, serves nicely executed upscale Cantonese food and high-quality dim sum in a luxurious setting at less-than-luxurious prices. The raucous 24-hour branch of **Otto's Restaurant** offers for-the-people southern dishes, rarely found outside Guǎngdōng, Hong Kong, and the largest of U.S. Chinatowns. See p. 90 and 84, respectively.

- **Best Hotpot:** Searingly spicy Sìchuān-style hotpot in an unusually classy setting can be found at the immensely popular **Huángchéng Lǎo Mā.** Out of the way but well worth the trip, **Tàipó Tiānfú Shānzhēn** features a mouthwatering broth made from 32 kinds of mushrooms and a whole black-skinned chicken—the city's most delicious do-it-yourself dining experience. See p. 91 and 100, respectively.

- **Best Noodles:** Available in dozens of shapes and sauces, Shānxī-style noodles at the fashionable and aptly named **Noodle Loft** are among the most satisfying in Běijīng, and without the crimes of hygiene perpetrated by the more typical noodle joints. See p. 96.

- **Best Karma** (Vegetarian): Clean, bright, and colorful **Lotus in Moonlight** serves food to match its decor: mushrooms and tofu masquerading as meat, light and flavorful vegetables, and a wide range of colorful teas. No animals anywhere, but you won't miss them. No smoking either. See p. 95.

- **Best European: Justine's** (p. 89) in the Jiànguó Hotel serves the city's finest French cuisine. **Danieli's** (p. 88) and the **Astor Grill** (p. 88), both in the St. Regis Hotel, are the best options for Italian and upscale American food, respectively. And the unassuming Belgian restaurant **Morel's** (p. 92), once considered the greatest Western eatery in Běijīng, is your best source of waffles, beef stew, and beer.

- **Best Asian** (non-Chinese): Stylish decor and creative rolls make **Hatsune** (p. 90) the best Japanese option in Běijīng. **Chingari** (p. 89) serves the most authentic Indian food. Overpriced but superbly decorated, **Nuage** (p. 86) in the Back Lakes offers creative Vietnamese. **Cafe Sambal** (p. 85) is much the same for Malaysian cuisine. Not flashy at all, **Pamer** (p. 100) provides Běijīng with its best Uighur food, including some divine lamb skewers.

- **Best Fusion:** Another contender for the title of best non-Chinese restaurant in Běijīng, **Aria** is one of the capital's most thoroughly satisfying dining experiences, from *amuse-bouche* to dessert. More than one visit may be necessary to do justice to a menu of thoroughly intelligent yet understated fusion dishes, served with helpful suggestions for accompanying wines in very comfortable and relaxingly woody surroundings. See p. 88.

- **Best Wine List:** High import duties and poor selection make life in Běijīng tough on wine drinkers. But **The Courtyard,** one of the city's most celebrated restaurants, both for its excellent fusion menu and for its location in a courtyard house overlooking the Forbidden City moat, offers an astonishingly sophisticated wine selection you'd have to go to Hong Kong to equal, with many top wines available even by the glass, and at prices far too low to be economically viable. See p. 82.

- **Best Quintessential Bĕijīng Setting:** Built inside the prayer hall of an old Daoist temple in a sea of crumbling residences near the Back Lakes, **Dào** eschews the polished gardens and pavilions of the city's other atmospheric restaurants in favor of something far more appropriate: the fast-fading intimacy of one of Bĕijīng's last *hútòng* neighborhoods. See p. 85.
- **Best Decor:** With its open kitchens, pleasing juxtaposition of glass and metal, and contributions from a Hong Kong video artist, the Peninsula Palace hotel's **Jing** is

easily the most stylish restaurant in Bĕijīng. Flavorful and artfully arranged fusion dishes complete the visual package. See p. 83.
- **Best for Children:** The servers in **Afunti** clear away plates at around 9pm to make way for "spontaneous" table-top dance parties, which happen every night. Children love it. Parents love it. And the food—Uighur minority dishes from Muslim-dominated Xīnjiāng—is pretty good. See p. 85.
- **Best Coffee:** The superbly comfortable **Rive Gauche,** on the west bank of Qián Hǎi, is more bar than cafe but is nevertheless the city's best alternative to Starbucks. The owners are friendly, the views of the lake are excellent, and the coffees come fortified with a variety of spirits for those in need of an extra kick. See p. 188.

2

Planning Your Trip to Běijīng

by Peter Neville-Hadley

Visiting China isn't as hard as you think it is. If you can manage Paris by yourself without speaking French, you can manage Běijīng without Mandarin. Tens of thousands of visitors travel in China independently each year, making arrangements as they go and without more than a guidebook and phrase book to help them. You can certainly arrange various levels of assistance, either on arrival or from home, but you can also travel just as freely as you would elsewhere, perhaps using agents to get your tickets and picking up the odd day tour.

But whether you plan to travel at random, with a pre-booked route, or with a fully escorted tour, it's *vital* that you read this chapter carefully in order to understand how the way you travel, even in many other developing nations, doesn't apply here. Much supposed wisdom on China travel is far from wise, what's good advice in the rest of the world is often the worst advice in China, and without absorbing what's below, some of the rest of this guide may seem inscrutable.

So put down your preconceptions, and read on. . . .

1 Visitor Information

NATIONAL TOURIST OFFICES
The mainland travel industry is, in general, a quagmire of deception that provides no truly reliable information either within China or via its overseas operations. The branches of the China National Tourism Administration in foreign countries are called **China National Tourist Offices.** Nominally nonprofit, they used to be little more than agents for the state-owned China International Travel Service (CITS), but they now offer links to a variety of operators. Don't expect them to be accurate about even the most basic visa or Customs regulations, and don't expect them to update their websites, which sometimes give conflicting information and can't even get the names of tour operators right.

Tourist offices are in the following locations:

- In the **United States:** 350 Fifth Ave., Suite 6413, Empire State Building, New York, NY 10118 (© 212/760-8218/8807/4002; fax 212/760-8809; ny@cnta.gov.cn); 600 W. Broadway, Suite 320, Glendale, CA 91204 (© 818/545-7505; fax 828/545-7506; la@cnta.gov.cn).
- In **Canada:** 480 University Ave., Suite 806, Toronto, ONT M5G 1V2 (© 416/599-6636; fax 416/599-6382; www.tourismchina-ca.com).
- In the **U.K.:** 4 Glentworth St., London NW1 5PG (© 020/7935-9787; fax 020/7487-5842; london@cnta.gov.cn).
- In **Australia:** Level 19, 44 Market St., Sydney, NSW 2000 (© 02/9299-4057; fax 02/9290-1958; sydney@cnta.gov.cn).

BĚIJĪNG ONLINE

Be cautious of official sources of information and unofficial Chinese-run sources alike, especially if they also offer travel services. Canadian-owned but Běijīng-based *Xiànzài* (www.xianzai.com) offers a weekly e-mail newsletter with hotel, restaurant, and airfare advertising (often including special offers only publicized locally), and a diary of events. The site also offers an assortment of other newsletters with information on travel in China.

Amateurish expat magazines, such as *that's Beijing* (www.thatsmagazines.com) and *City Weekend* (www.cityweekend.com.cn), have a certain amount of Běijīng news, information about what's on, and new restaurant reviews online, along with modest features on Běijīng life.

For an ad- and spam-free general discussion of any Běijīng (or other China) travel issues not covered in this book, subscribe to the e-mail discussion list *The Oriental-List,* moderated by one of this book's authors. To subscribe, send a blank e-mail to subscribe-oriental-list@list.xianzai.com.

2 Entry Requirements & Customs

ENTRY REQUIREMENTS

PASSPORT Visitors must have a valid **passport** with at least 6 months' validity and two blank pages remaining (you *may* get away with just one blank page).

VISAS All visitors to **mainland China** (as opposed to Special Administrative Regions of Hong Kong and Macau) must acquire a visa in advance. Visa applications typically take 3 to 5 working days to process, although this can be shortened to as little as 1 day if you apply in person and pay extra fees. "L" (tourist) visas are valid for between 1 and 3 months. Usually 1 month is granted unless you request more, which you may or may not get according to events in China at the time. Double-entry tourist visas are also available. It varies, but typically your visit must *begin* within 90 days of the date of issue.

You should apply for a visa in person at your nearest **consulate,** although it's possible to obtain Chinese visas in other countries while you're on an extended trip. To apply for a visa, you must complete an **application form,** which can be downloaded from many consular websites or acquired by mail. Visas are valid for the whole country, although some small areas require an extra permit from the local police. Temporary restrictions, sometimes for years at a time, may be placed on areas where there is unrest, and a further permit may be required to enter them. In general, do not mention Tibet or Xīnjiāng on your visa application, or it may be turned down flat.

Some consulates request that you show them an airline ticket, itinerary, or proof of sufficient funds, or they claim to issue visas only to those traveling in groups (while happily carrying on business with individuals who have none of the supporting documentation). Such guidelines provide consulates with a face-saving excuse for refusing a visa should there be unrest or political difficulties, or should Tibet or Xīnjiāng appear on the application.

One **passport photograph** is required per adult, as well as for any child traveling on a parent's passport.

A complete list of all Chinese embassies and consulates, including addresses and contact information, can be found at the Chinese foreign ministry's website: www.fmprc.gov.cn/eng (or various mirror sites around the world). Click on "Missions Overseas." Many consulates (including all those in the U.S. and Canada) will only accept applications in person; applications by post or courier must go through an agent, which charges additional fees. Contacting some embassies can be very difficult: Many telephone systems are automated, and reaching a human can be next to impossible; faxes and e-mails usually don't receive a reply; and websites are often out of date.

What follows are visa fees and requirements for some countries:

- **United States:** Single-entry visas are US$50; double-entry US$75. Visit www.china-embassy.org, which has links to all U.S. consular sites and a downloadable application form. Applications must be delivered and collected by hand, or sent via a visa agency.
- **Canada:** Single-entry visas are C$50; double-entry C$75. Visit www.chinaembassycanada.org for an application form. Applications must be delivered and collected by hand, or sent via a visa agency.
- **United Kingdom:** Single-entry visas are £30; double-entry £45. There's a supplementary charge of £20 for each package dealt with by mail. Visit www.chinese-embassy. org.uk for an application.
- **Australia:** Single-entry visas are A$30; double-entry A$45. Add A$10 per package dealt with by mail or courier, and a pre-paid return envelope. Visit www.china embassy.org.au or www.china consulatesyd.org for an application.
- **New Zealand:** Single-entry visas are NZ$60; double-entry NZ$90. Add NZ$15 per package dealt with by mail or courier, and a pre-paid return envelope. Visit www. chinaembassy.org.nz or www.china consulate.org.nz for an application.

Note: The visa **fees** quoted above for each country are the current rates for *nationals of that country,* and can change at any time. In addition to the visa fees quoted, there may be supplementary fees for postage. Payment must always be in cash or by money order.

VISA EXTENSIONS Single-entry tourist visas may be extended once for a maximum of 30 days at the PSB Exit/Entry Division offices in most cities. The office in Běijīng (© **010/ 8401-5292**) is on the south side of the eastern North Second Ring Road, just east of the Lama Temple (Mon–Sat 8:30am–4:30pm). Applications take 4 working days to process. Bring your passport and two passport photos (these can be taken at the office for ¥30/$4). Extension fees vary by nationality: U.S. citizens pay ¥125 ($16), U.K. citizens ¥160 ($20), Canadians ¥165 ($21), and Australians ¥100 ($12).

GETTING A VISA IN HONG KONG Nationals of most developed nations do not require a visa to enter Hong Kong, and visas for mainland China are more easily obtainable there than anywhere else.

For the cheapest visas go to **Grand Profit International Travel Agency,** 705AA, 7th Floor, New East Ocean Centre, 9 Science Museum Rd., Tsimshatsui (about a 15-min. walk east of Nathan Rd.; © **852/2723- 3288**). Here a single-entry tourist visa costs HK$150 (US$19), and is available the next day if you hand in your passport before noon. Same-day service is HK$180 (US$23). Double-entry and multiple-entry 6-month visas are also easily available.

CUSTOMS
WHAT YOU CAN BRING INTO CHINA
In general terms, you can bring anything into China for personal use that you plan to take back with you, with the usual exceptions of arms and

drugs, or plant materials, animals, and foods from diseased areas. There are no problems with cameras or video recorders, GPS equipment, laptops, or any other standard electronic equipment. Two unusual prohibitions are "old/used garments" and "printed matter, magnetic media, films, or photographs which are deemed to be detrimental to the political, economic, cultural and moral interests of China," as the regulations put it. Large quantities of religious literature, overtly political materials, or books on Tibet might cause you difficulties but, in general, small amounts of personal reading matter in non-Chinese languages do not present problems. Customs officers are for the most part easygoing, and foreign visitors are rarely searched. Customs declaration forms have now vanished from all major points of entry, but if you are importing more than US$5,000 in cash, you should declare it, or theoretically you could face difficulties at the time of departure—although, again, this is highly unlikely.

WHAT YOU CAN TAKE HOME FROM CHINA

An official seal must be attached to any item created between 1795 and 1949 that is taken out of China; older items cannot be exported. But, in fact, you are highly unlikely to find any genuine antiques, so this is moot (however, a genuine antiques dealer would know how to obtain the seal).

3 Money

CURRENCY

Although for most destinations it's usually a good idea to exchange at least some money before you leave home so you can avoid the less-favorable rates at airport currency-exchange desks, mainland China is different. RMB yuán are not easily obtainable overseas, and rates are worse when they can be found.

There is no legal private money-changing in mainland China. Nationwide outlets offer the same rates on a daily basis. You can exchange currency at the airport when you arrive, at larger branches of the Bank of China, at a bank desk in your hotel, or at major department stores in larger cities. Shops that offer to exchange money at other than formal Bank of China exchange counters do so illegally, and are known for rate shenanigans and passing fake bills, which are fairly common. *Do not deal with black market money-changers.*

Keep receipts when you exchange money, and you can **reconvert** excess ¥RMB into hard currency when you leave China, although sometimes not more than half the total sum for which you can produce receipts, and sometimes these receipts must be not more than 3 months old.

Hotel exchange desks will only change money for their guests but are open very long hours, 7 days a week. **Banking hours** vary from branch to branch but are limited on Saturday, and banks are closed on Sunday. For more information, see "Banks, Currency Exchanges & ATMs" in the "Fast Facts: Běijīng" section of chapter 3.

EXCHANGE RATE The yuán is pegged to the U.S. dollar, trading between ¥8.276 and ¥8.28 to 1 U.S. dollar, and is only allowed to move within a band of .2%. For all other currencies, strength in comparison to the yuán is a matter of strength in comparison to the U.S. dollar. The pound sterling has recently been trading at around $1.56 and ¥12.95, the euro at $1.07 and ¥8.87. The latest rates can be found at **www.xe.com/ucc**.

YUÁN NOTES   There are notes for ¥100, ¥50, ¥20, ¥10, ¥5, ¥2, and ¥1, which also appears as a coin. The word *yuán* is rarely spoken, and sums are referred to as *kuài qián,* "pieces of money," usually shortened to just *kuài. Sān kuài* is ¥3. Notes carry Arabic numerals as well as numbers in Chinese characters, so there's no fear of confusion. The next unit down, the *jiǎo* (¥0.10), is spoken of as the *máo.* There are notes of a smaller size for ¥0.50, ¥0.20, and ¥0.10, as well as coins for these values. The smallest and almost worthless unit is the *fēn* (both written and spoken), or cent. Unbelievably, when you change money you may be given tiny notes or lightweight coins for ¥0.05, ¥0.02, and ¥0.01, but this is the only time you'll see them except in the bowls of beggars or donation boxes in temples. The most useful note is the ¥10 ($1.25), so keep a good stock. Street stalls, convenience stores, and taxis are often unhappy to receive ¥100 ($13) notes.

ATMS

There are many ATMs in China, but with few exceptions, only a selection of Bank of China machines accept foreign cards. Check the back of your ATM card for the logos of the **Cirrus** (www.mastercard.com), **PLUS** (www.visa.com), and **Aeon** (www.americanexpress.com) systems, and then contact the relevant company for a list of working ATM locations in Běijīng, which is fairly well served. The capital also has one branch each of Citibank and the Hongkong and Shànghǎi Bank, whose machines take just about any card ever invented. Some Bank of China machines have a limit of ¥2,500 ($310) per transaction, but they often allow a second transaction the same day.

TRAVELER'S CHECKS

Traveler's checks are only accepted at selected branches of the Bank of China, at foreign exchange desks in hotels, and at the exchange desks of some department stores. In bigger bank branches, checks in any hard currency and from any major company are welcome, but at department-store exchange desks, currencies of the larger economies are preferred. You can exchange U.S. dollars in cash at most branches of almost any Chinese bank, so even if you plan to bring checks, having a few U.S. dollars in cash (in good condition) for emergencies is a good idea. Checks attract a marginally better exchange rate than cash, but the .75% commission on checks makes the result slightly worse (worse still if you paid commission when buying them).

CREDIT CARDS

Although Visa and MasterCard signs abound, credit cards are of limited use—in most cases only the Chinese versions of the cards are accepted. Usually all American Express, Diners Club, MasterCard, and Visa cards are accepted, or no credit cards at all. You can use foreign cards at many hotels, but they are accepted at only the most upmarket restaurants outside hotels, and at those souvenir shops where you are already paying well over the odds—in fact, if a shop accepts foreign credit cards, you should consider looking elsewhere.

You can also obtain cash advances on your MasterCard, Visa, Diners Club, or Amex cards at major branches of the Bank of China, with a minimum withdrawal of ¥1,200 ($150) and 4% commission, plus whatever your card issuer charges you—this expensive way to withdraw cash only makes sense for emergencies. If you do plan to use your card while in China, it's a good idea to call your issuer in advance to let them know that you'll do so.

EMERGENCY CASH   American Express runs an **emergency check**

What Things Cost in Běijīng	U.S.$	U.K.£
Taxi from airport to city center (use meter!)	8.00–12.00	5.00–8.00
Up to 4km (2½ miles) by taxi	1.25	77p
Metro ride	38¢	23p
Local telephone call	6¢	4p
Hearty bowl of beef noodles at a basic restaurant	60¢	38p
Regular coffee at Starbucks	1.50	92p
McDonald's set meal for one	2.25	1.38
Tasty dinner for two at a simple homestyle restaurant	3.75	2.30
Dinner for two in restaurants around foreigner-frequented bar areas	12.50	7.70
Dinner for two in top hotel restaurants	80.00	49.00
Bottle of beer at an ordinary restaurant or store	38¢	23p
Bottle of beer in a foreigner bar district	3.80	2.30
Admission to the Forbidden City	7.50	4.60
Admission to the Lama Temple	3.00	1.90

cashing system, which allows you to use one of your own checks or a counter check (more expensively) to draw money in the currency of your choice from selected banks. This works well in major cities but can cause confusion in less-visited spots, and the rules on withdrawal limits vary according to the country in which your card was issued. Consult American Express for a list of participating banks before leaving home.

You can also have money wired from **Western Union** (© **800/325-6000;** www.westernunion.com) to you at many post offices and branches of the Agricultural Bank of China across China, including 49 in Běijīng. You must present valid ID to pick up the cash at the Western Union office.

4 When to Go

The biggest factor in your calculations on when to visit Běijīng should be the movement of domestic tourists, who during the longer public holidays take to the road in tens or even hundreds of millions, filling transportation, booking out hotels, and turning even the quieter tourist sights into litter-strewn bedlam.

PEAK TRAVEL SEASONS Chinese New Year (Spring Festival) Like many Chinese festivals, this one operates on the lunar calendar. Solar equivalents for the next few years are January 22, 2004; February 9, 2005; January 29, 2006; February 18, 2007; and February 7, 2008. The effects of this holiday are felt from 2 weeks before the date until 2 weeks after, when anyone who's away from home attempts to get back, including an estimated 150 million migrant workers. If you are flying from overseas to Běijīng, this won't affect you, but a land approach may be difficult, except in the few days immediately surrounding the holiday. Banks, as well as smaller restaurants and businesses, may be shut for a week. But main attractions are mostly open.

Labor Day & National Day: In a policy known as "holiday economics," the May 1 and October 1 holidays have now been expanded to 7 days each (including 1 weekend—most people are expected to work through the weekend prior to the holiday in exchange for 2 weekdays, which are added to the official 3 days of holiday). These two holidays now mark the beginning and end of the domestic travel season, and mark the twin peaks of leisure travel, with the remainder of May, early June, and September also busy. The exact dates of each holiday are not announced until around 2 weeks before each takes place.

CLIMATE   For the best weather, visit Běijīng in September or October when warm, dry, sunny days with clear skies and pleasantly cool evenings are the norm. The second best time is spring, late March to mid-May, when winds blow away the pollution but also sometimes bring clouds of scouring sand for a day or two, turning the sky a livid yellow. Winters can be bitter, but the city is much improved visually under a fresh blanket of snow: The gaudy colors of the Forbidden City's palaces are emphasized, as is the Great Wall's bleakness. Summers are humid and hot, but air-conditioning makes them tolerable. The number of foreign visitors is high during summer, but the Chinese themselves mostly wait until the weather cools before traveling.

Běijīng's Average Temperatures & Rainfall

	Jan	Feb	Mar	Apr	May	June	July	Aug	Sept	Oct	Nov	Dec
Temp. (°F)	26	31	43	57	68	76	79	77	69	57	41	30
Temp. (°C)	-3	0	6	13	20	24	26	25	20	13	5	-1
Days of Rain	2.1	3.1	4.5	5.1	6.4	9.7	14.5	14.1	6.9	5.0	3.6	1.6

HOLIDAYS   A few years ago the Chinese were finally granted a 2-day weekend, but while offices close, shops, restaurants, post offices, transportation, and sights all operate the same services 7 days a week. Most sights, shops, and restaurants are open on public holidays, too, but offices and anything government-related close for as much time as possible. Although China switched to the Gregorian calendar in 1911, some public holidays (and many festivals—see the following "Běijīng Calendar of Events") are on a lunar cycle, with solar dates varying from year to year. Holidays are **New Year's Day** (Jan 1), **Spring Festival** (Chinese New Year's day and the following 2 days—see "Peak Travel Seasons" above, for exact dates in coming years), **Labor Day** (May 1 plus up to 4 more weekdays and a weekend), **National Day** (Oct 1 plus extra days, as for Labor Day).

BĚIJĪNG CALENDAR OF EVENTS

Festivals are more family affairs in Běijīng, which doesn't have much of a calendar of public events compared with some other parts of China.

Winter

Spring Festival (Chūn Jié), or Chinese New Year, is still the occasion for large lion dances and other celebrations in Chinatowns worldwide, but in mainland China it's mainly a time for everyone to return to his or her ancestral home and feast. Fireworks are now banned in Běijīng, however. Temple fairs have been revived in Běijīng but are mostly fairly low-key shopping opportunities without much of the color or professional entertainers of old. But in the countryside, there's been a gradual revival of stilt-walking and masked processions. New Year is on the day of the first new moon after

January 21, and can be no later than February 20.

Lantern Festival (Dēng Jié) perhaps reached its peak in the late Qīng dynasty, when temples, stores, and other public places were hung with fantastically shaped and decorated lanterns. Many people paraded through the streets with lightweight lanterns in the shapes of fish, sheep, or other animals, and hung others, often decorated with riddles, outside their houses. There are modest signs of a revival. This festival always falls 15 days after Spring Festival.

Spring

Tomb-Sweeping Festival (Qīng-míng), frequently observed in Chinese communities overseas, and more often in rural areas of China, as a family outing on a free day near the festival date. It's a day for honoring ancestors by visiting and tidying their gravesites, and making offerings of snacks and alcohol, which often turns into a picnic. Takes place April 5.

Autumn

The last remnant of the **Mid-Autumn Festival (Tuányuán Jié)**, except among literary-minded students, is the giving and eating of *yuèbing* (moon cakes), circular pies with sweet and extremely fattening fillings. Traditionally it's a time to sit and read poetry under the full moon, but pollution has made the moon largely invisible. Takes place the 15th day of the 8th lunar month (usually Sept).

National Day itself is for avoiding Tiān'ān Mén Square, especially if the government considers the anniversary important enough for one of its military parades, when the square may be blocked to you anyway. Takes place on October 1.

5 Travel Insurance

Check your existing insurance policies and credit card coverage before you buy travel insurance. You may already be covered for lost luggage, cancelled tickets, or medical expenses. The cost of travel insurance varies widely, depending on the cost and length of your trip, your age, your health, and the type of trip you're taking.

Purchase insurance from a broker or from an online or telephone-based insurer, as they're invariably cheaper than travel agents, banks, foreign exchange operations, or services at the airport.

TRIP-CANCELLATION INSURANCE Trip-cancellation insurance helps you get your money back if you have to back out of a trip, if you have to go home early, or if your travel supplier goes bankrupt. Allowable reasons for cancellation can range from sickness to natural disasters to a government department declaring your destination unsafe for travel. Insurers usually won't cover vague fears, though, and in 2003 travelers were not given refunds for SARS-related cancellations.

MEDICAL INSURANCE For China, purchase travel insurance that includes an air ambulance or scheduled airline repatriation. Be clear on the terms and conditions—is repatriation limited to life-threatening illnesses, for instance? While there are advanced facilities staffed by foreign doctors in Běijīng, regular Chinese hospitals are to be avoided if at all possible. They may charge you a substantial bill, which you must pay in cash before you're allowed to leave. If this happens to you, you'll have to wait until you return home to submit your claim, so make sure you have adequate proof of payment.

LOST-LUGGAGE INSURANCE On U.S. domestic flights, checked baggage is covered up to $2,500 per ticketed passenger. On international flights (including U.S. portions of international trips), baggage is limited to approximately $9.07 per pound, up to approximately $635 per checked bag. If you plan to check items more valuable than the standard liability, see if your valuables are covered by your homeowner's policy, or get baggage insurance as part of your comprehensive travel-insurance package. Read the policy carefully—some valuables

are effectively uninsurable, and others have such high excess charges that the insurance is not worth buying.

If your luggage is lost, immediately file a lost-luggage claim at the airport. For most airlines, you must report delayed, damaged, or lost baggage within 4 hours of arrival. The airlines are required to deliver luggage, once found, directly to your house or destination free of charge, although don't expect that necessarily to work with domestic Chinese airlines.

6 Health & Safety

STAYING HEALTHY
GREATEST RISKS

The greatest risk to the enjoyment of a holiday in China is one of **stomach upsets** or more serious illnesses arising from low hygiene standards. Keep your hands frequently washed and away from your mouth. Only eat freshly cooked hot food, and fruit you can peel yourself—avoid touching the part to be eaten once it's been peeled. Drink only boiled or bottled water. *Never* drink from the tap. Use bottled water for brushing your teeth.

The second most common cause of discomfort is the **upper respiratory tract infection, common cold,** or similar symptoms, often mistaken for cold or flu, which is caused by **heavy pollution.** Many standard Western remedies or sources of relief (and occasionally fake versions of these) are available over the counter, but bring a supply of whatever you are used to. If you have sensitive eyes, you may wish to bring an eye bath and solution.

If you regularly take a nonprescription medication, bring a plentiful supply with you and don't rely on finding it in China. Feminine hygiene products such as panty-liners are widely available in Běijīng, but tampons are not.

GENERAL AVAILABILITY OF HEALTHCARE

See "Fast Facts: Běijīng" in chapter 3 for a list of reliable (and very expensive) clinics with up-to-date equipment and English-speaking foreign-trained doctors. Should you begin to feel unwell in China, your first contact should be your hotel reception. Many major hotels have doctors on staff who will give a first diagnosis and treatment for minor problems, and who will be aware of the best places to send foreigners for further treatment.

Be very cautious about what is prescribed for you. Doctors are poorly paid, and many earn kickbacks from pharmaceutical companies for prescribing expensive medicines. Antibiotics are handed out like candy; indeed, dangerous and powerful drugs of all kinds can be bought over the counter at pharmacies. In general, the best policy is to stay as far away from Chinese healthcare as possible. Much of it is not good for your health.

BEFORE YOU LEAVE

Plan well ahead. If you intend merely to visit Běijīng, you may not need to bother with some of the inoculations listed below, but take *expert* advice (not website hearsay) on the latest situation. Some inoculations are expensive, some need multiple shots separated by a month or two, and some should not be given at the same time as others. So start work on this 3 or 4 months before your trip.

For the latest information on infectious diseases and travel risks, and particularly on the constantly changing situation with malaria, consult the World Heath Organization (www. who.int) and the Centers for Disease Control in Atlanta (www.cdc.gov). Look for the latest information on SARS, which may continue long after the media have become bored of reporting it. Note that family doctors are rarely up to date on vaccination requirements, so when looking for advice at home, consult a specialist travel clinic.

To begin with, your standard inoculations, typically for **polio, diphtheria,** and **tetanus,** should be up to date. You may also need inoculations against **typhoid fever, meningococcal meningitis, cholera, hepatitis A and B,** and **Japanese B encephalitis.** If you will be arriving in mainland China from a country with **yellow fever,** you may be asked for proof of vaccination, although border health inspections are cursory at best. See also advice on **malaria,** below.

WHILE YOU ARE THERE

Mosquito-borne **malaria** comes in various forms, and you may need to take two different prophylactic drugs, depending upon the time you travel, whether you venture into rural areas, and where you go. You must begin to take these drugs 1 week *before* you enter an affected area and *for 4 weeks after you leave it, sometimes longer.* For a visit to Běijīng and other major cities only, prophylaxis is usually unnecessary.

Standard precautions should be taken against exposure to **strong summer sun.** Its brightness may be dimmed by Běijīng's pollution, but the sun's power to burn is undiminished.

The Chinese are phenomenally ignorant about **sexually transmitted diseases,** which are rife. As with the respiratory disease SARS, the government denied there was any AIDS problem in China until it grew too large to be contained. Estimates of the spread of infection are still highly conservative. Condoms, including Western brands, which should be your first choice, are widely available in Běijīng.

STAYING SAFE

China is one of Asia's safest destinations. As anywhere else, though, you should be cautious of theft in places such as crowded markets, popular tourist sites, bus and railway stations, and airports. Take standard precautions against pickpockets (distribute your valuables around your person and wear a money belt inside your clothes). The main danger of walking the ill-lit streets at night is of falling down an uncovered manhole. There's no need to be concerned about dressing down or not flashing valuables— it's automatically assumed that all foreigners, even the scruffiest backpackers, are astonishingly rich, and the average Chinese cannot tell a Cartier from any other shiny watch.

Visitors should be cautious of various **scams,** especially in areas of high tourist traffic, and of Chinese who approach and say in English, "Hello friend! Welcome to China!" or similar. Scam artists who want to practice their English and suggest moving to some local haunt may leave you with a bill which has two zeros more than it should, and with trouble should you decline to pay. "Art students" are a pest, approaching you with a story about raising funds for a show overseas, but in fact enticing you into a shop where you will be lied to extravagantly about the authenticity, uniqueness, originality, and true cost of various paintings you will be pressured into buying. The man who is foolish enough to accept an invitation from pretty girls to sing karaoke deserves all the hot water in which he will find himself, up to being forced by large, well-muscled gentlemen to visit an ATM and withdraw large sums to pay for services not actually provided.

If you are a **victim of theft,** make a police report (go to the same addresses given for visa extensions earlier in this chapter; you are most likely to find an English-speaking policeman there). But don't necessarily expect sympathy, cooperation, or action. The purpose is to get a theft report to give to your insurers for compensation.

Harassment of **solo female travelers** is very rare, but slightly more likely if the traveler appears to be of Chinese descent.

Traffic is a major hazard for the cautious and incautious alike. In mainland China, driving is on the right, at least occasionally. Safe crossing of the road would be aided by the use of an *Exorcist*-style revolving head. The rules of the road are routinely ignored for the one overriding rule, "I'm bigger than you so get out of my way," and pedestrians are at the bottom of the pecking order. Cyclists come along the sidewalk, and cars mount it right in front of you and park across your path as if you don't exist. Cyclists go in both directions along the bike lane at the side of the road, which is also invaded by cars looking to mount the sidewalk to park. The edges of the main road also usually have cyclists going in both directions. The vehicle drivers are gladiators, competing for any way to move into space ahead, constantly changing lanes and crossing each other's paths. Pedestrians are like matadors pausing between lanes as cars sweep by to either side of them. Pedestrians often edge out into traffic together, causing cars to swerve away from them, often into the paths of oncoming vehicles, until one lane of traffic parts and flows to either side, and the process is repeated for the next lane.

DEALING WITH DISCRIMINATION

In mainland China, in casual encounters, non-Chinese are treated as something between a cute pet and a bull in a china shop, and sometimes with pitying condescension because they are too stupid to speak Chinese. At sights, Chinese tourists from out of town may ask to have their picture taken with you, which will be fun to show friends in their foreigner-free hometowns. ("Look! Here's me with the Elephant Man!") Unless you are of Chinese descent, your foreignness is constantly thrust in your face with catcalls of *"lǎowài,"* a not particularly courteous term for foreigner, and a bit like shouting "Chinky" at a Chinese you encounter at home. Mocking, and usually falsetto, calls of "Helloooooo" are not greetings but are similar to saying "Pretty Polly!" to a parrot. Whether acknowledged or not (and all this is best ignored), these calls are usually followed by giggles. But there's little other overt discrimination, other than persistent overcharging wherever it can possibly be arranged. In general, however, once some sort of communication is established, foreigners get better treatment from Chinese, both officials and the general public, than the Chinese give each other. People with darker skin do have a harder time than whites, but those who do not speak Mandarin will probably not notice.

7 Specialized Travel Resources

TRAVELERS WITH DISABILITIES

China is not a good choice for travelers with disabilities. If you do choose to come here, travel with a specialist group (although such tours to China are rare) or with someone fully familiar with your particular needs. The

Chinese hide people with disabilities, who are rarely seen unless reduced to begging, when they may even be subjected to taunting (although this won't happen to foreigners).

China is difficult for those with limited mobility. The sidewalks are very uneven, and public buildings, sights, and hotels almost always have stairs with no alternative ramps. In theory, some major hotels in the largest cities have wheelchair accessible rooms, but rarely are they properly executed. Metro stations do not have lifts, and any escalators usually run up only.

GAY & LESBIAN TRAVELERS

Don't travel to Běijīng for the gay scene anymore than you'd travel to Mexico for the icebergs. Homosexuality was only removed from an official list of mental illnesses in 2001. Běijīng has only a single gay bar of any note, but it is not permitted to describe it as such in print. The city has even less to offer lesbians. **The International Gay & Lesbian Travel Association (IGLTA)** (*(C)* **800/448-8550** or 954/776-2626; www.iglta.org) lists no gay-friendly organizations dealing with in-bound visitors to China.

SENIOR TRAVEL

There are no special arrangements or discounts for seniors in China, with the exception that some foreign brand-name hotels may offer senior rates if you book in advance (although you'll usually beat those prices simply by showing up in person, if there are rooms available).

FAMILY TRAVEL

Běijīng is not the place to make your first experiment in traveling with small children, although it's a better choice that anywhere else in China. Your biggest challenges will be the lack of services or entertainment aimed at children, the lack of familiar foods outside the bigger hotels and fast-food chains (unless your children have been brought up with Chinese food), and hygiene.

Some children find Chinese strangers a little too hands-on, and may tire of forced encounters (and photo sessions) with Chinese children met on the street. But the Chinese put their children firmly first, and stand up on buses while the young ones sit.

China is grubby at best, and for children who still have a tendency to put their hands in their mouths, constant vigilance will be necessary, or constant toilet visits the result. Older children should be instructed on frequent hand-washing and special caution with food.

Some familiar Western brands of disposable diapers, along with familiar creams and lotions, are available in Běijīng.

China accepts children traveling on a parent's **passport,** although the child's photo must be submitted along with the parent's when a visa application is made.

Běijīng **hotels** generally don't charge for children 12 and under who share a room with their parents. Almost all hotels will add a bed, turning a double room into a triple, for an extra ¥80 to ¥100 ($10–$13), which you can often bargain down.

Although **babysitting** services are not uncommon in the best hotels (the Sino-foreign joint-ventures with familiar names, in particular), in most cases the babysitters will speak very little English or none at all, will have no qualifications in child care, and will simply be members of the housekeeping staff.

All **restaurants** welcome children, but outside the Western fast-food outlets, some Chinese copies of those, and major hotels, don't expect high chairs or special equipment except very occasionally. The general Chinese eating method of ordering several dishes to share will at least allow your child to order whatever he or she deems acceptable (although it will not taste the same in any 2 restaurants), while allowing you to try new dishes at each meal.

Although Chinese food in Běijīng is different from (and mostly vastly superior to) Chinese food served in the West, it would still be wise to acclimatize children as much as possible before leaving by making trips to the local Chinese restaurant. In many cases only chopsticks will be available, so consider taking forks and spoons with you to China. You can now find McDonald's (complete with play areas), KFC, and Pizza Hut in Běijīng, and almost all hotels of four stars or up have coffee shops which deliver poor attempts at Western standards.

Keep in mind that although Western cooking is available at many excellent Běijīng restaurants, authenticity comes at a price. Cheap bakeries, however, often sell buttery cakes and close relatives of the muffin containing raisins and chopped walnuts.

In general, **attractions** for children are few, and exploring temples may quickly pall. Success here will depend upon your ability to provide amusement from nothing, and the sensitivity of your antennae to what captures your child's imagination.

Discounts for children on travel tickets and entrance fees are based on height, not age. There are variations, but typically children below 1.1m (3 ft., 7 in.) enter free and travel free if they do not occupy a seat on trains and buses. Children between 1.1m and 1.4m (4 ft., 2 in.) pay half price. Many ticket offices have marks on the wall at the relevant heights so that staff can quickly determine the appropriate price.

STUDENT TRAVEL

There are no particular benefits or discounts available to foreign students traveling in China unless they are registered at Chinese educational institutions (and then not many).

8 Planning Your Trip Online

SURFING FOR AIRFARES

The "big three" online travel agencies, **Expedia.com**, **Travelocity.com**, and **Orbitz.com**, sell most of the air tickets bought on the Internet. (Canadian travelers should try Expedia.ca and Travelocity.ca; U.K. residents try Expedia.co.uk and Opodo.co.uk.) Also remember to check **airline websites** for Web-only specials. For the websites of airlines that fly to and from your destination, go to section 10, "Getting There" in this chapter.

Do *not* buy China domestic travel online from English-language sites, as the markups are horrendous.

SURFING FOR HOTELS

Booking hotel rooms online in China is not a good idea, unless money is no object or you absolutely must stay at a specific hotel at a very busy time of the year. There are no online services offering Chinese hotel rooms at discounts lower than you can get for yourself, whatever they may tell you.

9 The 21st-Century Traveler

INTERNET ACCESS AWAY FROM HOME

Despite highly publicized clampdowns on cybercafes, monitoring of traffic, and blocking of websites, China remains one of the easiest countries in the world in which to get online.

WITHOUT YOUR OWN COMPUTER

In central Běijīng, government clampdowns have significantly reduced the number of Internet cafes (*wǎng bā*). Those still in operation tend to charge from ¥8 to ¥20 ($1–$2.50) per hour.

For a list of locations, see "Fast Facts: Běijīng" in chapter 3. Also keep your eyes open for the *wǎng bā* characters; see Appendix B.

Many media websites, and those with financial information or any data whatsoever on China which disagrees with the usually mendacious Party line, are blocked from mainland China, as are even some search engines.

WITH YOUR OWN COMPUTER

Don't bother looking for a local access number for your ISP in Běijīng. You can connect by using the number 95962 and making the account name and password both 263. Speeds vary but are usually fine for checking e-mail directly, although variable for checking mail via a Web interface. The service is paid for through a tiny increment in the low cost of a local phone call.

Mainland China uses the standard U.S.-style RJ11 telephone jack also used as the port for laptops worldwide. Cables with RJ11 jacks at both ends can be picked up for around ¥8.30 ($1) in Běijīng department stores and electrical shops. Standard electrical voltage across China is 220v, 50Hz, which most laptops can handle, but North American users in particular should check. For power socket information see "Fast Facts: Běijīng" in chapter 3.

Those with on-board Ethernet can take advantage of broadband services, which are sometimes free in major

---

Online Traveler's Toolbox

- **ATM Locators:** Visa ATM Locator (www.visa.com) gives locations of PLUS ATMs worldwide; MasterCard ATM Locator (www.mastercard.com) provides locations of Cirrus ATMs worldwide.
- **Online Chinese Tools** (www.mandarintools.com) has dictionaries for Mac and Windows users, Chinese calendars for conversions between the solar and lunar calendars (on which most Chinese festivals are based), and more.
- **The Oriental-List** is a noncommercial mailing list dedicated solely to the discussion of travel in China. This spam-free list, moderated to stay on-topic, offers swift answers to just about any China travel question not already dealt with in these pages. To subscribe, send a blank e-mail to subscribe-oriental-list@list.xianzai.com.
- **Travel Warnings** are available at: http://travel.state.gov/travel_warnings.html, www.fco.gov.uk/travel, www.voyage.gc.ca, and www.dfat.gov.au/consular/advice.
- **Universal Currency Converter** (www.xe.com/ucc) posts the latest exchange rates of any currency against the ¥RMB.
- **Weatherbase** (www.weatherbase.com) gives month-by-month averages for temperature and rainfall for individual cities in China.
- **Xianzai.com** (www.xianzai.com) provides free entertainment listings for Běijīng and other Chinese cities, as well as special offers from China for hotels and air tickets.
- **Zhongwen.com** (www.zhongwen.com), an online dictionary, looks up English and Chinese and provides explanations of Chinese etymology using a system of family trees.

hotels. Ethernet cables are often provided but it's best to bring your own. Occasionally Internet access is provided via the TV and a keyboard with an infrared link, but this is slow and clumsy. At least one Běijīng hotel (the Kempinski) offers wireless access in a public area for those with a wireless card installed.

USING A CELLPHONE IN CHINA

All Europeans, most Australians, and many North Americans use GSM (Global System for Mobiles). But while everyone else can take a regular GSM phone to China, North Americans, who operate on a different frequency, need a more expensive tri-band model.

International roaming charges can be horrendously expensive. Buying a pre-paid chip in China with a new number is far cheaper. You may need to call up your cellular operator to "unlock" your phone in order to use it with a local provider.

For Běijīng, **buying a phone** is the best option. Last year's now unfashionable model can be bought, with chip and ¥100 ($13) of pre-paid airtime, for about ¥800 ($100); you pay less if a Chinese model is chosen. Europeans taking their GSM phones, and North Americans with tri-band phones, can buy chips *(quánqiútōng)* for about ¥100 ($13). Recharge cards *(shénzhōuxíng)* are available at post offices and mobile-phone shops. Calling rates are low, although those receiving calls pay part of the cost.

10 Getting There

BY PLANE

On direct, nonstop flights, China's own international airlines always offer rates slightly lower than those of foreign carriers. Cabin staff try to be helpful but are never quite sure how, and the in-flight movies may be 40 years old. Air China only recently suffered its first and only fatal accident and should not be confused with China Airlines from Táiwān, at quite the other end of the scale.

Note that when leaving the country, there's a **departure tax,** currently ¥90 ($11), payable only in cash. Departure tax on domestic flights is ¥50 ($6.25), and flights from the mainland to Hong Kong and Macau are treated *as international flights.*

FROM NORTH AMERICA

Among North American airlines, **Air Canada** (www.aircanada.com), **Northwest Airlines** (www.nwa.com) (via Tokyo), and **United Airlines** (www.ual.com) fly to Běijīng.

Japan Airlines (www.jal.co.jp) flies via Tokyo to Běijīng, as does **All Nippon Airways** (www.ana.co.jp). **Korean Air** (www.koreanair.com) and **Asiana Airlines** (us.flyasiana.com) fly via Seoul.

FROM THE UNITED KINGDOM

British Airways (www.britishairways. com) flies to Běijīng. Fares with **KLM Royal Dutch Airlines** (www.klm. com) via Amsterdam, **Lufthansa** (www.lufthansa.com) via Frankfurt, or **Finnair** (www.finnair.com) via Helsinki, can often be considerably cheaper. Fares with eastern European airlines such as **Tarom Romanian Air Transport** (www.tarom.ru) via Bucharest, and **Aeroflot** (www.aeroflot.com) via Moscow, or with Asian airlines such as **Pakistan International Airlines** (www.piac.com.hk) via Islamabad or Karachi, **Malaysia Airlines** (www.mas.com.my) via Kuala Lumpur, or **Singapore Airlines** (www.singaporeair.com) via Singapore, can be cheaper still. There are even more creative routes via Ethiopia or the Gulf States.

> ### *Tips* Flying for Less: Tips for Getting the Best Airfare
>
> Passengers sharing the same airplane cabin rarely pay the same fare. Travelers who need to purchase tickets at the last minute, change their itinerary at a moment's notice, or fly one-way often get stuck paying the premium rate. Here are some ways to keep your airfare costs down.
>
> - Passengers who can book their ticket **long in advance,** who **stay over Saturday night,** or who **fly midweek** or **at less-trafficked hours** will pay less. If your schedule is flexible, say so, and ask if you can secure a cheaper fare by changing your flight plans.
> - Fly via an **intermediate country** rather than directly. In Europe considerable discounts can be obtained just by using a neighboring nation's airline and changing planes once. But North Americans can save by changing planes in Tokyo, Seoul, or Taipei, and Europeans save even more by picking eastern European airlines or those of intermediate Asian nations such as Malaysia, India, and Pakistan. Stopovers in one direction are often free or are allowable at minimum cost, giving you a chance to see two nations for the price of one ticket.
> - Fly with one of **China's carriers,** such as Air China, China Eastern, or China Southern. These undercut your own country's airline prices.
> - Fly with a carrier, such as Japan Airlines, serving **smaller regional** |airports.
> - Search the **Internet** for cheap fares (see section 8, "Planning Your Trip Online" above).
> - **Consolidators,** also known as bucket shops, are the best sources for international tickets. Start by looking in Sunday newspaper travel sections and "what's on" magazines. Small travel agents in your local Chinatown often have the best deals. *Beware:* Bucket shop tickets are usually nonrefundable or rigged with stiff cancellation penalties. Several reliable consolidators are worldwide and available on the Net. **STA Travel** (www.sta.com) offers competitive fares for travelers of all ages, as does **TravelCUTS** (www.travelcuts.com) of Canada and the U.K. **Flight Centre** (www.flightcentre.com) guarantees to beat the lowest written quote you can get elsewhere, and has offices all over Australia, Canada, New Zealand, South Africa, the U.K, and the U.S.

FROM AUSTRALASIA There's not much choice to the mainland from Down Under, although Sydney is served by **China Eastern** and **Air China** to Bĕijīng and Shànghăi, and by **Air China** and **China Southern** to Guăngzhōu, where you can catch a connecting flight to Bĕijīng. **Qantas** (www.qantas.com.au) and **Air New Zealand** (www.airnewzealand.com) fly to Hong Kong, and there are possible indirect routes with **Philippine Airlines** (www.pal.com.ph) via Manila, **Garuda Indonesia** (www.garuda-indonesia.com) via Jakarta, and **Malaysian Airlines** (www.malaysia airlines.com.my) via Kuala Lumpur. Hong Kong's **Cathay Pacific** (www.cathaypacific.com) flies directly from six Australian cities and Auckland.

BY ROAD

Foreign visitors are not permitted to drive their own vehicles into China, unless arrangements are made far in advance with a state-recognized travel agency for a specific itinerary. The agency will provide a guide who will travel in your vehicle, or in a second vehicle with a driver, and make sure you stick to the planned route. You will have to cover all the (marked-up) costs of guide, driver, and extra vehicle if needed, and of Chinese plates for your vehicle. The agency will book and overcharge you for all your hotels and for as many excursions as it can. Forget it.

BY TRAIN

From Hung Hom station in Kowloon (Hong Kong), expresses run directly to Běijīng's West Station on alternate days (see www.kcrc.com for schedules and fares). From Moscow there are weekly trains via Ulaan Baatar in Mongolia to Běijīng, and weekly via a more easterly route directly to Harbin in China's northeast and down to the capital. There's also a separate weekly run from Ulaan Baatar to Běijīng. Trains run twice-weekly from Hanoi in Vietnam to Běijīng West via Guìlín. There's also a service between Běijīng and Pyongyang in North Korea, but you'll only be on that if you've joined an organized tour.

BY SHIP

There are ferry connections from Incheon in South Korea (english.tour 2korea.com/coming/getting/bysea.asp) and from Shimonoseki and Kobe in Japan (www.celkobe.co.jp) to Tiānjīn, a couple of hours from Běijīng.

11 Packages for the Independent Traveler

For many destinations around the world, buying an unescorted package tour of pre-booked flights, internal travel, and hotels is a way of tapping into lower prices than you can obtain by buying each individual element yourself. China, as in so many other ways, is different.

Since China re-opened to foreign tourism in the early 1980s, all foreign tour operators have been required to use official state-registered travel companies as ground handlers. All arrangements in China were usually put together by one of three companies, China International Travel Service (CITS), China Travel Service (CTS), or China Youth Travel Service (CYTS). Controls are now loosening, foreign tour companies are now allowed some limited activities in China, and the range of possible Chinese partners has increased, but in effect, CITS and the like are the only companies with nationwide networks of offices, and most foreign tour companies still turn to them. They work out the schedule at the highest possible prices and send the cost to the foreign package company, which then adds its own administration charges and profit margins, and hands the resulting quote to you. You can get the same price yourself by dealing with CITS (which has many offices overseas) directly. But if things go wrong, you will be unlikely to obtain any compensation whatsoever. If you book through a tour operator in your home country, you can expect to obtain funds and compensation if this becomes necessary.

Other than convenience, there's little benefit and a great deal of unnecessary cost in buying a package. You'll get better prices by organizing things yourself as you go along.

Warning: Never book directly over the Web with a China-based travel service or "private" tour guide. Many are not licensed to do business with foreigners, many individuals have not been licensed as guides, and both will hugely overcharge and frequently mislead you (in the most charming way possible).

If money is no object, then start with the list of tour companies in the next section, nearly all of whom will arrange individual package tours (particularly Abercrombie and Kent, and Steppes East). Or you can contact the China National Tourist Offices (see section 1 in this chapter) to find properly registered Chinese agencies who can help you.

12 Escorted General-Interest Tours

Escorted tours are structured group tours with a group leader. The price usually includes everything from airfare to hotels, meals, tours, admission costs, and local transportation, but not usually domestic or international departure taxes. Almost all include a visit to Běijīng, but very few tackle Běijīng alone, or in any depth. For that you'll need to ask the companies below to organize an independent tour for you (but you'd be better off just to jump on a plane and be completely at liberty once you arrive).

Again, due to the distorted nature of the Chinese industry, escorted tours do not usually represent savings, but rather a significant increase in costs over what you can arrange for yourself. Foreign tour companies are for now required to work with state-owned ground handlers, although some book as much as they can directly or work discreetly with private operators they trust. But even as markets become more open, most arrangements will continue to be made with the official state operators, if only for convenience. Please read the brochures skeptically (one man's "scenic splendor" is another's "heavily polluted"), and carefully read the advice in this section.

As with package tours (see previous section), the arrangements within China itself are managed by a handful of local companies, whose cupidity often induces them to lead both you and your tour company astray. Various costs, which should be in the tour fee, can appear as extras; itineraries are altered to suit the pocket of the local operator; and there are all sorts of shenanigans to separate the hapless tourist from extra cash at every turn, usually at whatever point the tour staff appear to be most helpful. (The driver has bottles of water for sale on the bus each day? You're paying 3 times the shop price.)

EVALUATING TOURS

When choosing a tour company for China you must, of course, consider cost, what's included, the itinerary, the likely age and interests of other tour group members, physical ability required, and the payment and cancellation policies, as you would for any other destination. But you should also investigate:

Shopping Stops   These are the bane of any tour in China, designed to line the pockets of tour guides, drivers, and sometimes the ground handling company itself. A stop at the Great Wall may be limited to only an hour so as to allow an hour at a cloisonné factory. The better foreign tour operators design their own itineraries and have instituted strict contractual controls to keep these stops to a minimum, but they are often unable to do away with them altogether, and tour guides will introduce extra stops whenever they think they can get away with it. Other companies, particularly those companies that do not specialize in China, just take the package from the Chinese ground handler, put it together with flights, and pass it on uncritically. At shopping stops, you should never ask or accept your tour guide's advice on what is the "right price." You are shopping in the wrong place to start with, where prices will often be 10 to 15 times higher than they should be. Your driver gets a tip, and your guide gets 40% of sales. The "discount" card you are given marks you for yet higher initial prices and tells the seller to which guide commission is owed. So ask your tour company how many of these stops are included, and simply sit out those you cannot avoid.

Tipping There is *no* tipping in mainland China. If your tour company advises you to bring payments for guides and drivers, costs that should be included in your total tour cost are being passed on to you through the back door. Ask what the company's tipping policy is and add that sum to the tour price to make true comparisons. Some tour guides are making as much as *four hundred times* what an ordinary factory worker or shop assistant makes, mostly through kickbacks from sights, restaurants, and shops, all at your expense, and from misguided tipping. Some tour operators say that if they cut out the shopping stops, then they have to find other ways to cover the tour guides' income or there'll be no tour guide. Shopping-free trips are nearly always accompanied by a higher price or a higher tip recommendation (which is the same thing). The guides are doing so well that now, in some cases, rather than receive a salary from the ground-handling company, they have to *pay* for the privilege of fleecing you. The best tour companies know how China works, make what arrangements they find unavoidable, and leave you out of it. A middle path is to put a small sum from each tour member into a central kitty and disburse tips as needed, but only for truly exceptional service and at a proper local scale which short-time visitors from developed nations are incapable

of assessing. Foreign tour leaders can be tipped according to the customs of their country of origin, and most companies issue guidelines for this.

Guides Mainland guides rarely know what they are talking about, although they won't miss a beat while answering your questions. What they will have on the tip of their tongue is an impressive array of unverifiable statistics, amusing little stories of dubious authenticity, and a detailed knowledge of the official history of a place which may bear only the faintest resemblance to the truth. Their main concerns are to tell foreigners what they want to hear, and to impress them with the greatness of China. So you may be told that the Great Wall can be seen from outer space (silly), that China has 5,000 years of culture (what does this actually mean?), that one million people worked on building the Forbidden City (it was only 100,000 on last year's trip), and that the little old lady you just met in a village has never seen a foreigner before or heard of the United States (she tells every group the same thing). Guides are short-changed by China's shoddy and politically distorted education system, and also tend to put the potential profit from the relationship first.

Ask your tour company if it will be sending a guide and or tour manager from home to accompany the trip and to supplement local guides. This is worth paying more for, as this person's presence ensures a smoother trip and more authoritative information.

TOUR COMPANIES

Between them, the following tour companies (a tiny selection of what's available) serve just about all budgets and interests. The companies are from the United States, Canada, the United Kingdom, and Australia, but many have representatives around the globe. Plus you can often just buy the ground portion of the trip and fly in from wherever you like.

- **Abercrombie and Kent** (U.S.): Top-of-the-range small group tours, with the very best accommodation and transport. ℂ 800/323-7308, fax 630/954-3324, www.abercrombiekent.com (U.S.); ℂ 08450/700610, fax 08450/700608, www.abercrombie kent.co.uk (U.K.); ℂ 1300/851-800, www.abercrombiekent.com. au (Australia); ℂ 0800/441-638 (New Zealand).

- **Academic Travel Abroad** (U.S.): Tours in China for The Smithsonian (educational, cultural) and National Geographic Expeditions (natural history, soft adventure). ℂ 877/EDU-TOUR, fax 202/633-9250, smithsonianjourneys. org; ℂ 888/966-8687, fax 202/342-0317, www.nationalgeographic. org/ngexpeditions.

- **Adventure Center** (U.S.): Small group tours aimed at those who are usually independent travelers; one tour includes the Eastern Qīng Tombs and walking on several stretches of the Great Wall. ℂ 800/227-8747 (U.S.); ℂ 888/456-3522 (Canada); for representatives in Australia and New Zealand, see www.adventurecenter. com.

- **China Focus** (U.S.): Larger groups at budget prices, but with additional costs to cover extras. ℂ 800/868-8660 or 415/788-8660; fax 415/788-8665; www. chinafocustravel.com.

- **Elderhostel** (U.S.): Educational tours for seniors. ℂ 877/426-8056; www.elderhostel.org.

- **Gecko's Adventures** (Australia): Down-to-earth budget tours for small group tours of 20- to 40-year-olds, using smaller guesthouses, local restaurants, and public transport. ℂ 03/9662-2700; fax 03/9662-2422; with branches across Australia and representatives worldwide; see www. geckosadventures.com.

- **Intrepid Travel** (Australia): Slightly more adventurous tours with very small groups, following itineraries that are a deft mix of popular destinations and the less-visited. ℂ 613/9478-2626, fax 613/9419-4426, www.intrepid travel.com (Australia); ℂ 877/448-1616 (U.S).

- **Laurus Travel** (Canada): Small group tours from a Vancouver-based China-only specialist, run by a former CITS guide. ℂ 604/438-7718; fax 694/438-7715; www.laurustravel.com.

- **Pacific Delight** (U.S.): A large variety of mainstream trips for a wide range of different group sizes, with endless permutations for different time scales and budgets. Watch for extra costs. ℂ 800/221-7179; www.pacificdelight tours.com.

- **Peregrine Adventures** (Australia): Small group trips with good quality centrally located accommodation; includes visits to private houses and smaller restaurants frequented by local people and, possibly, walks and bike rides. ℂ 03/9663-8611, fax 03/9663-8618, www.peregrineadventures.com (Australia); ℂ 800/227-8747 (U.S.).

- **R. Crusoe & Son** (U.S.): Small group tours include extras such as a visit to an area of the Forbidden City usually closed to the public. ℂ 888/490-8045; www.rcrusoe. com.

- **Ritz Tours** (U.S.): Groups range in size from 10 to 40 people, and ages range widely; parents often bring children. Ritz is the foremost U.S. tour operator to China in terms of volume, and took over 20,000 visitors in 2002. ℂ 800/900-2446; www.ritztours.com.

• **Steppes East** (U.K.): Tours organized to very high standards. Its itineraries are merely suggestions that can be adapted to your specifications. ℭ 01285/651010; fax 01285/8858888; www.steppes east.co.uk.

13 Recommended Books

The best single-volume introduction to the people of China and their world is **Jasper Becker**'s *The Chinese* (John Murray, 2000). Longtime resident of Běijīng and former Běijīng bureau chief for the *South China Morning Post,* Becker delivers an immensely readable account of how the Chinese got to be who they are today; their pre-occupations, thoughts, and fears; and the ludicrous posturings of their leaders.

Old Běijīng can now only be found in literature. The origins of many Western fantasies of the capital, then called Khanbalik, lie in the ghost-written work of **Marco Polo,** *The Travels of Marco Polo.* Dover Publications' two-volume reprint (1993) of the Yule-Cordier edition is a splendid read (although only part of Polo's time was spent in Běijīng) because of its entertaining introduction and footnotes by famous explorers attempting to follow his route. **Frances Wood**'s *Did Marco Polo Go To China?* (Secker and Warburg, 1995) makes a good follow-up. Her answer is that he probably never went, but he still provides a useful compendium of what was known or believed about China at the time. One traveler who certainly visited was **Lord Macartney,** whose *An Embassy to China* (J. L. Cranmer-Byng [Ed.], Longman, 1962) gives a detailed account of Qīng China and particularly Běijīng at the end of the 18th century. This should be compulsory reading for modern businesspeople, as it prefigures recent WTO negotiations and the expectations of what will arise from them. Macartney's prediction that the Chinese would all soon by using forks and spoons is particularly relevant. **Hugh Trevor-Roper**'s *Hermit of Peking* (Eland Press, 1976), part history, part detective story, uncovers the life of Sir Edmund Backhouse, resident of Běijīng from the end of the Qīng dynasty into the Republic, who knew everyone in the city at the beginning of the century, and who deceived them all, along with a generation of China scholars, with his fake diary of a Manchu official at the time of the Boxer Rebellion. **Reginald F Johnston,** a Scot who was the last emperor's tutor, gives a measured account of life within the Forbidden City after the fall of the Qīng in *Twilight in the Forbidden City* (Gollanez, 1934; reprinted Oxford University Press, 1985). **John Blofeld**'s *City of Lingering Splendour: A Frank Account of Old Peking's Exotic Pleasures* (Shambala, 1961) describes the seamier side of Běijīng in the 1930s, by someone who took frank enjoyment in its pleasures, including adventures in "the lanes of flowers and willows"—the Qián Mén brothel quarter. In the same period, **George Kates,** an American, lived more decorously in the style of a Chinese gentleman-scholar in an old courtyard house of the kind now rapidly vanishing, and gives a sensitive and very appealing portrait of the city in *The Years That Were Fat* (Harper, 1955; reprinted by Oxford University Press, 1988). **Ann Bridge,** the wife of a British diplomat in Běijīng, wrote novels of life in the capital's Legation Quarter in the 1930s (cocktail parties, horse racing, problems with servants, love affairs—spicy stuff in its day, and best-selling, if now largely forgotten). *Peking Picnic* (Chatto and Windus, 1932; reprinted

Virago, 1989) features a disastrous trip to the outlying temples of Tánzhè Sì and Jiètái Sì (but one well worth undertaking yourself). *The Ginger Griffin* (Chatto and Windus, 1934; reprinted by Oxford University Press, 1985) offers the adventures of a young woman newly arrived in the city who attends the horse races, and has a happier ending. **David Kidd,** another American, lived in Běijīng for a few years before and shortly after the Communist victory of 1949, and gives an account of the beginning of the city's destruction in *Peking Story* (Eland Press, 1988; originally *All the Emperor's Horses,* John Murray, 1961). *Black Hands of Beijing* (John Wiley Inc., 1993), by **George Black and Robin Munro,** is the most balanced and least hysterical account of the Tiān'ān Mén protests of 1989, putting them in the context of other, better-planned movements for social change, all of which suffered in the fallout from the chaotic student demonstrations and their bloody suppression.

Chris Elder's *Old Peking: City of the Ruler of the World* (Oxford University Press, 1997) is a compendium of comments on the city from a wide range of literary and historical sources, sorted by topic. For those intent on digging out the last remains of the capitals' ancient architecture, **Susan Naquin**'s magisterial *Peking Temples and City Life, 1400–1900* (University of California Press, 2000) gives a scholarly yet readable background to many buildings now open to the public and many now long vanished.

3

Getting to Know Běijīng

by Peter Neville-Hadley

Since the 1920s, guidebook writers have complained that as quickly as they can write about one of Běijīng's historic buildings, it is pulled down.

Today we face the same problem with bars, clubs, and restaurants, whose lifetimes seem even shorter than the Chinese government's swiftness to suppress dissent. Whole streets and city blocks are often bludgeoned into oblivion almost overnight.

Historic buildings, other than ordinary housing, are not the problem. To be sure, some ancient temple buildings, long hidden by more modern construction, are demolished if the developer beats the culture cadres to the punch or induces them to look the other way. But others are emerging from roles as residences, offices, and storehouses spruced up to attract the tourist *yuán*. The choices of what to

do and see in a city already packed with pleasures increase all the time.

This chapter deals with everything you need to know to get yourself around Běijīng, a city better supplied with taxis and public transport than almost any in the United States or Europe. Běijīng's layout is simple, navigation is mainly by landmark, and the only confusion lies in the fact that any particular landmark may well be pulled down by the time you reach the city, taking two or three of our favorite restaurants with it.

In the next few years leading up to the 2008 Olympics, the massive and chaotic transformation of the city, a process which has been hiccupping along destructively for nearly a century, will become faster and ever more feverish.

So go now, before we have to start all over again.

1 Orientation

ARRIVING

Běijīng's Capital Airport (Shǒudū Jīchǎng), one of three in the city but the only one to see foreigners, and which for now handles all international and nearly all domestic flights, is 25km (16 miles) northeast of the city center (℡ **010/ 6457-1666,** information in Mandarin only; ℡ **010/6601-3336** domestic ticketing; ℡ **010/6601-6667** international ticketing). The new terminal building, opened in October 2000 and resembling other airports the world over, is straightforward to navigate, with a departures level stacked on top of an arrivals level.

There is a notional, usually nonexistent, **health check** as you approach immigration. Health declaration forms are no longer distributed, although temporary issues like SARS may cause them to be reinstated. **Immigration forms** are usually supplied in-flight or are available as you approach the immigration counters, which typically take 10 to 15 minutes to clear on arrival. Have the form completed and your passport ready.

Běijīng

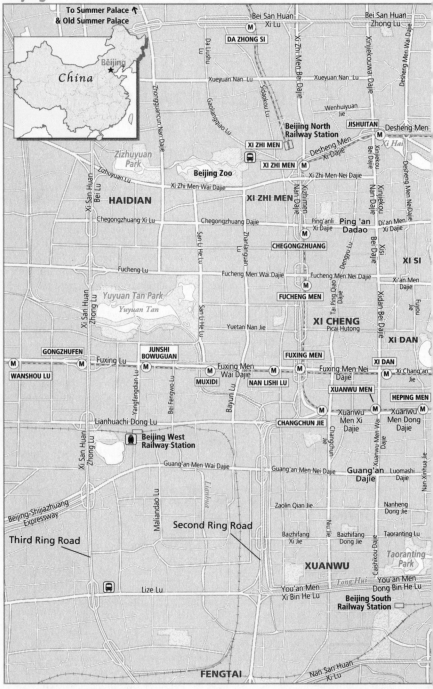

To Summer Palace ↑
& Old Summer Palace

China

Běijīng

Bei San Huan Xi Lu

Bei San Huan Zhong Lu

DA ZHONG SI

Xinjiekouwai Dajie

Desheng Men Wai Dajie

Da Liushu Lu

Xi Zhi Men Bei Dajie

Xueyuan Nan Lu

Xueyuan Nan Lu

Gaoliangqiao Lu

Sidaokou Lu

Wenhuiyuan Jie

Beijing North Railway Station

JISHUITAN

Desheng Men

Zhongguancun Nan Dajie

Desheng Men Xi Dajie

Xi Hai

Xinjiekou Bei Dajie

Desheng Men NeiDajie

XI ZHI MEN

Zizhuyuan Park

XI ZHI MEN

Xi Zhi Men Nei Dajie

Xinjiekou Nan Dajie

Zizhuyuan Lu

Beijing Zoo

Nan Dajie

Xizhimen

Xi San Huan Bei Lu

Xi Zhi Men Wai Dajie

HAIDIAN

XI ZHI MEN

Ping'anli Xi Dajie

Ping 'an Dadao

Di'an Men Xi Dajie

Chegongzhuang Xi Lu

Chegongzhuang Dajie

Xisi Bei Dajie

XI SI

San Li He Lu

Zhanlanguan Lu

Xi'an Men Dajie

Fuchéng Lu

Dengshi Lu

Xidan Bei Dajie

Fuyou Jie

Fucheng Men Wai Dajie

Fucheng Men Nei Dajie

CHEGONGZHUANG

Tai Ping Qiao Dajie

Yuyuan Tan Park

FUCHENG MEN

Yuyuan Tan

San Li He Lu

XI CHENG

Picai Hutong

XI DAN

Yuetan Nan Jie

Xi San Huan Zhong Lu

GONGZHUFEN

JUNSHI BOWUGUAN

FUXING MEN

XI DAN

Fuxing Lu

Fuxing Men Wai Dajie

Fuxing Men Nei Dajie

Xi Chang'an Jie

WANSHOU LU

MUXIDI

NAN LISHI LU

XUANWU MEN

HEPING MEN

Yangfangdian Lu

Bei Fengwo Lu

Bayun Lu

XUANWU MEN

Xuanwu Men Xi Dajie

Xuanwu Men Dong Dajie

Lianhuachi Dong Lu

Changchun Jie

Xuanwu Men Wai

CHANGCHUN JIE

Beijing West Railway Station

Nan Xinhua Jie

Guang'an Men Wai Dajie

Guang'an Men Nei Dajie

Guang'an Dajie

Luomashi Dajie

Mailiandao Lu

Zaolin Qian Jie

Nanheng Dong Jie

Beijing-Shijiazhuang Expressway

Lianhua

Second Ring Road

Baizhifang Xi Jie

Niu Jie

Baizhifang Dong Jie

Taoranting Jie

Third Ring Road

Caishikou Dajie

Taoranting Park

XUANWU

Tong Hui

You'an Men Dong Bin He Lu

Lize Lu

You'an Men Xi Bin He Lu

Beijing South Railway Station

Nan San Huan Xi Lu

FENGTAI

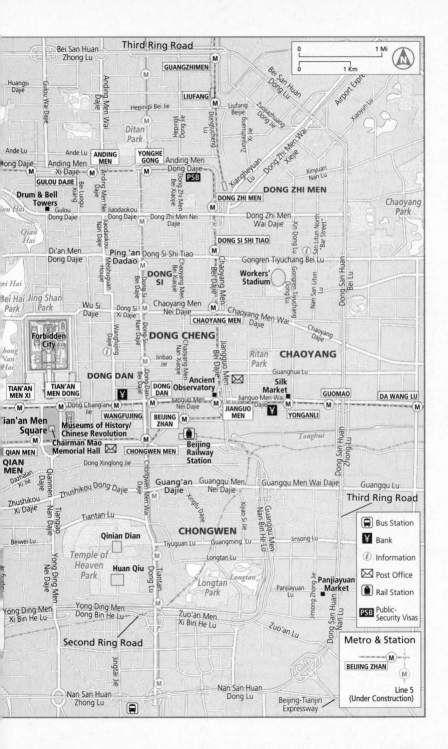

There are no longer **Customs declaration forms,** and foreigners are rarely stopped. Immediately after Customs, you may be asked to put your larger bags through an **X-ray machine,** which may or may not be photo-safe.

There are signposted **money-changers** (branches of various Chinese banks, all of which can help you), ATMs accepting foreign cards (two at arrivals level and two at departures level), and even automated money-changing machines. Exchange rates are the same here as everywhere else, although this may change eventually. So exchange as much currency as you think you'll need, and try to get at least ¥100 in ¥10 notes.

GETTING INTO TOWN

TAXIS   You will be pestered by **taxi** touts as soon as you emerge from Customs. *Never* go with these people. The signposted taxi rank is straight ahead and has a line that mostly works, although a few people will always try to cut in front of you. Line up at the two-lane rank, and a marshal will direct you to the next available vehicle as you reach the front of the line. Rates are clearly posted on the side of each cab. (The cheapest taxis are not allowed to pick up at the airport.) If you prefer a ¥1.60 (20¢) per-kilometer cab to a ¥2 (25¢) one, you can simply wait for it. After 15km (9 miles), rates increase by 50%, making a higher-priced taxi substantially more expensive, especially if you are heading for the far side of town. If you only want to go to the hotels (such as the Kempinski, Hilton, or Sheraton) in the Sān Yuán Qiáo area, where the Airport Expressway meets the Third Ring Road, your taxi driver may be a bit grumpy, but that's his bad luck.

In a ¥1.60 (20¢) cab, expect to pay under ¥80 ($10) to reach the eastern part of the city and around ¥100 ($13) to reach the central hotels. These estimates include the meter rate and a ¥10 ($1.25) expressway toll, which you'll see the driver pay en route. Fares to the central hotels will increase significantly if you travel during rush hours (8–9am and 3:30–7pm). For most of the day, you can reach hotels on the Third Ring Road within about 30 minutes, and central hotels in about 45 minutes—the latter trip may rise to more than an hour during rush hours. During the life of this book, the Běijīng taxi fleet will be replaced with new Hyundai *(Xiàndài)* vehicles, after which rates are likely to rise. Make sure you to read the box "Ten Tips For Taking Taxis Around Town," in this chapter.

HOTEL SHUTTLES   If you book a hotel room in advance, ask about shuttle services. Some hotels, such as the Kempinski, offer guests free transportation with a regular schedule of departures. The Palace Hotel will send a Rolls-Royce for you, but for a fee.

AIRPORT BUSES   Air-conditioned services, run by two different companies, leave from in front of the domestic arrivals area. The Airport Shuttle Bus runs three routes; the most useful, Line A, runs 24 hours a day, departing every 15 minutes from 8am to 10pm, less frequently through the night. The fare is ¥16 ($2). Destinations include Sān Yuán Qiáo (near the Hilton and Renaissance hotels), the Dōng Zhí Mén and Dōng Sì Shí Tiáo metro stations, Běijīng Railway Station, the CAAC ticket office in Xī Dān, and Háng Tiān Qiáo (near the Marriott West). Lines A, B, and C all pass through Sān Yuán Qiáo, but only Line A lets off passengers at a location convenient for picking up taxis to continue to other destinations. Most hotels in the center of the city can be reached by taxi for under ¥20 ($2.50) from there. The Civil Aviation Traveler Regular Bus, to the left of the exit, runs the same routes, but it also offers stops at the CAAC ticket office at the north end of Wángfǔjǐng Dàjiē.

TRAINS Twice-weekly Trans-Siberian services from Moscow (one via Ulaan Baatar in Mongolia, and one via Harbin), weekly services from Ulaan Baatar only, and services from Pyongyang in North Korea (which you'll only take if on a pre-arranged tour) all arrive at **Běijīng Zhàn,** Běijīng's original main railway station, built with Soviet assistance in the late 1950s to replace one built by the British in 1901. Twice-weekly trains from Hanoi in Vietnam, and trains from Kowloon in Hong Kong which run on alternate days, arrive at the new and far larger but already disintegrating **Xī Kè Zhàn** (also known as Běijīng Xī Zhàn), the West Station. Neither station has any currency exchange facility or ATM, although there are banks and ATMs accepting foreign cards 5 minutes' walk north of Běijīng Zhàn, at Citibank next to the Běijīng International Hotel, and at the Hong Kong and Shànghǎi Bank (HSBC) on the north side of the COFCO shopping complex.

Domestic train services from Shànghǎi and most of the south, southeast, east, and northeast arrive at Běijīng Zhàn, which has its own metro station on the circle line, with entrances across the forecourt to the right and left as you leave the railway station. The West Station will gain its own metro connection in a few years' time.

DEPARTING BĚIJĪNG

Check with your airline for the latest advice, but for international flights make sure you are at the airport *at least* 1½ hours before departure; 1 hour for domestic flights. As you face the terminal, international departures are to the right, and domestic to the left. Before proceeding through initial security and X-ray to the check-in counters, you must pay a departure tax, which is currently ¥90 ($11) for international flights (including those to Hong Kong and Macau) and ¥50 ($6.25) for domestic flights. Payment is in ¥RMB cash only at a counter near the entrance to the check-in area. Before joining lines for emigration, pick up and complete a departure card. Have your passport, departure card, departure tax receipt, and boarding card ready.

TRAVELING BEYOND BĚIJĪNG

BY PLANE There are daily **direct flights** from Capital Airport to nearly every major Chinese city, including Shànghǎi (¥1,040/$130), Guǎngzhōu (¥1,510/$189), Xī'ān (¥970/$121), Chéngdū (¥1,300/$163), and Lhasa (¥2,090/$261). Prices vary widely, according to season and your bargaining skills, and may be reduced to half the amounts quoted here. Much Chinese domestic flying is done on a walk-up basis, but the best discount is never available at the airport. The aviation authority officially permits the airlines to discount to a maximum of 40% on domestic flights, but discounts of 50%, sometimes even more, are not uncommon at ticket agencies.

Tickets for domestic flights (and international flights) on Chinese airlines are best purchased through a travel agent, such as **Airtrans** (next to the Jiànguó Hotel; ✆ **010/6595-2255**), or in one of two main ticketing halls: the Aviation Building (Mínháng Dàlóu; ✆ **010/6601-7755;** fax 010/6601-7585; 24 hr.) at Xī Cháng'ān Jiē 15, just east of the Xī Dān metro station; or at the Airlines Ticketing Hall (Mínháng Yíngyè Dàtīng; ✆ **010/8402-8198;** fax 010/6401-5307; 8am–5pm), opposite the north end of Wángfǔjǐng Dàjiē at Dōng Sì Xī Dàjiē 155. Both ticketing halls accept credit cards and offer discounts similar to those of an agent. For some of the lowest prices, check with the ticket agency representatives who wait outside the PSB visa extension office, where Chinese acquire their exit visas. If you see the characters for your destination on a representative's flier and you like the corresponding price, the tout will point you in the right direction. When pricing tickets, *always* shop around and *always* bargain for a discount. And don't expect agents inside major hotels to give you anything like the reductions you'll find elsewhere.

Booking from overseas via websites offering tickets for Chinese domestic flights, most of which do not appear on international ticketing systems, is *always* a mistake. You'll be charged the full price, which is generally only paid by a handful of people traveling at peak times at the last minute, and probably a booking fee, too.

Most hotels can arrange tickets for flights on **foreign airlines,** but they tend to levy hefty service fees. The airline offices themselves do not usually attempt to match the prices offered by agents, but are merely a source of the price to beat elsewhere. Special offers are often published in *Xianzai Beijing,* a weekly e-mail newsletter (www.xianzai.com), but sometimes agents undercut even these, or they bend the rules on advance booking requirements to give an advance-purchase price at the last minute.

BY TRAIN   The main railway stations are **Běijīng Railway Station (Běijīng Zhàn;** ✆ **010/5183-4122)** and **West Station (Xī Kè Zhàn;** schedule information ✆ **010/5182-6253).** Tickets can be purchased at these stations for any train leaving Běijīng up to 4 days in advance, and during the busiest seasons up to 10 days in advance. It is now possible to buy **round-trip tickets** *(fǎnchéng piào)* to major destinations like Shànghǎi or Xī'ān up to 12 days in advance, subject to availability. **Satellite ticket offices** *(tiělù shòupiào chù)* scattered throughout the city charge a negligible ¥5 (60¢) service fee; convenient branches are just inside the main entrance of the Sānhé Bǎihuò (department store), south of the Xīn (Sun) Dōng Ān Plaza on Wángfǔjǐng Dàjiē (9am–9pm; ✆ **010/9511-4669);** and at the Shātān Shòupiào Chù further north at Píng'ān Dàdào 45, west of Jiāodàokǒu Nán Dàjiē (8am–6pm; ✆ **010/6403-6803).** Tickets for all trains from Běijīng can also be booked free of charge at Běijīng South Station (Běijīng Nán Zhàn) and at Běijīng North Station (Běijīng Běi Zhàn), which is rather more conveniently located at Xī Zhí Mén metro station. Ordinary travel agents without computers on the railway system will usually also handle rail-ticket bookings. The fee per ticket should be no more than ¥20 ($2.50), including delivery to your hotel, although some agencies like to take foreign visitors for a ride in more than one sense. Ticket desks in hotels may charge up to ¥50 ($6.25) per ticket. Mandarin speakers can check train times and book tickets using one of several hot lines (✆ **010/6321-7188,** 010/5182-7188, or station numbers below).

At **Běijīng Railway Station (Běijīng Zhàn;** ✆ **010/5183-4122),** the best place to pick up tickets is the "ticket office for foreigners" inside the soft-berth waiting room on the ground floor of the main hall, in the far left corner (5:30am–11pm). Tickets for both versions of the **Trans-Siberian,** the Russian T19 via Manchuria (Sat 10:50pm) and the Chinese T3 via Mongolia (Wed 7:40am), must be purchased from the CITS international railway ticket office inside the International Hotel (Mon–Fri 8:30am–noon and 1:30–5pm, weekends 9am–noon and 1:30–4pm; ✆ **010/6512-0507)** 10 minutes' walk north of the station on Jiànguó Mén Nèi Dàjiē (metro: Dōng Dān). Both trains travel to Moscow (¥2,360/$295 soft sleeper), but only the T3 passes through Mongolia and stops in Ulaan Baatar (¥778/$97 soft sleeper); there's a separate Saturday train to Ulaan Baatar as well.

At the **West Station** (Xī Kè Zhàn; schedule information ✆ 010/5182-6253), the best ticket outlet is not the main ticket hall but a second office inside the main building, on the second floor to the left of the elevators (signposted in English); this is also where you go to purchase tickets for the **T97 express to Kowloon/Jiǔlóng** (10:06am; 27 hr.; ¥1,028/$129 soft sleeper, ¥662/$83 hard). The West Station is also the starting point for **trains to Hanoi,** but you have to buy tickets (¥1,023/$128 soft sleeper only) at a "travel service" booth (9am–4:30pm; ✆ **010/6398-9485**) inside the Construction Bank on the east side of the station complex. The nearest **airport shuttle** stops at the Aviation Building in Xī Dān (see above), reachable by bus no. 52 from the station's east side. The taxi rank is on the second floor.

Warning: Larger baggage is X-rayed at the entrances to most Chinese railway and bus stations. Keep film in your hand baggage.

VISITOR INFORMATION

The Běijīng Tourism Administration maintains a 24-hour **tourist information hot line** at ✆ **010/6513-0828.** Surprisingly, staff actually speak some English, so it's unfortunate that they rarely have the answers to your questions. Hotel concierges and guest relations officers are at least close at hand, although they often have little knowledge of the city, will be reluctant to work to find the answers if they can convince you to do something else instead, and, when they do find the answer to a question, they do not note it down for the next time a guest asks. Beware of strong recommendations to visit dinner shows or other expensive entertainments, as they are often on a kickback.

You can also try the new BTA-managed **Běijīng Tourist Information Centers (Běijīng Shì Lǚyóu Zīxún Fúwù Zhōngxīn)** located in each district and all marked with the same aqua-blue signs. The most competent branch is in Cháoyáng, on Gōngtǐ Běi Lù across from the City Hotel and next to KFC (✆ 010/6417-6627; fax 010/6417-6656; chaoyang@bta.gov.cn; daily 10am–6pm). Free simple maps are available at the door, and staff can sometimes be wheedled into making phone calls. Ignore the extortionist travel service, attached.

For the most current information on life in Běijīng, particularly restaurants and nightlife, see the intermittently accurate listings in the free English-language expat-produced twice-monthly *City Weekend* or monthly *that's Beijing,* available in hotel lobbies and at bars in the major drinking districts (see chapter 9 for these). Online, *City Weekend* (www.cityweekend.com) manages to update its website with fair regularity. The e-mail newsletter *Xianzai Beijing* (see www.xianzai.com for more information) provides a list of each week's events, as well as special hotel, air ticket, and restaurant offers.

CITY LAYOUT & HISTORY

Modern Běijīng stands on the site of the capital founded in 1271 by the Mongols when the territory of modern-day China was merely a part of a far larger Mongol empire. Known to the Mongols as Khanbalik and to their Chinese subjects as Dà Dū or "Great Capital," it lay on a plain with limited and bitter water supplies, handy for the steppe from which the Mongols had emerged, but well away from the heartlands of the Hàn, as the main ethnic Chinese group still call themselves. When, in 1368, the Mongol Yuán dynasty was expelled, the foreigner-founded capital was abandoned for Nánjīng, the "Southern Capital." The third Míng emperor, who had formerly been in charge of resisting fresh

Mongol advances from the north, returned the city to capital status in 1420, renaming it Běijīng, or "Northern Capital."

Although retaining much of the plan and grid of the Mongol founders, the emperor otherwise remodeled the city extensively, creating a secondary, broader walled extension to the south of the Mongol original. Many of the capital's major monuments also date from this period, and its most extensive, the Forbidden City, right at the city's heart, is the one around which the remainder of the capital is still more or less arranged. The key ceremonial halls lie on a nearly north-south axis (actually aligned on the Pole Star), which bisects the city. Most north-south streets parallel this, and main east-west routes cross them at right angles. There are very few major streets running diagonally. The grid created was originally filled in with a maze of lanes peculiar to Běijīng and to a handful of other northern cities, called *hútòng* (both singular and plural), derived from a Mongol word. But most of these narrow streets have now been destroyed.

In 1644 the Míng dynasty was overthrown by a peasant rebellion, and the peasants were driven out shortly afterwards by invading Manchu forces from beyond the Great Wall to the northeast. China was absorbed into the Qīng empire, and foreigners ruled from Běijīng until the Qīng abdication of 1912. Including occupation by foreign forces in 1860 and from 1900 to 1901, and Japanese occupation during World War II, Běijīng has been under foreign control for more than half of its existence.

Běijīng was once a set of walls within walls. The Qīng took over the walled Forbidden City and the walled Imperial City within which it sat, and their followers took over the remainder of the northern section of the walled city. This area was known to other foreigners as the Tartar City, while the broader but separate walled section to the south of the Qián Mén (Front Gate) became the Chinese City—the Chinese quarter of Běijīng.

The enemy was now within the gates, and the outer city walls were neglected, but the Qīng built many temples and palaces, leaving the city's basic grid largely unchanged while building extensive gardens to the northwest.

With the exception of a limited number of Russians and small groups of missionaries, some of whom were allowed to erect churches, Běijīng remained free of Western influence or a Western presence until 1860, when emissaries sent to complete ratification of a treaty forced on the Qīng at the end of the Second Opium War by the British and French were put to death or imprisoned. Revenge took the form of the occupation of the city by British and French troops, who torched the vast area of palaces and gardens to the northwest of the city, of which now only fragments remain at the Summer Palace and Old Summer Palace.

For the first time, Western powers were allowed to station ministers in Běijīng, and accommodation was allocated to them just inside the Tartar City, east of the Qián Mén and what is now Tiān'ān Mén Square. At the end of the 19th century, resentment at the expansion of foreign influence in China led to attacks on Chinese who had converted to Christianity, attacks on railway lines and foreign property, and eventually to a siege of the Legation Quarter during which the attackers destroyed much of the surrounding housing, a fabulous library of ancient learning, and part of the Qián Mén. The siege was only lifted 2 months and many deaths later by the forces of eight allied powers who marched from the coast. Imperial troops, Boxers, Běijīng residents, and foreign troops indulged in an orgy of looting and destruction, which supplemented the burning of shops selling foreign goods and the destruction of churches already accomplished by the Boxers. The Legation Quarter subsequently became a further walled enclave, with many foreign banks, offices, and legation (embassy) buildings. In the early 20th century it was still the only area with paved roads and proper drainage and sewerage in an otherwise notably malodorous city.

The churches were rebuilt (and still stand), but the temples that had been collateral damage were mostly left in ruins. The Qīng were in decline, and after their fall in 1912, much else went into decline, too, ancient buildings being the victims of neglect or casual destruction. This process continued during the 1911/1912–1949 Republic and accelerated following the Communist Party victory and the creation of the People's Republic of China.

Signs at the Old Summer Palace and elsewhere harp in an unbalanced way on foreign destruction in 1860 and 1900, but since 1949 the Chinese themselves have almost completely demolished their city. Temples have been turned into housing, warehouses, industrial units, offices, and police stations. The slender walled space south of the Tiān'ān Mén was smashed open to create the vast expanse of the modern square, lined by hideous Soviet-influenced halls of rapidly down-at-heel grandeur. The city walls and most gate towers were pulled down to allow the construction of the Second Ring Road and the first metro line. Areas of traditional courtyard houses were pulverized for the construction of hideous six-story concrete dormitory blocks. Political campaigns against all traditional culture led to the defacing, damage, or destruction of many ancient buildings and their contents, particularly during the 1966–76 Cultural Revolution.

The *hútòng,* once "numberless as the hairs on an ox," will soon be no harder to count than your fingers and toes, because China's increasing, if exaggerated, wealth has seen the government trying to turn the capital from a sleepy backwater into a city of international standing. The broad boulevards apparently required by Marxist theory have become ever more numerous, and the last few years have seen several new routes blasted across the city. An assortment of often hideous towers representing no particular style or culture but sometimes with cheesy Chinese toppings have sprung up within the vanished city walls, dwarfing the Forbidden City and the few older buildings which remain.

The awarding of the 2008 Olympics to Běijīng has delivered the *coup de grâce.* Whole blocks of housing disappear every few weeks as developers, hand-in-glove with the government, expel residents. Developers race to destroy the remaining halls of ancient and largely forgotten temples before those charged with preserving them can catch up, although a few are given ham-fisted restoration and reopened to the public for a fee. The city has been encircled by a third ring road, then a fourth ring road, and a fifth is underway, at ever increasing distances from the center. Another 12 metro and light rail lines are to be constructed. When the Olympic inspectors came to town, factories were shut down to reduce the omnipresent pollution, and the streets were spruced up by "volunteers," who even painted the grass green. The authorities are determined that by 2008 we should be impressed by the city's modernity, and all but the basic grid of the Yuán and Míng plan will have been swept away for shiny towers and gridlock. The most noticeable buildings will be those most alien to China—a three-venue National Theatre resembling a flying saucer which has landed in a lake, under construction in the heart of the city just west of Tiān'ān Mén Square and designed by Frenchman Paul Andreu; and the vast venues for the Běijīng Olympics including the $100 million National Swimming Centre, which *China Daily* chillingly reported "could become the defining architecture of the new century in Běijīng."

MAIN STREETS

The main west-to-east artery of interest to visitors runs across the top of Tiān'ān Mén Square, past the Tiān'ān Mén (Gate of Heavenly Peace) itself. It changes names several times, but is most importantly Xī Cháng'ān Jiē to the west of the square, Dōng Cháng'ān Jiē to the east, then Jiànguó Mén Nèi Dàjiē until it crosses the Second Ring Road, when it becomes Jiànguó Mén Wài Dàjiē. Compass points such as *xī* (west) and *dōng* (east) turn up very frequently in street names, as do words such as *mén* (gate), *nèi* (inside), and *wài* (outside). Metro Line 1 runs under this route, passing several major hotels and shopping areas. The Xī Dān Běi Dàjiē and Wángfǔjǐng Dàjiē shopping streets run north from this route. The Second Ring Road runs around the combined outer perimeter of the old city walls they replaced, still showing the bulge of the wider Chinese City to the south and, depending on the time of day, usually provides a quicker route around the city center than going though it. Further out and quicker still, the Third Ring Road, which links with the airport expressway and routes to the Summer Palace, is the site of several major long-distance bus stations, numerous upmarket joint-venture hotels, and important restaurants. Beware the taxi driver who suggests using the Fourth Ring Road. Speeds on this route are higher, but the kilometer count for getting round the city will also be significantly greater, and so will the cost.

FINDING AN ADDRESS

Maps of Běijīng are rarely accurate—the cartographers don't seem to feel it necessary to do more than sketch the main roads—and the smashing of new routes across and around the city is so rapid they can't keep up. Although some claim to issue half a dozen editions a year, the presence of *zuì xīn* or "newest" on the map cover is only an indication that the characters *zuì xīn* or the word "newest" have been put on the cover. The rest of the map may be identical to the last edition, which carried the same message, as did all its predecessors. Bilingual maps, or maps with Romanized Chinese, tend to be less accurate to start with, and are printed less often. Regardless of this, **always buy a map,** available from vendors at all arrival points and at all bookstores, for around ¥5 (65¢). The small pages of this book cannot hope to give you a detailed picture of any area, but the characters on the map keys can be used to help you find your way around the Chinese map. The staff at your hotel can mark where you are and where you want to go, and you can compare the street-name characters with those on the road signs so you can keep track of your route. There's no question of really getting lost, and you can always flag down a cab and show the driver the characters for where you want to go. Note that street numbers are given in this book, but no one actually uses them. Navigation is by street name and landmark.

NEIGHBORHOODS IN BRIEF

Citywide architectural uniformity makes the boundaries of Běijīng's official districts rather arbitrary, so we've avoided them in favor of maps showing in more detail the areas of most interest to visitors for their clusters of accommodations, restaurants, and attractions. Beyond the districts listed below, the metropolitan area stretches far into the countryside, adding perhaps another four million people to the urban population of around seven million.

Dōng Chéng

Dōng Chéng (East City) occupies the eastern half of the city center, spreading north and east from the southwest corner of Tiān'ān Mén Square until it reaches the Second Ring Road, and occasionally spills over it. It includes the square itself, the Forbidden City, major temples such as the Yǒnghé Gōng (Lama Temple) and Confucius Temple, and the major shopping streets of Wángfǔjǐng and Dōng Dān. It's essentially the eastern half of the Qīng-era Tartar City, north of the wall separating it from the Chinese City, of which the twin towers of the Qián Mén (Front Gate) are the most significant remaining fragments.

Xī Chéng

The western half of the old Tartar City, Xī Chéng is spreading farther west beyond the line of the original city wall at the Second Ring Road.

It is home to Zhōng Nán Hǎi, the off-limits central government compound otherwise known as the new Forbidden City, Běi Hǎi Gōngyuán, and the Bái Tǎ Sì (White Dagoba Temple). The Shíchà Hǎi (Back Lakes) and Dì'ān Mén area within Xī Chéng, with its string of lakes and relatively well-preserved *hútòng,* is where the last fading ghosts of (pre-1949) Old Běijīng reside. It's popular among writers, musicians, foreigners teaching in Běijīng, and other younger expatriates who haunt a collection of trendy, nameless bars and cafes at the waters' edge. Several minor sights here provide the excuse for a day's wandering.

Cháoyáng

Part urban, part suburban, Cháoyáng sprawls in a huge arc around the northeast and eastern sides of the city, housing the two main diplomatic compounds (and a 3rd new one on the way), the Sānlǐtún and Cháoyáng drinking districts, and the newly coined CBD (Central Business District) around the China World Trade Center. This is the richest district in Běijīng, the result, according to some, of the district's good *fēngshuǐ*.

The South

If Cháoyáng has Běijīng's best *fēngshuǐ*, the old Chinese City south of the Qián Mén, made up of Chóngwén (east) and Xuānwǔ (west), both enclosed by the suburban sprawl of Fēngtái to the south

and southwest, has the worst. Squalid since its construction in the Míng dynasty, this is where you'll find the city's grittiest *hútòng* and some of its best bargains on fake antiques, as well as Míng architectural jewels such as the Temple of Heaven (Tiān Tán).

Hǎidiàn

Sprawling to the northwest, this is the university and high-tech district, referred to optimistically in local media as "China's Silicon Valley," but home also to the Summer Palace and other easily reached "scenic areas."

2 Getting Around

The major street layouts in Běijīng are often well planned: sidewalk for pedestrians, a fenced-off bike lane, two lanes for cars, another bike lane, and then sidewalk again. This is one of the benefits of the hideous boulevardization, or would be if only the inhabitants used these layouts properly. However, cars are parked on the pavement, usually at an angle so as to drive pedestrians into the bike lanes, and even pushbikes are usually parked so as to cause quite unnecessary obstruction to pedestrians. So the pedestrians are forced to get in the way of the cyclists, who are anyway going in both directions in the lanes on each side of the road, as well as along the edges of the lanes for cars, often in the wrong direction. Meanwhile, cars come along the bike lanes, also often in the wrong direction, so as to get access to the pavements and drive at a few pedestrians before parking.

Although residents quickly become inured to all this madness, and although if visitors use taxis and buses they are unlikely to get injured, they'll certainly see a few accidents and injuries. The best way to get around the city is by metro or by taxi, or often by a combination of the two.

BY METRO

The Běijīng metro system *(dìtiě)* is undergoing a process of rapid expansion, which is contributing to the traffic snarls at ground level, which make using the existing three lines (two underground, one light rail or *chéngtiě*) essential. Although other cities have involved foreign companies in the construction of up-to-date rolling stock, Běijīng seems to have stuck to a locally made product, which is slow and squeaky. And whereas other cities have switched to modern electronic gates to read your ticket, Běijīng has stuck with a paper ticket system and lots of staff to check the tickets, although modernization is on the way.

According to current plans, eventually there will be 15 metro and light-rail lines, but for now the system consists of the **Circle Line** (sometimes known as **Line 2**), which follows the upper portion of the Second Ring Road, cutting across under Qián Mén, effectively following the line of the Tartar City walls that were demolished to make its construction possible. **Line 1** runs from Píngguǒ Yuán in the west, the site of Capital Iron and Steel and other heavy industry

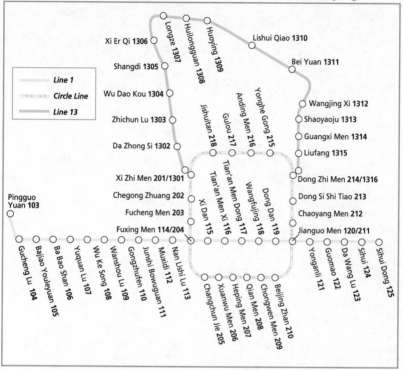

which are the sources of much of Běijīng's throat-tickling pollution, right across town beneath Cháng'ān Jiē and its extensions to Sì Huì Dōng in the east. The light-rail **Line 13** swings in a suburban loop to the north, from the Circle Line's Xī Zhí Mén to Dōng Zhí Mén stations. Several other lines, such as north-south Line 5, and one to the airport, will be completed by 2008. Stations are numbered (see Běijīng metro map), signs on platforms tell you which station is the next in each direction, and English announcements are made on trains, so navigation is not difficult.

For now, ticket booths are below ground, and a ticket costs ¥3 (35¢) for a ride anywhere from any Circle Line or Line 1 station to any other on those two lines, with free interchange. Because there's a fair bit of pushing and shoving at the ticket counters, buy a few tickets at one time (just hold up a number of fingers), but note that the two lines have different colored tickets, and you must use the right color as you start your journey. A ticket allowing you to start from or switch to Line 13, a *huànchéng piào,* is ¥5 (65¢). After the system switches to machine-readable tickets, the cost will be ¥2 (25¢) for the first three stops on any line, and ¥1 (10¢) for every three stops after that. You'll need to retain your ticket so you can insert it into an exit barrier as you leave. For the current paper ticket system, this is unnecessary.

Entrances are not clearly marked. Find them on maps, marked with a D (for *dìtiě*) in a circle, and look for the same sign at entrances. Escalators are up only, staircases are long, and there are no elevators. Those with limited mobility should stay on the surface.

> **Tips   Ten Tips for Taking Taxis Around Town**
>
> 1. **Never** go with a driver who approaches you at the airport (or rail-way stations). Leave the building and head for the rank. As with everywhere else in the world, airport taxis are the most likely to cause trouble. Drivers who approach you are usually *hēi chē*—illegal and meterless "black cabs."
> 2. Cabs waiting for business outside major tourist sights, especially those whose drivers call out to foreigners, should generally be avoided, as should cabs whose drivers ask you where you want to go before you even get in. Always flag down a passing cab, and nine times in ten the precautions listed here will be unnecessary.
> 3. If you're staying in an upmarket hotel, do not go with taxis called by the doorman or waiting in line outside. Even at some famous hotels, drivers pay kickbacks to the doormen to allow them to join the line on the forecourt. Some cabs are merely waiting because many guests, Chinese and foreign alike, will be out-of-town people who can be easily misled. Instead, flag down a passing cab for yourself. Take the hotel's business card to show to a taxi driver when you want to get back.
> 4. Better hotels give you a piece of paper with the taxi registration number on it as you board or alight, so that you can complain if something goes wrong. Often you won't know if it has, of course, and there's no guarantee that anything will happen if you complain to the hotel, but hang onto it anyway.
> 5. Look to see if the supervision card, usually with a photo of the driver and a telephone number, is prominently displayed, as

BY TAXI

Běijīng's rapid conversion from a city for bicycles to one for cars has brought the inevitable traffic jams. Get on the road well before 8am to beat the rush, or forget it until about 9:30am. The city's arteries start to clog again about 3:30pm, and circulation slows to a crawl until 7:30pm. Take the metro to the point nearest your destination and jump in a cab from there.

The more than 67,500-strong Běijīng taxi fleet is due to be replaced with vehicles manufactured in Běijīng by a joint-venture with Hyundai (Xiàndài in Mandarin). But for now there are essentially three types of vehicle available, with their per-kilometer rates posted on the side window. In most cases a cage protects the driver.

The **Xiàlì,** identified by the ¥1.20 sticker on the side window, is manufactured in Tiānjīn with a Japanese engine in its newer version. In general, it's a poorly air-conditioned rattletrap. An initial charge of ¥10 ($1.25) includes 4km (2½ miles). Subsequent kilometers are ¥1.20 (15¢) each.

The **Fùkāng,** a Citroën joint-venture built in Wǔhàn on the Yángzǐ River, is a slightly larger and more robust vehicle, with a superior engine and air-conditioning that actually works. It's a better choice for longer trips out of town. Fùkāng and Xiàlì, both of which come in "two-box" and "three-box" versions, can be hard to tell apart at a distance. The Fùkāng has its radio antenna over the regulations require. If it isn't, you may have problems. Choose another cab.

6. Can you clearly see the meter? If it's recessed behind the gear stick, partly hidden by an artfully folded towel, for example, choose another cab.

7. Always make sure you see the meter reset. If you didn't see the flag pushed down, which shouldn't happen until you actually move off, then you may end up paying for the time the cab was in the rank. This is a particularly popular scam outside better hotels.

8. If you are by yourself, sit in the front seat. Have a map with you and look as if you know where you are going (even if you don't).

9. Rates per kilometer are clearly posted on the side of the cab and vary by vehicle type. The flag drop of ¥10 ($1.25) includes 3km or 4km (2–2½ miles), after which the standard kilometer rate begins. But in Běijīng, after 15km (9 miles), the rate jumps by 50% if the driver has pushed the "one-way" button on the front of the meter. This button is for one-way trips out of town and usually should not be pushed, but always is. As a result, it's rarely worthwhile to have a cab wait for you and take you back.

10. Pay what's on the meter, and don't tip—the driver will insist on giving change. Always ask for a receipt (fā piào). Should you leave something in a cab, there's a remarkably high success rate at getting even valuable items back if you call the number on the receipt and provide the details. You'll need the assistance of a Mandarin speaker.

windshield in the middle. An initial charge of ¥10 ($1.25) includes 3km (2 miles), and each subsequent kilometer is ¥1.60 (20¢).

The **Santana** and **Jetta** are roomier vehicles built in various Volkswagen joint-ventures around China. They're similar to popular Volkswagen models in the West and are equally solid. The smaller versions have the same charges as the Fùkāng above; the larger ones charge ¥2 (25¢) per kilometer after 3km (2 miles). Occasionally, there are larger vehicles charging as much as ¥3 (35¢) per kilometer. Some of these have dodgy meters and hang around larger hotels where corrupt bellhops call them for you. Always follow the advice in the box "Ten Tips For Taking Taxis Around Town."

All taxis are metered. But on the front of the meter they also have a button, for one-way trips out of town, which is pushed regardless of the type of trip to be taken. This causes the rate per kilometer to increase by 50% after 15km (9 miles). If you are hiring the vehicle to take you somewhere, wait, and bring you back, or to run you around town all day, then you should insist that the button is not pushed. As elsewhere in the world, the meter also ticks over slowly when the vehicle is stationary or moving very slowly.

Taxi rates are also 30% higher between 11pm and 5am, but the meter's clock may decide that 11pm has arrived a little before your watch says so.

Consider taking taxis for **trips out of town.** Your hotel's transport depart-ment would love for you to take one of their cars for the day—and they would love to separate you from up to ¥1,200 ($150) for a trip you can bargain for yourself for ¥300 ($37). Xiàlì drivers typically take in around ¥500 ($63) a day; Fùkāng drivers take in around ¥300 ($37), despite their higher per-kilometer rate (the cheaper taxis do more business). Even after overheads, this puts the drivers well above the average Běijīng resident in income, but they often work 12 hours a day, 7 days a week to obtain it, and the vehicle often works 24 hours, with a separate driver on the night shift. A trip out of town is often a welcome change, and better than spending much of the day cruising the city empty. But the rate you pay should be well under the official per-kilometer rate, and a price should be negotiated. Again, deal with drivers stopped at random and not those targeting foreigners or better hotels, and begin getting quotes the day before you want to travel. The lack of a common language need not deter you, as long as you have the characters for the name of your destination and can write down the start and return times. Prices can be negotiated using pen and paper or a calcu-lator. ¥300 ($37) for a round-trip of around 200km (124 miles) is fine. You should also be prepared to pay road tolls and parking fees (probably in total no more than about ¥60/$7.50), and it's a nice gesture to buy the driver lunch.

BY BUS

Unless you are on the tightest of backpacker budgets and are traveling alone, your first choice for getting around town is the metro, your second choice is taxi, and your last resort should be the bus, although some of the air-conditioned 800 series routes are worth considering. Regular buses charge a flat fare of ¥1 (10¢), while air-conditioned buses charge ¥2 (25¢). Fees are payable into a slot at the front of the bus with no change given. Entrance and exit doors are marked with the *shàng* and *xià* characters respectively (see Appendix B). Some buses have con-ductors who'll need to know your destination in order to work out how much to charge you.

BY PEDICAB

Unless you are competent in Mandarin and obviously familiar with the city, a ride in a pedicab will always end in grief, and arguments over the agreed fare ("No! Thirty *dollars!*"). A taxi is cheaper, quicker, and less stressful, and it won't make you look like an idiot tourist.

BY BICYCLE

There used to be considerable charm in being one fish in a vast shoal of bicy-cles, but cycling is now ill-advised for the timid (or sensibly cautious). (See "By Car," below.) But enthusiasts for two-wheeled travel will certainly find that at some times of day they can get around more quickly than anyone else. Many upmarket hotels will rent you a bicycle for around ¥80 to ¥100 ($10–$13) for the day—around one-third to one-quarter what it would actually cost to buy one, so if you're going to be using a bike for a few days (and if you survive), buy-ing one is a better deal. Don't expect sophisticated accessories such as gears on rental bikes or bikes purchased for these prices. Flat Běijīng does not require them anyway. Budget accommodations and the occasional independent outlet will charge a more appropriate ¥10 ($1.25) for the day. Check the bike's condi-tion carefully, especially the brakes and tires. Sidewalk bicycle-repair operations are everywhere and will make repairs for a few *yuán,* if the worst comes to the worst. Always park the bike in marked and supervised enclosures, using the lock, which is built in or provided, or expect the bike to be gone when you get back. The parking fee is usually ¥0.20 (2¢).

ON FOOT

The vast width of Běijīng's boulevards make maps deceiving. Blocks are long, and everything is further away than it seems. Save your feet for getting around temples, palaces, and markets, which can be very extensive, or for the walking routes in chapter 7. Use pedestrian underpasses and footbridges wherever available, or be prepared to adopt the matador approach of the locals, letting cars sweep past you to either side as you wait for the opportunity to cross to the next lane. Traffic turning right at lights does not give way to pedestrians, nor does any other traffic unless forced to do so by large groups of people bunching up to cross the road.

BY CAR

The rule of the road is "me first," regardless of signs, traffic lights, road markings, safety considerations, or common sense, unless someone with an ability to fine or demand a bribe is watching. In general, the bigger your vehicle, the more authority you have. Maximum selfishness in the face of common sense characterizes driving in general, and there is no maneuver so ludicrous, unreasonable, or unexpected that someone will not attempt it. Residents have time to adapt—visitors do not.

As soon as traffic lights turn green, those cars turning left make a dash straight across the path of oncoming vehicles, each car nose-to-tail a paint layer's distance apart, forming a long string to prevent those with the right of way from going straight on. The oncoming traffic edges forward, causing those turning left to do so ever more sharply until they are almost turning back on themselves before turning right up the inside of the oncoming traffic and then left again at the junction. Only when the lights change do the oncoming vehicles get a chance to move, which involves swerving ever more sharply to avoid those who now have the theoretical right of way to cross their paths, themselves also thwarted by the new string of left-turners from the opposite direction.

Wing mirrors and indicators are purely decorative. Drivers simply pull out without looking. Accidents are commonplace, and while they are resolved, the vehicles involved are simply left in the middle of the road or junction, regardless of how busy they may be. An instant court of loafers and passers-by convenes, and those involved play out their arguments about fault to an ever-increasing audience which appoints itself jury. Meanwhile, traffic oozes around to either side, mounting the sidewalk if necessary or swerving to the other side of the road to block oncoming traffic.

Bicyclists, none of whom use lights, enter traffic streams as if blindfolded and expect vehicles to avoid them. However, cars turning right, for instance, will turn straight across the path of cyclists alongside them as if they don't exist. But why do Chinese cyclists almost never have their seats at optimum height? Because they rarely bother to replace the brake blocks on their bikes, and they need their feet to help them stop. Collisions are inevitable.

When cars pull out from side streets into the stream of cyclists, the cyclists still keep coming, swerving ever further out from the curb around the emerging noses of the cars until they cross into the opposite lane and cause oncoming vehicles to swerve to avoid them. In general, in any collision between car and bicycle, the bicyclist is always deemed to be the victim. Some exploit this and will use the slightest contact, even if it's entirely their own fault and no damage is done or hurt caused, to extort some kind of compensation. The instant self-convening pedestrian court of public opinion will be on their side.

In the case of an accident, the court of public opinion will usually designate you the loser simply because you are foreign, and if Chinese are hurt, it's not unknown for foreigners to be beaten up and their vehicles damaged (regardless of fault), especially at times when the government has been running one of its frequent anti-foreigner campaigns in the media.

FAST FACTS: Běijīng

Airport See "Arriving" under "Orientation" at the beginning of this chapter.

American Express Běijīng: Room 2101, China World Tower 1, China World Trade Center; ℂ **010/6505-2639**. After hours: U.S. hot line ℂ 001336/393-1111. Emergency card replacement: 00852/2277-1010. Stolen traveler's checks: 010800/610-0276 (toll-free).

Area Codes In mainland China, area codes begin with a zero, which must be dropped when calling China from abroad. The whole area code can be dropped when calling another number in the same area.

Babysitters Babysitting services are widely available in hotels but are usually carried out by regular members of the housekeeping staff. Don't expect special qualifications, but do expect your children to be spoiled rotten.

Banks, Currency Exchanges & ATMs Larger branches of the **Bank of China** typically exchange cash and traveler's checks on weekdays only, from 9am to 4pm, occasionally with a break for lunch (11:30am–1:30pm). Most central is the branch at the bottom of Wángfǔjǐng Dàjiē, next to the Oriental Plaza, with currency exchange and credit card cash advances handled at windows 5 to 11 (until 5pm). Other useful branches include those at Fùchéng Mén Nèi Dàjiē 410; on Jiànguó Mén Wài Dàjiē, west of the Scitech Building; in the Lufthansa Center, next to the Kempinski Hotel; and in Tower 1 of the China World Trade Center. Outside the airport, Bank of China **ATMs** accepting international cards 24 hours a day include those outside the Wángfǔjǐng Dàjiē branch mentioned above. Others exist further north on Wángfǔjǐng Dàjiē, outside the Xīn (Sun) Dōng Ān Plaza; on the left just inside the Pacific Century Plaza on Gōngtǐ Běi Lù east of Sānlǐtún (only 9am–9pm); and adjacent to the Bank of China branch next to the Scitech Building (see above; also 24 hr.). The Citibank ATM east of the International Hotel, and the Hongkong and Shanghai Bank machine at the entrance to COFCO Plaza, roughly opposite each other on Jiànguó Mén Nèi Dàjiē, are Běijīng's most reliable. There are also four ATMs at the airport; two at departures level and two at arrivals level. See "Money" in chapter 2 for further details on using ATMs.

Books The best selection of English-language books in Běijīng can be found at the clearly marked **Foreign Languages Bookstore** (Wàiwén Shūdiàn; 9am–8:30pm) at Wángfǔjǐng Dàjiē 235, opposite the Xīn (Sun) Dōng Ān Plaza. Look on the right side of the first floor for China-related nonfiction, glossy *hútòng* photo books, cookbooks, the full range of

Asiapac's cartoon renditions of Chinese classics, and even Frommer's guides. Cheap paperback versions of a huge chunk of the English canon, as well as a number of contemporary works, are sold on the third floor. The newsstand on the first floor of the **Friendship Store,** at Jiànguó Mén Wài 17, carries a respectable selection of foreign magazines and newspapers, also available in many five-star hotel lobbies. *Warning:* Nearly everything mentioned above is wildly overpriced.

Business Hours Offices are generally open 9am to 6pm, but closed Saturday and Sunday. All shops, sights, restaurants, and transport systems offer the same service 7 days a week. Shops are typically open at least 8am to 8pm. Bank opening hours vary (see "Banks, Currency Exchanges & ATMs" above).

Car Rentals Because of the many driving hazards in Běijīng, renting a car is not recommended for visitors. Taking taxis is cheaper and easier. For the fearless (and wealthy), cars can be rented from your hotel or through a travel agency, but these come with drivers, which is how you want it. There is a highly expensive car-rental agency at Běijīng's Capital Airport, **BCNC Car Rental,** which will rent you a vehicle if you can show an air ticket and have an *international* driving license. Rates are high, deposits huge, and further payments for permission to venture beyond the city are also high. To reserve a vehicle, call toll-free in China ℂ **010800/810-9001.** From overseas, inquire by e-mail: thompsonwest@mindspring.com.

Currency See "Money" in chapter 2.

Doctors & Dentists For comprehensive care, the best choice is **Běijīng United Family Hospital (Hémùjiā Yīyuàn;** ℂ **010/6433-3960)** at Jiàngtái Lù (2 blocks southeast of the Holiday Inn Lido); it is open 24 hours, is staffed with foreign-trained doctors, and has a pharmacy, dental clinic, in- and out-patient care, and ambulance service. Other reputable health-service providers, both with 24-hour ambulance services, are the **International Medical Center** (ℂ **010/6456-1561**), inside the Lufthansa Center; and the **International SOS Clinic and Alarm Center** (ℂ **010/6492-9111**), in Building C of the BITIC Leasing Center.

Driving Rules "I'm bigger than you, so get out of my way," sums it up. See "By Car" earlier in this chapter.

Drugstores Bring supplies of your favorite over-the-counter medicines with you because supplies of well-known Western brands are unreliable and sometimes fake. The real thing can be found in the lobbies of international five-star hotels. Better still, branches of **Watson's** (on the 1st floor of Full Link Plaza at Cháoyáng Mén Wài Dàjiē 19, and in the basement of the Oriental Plaza at the bottom of Wángfǔjǐng Dàjiē 1; 10am–9pm) stock most common remedies and toiletries, mostly in the British versions. For more specific drugs, try the pharmacy in the Běijīng United Family Hospital (see "Doctors & Dentists" above).

Electricity The electricity used in all parts of China is 220 volts, alternating current (AC), 50 cycles. Most devices from North America, therefore, cannot be used without a transformer. The most common outlet takes the North American two-flat-pin plug (but not the three-pin version, or those with one pin broader than the other). Nearly as common are outlets for the two-round-pin plugs common in Europe. Outlets for the three-flat-pin (two pins at an angle) used in Australia, for instance, are also frequently seen. Most hotel rooms have all three, and indeed many outlets are designed to take all three plugs. Adapters are available for only ¥8.25 to ¥17 ($1–$2) in department stores. Shaver sockets are common in bathrooms of hotels from three stars upwards. British-style three-chunky-pin plugs also often occur in mainland joint-venture hotels built with Hong Kong assistance, but hotels of this caliber will have adapters available.

Embassies & Consulates Běijīng has two main embassy areas—one surrounding Rìtán Gōngyuán north of Jiànguó Mén Wài Dàjiē, and another in Sānlǐtún north of Gōngtǐ Běi Lù. A third district, future home of the new U.S. Embassy, has sprouted up next to the Hilton Hotel outside the north section of the East Third Ring Road. Embassies are typically open Monday through Friday from 9am to between 4 and 5pm, with a lunch break from noon to 1:30pm. The **U.S. Embassy** is in Rìtán at Xiùshuǐ Dōng Jiē 2 (American Citizen Services: ☏ 010/6532-3431, ext. 5344 or, after hours, 010/6532-1910; fax 010/6532-4153). The **Canadian Embassy** is at 19 Dōng Zhí Mén Wài Dàjiē (☏ **010/6532-3536**; beijing-cs@dfait-maeci.gc.ca). The **British Embassy** consular section is in Rìtán at Guānghuá Lù 1 (☏ **010/8593-6076**; fax 010/8529-6081). The **Australian Embassy** is in Sānlǐtún at Dōng Zhí Mén Wài Dàjiē 21 (☏ **010/6532-2331**; fax 010/6532-4605). The **New Zealand Embassy** is in Rìtán at Dōng Èr Jiē 11 (☏ **010/6532-2731**, ext. 220; fax 010/6532-4317).

Emergencies No one speaks English on emergency numbers in China, although your best bet will be **110**. Find help nearer at hand.

Etiquette & Customs **Appropriate attire:** Wear whatever you find comfortable. Some of the diaphanous or apparently spray-on dressing of younger women is more likely to surprise you than your attire will surprise them. Foreigners are stared at regardless of what they wear. Swimwear should tend towards the conservative by Western standards—shorts rather than briefs for men, swimsuits rather than bikinis for women—but not if you are using pools in deluxe hotels with plenty of foreign guests. Business attire is similar to that of the West. For most visitors, opportunities to dress up formally are few, and there are no restaurants or hotels absolutely requiring jacket or tie (nor would they be likely to turn foreigners away even if they did).

Greetings and gestures: The handshake is now used as it is in the West, although there's a tendency to hang on rather longer. Take business cards if you have them, as an exchange of cards almost always follows. Present yours with two hands, and then hold the one you're given with two hands. If you can speak even two words of Mandarin, you will be told that you speak very well. But even if you are fluent, this is something you should deny.

Avoiding offense: However great the provocation, do not lose your temper and shout at someone in public or cause them to experience public shame (loss of face). Even flatly contradicting someone in front of others (so he loses face) is also best avoided if harmony is to be maintained. Instead, complain calmly and privately, and directly to a superior if you wish. Punctuality is very important in China, and the traffic situation in most cities makes that difficult, so allow plenty of time.

Eating and drinking: Master the use of chopsticks before you go. Suggestions that the food is lacking in some way, made by the host, should always be greeted with firm denials. Serve yourself from main dishes using the spoon provided, then eat with chopsticks. Do not leave them sticking up out of your bowl. Your cup of tea will constantly be topped up—when you want no more, leave it full. There's a great deal of competitive drinking at banquets, which is done by the simultaneous drinking of toasts in *bái jiǔ* (Chinese spirits), to cries of *"Gān bēi!"* ("dry cup"—down in one). Avoid participation by drinking beer or mineral water instead, but if toasts of welcome are made, be sure to make one in reply. Dining tends to happen fairly early, and at the end of the meal everyone disappears quickly. If you are invited to eat at someone's home, be sure to take off your shoes at the entrance (your host's protestations that it's not necessary are merely polite).

Holidays See "Calendar of Events" earlier in this chapter.

Hot Lines Hot lines and all kinds of telephone booking and information numbers are given throughout this book. But in almost no cases will English be spoken at the other end. Ask English-speaking staff at your hotel to find answers to your questions and to make any necessary calls on your behalf.

Information See "Visitor Information" earlier in this chapter.

Internet Access Internet bars in Běijīng are subject to numerous regulations (no one under 18, no smoking) and are restricted in number. The best bet for affordable Internet access is any of the city's various **youth hostels**; the cost is usually ¥10 ($1) per hour. There are two conveniently located Internet bars on the third floor of the Lǎo Chē Zhàn (Old Train Station) shopping center next to Qián Mén. **Qiányì Wǎngluò Kāfēiwū** is open from 9am to 11pm and charges ¥20 ($2.50) per hour in a cafe setting with a full coffee menu. A simpler, nameless place next door, open from 9am to midnight, charges ¥6 (80¢) per hour. The fastest in-room **dial-up** service is **95962** (user name and password 263). See "The 21st-Century Traveler" in chapter 2 for a full explanation.

Language English is rare in Běijīng, although there will be someone at your hotel who speaks at least a little. Ask him or her to help you with phone calls and bookings. Almost no information, booking, complaint, or emergency lines in Běijīng have anyone who speaks English.

Legal Aid If you get on the wrong side of what passes for the law in China, contact your consulate immediately.

Liquor Laws With the exception of some minor local regulations, there are no liquor laws in Běijīng. Alcohol can be bought in any convenience store, supermarket, restaurant, bar, hotel, or club, 7 days a week, and may be drunk anywhere you feel like drinking it. If the shop is open 24 hours, then the alcohol is available 24 hours, too. Closing times for bars and clubs vary according to demand, but typically it's all over by 3am.

Lost & Found Be sure to contact all of your credit card companies the minute you discover your wallet has been lost or stolen. Your credit card company or insurer may require a police report number or record of the loss, although many Public Security Bureau (police stations) will be reluctant to do anything as energetic as lift a pen. Most credit card companies have an emergency toll-free number to call if your card is lost or stolen: In **mainland China,** Visa's emergency number is ☏ **010/800-440-0027;** American Express cardholders and traveler's check holders should call ☏ **010/800-610-0277;** MasterCard holders should call ☏ **010/800-110-7309.** Diners Club members should call Hong Kong at ☏ **852/2860-1800,** or call the U.S. collect at ☏ **416/369-6313.** Also see "Emergency Cash" under "Money" in chapter 2.

Mail Sending mail from China is remarkably reliable, although sending it to private addresses within China is not. Take the mail to post offices rather than use post boxes. Some larger hotels have postal services on-site. It helps if mail sent out of the country has its country of destination written in characters, but this is not essential, although hotel staff will often help. Letters and cards written in red ink will occasionally be rejected, as this carries extremely negative overtones. Costs are as follows: Overseas mail: **postcards** ¥4.20 (50¢), **letters under 10g** (.35 oz.) ¥5.40 (70¢), **letters under 20g** (.70 oz.) ¥6.50 (80¢). **EMS (express parcels** under 500g/18 oz.): to the U.S. ¥180 to ¥240 ($23–$30); to Europe ¥220 to ¥280 ($28–$35); to Australia ¥160 to ¥210 ($20–$26). **Normal parcels** up to 1kg (2.2 lb.): to the U.S. by air ¥95 to ¥159 ($12–$20), by sea ¥20 to ¥84 ($2.50–$14); to the U.K. by air ¥77 to ¥162 ($10–$20), by sea ¥22 to ¥108 ($11–$13); to Australia by air ¥70 to ¥144 ($8.75–$18), by sea ¥15 to ¥89 ($1.90–$11). Letters and parcels can be registered for a small extra charge. Registration forms and Customs declaration forms are in Chinese and French.

Maps Purchasing city maps as you go is absolutely essential, even though few are bilingual. These are available at bus and railway stations and at airports for around ¥5 (65¢). Get your hotel staff to circle the characters for your hotel on the map, and the characters for the main sights you plan to see. You can then jump in a taxi at any point, show the driver the characters for where you want to go, and keep an eye on the route he takes.

Newspapers & Magazines Sino-foreign joint-venture hotels in the bigger cities have a selection of foreign newspapers and magazines available, but these are not otherwise on sale. The government distributes a propaganda sheet called *China Daily,* usually free at hotels. Běijīng also supports a number of self-censoring entertainment magazines usually produced by resident foreigners, and only slightly more bland when produced by Chinese aiming at the same market. Nevertheless, these do have intermittently accurate entertainment listings, as well as restaurant reviews. See "Visitor Information" earlier in this chapter.

Police Known to foreigners as the PSB (Public Security Bureau, *gōng'ān jú*), this is only one of several different bureaus in mainland China. The police (*jǐngchá*) are quite simply best avoided. Since they are keen to avoid doing any work, you have the same interests at heart. If you must see them for some reason, approach your hotel for assistance first, and visit the office listed under "Visa Extensions," under "Entry Requirements & Customs" in chapter 2, where you are likely to find an English speaker of sorts.

Post Office There are numerous post offices across the city, including one a long block north of the Jiànguó Mén metro station on the east side of Jiànguó Mén Běi Dàjiē (8am–6:30pm), one inside the Landmark Tower (next to the Great Wall Sheraton), one next to the Friendship Store on Jiànguó Mén Wài Dàjiē, one on Gōngtǐ Běi Lù (opposite the Workers' Stadium), the main office on Jiànguó Mén Nèi Dàjiē on the corner of Běijīng Zhàn Kǒu leading to Běijīng Station (almost opposite the International Hotel), and the EMS Post Office (Běijīng Yóuzhèng Sùdì Jú) at the corner of Qián Mén Dōng Dàjiē and Zhèngyì Lù. There is a **FedEx** office at the Oriental Plaza (intersection of Wángfǔjǐng Dàjiē and Cháng'ān Dōng Dàjiē), in Room 107, No. 1 Office Building. **DHL-Sinotrans** has a branch in the Lufthansa Center, and **UPS** is at Guānghuá Lù 12A.

Restrooms Street-level public toilets in China are common, many detectable with the nose before they are seen. Entrance fees have been abolished in Běijīng, but someone may still try to charge you for toilet paper ¥0.20. In many cases you merely squat over a trough. So, use the standard Western equipment in your hotel room, in department stores and malls, and in branches of foreign fast-food chains. This is the principal benefit of the presence of so many branches of KFC and McDonald's.

Safety See "Health & Safety" in chapter 2.

Smoking The government of China is the world's biggest cigarette manufacturer. China is home to 20% of the world's population but 30% of the world's cigarettes. About one million people a year in China die of smoking-related illnesses. Nonsmoking tables in restaurants are almost unheard of, and NO SMOKING signs are favorite places beneath which to smoke, especially in elevators. Smokers are generally sent to the spaces between the carriages on trains, but they won't bother to go there if no one protests. Similarly on air-conditioned buses: Some people will light up to see if they can get away with it (but usually they'll be told to put it out).

Taxes Běijīng's bed tax (of ¥6/75¢ per bed) has now been abolished, but you may need to remind some hotels of this. Service charges mostly only appear in Sino-foreign joint-venture hotels, and range from 10% to 15%. Departure taxes must be paid in cash at the airport before flying: domestic ¥50 ($6.25), international (including flights to Hong Kong and Macau) ¥90 ($11).

Telephone The international country code for mainland China is **86**.
To call China:
1. Dial the international access code: 011 in the U.S., 00 in the U.K., for example.
2. Dial the country code: 86 for China.
3. Dial the city code, omitting the leading zero, and then dial the number. To reach Běijīng from the U.S., you would dial 011-86-10-XXXX-XXXX.

To call within China: For calls within the same city, omit the city code, which always begins with a zero when used (010 for Běijīng, 020 for Guǎngzhōu, for example). All hotel phones have direct dialing, and most have international dialing. Hotels are only allowed to add a service charge of up to 15% to the cost of the call, and even long-distance rates within China are very low. To use a public telephone you'll need an IC (integrated circuit) card *("àicēi" kǎ)* available from post offices, convenience stores, and street stalls, in values beginning at ¥20 ($2.50) wherever you can make out the letters "IC" among the Chinese characters. A brief local call is typically ¥0.30 to ¥0.50 (4¢–6¢). Phones show you the value remaining on the card when you insert it, and count down as you talk.

To make international calls: First dial 00 and then the country code (U.S. or Canada 1, U.K. 44, Ireland 353, Australia 61, New Zealand 64). Next dial the area or city code, omitting any leading zero, and then dial the number. For example, if you want to call the British Embassy in Washington, D.C., you would dial 00-1-202-588-7800. Forget taking access numbers for your local phone company with you—you can call internationally for a fraction of the cost by using an IP (Internet protocol) card *(àipì kǎ),* available wherever you see the letters "IP." You should bargain to pay less than the face value of the card—as little as ¥70 ($8.75) for a ¥100 ($13) card from street vendors. Instructions for use are on the back, but you simply dial the access number given, choose English from the menu, and follow the instructions to dial in the number behind a scratch-off panel. Depending on where you call, ¥50 ($6.25) can give you an hour of talking. If using a public phone, you'll need an IC card (see above) to make the local call. In emergencies, dial 108 to negotiate a collect call, but again, you'll need help from a Mandarin speaker.

For directory assistance: Dial 114. No English is spoken, and only local numbers are available. If you want numbers for other cities, dial the city code followed by 114—a long-distance call.

For operator assistance: Just ask for help at your hotel.

Toll-free numbers: Numbers beginning with 800 within China are toll-free, but calling a 1-800 number in the States from China is a full tariff international call, as is calling one in Hong Kong from mainland China, or vice versa.

Time Zone The whole of China is on Běijīng time—8 hours ahead of GMT (and therefore of London), 13 hours ahead of New York, 14 hours ahead of Chicago, and 16 hours ahead of Los Angeles. There's no daylight savings time (summer time), so subtract 1 hour in the summer.

Tipping In **mainland China,** as in many other countries, there is *no tipping,* despite what tour companies may tell you (although if you have a tour leader who accompanies you from home, home rules apply). Until recently, tipping was expressly forbidden, and some hotels still carry signs requesting you not to tip. Foreigners, especially those on tours, are overcharged at every turn, and it bemuses Chinese that they hand out free money in addition. Chinese never do it themselves, and indeed if a bellhop or other hotel employee hints that a tip would be welcome, he or she is likely to be fired. Waitresses may run out of restaurants after you to give you change, and all but the most corrupt of taxi drivers will insist on returning it, too. Hotel employees and taxi drivers are already far better paid than the average Chinese, and to be a tour guide is already a license to print money. In China, the listed price or the price bargained for is the price you pay, and that's that.

Water Tap water in mainland China is not drinkable, and should not even be used for brushing your teeth. Use bottled water, widely available on every street, and provided for free in all the better hotels.

Weather For daily weather forecasts, check *China Daily* or CCTV 9, China Central Television's English channel (broadcast in most hotels). There is also a weather hot line (© 121); dial 6 after a minute or so for the report in English (¥3/45¢ per min.).

4

Where to Stay

by Josh Chin, Graeme Smith, and Peter Neville-Hadley

There are two types of hotel in mainland China: the **Sino-foreign joint-venture** hotels with familiar brand names, and **Chinese-owned and -managed** hotels. At the four- and five-star levels (see below for details on local star ratings), the Chinese-owned and -run hotels want you to think they are on par with the joint ventures. At lower levels they can range from indescribably battered and grubby to friendly, clean, and comfortable. (*Note:* We awarded the star ratings shown at the beginning of each review in this chapter. Our 0–3 star scale does not coincide with the Chinese star-rating system.)

Your **first choice** at the four- or five-star level should be a familiar brand name, or a property from one of the Asian luxury chains. In most cases, the buildings are Chinese-owned, and the foreign part of the joint venture is the management company, which supplies world-wide marketing efforts, staff training, and senior management, while ensuring conformity with brand standards (never entirely possible; you'll generally find 90% of what you'd expect from the same brand at home).

Your **second choice** should be a wholly Chinese-owned and -run hotel with foreigners in senior management whose main purpose is to be there and make sure that things actually happen. But in both types of hotel, the general manager may have far less idea than he thinks he has to what's going on: The transport department uses hotel vehicles for private hires to make money on the side; the human resources manager rejects applicants whose experience may be threatening and makes a good income from bribes (to ensure that the housekeeper's nephew gets a job in security, for instance); the front office manager institutes a system of fines, and pockets them himself; or the doormen charge taxis to be allowed to wait in the rank.

Entirely **Chinese-owned and -run** hotels at four- and five-star levels usually have only one thing in common with their counterparts: They charge the same (or, at least, attempt to do so); but you'll rarely get value for your money. At the four-star level and below, the best choice is almost always the newest hotel—teething troubles aside, most things will work, staff will be eager to please (if not quite sure how), rooms will be spotless, and rates can be easily bargained down, since few hotels spend any money on advertising. The aim is to find sweetly inept but willing service rather than the sour leftovers of the *tiěfànwǎn* (iron rice bowl) era of guaranteed employment, for whom everything is too much effort.

A drawback for all hoteliers is that the government requires them to employ far more people than they need, and it's nearly impossible to obtain staff with any experience in hotel work. The joint-venture hotels are the training institutions for the rest of the Chinese hotel industry, which steals their local staff as soon as possible. Lower-level hotels are run by half-understood rules, with which there's half-compliance, half the time. A hotel may have designated nonsmoking rooms, but that doesn't mean they don't have ashtrays in them.

Until recently throughout China, only hotels with **special licenses** were allowed to take foreign guests. This requirement has now vanished from Běijīng. In theory, all hotels with such licenses have at least one English speaker, usually of modest ability.

The Chinese **star-rating system** is meaningless. Nationwide, five-star ratings are awarded by a central authority, but four-star and lower ratings depend upon local standards, and both depend upon compliance with a checklist, which in Běijīng now includes having a bowling alley. The bowling alley may be permanently out of order, but the hotel will retain its four stars, as long as it banquets the inspectors adequately. (Inspectors have no idea how to run a hotel anyway.) In general, Chinese hotels receive almost no maintenance after they open. There are Chinese "five-star" hotels in Běijīng which have gone a decade without proper redecoration or refurbishment. Foreign managements force the issue with building owners, but it's rare for standards to be maintained. A new three-star will usually be better than an old four-star.

Outside of joint-venture hotels, don't rely on finding **amenities;** even if we list them in this book, there's no guarantee that you'll find them fit to use. Salons, massage rooms, nightclubs, and karaoke rooms are often merely the bases for other kinds of illegal entertainment (for men). Fitness equipment may be broken and inadequately supervised, and Jacuzzis may have more rings than a sequoia, so proceed with care.

You may receive unexpected **phone calls.** If you are female, the caller may hang up without saying anything, as may be the case if you are male and answer in English. But if the caller persists and is female, and if you hear the word *ànmó* (massage), then what is being offered probably needs no further explanation, but a massage is only the beginning. Unplug the phone when going to sleep.

Almost all rooms, however basic, have the following: A telephone whose line can usually be unplugged for use in a laptop; air-conditioning, which is either central with a wall-mounted control or individual to the room with a remote control, and which may double as a heater; a television, usually with no English channels except CCTV 9 (although no buttons may actually be tuned to that channel) and possibly an in-house movie channel using pirated DVDs or VCDs; a thermos of boiled water or a kettle to boil your own, usually with cups (which you should wash before using) and free bags of green tea; and an array of switches, which may not control what they say they control, found near the bed. The bathrooms have free soap and shampoo, and in better hotels a shower cap and toothbrush/toothpaste package (but bring your own).

Ordinary Chinese hotels usually contain a *biāozhǔn jiān,* or "standard room," which means a room with twin beds or a double bed, and with a private bathroom. In older ordinary hotels, double beds may have only recently been installed, the switches are all in the wrong place, and the room is now referred to as a *dān rén jiān* or single room. Nevertheless, two people can stay there and the price is lower than for a standard room with twin beds. In older hotels, genuine single rooms are available; and in many hotels below four-star level, there are triple rooms and quads, which can also serve as dorms, shared with strangers.

Foreign **credit cards** are increasingly likely to be accepted in three-star hotels and above, but never rely on this. Most hotels accepting foreigners will exchange foreign currency on the premises, although some may send you elsewhere to traveler's checks. Almost all hotels require **payment in advance,** plus a deposit *(yājīn)*, which is refundable when you leave. Some hotels add a 5% to 15% **service charge** on top of their room rates (our listings indicate where this is done).

Keep all **receipts** you are given, as you may need to show one to floor staff to get your key, and you may in fact need to hand the key back and retrieve the receipt again before you can leave. To get your deposit back, you'll need to hand over the receipt for it when you check out, and since staff occasionally forget to enter payments in computers or ledgers, you may need receipts to prevent yourself from being charged twice.

To **check in** you'll need your passport, and you must complete a registration form (which will usually be in English). Always inspect the room before checking in. You'll be asked how many nights you want to stay, and you should always say just 1, because if you say 4, you'll be asked for 4 nights' money in advance (plus a deposit), and because it may turn out that the hot water isn't hot enough, the karaoke rooms are above your head, or a building site behind the hotel starts work at 8am sharp. Once you've tried 1 night, you can pay for more.

When you **check out,** the floor staff will be called to verify that you haven't stolen anything. This step may not happen speedily, so allow extra time.

Children 12 and under stay free. Hotels will add an extra bed to your room for a small charge, which you can bargain down.

SAVING ON YOUR HOTEL ROOM

The **rack rate** is the maximum rate that a hotel charges for a room. In China these rates are nothing more than the first bid in a bargaining discussion, designed to keep the final price as high as possible. You'll almost never pay more than 90%, usually not more than 70%, frequently not more than 50%, and sometimes as little as 30% of this first asking price. To lower the cost of your room:

- **Do not book ahead.** Just show up and bargain. In China this applies to the top class joint-venture names as much as all the others. The best price is available over the counter, as long as there's room. For most of the year there are far more rooms than customers at every level. For ordinary Chinese hotels you may well pay double by booking ahead, and there's no guarantee that your reservation will be honored if someone else arrives before you, cash in hand. E-mail is almost never answered, and faxes get ignored. Chinese mostly just show up and bargain.

- **Book online.** If you want to reserve a room in a particular joint-venture hotel during a busy period, look at its website for rates. Major hotel chains operating in China often have their best *published* rate on their websites. However, these rates fluctuate constantly according to demand, and are sometimes linked to inventory systems that alter prices at frequent intervals, sometimes hourly. Prices for any time of year quoted far in advance will always look uninviting. Rates are much cheaper nearer the time, unless some major event is taking place. Ordinary hotels, if they have a website, will just quote rack rates.

- **Dial any central booking number.** Contrary to popular wisdom, as the better hotels manage their rates with increasing care, the central booking number is likely to have a rate as good as or better than the rate you can get by calling the hotel directly, and the call is usually toll-free.

- **Avoid booking through Chinese hotel agencies and websites specializing in Chinese hotels.** You'll obtain the same discount if you contact the hotels directly. In fact, you can usually beat the agency's discount because you won't be paying their markup. Many agencies have no affiliations with hotels, and simply jump on the phone to book a room as soon as they hear from you.

HOW TO CHOOSE THE LOCATION THAT'S RIGHT FOR YOU

On short visits, the best option is to stay in the **city center,** within walking distance of the Forbidden City and Tiān'ān Mén Square, on Wángfǔjǐng Dàjiē or nearby. The range of accommodation in this area—from super-luxury to rock-bottom—is unmatched.

The greatest luxury and highest standards of service can be found in **Cháoyáng,** near the two main diplomatic areas just outside the East Second Ring Road. The district's southern half, also known as the CBD (Central Business District), is filled almost exclusively with high-end hotels and is the city's glitziest shopping area. The north boasts proximity to the airport and to the dining and nightlife options of Sānlǐtún.

A wide variety of mid-range and budget accommodation options are offered in the **southern districts** of Xuānwǔ (southwest) and Chóngwén (southeast). Hotels here offer convenient access to the metro line, Běijīng Railway Station, and Běijīng West Railway Station.

A district that has blossomed markedly in the past few years, the **Back Lakes (Hòu Hǎi** or **Shíchà Hǎi)** area is the most picturesque place to stay. Here you'll find interesting cafes, narrow lanes called *hútòng,* and a last glimpse of Old Běijīng.

The **western** part of the city, where most universities are located, is the least charming area in which to park your luggage, but hotels are generally cheaper and are near the Summer Palace.

---

1 Běijīng City Center, Around Wángfǔjīng Dàjiē

VERY EXPENSIVE

Běijīng Hotel (Běijīng Fàndiàn) *Overrated*   In a city where hotels are deemed historic if open for more than a decade, it's a shame the genuinely old Běijīng Hotel is so bent on maintaining a bland semblance of youth. The original French-owned Hotel de Pekin, considered among the finest hotels in prewar China, was destroyed in the Boxer Rebellion (1900) and moved to this location, at the bottom of Wángfǔjǐng Dàjiē, in 1917. It was taken over by the government after 1949 and was until the mid-1980s one of the only hotels where foreigners could stay. A renovation between 1999 and 2001 buried most reminders of the hotel's past behind an unimaginative mix of marble and glass, the lone exception being a 100-year-old Bosendorfer piano that sits forlornly in the original lobby. Rooms are spacious but boring, offering the same lackluster luxury found in most government-affiliated high-end hotels. Many visitors still stay here, if only for nostalgia's sake, but facilities and service don't match the hotel's five-star rating.

Dōng Cháng'ān Dàjiē 33, Dōng Chéng Qū; see map p. 104. ℃ 010/6513-7766. Fax 010/6513-7307. business@chinabeijinghotel.com.cn. 891 units. ¥2,100 ($263) standard room (summer discount rate around ¥1,250/$156), plus 15% service charge. AE, DC, MC, V. Metro: Wángfǔjǐng (118). **Amenities:** 4 restaurants (regional, Cantonese, Western, Japanese), bar; indoor pool; indoor and outdoor tennis courts; exercise room; Jacuzzi; sauna; concierge; tour desk; business center; shopping arcade; salon; 24-hr. room service; same-day dry cleaning/laundry service; executive-level rooms; currency exchange; squash courts. *In room:* A/C, satellite TV, dataport, minibar, hair dryer, safe.

Grand Hotel (Běijīng Guìbīnlóu Fàndiàn)   The Grand Hotel, a separately managed 1990 addition to the west end of the Běijīng Hotel (see above), has marginally better service than its neighbor and a pleasant central atrium with glass elevators, cascading greenery, and a handful of elaborate fountains. Decently sized rooms are elegantly outfitted with rosewood furniture; those on the west side offer clear views of the Forbidden City (within walking distance). Bathrooms have separate shower and bathtub. Rates are unreasonably inflated, however. As with the Běijīng Hotel, your money is better spent elsewhere.

Dōng Cháng'ān Dàjiē 35, Dōng Chéng Qū (at Nán Hé Yàn); see map p. 104. ✆ 010/6513-7788. Fax 010/ 6513-0048. www.grandhotelbeijing.com.cn. 217 units. ¥2,200–¥2,400 ($275–$300) standard room (summer discount rate around ¥1,700/$212), plus 15% service charge. AE, DC, MC, V. Metro: Wángfǔjīng (118). **Amenities:** 4 restaurants (Cantonese, Sìchuān, Imperial, Western); 2 bars; indoor pool; exercise room; Jacuzzi; sauna; concierge; tour desk; business center; shopping arcade; salon; 24-hr. room service, same-day dry cleaning/laundry service; executive-level rooms; currency exchange. *In room:* A/C, satellite TV, free broadband, dataport, minibar, hair dryer, safe.

The Peninsula Palace Běijīng (Wángfǔ Fàndiàn) ★★★   No other hotel in mainland China will pick you up at the airport in a Rolls Royce and whisk you to its very central location. The Peninsula Palace is run by the same people who operate Hong Kong's legendary Peninsula Hotel, and while not as charismatic, this property features many of the same luxuries, such as bedside controls for almost everything in the room. Deluxe marble bathrooms have separate faucets with sterilized drinking water. The hotel sits at the heart of Běijīng's principal shopping district above the capital's most exclusive boutiques, built around a high-tech computerized fountain. Also in the shopping arcade below is Jing (p. 83), one of the city's finest and best-decorated fusion restaurants.

Jīnyú Hútòng 8, Dōng Chéng Qū (1 block east off Wángfǔjīng Dàjiē), ✆ 0800/262-9467 or 010/6512-8899. Fax 010/6512-9050. www.peninsula.com. 530 units. $320 standard room, plus 15% service charge. AE, DC, MC, V. **Amenities:** 3 restaurants (Western-Asian fusion, Cantonese, coffee shop); indoor pool; fully equipped fitness center; saunas and steam rooms; 24-hr. concierge; tour desk; Rolls-Royce and Mercedes limousines; business center; shopping arcade (with ATM and bank); Clarins Beauty Institute; 24-hr. room service; sports message; babysitting; same-day dry-cleaning/laundry service; medical clinic. *In room:* A/C, satellite TV, dataport, minibar, hair dryer, safe.

EXPENSIVE

Crowne Plaza Hotel (Guójì Yīyuàn Huángguān Fàndiàn)   The Crowne Plaza, like the Great Wall Sheraton, was one of Běijīng's earlier joint-venture five-stars and is now a little tired. The hotel is still one of the finer places near the Forbidden City, however, and plans exist to renovate the oft-imitated but now outdated central atrium in mid-2003. Rooms could stand a renovation of their own. They are spacious and comfortable enough, but with an odor of age, ancient bedside control consoles, and slightly battered bathrooms. A small gallery on the first floor and weekly events in the "art salon" on the mezzanine floor give the hotel a certain credibility with the art world, and added interest for the guest. The hotel's Plaza Grill, a respectable French restaurant, serves as the backdrop to a popular local TV show on Western table manners.

Wángfǔjīng Dàjiē 48, Dōng Chéng Qū (corner of Dēngshìkǒu Dàjiē). ✆ 877/932-4112 in the U.S. and Canada, 1800/36-300 in Australia, 0800/80-1111 in New Zealand, 0800/917-1587 in the U.K., or 010/6513-3388. Fax 010/6513-2513. www.sixcontinentshotels.com. 358 units. $200 standard room, plus 15% service charge. AE, DC, MC, V. **Amenities:** French restaurant; tiny indoor pool; small health club with new equipment; underwhelming Jacuzzi, sauna, and solarium; concierge; Panda Tours desk; business center; salon; 24-hr. room service; babysitting; same-day dry cleaning/laundry service. *In room:* A/C, satellite TV, minibar, hair dryer, safe.

Grand Hyatt Běijīng (Běijīng Dōngfāng Jūnyuè) ★★★   The newest luxury hotel in the city, the Grand Hyatt also has the best position: directly over the Wángfǔjǐng metro station, at the foot of the capital's most famous shopping street, within walking distance of the Forbidden City. The theatrically lit, palatial lobby is already a popular meeting place, with live music in the evenings and Běijīng's best chocolate shop at one end. Rooms offer signature Grand Hyatt comfort and modernity, with convenient dataports and free broadband Internet access. Well-equipped bathrooms have separate shower cubicles. The vast swimming pool, buried among mock-tropical decor and a ceiling of electric stars, is very kitsch and un-Hyatt—it's worth visiting even if you have no plans to swim. Some of Beijing's best restaurants—including Noble Court (p. 83) and Da Giorgio (p. 83)—are scattered throughout.

Dōng Cháng'ān Jiē 1, Dōng Chéng Qū (within the Oriental Plaza complex at the foot of Wangfujing Dàjiē); see map p. 104. ✆ 800/633-7313 in the U.S. and Canada, 0845/888-1226 in the U.K., 1800/13-1234 in Australia, 0800/44-1234 in New Zealand, or 010/8515-1234. Fax 010/6512-9050. beijing.grand.hyatt.com. 531 units. $300 standard room, plus 15% service charge. AE, DC, MC, V. Metro: Wángfǔjǐng (118). **Amenities:** 4 restaurants (Cantonese, Italian, International, coffee shop); indoor resort-style pool (50m/55 yards); fitness center with latest equipment; Jacuzzi; sauna; solarium; children's pool and playroom; airport limousine pick-up; business center; shopping arcade; 24-hr. room service; massage; doctor/nurse on call; jogging path. *In room:* A/C, satellite TV, free broadband, dataport, minibar, hair dryer, safe.

Wángfǔjǐng Grand (Wángfǔjǐng Dàjiǔdiàn) ★   At this price level, this is one of the better city-center hotels, offering views of the Forbidden City and a fresher feel than the nearby Crowne Plaza. "Superior" rooms, available for roughly the same rate as a standard room at the Crowne Plaza, are bright and modern, with cheap but new fixtures and cramped but nicely outfitted bathrooms. Prices are the same on both sides of the hotel; ask for a west-facing unit on one of the higher floors if you want to see the palace. The hotel's standard rooms, usually only ¥50 ($6) cheaper than rooms in superior class, were refurbished less recently. Go for the upgrade.

Wángfǔjǐng Dàjiē 57, Dōng Chéng Qū (south of Cháoyáng Mén Nèi Dàjiē intersection, west side of street); see map p. 104. ✆ 010/6522-1188. Fax 010/6522-3816. www.WangfujingHotel.com. 428 units. ¥1,490 ($186) superior rooms (summer discount rate around ¥950/$118), plus 15% service charge. AE, DC, MC, V. **Amenities:** 3 restaurants (Cantonese, Western, Korean); bar; small indoor pool; exercise room with new equipment; simple sauna; concierge; tour desk; business center; salon; 24-hr. room service; same-day dry cleaning/laundry service; executive-level rooms; currency exchange. *In room:* A/C, satellite TV, free broadband, minibar, hair dryer, safe.

MODERATE

Cuìmíng Zhuāng Bīnguǎn   This sleepy little three-star, built inside a Republican-era government complex west of Wángfǔjǐng Dàjiē, is just a 10-minute walk east of the Forbidden City. The structure was admirably restored in 1998 and has been well maintained since then. Rooms are smallish and simply but comfortably furnished, and the staff is friendlier than you might expect at a state-run hotel. (For history fans: The building originally housed offices of the Communist Party half of the Běipíng Military Mediation Section, a government body that maintained a cease-fire between the Communists and Nationalists so China could fight a Japanese invasion during World War II.)

Nán Hé Yàn 1, Dōng Chéng Qū (at intersection with Dōng'ān Mén Jiē); see map p. 104. ✆ 010/6513-6622. Fax 010/6525-7387. www.cuimingzhuanghotel.com. 134 units. ¥600 ($75) standard room (summer discount rates around ¥480/$60). AE, DC, MC, V. **Amenities:** Restaurant (Chinese); bar; small exercise room with new equipment; business center; laundry service; currency exchange. *In room:* A/C, satellite TV, fridge, safe.

Fùháo Bīnguǎn *Value*   The Fùháo boasts few facilities and seems to literally cower in the shadows of the much larger Wángfǔjǐng Grand; however, it wins consideration for its mix of affordability and address. Rooms are small and tidy, with slightly hard beds. Bathrooms are worn but wired to receive phone calls. Several decent restaurants stand just outside the main entrance. The location is within walking distance of the Forbidden City and the Wángfǔjǐng shopping area.

Wángfǔjǐng Dàjiē 45, Dōng Chéng Qū. ⓒ **010/6523-1188.** Fax 010/6513-0523. 104 units. ¥480 ($60) standard room (summer discount rates around ¥400/$50), plus 10% service charge. AE, MC, V. **Amenities:** Restaurant (Chinese); bar; laundry service. *In room:* AC, TV, minibar, fridge.

Hǎoyuán Bīnguǎn ⭐ Located down a lane just off one of Běijīng's trendiest shopping streets, the 19-room Hǎoyuán is among the most exclusive of the city's popular courtyard-style hotels. Red doors hung with lanterns and flanked on either side by stone lions mark the entrance. Inside is a neatly restored Qīng-era house, with a small unadorned courtyard in front and a sublime larger courtyard in back decorated with flowers and tree-shaded, stone chess tables. Larger rooms in the rear courtyard are furnished with canopy beds and custom-made Míng reproduction furniture. A bonus for fans of obscure Communist Party history: The house once belonged to Huá Guófēng, Party chair after Máo, who succeeded in aping the Great Helmsman's coiffure but alas, not his stature.

Shíjiā Hútòng 53, Dōng Chéng Qū (blue sign points way on Dōngdān Běi Dàjiē); see map p. 104. ⓒ **010/6512-5557.** Fax 010/6525-3179. 19 units. ¥585–¥715 ($73–$89) standard room (discounts extremely rare, even in winter). AE, DC, MC, V. **Amenities:** Restaurant (Chinese/Western); bike rental; tour desk, laundry service; Internet access. *In room:* A/C, satellite TV, hair dryer, fridge.

Novotel Peace Běijīng (Běijīng Nuòfùtè Hépíng Bīnguǎn) This French-managed hotel, part of the Accor stable, has surprisingly average service, but its reasonable rates make it an affordable alternative to the Peninsula Palace across the street. "Deluxe" rooms renovated in 2002 are spacious and comfortable despite the overdone blue color scheme (probably meant to soothe); corner rooms cost the same and are even larger. Standard rooms in the older building were undergoing renovations at press time, and management was mysteriously tight-lipped about how they would look.

Jīnyú Hútòng 3, Dōng Chéng Qū (west of Dōng Sì Nán Dàjiē); see map p. 104. ⓒ **0800/610–0171** or 010/6512-8833. Fax 010/6512-6863. www.accorhotels-asia.com. 344 units. ¥1,040 ($130) deluxe room (summer discount rate around ¥760/$95), plus 15% service charge. AE, DC, MC, V. **Amenities:** 4 restaurants (Cantonese, Sìchuān, Korean, French/International), bar; small indoor pool; small but well-equipped exercise room; Jacuzzi; disappointing sauna; concierge; tour desk; business center; 24-hr. room service; same-day dry cleaning/laundry service; executive-level rooms; bakery; currency exchange. *In room:* A/C, satellite TV, dataport, minibar, hair dryer, safe, video on demand.

Sōnghè Dàjiǔdiàn *Value* The three-star Sōnghè was abandoned by Accor Hotels in 1995 but has slipped surprisingly little after years under Chinese management. It still offers some of the best value for money in the Wángfǔjǐng area. This place is often ignored because of its bland and somewhat battered exterior, or more because of its location opposite the better-known Crowne Plaza. However, the interior is on a par with some of the city's four-stars' interiors. Standard rooms are mid-size and bright, although a bit banged up. Deluxe rooms, roughly ¥50 ($6) more per night, are larger and more comfortable, with new carpets and furniture.

Dēngshìkǒu Dàjiē 88, Dōng Chéng Qū (diagonally across from Crowne Plaza); see map p. 104 ⓒ **010/6513-8822.** Fax 010/6513-9088. www.songhetl.com. 310 units. ¥750 ($93) standard room (summer discount rates around ¥450/$56), plus 15% service charge. AE, DC, MC, V. **Amenities:** 4 restaurants (Cantonese, Sìchuān, hotpot, Western); bar; small exercise room; business center; limited room service; laundry service; currency exchange. *In room:* AC, satellite TV, fridge, free bottled water.

INEXPENSIVE

International Youth Hostel (Guójì Qīngnián Lǚxíngshè)   News of the International's demise spread quickly after backpackers found its doors locked in late 2002, but the hostel's ex-manager (temporarily ensconced at the Fēiyīng) says it has only been closed for renovations and will reopen with better facilities at the end of 2003. The old per-bed rate, listed below, is supposed to stay the same.

Jiànguó Mén Nèi Dàjiē 9, Dōng Chéng Qū (behind International Hotel). Phone number not yet established. biy-yh@sohu.com. ¥60 ($8) dorm bed.

Saga Youth Hostel (Shíjiā Guójì Qīngnián Lǚxíngshè)   Opened in May 2002 in one of Běijīng's most famous *hútòng*, the Saga is the current favorite among savvy backpackers. The view west from the third-floor balcony across well-preserved old courtyard houses is a joy, especially at sunrise. To the east, alas, hastily-built six-story monstrosities are rising from the rubble of Old Běijīng. Sunnier dorm rooms on the third floor are preferable, although their proximity to the kitchen means an early night's sleep is not guaranteed. The large, clean, communal kitchen is a huge plus, and staff is incredibly helpful. Unfortunately, the cost of popularity shows in the bathrooms, which are starting to look tatty.

Shíjiā Hútòng 9, Dōng Chéng Qū (just west of the intersection with Cháoyáng Mén Nán Xiǎojiē on north side of street), Dóng Chéng Qū; see map p. 104. ✆ 010/6257-2773. Fax 010/6524-9098. 24 units (12 with in-room shower). ¥180 ($22) twin, ¥50–¥60 ($5–$6) dorm bed. No credit cards. Bus: 24 from Běijīng Zhàn to Lùmǐcāng. **Amenities:** Cafe; useful travel service; self-service laundry; cheap Internet access; self-service kitchen; table soccer. *In room:* A/C, no phone.

2 Back Lakes & Dōng Chéng

MODERATE

Bamboo Garden Hotel (Zhú Yuán Bīnguǎn) ★★   Bamboo Garden was the first major courtyard-style hotel in Běijīng (the brochure still claims it's the only one) and among the most beautiful. It's slightly more luxurious than the Lǚsōng Yuán (see below), but with less character. Rooms border three, different-size courtyards, each filled with rock gardens, clusters of bamboo, and covered corridors. Standard rooms in two multi-story buildings at opposite ends of the complex are decorated with Míng-style furniture and traditional lamps that cast pleasant shadows on the high ceilings. A restaurant looks out on the rear courtyard; next door is a pleasant bar with a glass-covered fishpond as part of the floor.

Xiǎoshí Qiáo Hútòng 24, Xī Chéng Qū (6th *hútòng* on left walking north on Jiù Gǔlóu Dàjiē, west of Drum Tower); see map p. 104. ✆ 010/6403-2229. Fax 010/6401-2633. www.bbgh.com. 40 units. ¥480–¥580 ($60–$72) standard room (discounts rare). AE, DC, MC, V. **Amenities:** Restaurant (Chinese); bar; concierge; travel service; business center; salon; laundry service; currency exchange. *In room:* A/C, satellite TV, fridge, free bottled water.

Héjìng Fǔ Bīnguǎn *Finds*   This elaborate imperial complex was the home of Qiánlóng's third daughter (Gùlún Héjìng), and more recently the ominously named Central Records and Investigation Committee, responsible for investigating corrupt officials. The spooks have moved to premises unknown, but their presence helped spare some of Běijīng's most spectacular courtyard buildings from Cultural Revolution–inspired damage. Exquisitely carved stone statues of camels, lions, and mythical beasts dot the rear and middle courtyards, where bamboo and peach trees flourish. Ornate wooden carvings recently fitted to the walls and the huge slate-tiled bathrooms bode well, but there is talk of glassing-over the balconies and laying a lawn over the cobblestones. Pray that good taste prevails. Suites should be in the ¥1,000 ($125) range, a steal for the plushest courtyard rooms in the capital. A lavish new restaurant is also promised. For the moment, rooms are available in the unspectacular rear building. Rooms on the first and second floors are spacious, if a little musty. Smaller, more recently renovated rooms on the third and fourth floors contain less-scarred bathrooms and well-sprung mattresses, but the ¥160 ($20) premium is robbery.

Zhāngzìzhōng Lù 7, Dōng Chéng Qū (a block west of Dōng Sì Běi Dàjiē); see map p. 104. ✆ **010/6401-7744.** Fax 010/8401-3570. hjf_hotel@china.com. 137 units. ¥320–¥480 ($40–$60) standard room; ¥960 ($120) suites. Occasional discounts up to 30%. AE, DC, MC, V. Metro: Dōng Sì Shí Tiáo (213; exit A). **Amenities:** Restaurant (homestyle); bar; tiny exercise room; business center; same-day laundry service; currency exchange. *In room:* A/C, TV.

Lǔsōng Yuán Bīnguǎn ★★★   The Lǔsōng Yuán, situated inside a former imperial house down a quaint *hútòng* north of Píng'ān Dàdào and nicely renovated in 2001, is for now the most charming courtyard hotel in Běijīng. Smaller and more intimate than the Bamboo Garden, with more traditional rooms, it wins with the details—bright paneled ceilings in the hallways, faux rotary phones in-room, and Chinese-style wall-mounted lamps over the beds. A few rooms open directly onto quiet, semi-private courtyards, adorned with potted plants and presided over by white stone busts of "the father of modern China" (Sun Yat-sen) and "the father of modern Chinese literature" (Lǔ Xùn). Comfortable dorms are still available in the basement, and a teahouse with stone floors and low-backed Míng-style chairs is next to the lobby.

Bǎnchǎng Hútòng 22, Dōng Chéng Qū (walking north from Dì'ān Mén Dōng Dàjiē on Jiǎodàokǒu Nán Dàjiē, 2nd *hútòng* on left); see map p. 104. ✆ **010/6404-0436.** Fax 010/6403-0418. www.the-silk-road.com. 59 units. ¥480–¥600 ($60–$75) standard room (summer discounts rare, 40% discounts in winter). AE, DC, MC, V. **Amenities:** Restaurant (Chinese); bike rental; business center with cheap Internet access (¥10/$1 per hr.); laundry service. *In room:* AC, satellite TV.

Qílǔ Fàndiàn *Value*   The bland, white-tiled exterior promises little, but the rooms are a pleasant surprise—freshly painted and carpeted and containing new, firm mattresses. Best of all, you're within sight of the delightful Shíchà Lakes area and the north gate of Běi Hǎi. The friendly staff speak little English, but at least they're willing to try. Owned by the Women's Federation, the hotel hosts mostly business travelers. A nice bonus: Guests receive a fresh bowl of fruit each night.

Dì'ān Mén Xī Dàjiē 103, Xī Chéng Qū; see map p. 104. ✆ **010/6618-0099.** Fax 010/6618-0969. 126 units (10 shower only). ¥340–¥426 ($42–$53) standard rooms; ¥860 ($107) suite (summer discounts 20%, up to 40% in winter). AE, DC, MC, V. Bus: 810 from Jīshuǐ Tán metro to Běi Hǎi Hòu Mén. **Amenities:** Restaurant (Sìchuān); concierge; business center; next-day dry cleaning/laundry service; limited currency exchange (no traveler's checks). *In room:* A/C, TV.

3 Cháoyáng

VERY EXPENSIVE

China World Hotel (Zhōngguó Dàfàndiàn) ★★★   Long thought by many to be the city's top business hotel, China World now aims to be the best Běijīng hotel altogether, with a just-completed $30-million renovation. Guests include CEOs and, occasionally, visiting world leaders. Praised for its comfort and sterling service, the hotel, managed by Shangri-La, has used its most recent face-lift to add several up-to-date luxuries, including an oxygen chamber in the health club. Refurbished standard rooms are somewhat narrow but modern, with glass-topped desks and vaguely Asian *objets d'art* on walls and shelves. Comfortably elegant Aria (p. 88), tucked away up a spiral staircase, serves the city's finest Continental cuisine. A new fusion restaurant, as yet unnamed, is scheduled to open inside the hotel in mid-2003. The attached China World shopping complex boasts several upmarket boutiques, a well-stocked supermarket, an ice rink, and a Starbucks. A metro stop connected to the shopping area means quick (15 min.) access to the city center.

Jiànguó Mén Wài Dàjiē 1, Cháoyáng Qū (at intersection with East Third Ring Road); see map p. 115. (C) 010/6405–2266. Fax 010/6505–0828. www.shangri-la.com. 716 units. ¥2,400 ($300) standard room (discount rates down to ¥1,240/$155), plus 15% service charge. AE, DC, MC, V. Metro: Guómào (122). **Amenities:** 4 restaurants (Chinese, Western, Japanese, Italian) plus several more and supermarket in attached mall; indoor pool (25m/27 yards); golf simulator; 3 indoor tennis courts; full-service health club; separate spa with aromatherapy; concierge; business center; shopping complex; salon; 24-hr. room service; same-day dry cleaning/laundry service; executive-level rooms; nonsmoking rooms; currency exchange. *In room:* A/C, satellite TV, free broadband, dataport, minibar, hair dryer, safe.

Great Wall Sheraton (Cháng Chéng Fàndiàn)

Běijīng's largest hotel by far, the Great Wall was also the city's first international five-star when it opened in 1984. The building is well maintained considering its age, but it now seems to have fallen behind some of its competitors in terms of refurbishment. Standard rooms, which are typically pawned off on tour groups, are large but dark with outdated fixtures. The only slightly more expensive deluxe rooms on the seventh and eighth floors, renovated in 2000, are bright and comfortable. The beautifully refurbished 21st Floor Restaurant now serves first-class Sìchuān food together with commanding views of eastern Běijīng.

Běi Sān Huán 10, Cháoyáng Qū (south of Lufthansa Centre); see map p. 115. (C) 800/810–3088 or 010/6590–5566. Fax 010/6590–5938. www.starwood.com. 1,007 units. ¥1,780 ($215) deluxe room, ¥1,490 ($180) standard room (summer discounts around ¥800/$100), plus 15% service charge. Most rates include breakfast. AE, DC, MC, V. **Amenities:** 3 restaurants (Cantonese/Sìchuān, Italian/International, French); bar; small indoor pool with sun deck; 2 outdoor tennis courts; aging exercise room; Jacuzzi; sauna; concierge; tour desk; business center; salon; 24-hr. room service; same-day dry cleaning/laundry service; executive-level rooms; currency exchange. *In room* (deluxe): A/C, satellite TV, broadband/dataport; minibar, hair dryer, safe.

Hilton Běijīng (Běijīng Xīĕrdùn Fàndiàn)

This popular business hotel stands a little in the shadow of the feature-packed Kempinski to the south and the brand-new, more luxurious Renaissance to the north. Very slightly tired rooms have Japanese-style sliding screens offering bright illumination without direct sunlight, and well-fitted bathrooms have separate shower cubicles. Louisiana, a favorite among long-time expats, offers quality American-Cajun fare and a long wine list.

Dōngfāng Lù 1, Dōng Sān Huán Běi Lù, Cháoyáng Qū (east side of North Third Ring Road, north of Xiāoyún Lù); see map p. 115. (C) 800/445-8667 in the U.S. and Canada, 0800/909090 in the U.K., 1800/22-2255 in Australia, 0800/44-8002 in New Zealand, or 010/6466-2288. Fax 010/6465-3052. www.beijing.hilton.com. 340 units. $170 standard room, $205 executive floor; plus 15% service charge. AE, DC, MC, V. **Amenities:** Restaurant (American-Cajun); indoor pool; outdoor tennis court; fitness club; Jacuzzi; sauna; bike rental; concierge; tour desk; small 24-hr. business center; salon; 24-hr. room service; massage; babysitting; same-day dry cleaning/laundry service; 2 squash courts; wheelchairs; valet. *In room:* A/C, satellite TV, broadband/dataport, minibar, hair dryer, safe.

Kempinski Hotel (Kǎibīnsījī Fàndiàn) 🦅

The Kempinski's plain but large and very comfortable rooms have recently been refurbished to a high standard, and its position in the vast Lufthansa Centre shopping, office, and apartment complex means every facility imaginable is at hand. These include a specialist wine store, endless airline offices and ticket agents, medical and dental clinics with Western staff and equipment, eight restaurants and cafes, a supermarket, a bookshop, and a department store. This is the perfect location for business visitors; other than for sightseeing, there's scarcely any need to venture out. If you do, large numbers of long-staying expats from the Kempinski's well-fitted apartments help support an assortment of other Western and wannabe-Western enterprises in the neighborhood, including Běijīng's branch of the Hard Rock Cafe. The Paulaner Bräuhaus offers top-of-the-range beers brewed on-site and hearty German dishes. The Kempi Deli has an excellent range of baked goods (half price after 9pm).

Liàngmǎ Qiáo Lù 50, Cháoyáng Qū (east of North Third Ring Road, near airport expressway junction); see map p. 115. ⓒ 010/6465-3388. Fax 010/6465-3366. 486 units. ¥2,000 ($270) standard room (discount rates around ¥1,280/$160), plus 15% service charge. AE, DC, MC, V. **Amenities:** 8 restaurants (including Cantonese, Mexican, Japanese, and German); indoor pool; outdoor tennis court; fitness center; Jacuzzi; sauna; concierge; free shuttle to airport and city center; business center; shopping complex; 24-hr. room service; same-day dry cleaning/laundry service; executive-level rooms; nonsmoking rooms; currency exchange squash courts. *In room:* A/C, satellite TV, broadband/dataport, minibar, hair dryer, safe.

Kerry Centre Hotel (Běijīng Jiālì Zhōngxīn Fàndiàn) ★★★ Kids The latest addition to the Shangri-La–managed properties in the city, the Kerry Centre is also the most trendy, with a clean, stylish, modern design to its warm, comfortable, and unusually high-ceilinged rooms. Full facilities, such as shower cubicles in bathrooms, free in-room broadband Internet access, and particularly attentive staff, have all helped make it one of Běijīng's most successful hotels. Executive-floor rooms have luxuries such as CD players. The Kerry Centre complex has several noteworthy restaurants, including Horizon (p. 90), one of the city's best Cantonese restaurants, which also serves Chinese regional dishes prepared by Hong Kong chefs.

Guānghuá Lù 1, Cháoyáng Qū (on west side of Kerry Centre complex, north of Guómào metro station); see map p. 115. ⓒ 010/8529-6999. Fax 010/8529-6333. www.shangri-la.com. 487 units. ¥1,760 ($220) standard room (summer discounts around ¥1,200/$150), plus 15% service charge. AE, DC, M, V. Metro: Guómào (122). **Amenities:** 3 restaurants (Cantonese, Pan-Asian, Western); bar; indoor pool (25m/27 yards); indoor basketball/tennis/badminton courts; fitness center; children's play area; concierge; tour desk; business center; shopping arcade; 24-hr. room service; same-day dry cleaning/laundry service; executive-level rooms; nonsmoking rooms; currency exchange; roof-top track for running and in-line skating; sun deck. *In room:* A/C, satellite TV, free broadband, dataport, minibar, hair dryer, safe.

Renaissance Běijīng (Guóháng Wànlì Jiǔdiàn) ★ Just opened north of Sān Yuán Qiáo near the new embassy area in 2003, the Renaissance is understated but elegant in the St. Regis mold (see below) and destined to steal a fair amount of business from surrounding hotels. Rooms are palatial, with pillows piled high on generous beds. Association with Air China (which owns the building) means you can check flight schedules on your TV and, if you're flying with Air China, check in for your flight at the hotel desk. A few problems with facilities and service—faulty light switches and front desk confusion—should be resolved by the time you read this.

Xiāoyún Lù 36, Cháoyáng Qū (behind Air China Building, east of Sān Yuán Qiáo); see map p. 115. ⓒ 0800/852-0469 or 010/6468-9999. Fax 010/6468-9913. www.renaissancehotels.com. 212 units. ¥2,080 ($260) standard room (discount rates in summer ¥960–¥1,320/$120–$165), plus 15% service charge. AE, DC, M, V. **Amenities:** 2 restaurants (Cantonese/Sìchuān, International buffet); Roman-style indoor pool with skylight; sauna; concierge; business center; salon; 24-hr. room service; same-day dry cleaning/laundry service; executive-level rooms; currency exchange. *In room:* A/C, satellite TV, broadband/dataport, minibar, hair dryer, safe.

St. Regis Běijīng (Běijīng Guójì Jùlèbù Fàndiàn) ★★★ The variety of fine hotels in Běijīng is too wide now to label any one the unequivocal best, but if a

choice has to be made, the St. Regis would be near the top of the shortlist. The white marble lobby, with its towering palms and afternoon tea, is the city's most elegant. The new health club is world class (basketball superstar Kobe Bryant worked out here during a recent stay in Běijīng). And the hotel's extremely personalized service, provided on every floor by on-call "butlers," is as close to perfect as you'll find in China. If there's a complaint, it's the smallness of the rooms, but all are beautifully appointed with traditional Chinese furniture, Běijīng's deepest bathtubs, and a full range of extras (including DVD players). Danieli's (p. 88) on the second floor is perhaps the city's best Italian restaurant.

Jiànguó Mén Wài Dàjiē 21, Cháoyáng Qū (west side of Rì Tán Park); see map p. 115. © 010/6460-6688. Fax 010/6460-3299. www.stregis.com/beijing. 273 units. ¥2,720 ($340) standard room (summer discount rates ¥1,400–¥1,600/$180–$200), plus 15% service charge. AE, DC, MC, V. Metro: Jiànguó Mén (120/211, 2 blocks away). **Amenities:** 5 restaurants (Cantonese, Japanese, American, Italian, International); bar; gorgeous indoor pool (25m/27 yards); outdoor putting green and driving area; nicely equipped exercise room; full-service spa; bowling alley; billiards room; concierge; business center; salon; 24-hr. room service; same-day dry cleaning/laundry service; nonsmoking rooms; cigar and wine-tasting rooms; currency exchange; 24-hr. "butler" service; squash courts. *In room:* A/C, satellite TV, broadband/dataport, minibar, hair dryer, safe, DVD player.

EXPENSIVE

Jiànguó Hotel (Jiànguó Fàndiàn) ★ This four-star property, opened in 1982, was the first joint-venture hotel in Běijīng. It's one of the few older hotels to have kept up standards with constant refurbishment, and it still retains foreigners in its senior management, keeping staff up to the mark. The ground floor contains the best rooms, with French windows opening onto small patios alongside goldfish-stocked pools. Běijīng's bustle is pleasantly excluded. A popular meeting place for expats and business visitors, the large lobby boasts afternoon tea, a string quartet every evening, and an orchestra during Sunday morning coffee. Justine's (p. 89), Běijīng's first serious French restaurant, now faces massive competition but is still worth a visit, particularly for the set-price Sunday lunch.

Jiànguó Mén Wài Dàjiē 5, Cháoyáng Qū (east of Silk St. Market); see map p. 115. © 010/6500-2233. Fax 010/6500-2871. 399 units. ¥1,520 ($190) standard room (summer discount rates around ¥1,080/$135), plus 15% service charge. AE, DC, MC, V. Metro: Yǒng'ānlǐ (121). **Amenities:** 3 restaurants (Chinese, French, International); bar; indoor pool; fitness center; Jacuzzi; sauna; concierge; tour desk; business center; shopping arcade; salon; 24-hr. room service; same-day dry cleaning/laundry service; executive-level rooms; currency exchange. *In room:* A/C, satellite TV, minibar, hair dryer, safe.

Traders Hotel Běijīng (Guómào Fàndiàn) ★ *Value* The greatest advantage to staying in this Shangri-La four-star hotel is access to the five-star health club facilities in the China World Hotel next door. (These two sister hotels are joined by an underground shopping center, complete with ice-skating rink.) Otherwise, Traders is a straightforward business hotel, with slightly small and plain but nicely outfitted rooms, unobtrusive service, and easy access to the metro. The only major drawback is the tiny bathrooms, but this is more than compensated for by surprisingly low (after-discount) room rates. The West Wing has the slightly nicer (and more expensive) rooms, renovated in 2001.

Jiànguó Mén Wài Dàjiē 1, Cháoyáng Qū (behind China World Hotel); see map p. 115. © 010/6505-2277. Fax 010/6505-0818. www.shangri-la.com. 552 units. ¥1,360 ($170) standard room (discount rates around ¥820/$102), plus 15% service charge. AE, DC, MC, V. Metro: Guómào (122). **Amenities:** 3 restaurants (Chinese, Western, Malaysian); small exercise room; concierge; business center; shopping complex; salon; 24-hr. room service; same-day dry cleaning/laundry service; executive-level rooms; nonsmoking rooms; currency exchange. *In room:* A/C, satellite TV, free broadband, minibar, hair dryer, safe.

MODERATE

Red House (Ruìxiù Bīnguǎn) ⭐ *Value*   Located in a large, red brick building, the Red House is the best choice for long stays. Spacious apartments, partially refurbished in late 2002, come with bedroom, small kitchen, and large sitting room now with faux hardwood floor and brand-new couch. Bathrooms are shower-only. Affordable 12-person dorms are a bit crowded but have in-room bathroom and extra sinks.

Chūnxiù Lù 10, Cháoyáng Qū (1 block south of Pizza Hut on Dōng Zhí Mén Wài Dàjiē); see map p. 115. ℂ 010/6416-7810. www.redhouse.com.cn. 36 units. ¥500 ($63) 1-bedroom apt (discount rates around ¥300/$36 for long stay). Rates include breakfast. AE, MC, V. **Amenities:** Free laundry service. *In room:* A/C, TV, fridge.

INEXPENSIVE

Gōngtǐ Youth Hostel (Gōngtǐ Qīngnián Lǚxíngshè) ⭐ *Value*   Located inside the Workers Stadium, a long block west of the Sānlǐtún bar area, Běijīng's newest YHA offers a quiet location above a three-star hotel (The Sports Inn), a view over pleasant gardens, and brand-new facilities. The fourth-floor rooms are agreeably curved, and all face southeast. The showers and toilets, although communal, are spotless. If you crave privacy, there are single rooms. However, the white tiled floors are a turn-off; this place will have to work hard to create some ambience. The manager hopes to arrange discounts for guests who use the sporting facilities within the complex.

Gōngrén Tǐyùchǎng 9 Tái, Cháoyáng Qū; see map p. 115. ℂ 010/6552-4800. Fax 010/6552-4860. 38 units (communal bathrooms and showers). ¥50–¥60 ($6–$7.50) 4-bed dorms; ¥80–¥90 ($10–$11) 2-bed dorms; ¥120 ($15) single room. No credit cards. **Amenities:** Bar; exercise room; bike rental; travel service; Internet access; reading room. *In room:* A/C, TV, no phone.

Poacher's Inn Youth Hostel (Yǒuyì Qīngnián Jiǔdiàn)   Run by the same people who manage Red House (see above), this youth hostel offers the liveliest budget accommodations in the Sānlǐtún area. The clean twin rooms are simple with no in-room bathrooms, but common bathrooms are similarly sanitary. Tidy four-person dorm rooms contain the city's most comfortable beds. As at Red House, breakfast and laundry are free. The attached bar, by far Běijīng's most raucous, is the only potential drawback if you value your sleep on weekends. If, on the other hand, you'd rather have cheap beer and a sexually charged atmosphere close at hand, there is no better choice. Look for the bright red brick building with white lettering.

Běi Sānlǐtún Nán, Cháoyáng Qū (west of the Sānlǐtún bar street, take left at the small Industrial and Commercial Bank of China branch, then take 1st right); see map p. 115. ℂ 010/6417-2597. Fax 010/6415-6866. www.poachers.com.cn. 35 units. ¥180 ($23) twin; ¥80 ($10) dorm bed (discounts 10%–20% depending on occupancy). All rates include breakfast. AE, DC, MC, V. **Amenities:** Bar; travel service; laundry service. *In room:* AC, TV, no phone.

Zhàolóng Qīngnián Lǚguǎn   Whether proximity to the Sānlǐtún bar area is a plus or a minus is open to question, but the Zhàolóng is a quiet alternative to the madness of its better-known cousin, Poacher's (see above). Most guests are Chinese backpackers, and doors close at 1am to discourage revelers. Twins and dorms are simple and clean; neither has in-room bathroom, but common showers are adequate. Facilities are minimal. Proximity to the East Third Ring Road means convenient bus access to all parts of town.

Gōngtǐ Běi Lù 2, Cháoyáng Qū (behind Great Dragon Hotel and Nirvana Health Club); see map p.115. ℂ 010/6597-2299, ext. 6111. Fax 010/6597-2288. outdoor@etang.com. 24 units. ¥120 ($15) twin; ¥50 ($6) dorm bed. AE, DC, M, V. Bus: 115 from Dōng Sì Shí Tiáo metro to Nóngzhǎnguǎn. **Amenities:** Travel service; self-service laundry. *In room:* A/C, no phone.

4 Běijīng South

EXPENSIVE

The Marco Polo (Mǎgē Bóluó Jiǔdiàn) ★★ (Value) We highly recommend this hotel, located in a brand-new 10-story building. The lobby, sumptuously decorated with white marble and rippling gold friezes, is stylish yet of a modest enough scale to suggest the atmosphere of a discreet boutique hotel. Rooms are among Běijīng's largest, however, and are fully fitted with broadband Internet access and every luxury. Although not among the main clusters of foreign hotels, the Marco Polo is as close to the center of things as any of them, and is quieter and better connected than most. (The location—just south of the No. 1 Line's Xī Dān station and north of the Circle Line's Xuānwǔ Mén station—enables guests to get in and out during even the worst of rush hour.) Cafe Marco features buffet or a la carte dishes from the Mediterranean, Middle East, Southeast Asia, and China in honor of the routes the great traveler took himself (at least according to his book). Heichinrou is China's first branch of the highly regarded 110-year-old Cantonese restaurant from Yokohama.

Xuānwǔ Mén Nèi Dàjiē 6, Xuānwǔ Qū (just south of Xī Dān metro stop); see map p. 108. ℂ 010/6603-6688. Fax 010/6603-1488. www.marcopolohotels.com. 296 units. ¥1,360 ($170) standard room (discount rates ¥820/$102), plus 15% service charge. AE, DC, MC, V. Metro: Xī Dān (115). **Amenities:** 3 restaurants (Cantonese, Western, Café Marco—see above); bar; indoor pool; fitness center; concierge; tour desk; business center; salon; 24-hr. room service; same-day dry cleaning/laundry service; executive-level rooms; currency exchange. In room: A/C, satellite TV, broadband/dataport, minibar, hair dryer, safe.

MODERATE

Hademen Hotel (Hādé Mén Fàndiàn) ★ The ongoing renovations at this massive three-star hotel will lift it above many lackluster rivals. Midsize rooms on the sixth floor are decorated with replica Míng furnishings and plush carpeting in a regrettable shade of green, and come with a broadband Internet connection—almost unheard-of at this price range. Location, right above the Chóngwén Mén metro, is the Hademen's biggest plus. Rooms facing south and east are quieter, while north-facing rooms come with a view of the newly restored wall in Míng City Wall Park (p. 137). Although front-desk staff can be brusque, they speak reasonable English. The celebrated roast duck restaurant, Biàn Yí Fáng, is to the right of the foyer.

Chóngwén Mén Wài Dàjiē 2A (just east of Chóngwén Mén metro), Chóngwén Qū; see map p. 108. ℂ 010/6711-244. Fax 010/6711-6865. www.hademenhotel.com. 229 units. ¥480–¥580 ($60–$72) standard room; ¥680–¥880 ($85–$110) suite (summer discounts of 20%). 5% service charge. AE, DC, MC, V. Metro: Chóngwén Mén (209; exit C). **Amenities:** 2 restaurants (Shāndōng, Thai); expensive bike rental; concierge; tour desk; business center with overpriced Internet; 24-hr. room service; same-day dry cleaning/laundry service; currency exchange. In room: A/C, limited satellite TV, broadband/dataport, fridge, safe.

Harmony Hotel (Huáměilún Jiǔdiàn) A stone's throw from Běijīng Railway Station, this small and slightly tattered three-star is ideal for those arriving late from the station or needing to catch an early train. Rooms are small for the price and renovations are overdue; however, staff is friendly, and after years of struggling to comprehend the broad accents of Australian tour leaders, their English is passable. "Luxury" rooms (háohuá jiān) are nearly double the size of standard rooms and come with bathtubs—well worth the extra ¥100 ($12). Ask for a quieter room on an upper floor facing the west side, as the railway area is predictably rowdy.

Sūzhōu Hútòng 59, Chóngwén Qū (from Běijīng Zhàn metro exit walk west, taking the 1st right onto Yóutòng Jiē and continuing for 100m/109 yard as it doglegs northwest); see map p. 108. ℂ 010/6528-5566. Fax

Finds In the Red Lantern District

Southwest of Qián Mén, beyond the mercantile madness of Dà Zhàlán, in the *hútòng* that never dreams of pedicab-tour salvation, is where you'll find the remains of Běijīng's once-thriving brothel district. Prior to the Communists' elimination of prostitution in the 1950s and its gradual reemergence since the 1980s, government officials, foreign diplomats, and other men of means would come here to pay for the pleasures of "clouds and rain."

The transaction was not always lurid. The women were closer to courtesans than whores, akin to Japanese geishas, and their customers often paid simply for conversation and cultured entertainment. The promise of another brand of entertainment always lurked in the background, and many of the women who worked south of Qián Mén were kidnapped from other provinces. Nonetheless, the dynamic was not half as base as its modern counterpart's. Money was necessary, but so was courtship.

Many of the old brothel buildings still stand. Most were converted into apartments or stores, but a few were restored and turned into cheap hotels. While those who can afford it will probably prefer to stay in a more luxurious hotel further north, travelers on a budget would be hard-pressed to find affordable accommodations with so much character.

Among the best restored of the old brothels is **Shǎnxī Xiàng Dì'èr Bīnguǎn** (© 010/6303-4609), at the north end of Shǎnxī Xiàng (once home to the most upmarket bordellos), a poorly marked and malodorous lane a few minutes' walk south of Dà Zhàlán. As with most buildings of its kind, it is recognizable by its multi-story height (rare in a neighborhood made up of single-floor houses) and by the glass that divides its roof, designed to let light into the central courtyard while

010/6559-9011. www.harmony-hotel.com. 122 units (112 shower only). ¥688–¥788 ($86–$98) standard room (summer discounts of 25%). Rates include breakfast. AE, DC, MC, V. Metro: Běijīng Zhàn (210). **Amenities:** 2 restaurants (Cantonese, cafe); bike rental; concierge; tour desk; business center; 24-hr. room service; same-day dry cleaning/laundry service; currency exchange. *In room:* A/C, satellite TV, minibar; fridge.

Howard Johnson Paragon Hotel (Bǎochén Fàndiàn)   Already the nicest hotel near the Běijīng Railway Station, the Paragon is now somewhat better equipped thanks to a minor refurbishment in 2001 after Howard Johnson took over. Standard rooms are small and simply furnished, with outdated fittings, but are pleasant enough for the price. Rooms on the sixth floor and higher now have in-room broadband. The pool table, plopped oddly in the middle of the second-floor hallway, should probably be moved. Good deals on executive-level rooms are sometimes available.

Jiànguó Mén Nèi Dàjiē 18A, Chóngwén Qū (north of eastern Běijīng Zhàn footbridge); see map p. 108. © 010/ 6526-6688. Fax 010/6527-4060. www.hojochina.com. 280 units. ¥656 ($82) standard room (summer discounts only, 10%–20%), plus 15% service charge. AE, DC, MC, V. Metro: Běijīng Zhàn (210). **Amenities:** 3 restaurants (Cantonese, Thai, Western); bar; outdoor tennis court; exercise room; sauna; bowling center; children's playroom; concierge; business center; salon; limited room service; dry cleaning/laundry service; bakery; currency exchange. *In room:* A/C, satellite TV, minibar, hair dryer, safe, video on demand.

blocking an outsider's view of the activities taking place inside. Far nicer than the late-night barber shops and karaoke parlors where Běijīng's working girls now do business, the hotel is spacious and lavishly decorated, with red columns and walls supporting colorfully painted banisters and roof beams, the latter hung with traditional lanterns. The rooms, arranged on two floors around the courtyard, are tiny and windowless, as befit their original purpose, but now have air-conditioning, TVs, and bathrooms (¥100/$12 per night). To reach the hotel, walk east from Far East Youth Hostel (see below) and turn left down the second *hútòng* on the right.

The 200-year-old **Qián Mén Chánggōng Fàndiàn** (© 010/6303-2665), at Yīngtáo Xiéjiē 11, is less well maintained than the Shǎnxī Xiàng Dì'èr but closer to the city center and far grander inside. The tell-tale roof peeks over the rest of the street but the facade has been pasted over with anonymous white tile, which makes the elaborate interior more surprising. A large sign by the door describes the building's history as a "black meeting hall." Beyond is a large, high-ceilinged central courtyard surrounded by green walls with traditional red pillars and banisters. Informal cross-talk performances and chess games take place here in summer. Standard rooms (¥140/$18) on the first floor are basic and have grotty bathrooms but are still livable, with air-conditioning and TV. The second floor has more luxurious rooms (¥180/$23), which are brighter and cleaner with a few pieces of traditional Chinese furniture. A gathering spot for elderly men from the neighborhood, the hotel is worth visiting for its Old Běijīng atmosphere even if you don't plan to stay overnight (see "Walking Tour 1: Liúlíchǎng & Dà Zhàlán" in chapter 7). To get here, walk west along Dà Zhàlán, and take a right at the fork.

INEXPENSIVE

Far East Youth Hostel (Yuǎn Dōng Qīngnián Lǔshè) ★★ *Finds* This is the best budget option in Běijīng. Buried deep inside one of the city's most interesting *hútòng* neighborhoods, but only a 10-minute walk from both the Hépíng Mén and Qián Mén metro stations, the Far East offers comfortable rooms with sparkling new everything at unbeatable rates. Even the hallways—partly adorned with faux brick and latticed, dark wood panels—are pleasant. The hostel maintains cheaper dorms behind a courtyard house across the street, but those in the main building are far better. The Far East makes a good choice even if you usually stay at mid-range places.

Tiěshù Xié Jiē 113, Xuānwǔ Qū (follow Dà Zhàlán Jiē west, left at fork); see map p. 108. © 010/6301-8811, ext 3118. Fax 010/6301-8233. 110 units. ¥298 ($37) standard room (often discounted to ¥200/$25); ¥60–¥75 ($8–$10) dorm bed. No credit cards. Metro: Hépíng Mén (207), Qián Mén (208). **Amenities:** Restaurant (Chinese); bike rental; tour desk; cheap coin-op laundry; self-catering kitchen; Internet access. *In room:* AC, TV, fridge.

Fēiyīng Bīnguǎn ★ The Fēiyīng became one of the top budget options in the city after completing a top-to-bottom refurbishment in 2002 and joining

Youth Hostelling International. It's the most "hotel-like" YHA you'll find. Standard rooms are bright and well equipped with low, slightly hard, twin beds; bathrooms have proper tubs. Dorms are also nice with in-room bathroom and brand-new floors. There's even a coffeemaker in the well-appointed kitchen. The hotel's best feature is its location, just southwest of the Xuānwǔ Mén metro stop and next to several useful bus stops.

Xuānwǔ Mén Xī Dàjiē 10, Xuānwǔ Qū (down alley east of Guóhuá Market); see map p. 108. ℂ **010/6317-1116.** Fax 010/6317-1116, ext. 4010. iyhfy@yahoo.com.cn. 46 units. ¥180 ($22) standard room; ¥50–¥60 ($6–$7.50) dorm bed. Discounts for YHA members. No credit cards. Metro: Xuānwǔ Mén (206), Chángchūn Jiē (205). **Amenities:** Restaurant (Cantonese); bar; travel service; self-service laundry; self-catering kitchen; small convenience store. *In room:* A/C, TV.

5 Běijīng West & Hǎidiàn

VERY EXPENSIVE

Shangri-La Běijīng Hotel (Xiānggélǐlā Fàndiàn) ✦ That Shangri-La is now the biggest player among foreign hotel managements in China (four properties in Běijīng alone) is due perhaps to its success with staff. Whereas elsewhere the best staff respond helpfully to guests' requests, here there's the anticipation of guests' needs that distinguishes superior service. The hotel has expanded since its original 1987 opening, and another major refurbishment is on the way. Currently, rooms are a good size and comfortably furnished, if less imaginative than rooms at other Běijīng hotels in this chain. Although off by itself in the northwest, the hotel benefits from having space for a large and lush garden, easy access to the Summer Palaces and the Western Hills, and quick routes around Běijīng via the third and fourth ring roads.

Zǐzhú Yuàn Lù 29, Hǎidiàn Qū (northwest corner of Third Ring Road); see map p. 112. ℂ **010/6841-2211.** Fax 010/6841-8002. www.shangri-la.com. 657 units. ¥1,520 ($190) standard room (discounted rates ¥1,100/$138), plus 15% service charge. AE, DC, MC, V. **Amenities:** 4 restaurants (Cantonese, Japanese, Italian, International); indoor pool; indoor tennis courts; indoor basketball court; recently renovated health club with sauna, solarium, exercise room; concierge; tour desk; business center; shopping arcade; salon; 24-hr. room service; same-day dry cleaning/laundry service; executive-level rooms; nonsmoking rooms; currency exchange; squash courts. *In room:* A/C, satellite TV, broadband/dataport, minibar, hair dryer, safe.

EXPENSIVE

Běijīng Marriott West (Běijīng Jīnyù Wànháo Jiǔdiàn) ✦ *Value* The first full-fledged Marriott in Běijīng, this hotel offers good value after the discount, although the location is far from the major sights. Along with the Shěnyáng Marriott (the first Marriott in China), it's among the country's most opulent hotels. The structure was an apartment building before the Marriott Group took over, so rooms are immense. Eighty percent have Jacuzzi tubs and all are furnished with sumptuous beds and overstuffed chairs. Guests have free access to the attached Bally fitness center.

Xī Sān Huán Běi Lù 98, Xī Chéng Qū (in Jīnyù Dàshà, at intersection with Fùchéng Lù); see map p. 112. ℂ **010/6872-6699.** Fax 010/6872-7302. www.marriotthotels.com/bjsmc. 155 units. ¥2,080 ($260) standard room (summer discount rates ¥700–¥800/$88–$100), plus 15% service charge. AE, DC, MC, V. **Amenities:** Restaurant (Western); bar; comprehensive health club with indoor pool and tennis courts; concierge; business center; salon; 24-hr. room service; same-day dry cleaning/laundry service; executive-level rooms; nonsmoking rooms; bowling center; currency exchange. *In room:* A/C, satellite TV, dataport, minibar, hair dryer, safe.

State Guest Hotel Presidential Plaza (Guóbīn Jiǔdiàn) *Value* The Presidential Plaza stole much of its staff from Radisson (the company originally contracted to manage it) and its lobby and room decor from the St. Regis, but it's a good choice for the money. Because the decision to create a hotel was

Airport Hotels

Plenty of hotels, all with free shuttle services, are located near the airport. The most pleasant choice is the **Sino-Swiss Hotel (Guódū Dàfàndiàn)** ★ (© 010/6456-5588; fax 010/6456-1588; www.sino-swiss hotel.com), formerly a Mövenpick, containing large rooms with two queen-size beds for around ¥830 ($104) after discount. Guests have free access to a pleasant resort-style pool complex, and regular shuttles go the airport (10 min.) and downtown. Almost within walking distance of the airport to the south is the very basic **Air China Hotel** (Guóháng Bīnguǎn; © 010/6456-3440), with standard rooms from ¥260 to ¥320 ($33–$40). Slightly nicer rooms can be had at the three-star **Blue Sky Hotel** (Lán Tiān Dàshà; © 010/8048-9108), 15 minutes away in the Kōngǎng Industrial Zone. A standard room costs ¥488 ($61). Further from the airport, in northern Cháoyáng, the **Holiday Inn Lido** (Lìdū Jiàrì Fàndiàn; © 010/6437-6688; fax 010/6437-6237; http://bejing-lido.holiday-inn.com) is part of an extensive complex with foreign restaurants and shops. Standard rooms are large but plain and in need of refurbishment (¥880/$110 after discount). The **Kempinski Hotel** (p. 69), on the Third Ring Road, also has free shuttle service to the airport.

made halfway through the building's construction, the hotel has more than 30 room types, some with odd but interesting arrangements, but all luxuriously appointed with a few pieces of traditional Chinese furniture and spacious, marble-heavy bathrooms. Proximity to the Fùchéng Mén metro station means convenient access to the major sights, but the surrounding neighborhood is a bore.

Fùchéng Mén Wài Dàjiē 9, Xī Chéng Qū (1 block west of Fùchéng Mén metro); see map p. 112. © 010/6800-5588. Fax 010/6800-5888. www.stateguesthotel.com. 500 units. ¥1,400 ($175) standard room (summer discount rates around ¥960/$120), plus 15% service charge. AE, DC, MC, V. Metro: Fùchéng Mén (203). **Amenities:** 3 restaurants (Cantonese, International buffet, American grill); bar; pleasant indoor pool; small but well-equipped exercise room; Jacuzzi; sauna; concierge; business center; salon; 24-hr. room service; same-day dry cleaning/laundry service; executive-level rooms; currency exchange. *In room:* A/C, satellite TV, dataport, minibar, hair dryer, safe.

INEXPENSIVE

International Exchange Center (Wàijiāo Xuéyuàn Guójì Jiāoliú Zhōngxīn) ★ *Finds*   This seldom-exploited international students' building on the Foreign Affairs College campus offers freshly refurbished dorm-style twins and large apartments at reasonable daily rates. The apartments have kitchens and washing machines, and regular rooms come with sparkling en suite bathrooms. There's a well-equipped self-catering kitchen on each floor, plus such amenities as Ping-Pong, Internet access, and laundry machines. Several buses pass by here.

Zhǎnlǎn Guǎn Lù 24, Xī Chéng Qū (in newish gray concrete apt structure behind main campus building); see map p. 112. © 010/6832-3000. Fax 010/6832-2900. faciec@mx.cei.gov.cn. 170 units. ¥195 ($24) standard room (discounts for long stay). No credit cards. **Amenities:** Coin-op laundry; Internet access; self-catering kitchens. *In room:* A/C, satellite TV, fridge upon request.

5

Where to Dine

by Josh Chin

This, most people tell themselves after their first meal in Běijīng, is not Chinese food. There's none of the lemon chicken you usually get delivered from the Ho-Ho Gourmet back home, the chicken you do get still has its head, and the sauce doesn't drip from it in gelatinous clumps. The rice comes at the end of the meal unless you ask for it early—and there are no fortune cookies.

Of all the vertigo first-time visitors experience in Běijīng, the worst spins often come from eating. In the past, fear of the food kept many travelers turning to their hotels and a few free-standing "Western" eateries for sustenance. This is no longer necessary, if it ever was.

Běijīng is China's best city for gastronomes. Nowhere is there a greater variety of restaurants. Better standards of hygiene have erased the biggest barrier to eating out in the past, making it almost criminal to stay in your hotel. And once you get over the shock of strange flavors, most travelers find the real Chinese food astronomically better than its Western corruption.

Restaurants in Běijīng open and close with such frequency, they are quite literally innumerable. The short life span of the average restaurant in Běijīng can create headaches—for guidebook writers and readers in particular, and restaurant owners most of all. But the volatility is also what makes the city such a wonderful place to eat, as establishments that manage to stick around have generally earned the right to exist.

Běijīng has its native cuisine, but it is by no means the dominant one. While there are entire restaurants devoted to producing the city's most famous local dish, Běijīng roast duck, local diners are fickle and fond of new trends. These sweep through the city like tornadoes through Kansas. A few years ago it was Cultural Revolution nostalgia dishes, then fish and sweet sauces from Shànghǎi, and now yuppified minority food from Yúnnán. Tomorrow it will be something else. Each leaves its mark on the culinary landscape after it has passed, making it possible for visitors to sample authentic dishes from nearly every corner of the country. (For a summary of the most popular cuisines, see "The Cuisines" box below.)

The choices expand well beyond China's borders. Most of Asia and Europe are well represented at close-to-authentic levels. Italian, American, French, Indian, and Japanese restaurants are particularly numerous, some of superb quality.

American fast-food outlets are ubiquitous. KFC, the most popular among locals, opened its 70th branch in the city in 2001 and has more than 80 now. McDonald's is a close second, with around 60. Subway and even A&W are also in the mix. For sandwiches, there are several other choices: Schlotsky's Delis (in the Oriental Plaza and China World Trade Center), the highly recommended Super 24 (halfway up Sānlǐtún bar street), and Sammie's next to the SilkStreet Market.

Among sit-down options are Pizza Hut, T.G.I. Friday's, Henry J. Bean's (in the China World complex), the American-owned Outback Steakhouse, and the Běijīng Hard Rock Cafe (check *City Weekend* for location details).

Běijīng frequently ranks among the most expensive cities in which to dine for business travelers, according to the Corporate Travel Index and other sources of such information. While it is certainly possible to spend a lot of money on food in the city, it is also possible to eat, and eat well, for very little. A typical dinner for two at a relatively upscale Chinese restaurant costs ¥80 to ¥140 ($10–$18), but prices can go much lower with little to no drop in food quality.

Main courses in almost every non-Western restaurant are placed in the middle of the table and shared between two or more people. The "meal for two" price estimates in this chapter include two individual bowls of rice and between two and four dishes, depending on size of portions, which tends to decrease as prices rise.

Credit cards are generally accepted in most restaurants above the moderately priced level. Hotels frequently levy a 15% service charge, but free-standing restaurants seldom do. Tips are not given; waitresses will frequently come running out into the street to give your money back if you try to leave one.

Restaurants in this chapter are a mix of established favorites and newer places creative enough or just plain good enough to survive. Běijīng's enthusiasm for the wrecking ball can sometimes take down even the most venerable of eating establishements, but new worthies inevitably rise to fill the gap. Most restaurants of note, especially those that cater to foreign clientele, are located in Cháoyáng, but excellent establishments exist all over the city. The most picturesque spot to dine in Běijīng is around the Back Lakes, north of Běihǎi Park, an area of well-preserved *hútòng* (narrow lanes) and idyllic man-made lake promenades that is home to several of the city's most compelling eateries.

Note: For tips on dining etiquette, see "Fast Facts: Běijīng" in chapter 3. For more tips and a menu guide to the city's most popular dishes, see "Appendix A: Běijīng in Depth."

1 Restaurants by Cuisine

AMERICAN
Astor Grill ✶ (Cháoyáng, $$$$, p. 88)

Grandma's Kitchen (Zǔmǔ de Chúfáng) (Cháoyáng, $$, p. 94)

BĚIJĪNG
Běijīng Dàdǒng Kǎoyā Diàn ✶✶ (Cháoyáng, $$, p. 94)

Dào Jiā Cháng ✶ (Cháoyáng, $, p. 99)

Fú Jiā Lóu (Dōng Chéng, $$, p. 86)

Jiǔhuā Shān ✶ (Hǎidiàn, $$, p. 101)

Sìhéxuān (Cháoyáng, $$, p. 98)

Quánjùdé Kǎoyā Diàn (Běijīng South, $$$, p. 100)

BELGIAN
Morel's (Mòláolongxǐ Xīcāntīng) ✶✶ (Cháoyáng, $$$, p. 92)

CANTONESE
Horizon (Hǎitiān Gé) ✶ (Cháoyáng, $$$, p. 90)

Noble Court (City Center, $$$$, p. 83)

Otto's Restaurant (Rìchāng Chá Cāntīng) ✶ (City Center, $$, p. 84)

DAOIST
Dào ✶✶ (Back Lakes, $$$, p. 85)

FRENCH
Flo (Fú Lóu) ✶ (Cháoyáng, $$$, p. 90)

Key to Abbreviations: $$$$ = Very Expensive $$$ = Expensive $$ = Moderate $ = Inexpensive

The Cuisines

China has between four and ten seminal cooking styles, depending on who you ask, but regional permutations, minority contributions, and specialty cuisines like Buddhist-influenced vegetarian and therapeutic medicinal dishes push the number into the dozens. Most of these have at least passed through Běijīng since privately owned restaurants really took off in the 1980s. Below are summaries of the most consistently popular styles, as well as the cuisines *du jour,* which may or may not be around next time you visit:

Běijīng This ill-defined cuisine was influenced over the centuries by the different eating habits of successive rulers. Emphasis is on lamb and pork, with strong, salty, and sometimes musky flavors. Staples are heavy noodles and breads rather than rice. *Jiǎozi,* little morsels of meat and vegetables wrapped in dough and usually boiled, are a favorite local snack.

Cantonese Among the most famous Chinese cooking styles, Cantonese tends to be light and crisp, with pleasing combinations of salty and sweet, elaborate presentations, and a fondness for rare animal ingredients at the high end. As with Sichuanese food, real Cantonese puts its American version to shame. It's available in both swanky and for-the-masses permutations.

Homestyle (Jiācháng Cài) The most pervasive style in Běijīng, homestyle food consists of simplified dishes from a variety of regions, primarily Sìchuān. It is cheap, fast, and gloriously filling, with straightforward flavors that run the gamut. This is the Chinese equivalent of downhome American cooking, but far healthier and more colorful.

Huáiyáng This ancient style from the lower reaches of the Yangtze River (Cháng Jiāng) is celebrated for delicate knife work and light, slightly sweet fish dishes. Vegetarian dishes often make interesting use of fruit. The tendency here is to braise and stew rather than stir-fry.

Shànghǎi   These richly sweet, oil-heavy dishes are no longer as trendy as they were a few years ago, are still easy to find. Shanghainese food tends to be more expensive than fare from Sìchuān or Běijīng, but affordable Shànghǎi-style snack shops dot the city. Best are the varieties of *bāozi*, or bread dumplings.

Sìchuān   The most popular of the pure cuisines in Běijīng, real Sichuanese is far more flavorful than the "Szechuan" food found in the United States. Main ingredients are vividly hot peppers, numbing black peppercorns, and garlic, as found in classics like *gōngbǎo jīdīng* (diced chicken with chilies and peanuts). Spicy Sìchuān-style hotpot is the city's best interactive food experience.

Southern Minority   The trend of the moment. Cuisine and rare ingredients from Nàxī-dominated regions of Yúnnán Province are especially fashionable, but Hakka, Dǎi, Miáo, and other ethnic traditions are also well represented. This is some of the city's most interesting food right now, but also its most inconsistent and overpriced.

Uighur   Uighur cooking is the more distinctive of Běijīng's two Muslim styles (the other being Huí), with origins in remote Xīnjiāng Province. The cuisine is heavy on lamb and chicken and is justly adored for its variety of thick noodles in spiced tomato-based sauces. Uighurs produce the city's favorite street snack: *yang ròu chuàn*, roasted lamb skewers with cumin and chili powder.

Vegetarian   An increasingly diverse style, the Běijīng version of vegetarian cuisine is moving away from its previous obsession with soy- and taro-based fake meat dishes. Decor and quality vary from restaurant to restaurant, but none allow smoking or booze.

HONG KONG

Be There or Be Square (Bú Jiàn Bú Sàn) (City Center, $$, p. 84)

Otto's Restaurant (Rìchāng Chá Cāntīng) ✿ (City Center, $$, p. 84)

HOTPOT

Bǎi Shì Jí Huǒguō (Cháoyáng, $$, p. 93)

Dǐng Dǐng Xiāng (Cháoyáng, $$, p. 94)

Huángchéng Lǎo Mǎ ✿ (Cháoyáng, $$$, p. 91)

Tàipó Tiānfǔ Shānzhēn ✿✿ (Běijīng South, $$, p. 100)

HUÁIYÁNG

Kǒng Yǐjǐ Jiǔlóu ✿✿✿ (Back Lakes, $$, p. 87)

INDIAN

Chingari (Xíngéi) (Cháoyáng, $$$, p. 89)

Taj Pavilion (Tàijī Lóu Yìndù Cāntīng) (Cháoyáng, $$$, p. 92)

ITALIAN

Annie's Café (Ānnī Yìdàlì Cāntīng) ✿ (Cháoyáng, $$, p. 93)

Da Giorgio (City Center, $$$$, p. 83)

Danieli's (Dānní'àilì) ✿✿ (Cháoyáng, $$$$, p. 88)

Mediterraneo (Dìzhōnghǎi) ✿
(Cháoyáng, $$$, p. 91)

JAPANESE
Hatsune (Yǐn Quán) ✿✿
(Cháoyáng, $$$, p. 90)
Matsuko (Sōngzǐ) (Cháoyáng, $$$,
p. 91)

JIǍOZI
Tiānjīn Bái Jiǎo Yuán (Běijīng
South, $, p. 101)

MALAYSIAN
Cafe Sambal (Back Lakes, $$$,
p. 85)

MIDDLE EASTERN
1001 Nights (Yìqiānlíngyī Yè)
(Cháoyáng, $$$, p. 92)

NORTHEASTERN
Xiàngyáng Tún (Hǎidiàn, $, p. 101)

SHÀNGHǍI
Hùjiāng Xiāng Mǎn Lóu (Dōng
Chéng, $$, p. 87)
Shànghǎi Fēngwèi Cāntīng ✿✿
(Cháoyáng, $$$$, p. 89)

SHĀNXĪ
Noodle Loft (Miàn Kù Shānxī
Shíyì) ✿ (Cháoyáng, $$, p. 96)

SÌCHUĀN
Gōng Wángfǔ Sìchuān Fàndiàn
(Back Lakes, $$$, p. 86)
Hóng Jīng Yú (Cháoyáng, $$,
p. 95)
Yúxiāng Rénjiā ✿ (Cháoyáng, $$,
p. 98)

SPANISH
Mediterraneo (Dìzhōnghǎi) ✿
(Cháoyáng, $$$, p. 91)

THAI
Red Basil (Zǐ Tiān Jiāo)
(Cháoyáng, $$$, p. 92)

TIBETAN
Makye Ame (Mǎjí Āmǐ)
(Cháoyáng, $$$, p. 91)

UIGHUR
Afunti (Āfántí) (Dōng Chéng,
$$$, p. 85)
Pamer (Pàmǐ'ěr Shífǔ) ✿ (Běijīng
South, $$, p. 100)

VEGETARIAN
Green Tiānshí (Lǜsè Tiānshí) (City
Center, $$$, p. 84)
Lotus in Moonlight (Hétáng Yuèsè
Sùshí) ✿ (Cháoyáng, $$,
p. 95)
Pure Lotus (Jìngxīn Lián)
(Cháoyáng, $$, p. 97)

VIETNAMESE
Nuage (Qìng Yún Lóu) ✿ (Back
Lakes, $$$, p. 86)

YÚNNÁN
Ānyuán No. 5 (Ānyuán Wǔ Hào
Cāntīng) (Cháoyáng, $$,
p. 93)
Middle 8th (Zhōng Bā Lóu)
(Cháoyáng, $$, p. 96)
Yúnnán Jīn Kǒngquè Déhóng
Dǎiwèi Cānguǎn ✿ (Hǎidiàn,
$$, p. 101)

2 Běijīng City Center, Around Wángfǔjǐng Dàjiē

VERY EXPENSIVE

The Courtyard (Sìhéyuàn) ✿✿ FUSION If you read the food magazines, this is the only Běijīng restaurant you're likely to know about. Owned by a Chinese-American lawyer with family roots in Běijīng, the Courtyard serves admirable fare but wins the most accolades for its setting, in a restored courtyard-style house next to the Forbidden City. The house's gray brick exterior still blends with its old Běijīng surroundings, but inside is a different world: modernist white and glass, with tall art-hung walls and a beckoning staircase that leads to a contemporary art gallery in the basement. The food is genuine fusion, competently executed though somewhat over-hyped. Cashew-crusted lamb chop and Alaskan black cod with baby bok choy are longtime favorites. The tender grilled chicken breast in lemon grass and coconut curry is among the best poultry dishes the city has to offer, justifying rave reviews almost by itself. The wine list is more comprehensive than anything this side of Hong Kong, with a surprisingly large number available by the glass. An intimate cigar lounge upstairs, furnished with leather couches, looks out across the Forbidden City's eastern moat. The Sunday brunch set menu is a deal at ¥150 ($19) for three courses.

Dōnghuá Mén Lù 95 (on north side of street); see map p. 104. ✆ 010/6526-8883. Reservations recommended on weekends. Main courses ¥160–¥320 ($20–$40). AE, DC, MC, V. Mon–Sat 6–10:30pm; Sun 11am–2pm. Metro: Tiān'ān Mén Dōng (117); east side of Forbidden City.

Da Giorgio ITALIAN   Within the Grand Hyatt (p. 65), this small restaurant with modest Italianate decor is in cozy contrast to the general grandeur of the hotel. Restaurants serving foreign cuisine in Běijīng tend to tone down the flavors so as not to frighten away still unadventurous and unsophisticated richer Chinese, but if that's been done here, it's only served to release the honest flavors of the ingredients on a concise but well-executed menu. The beef carpaccio has a liquid freshness, the minestrone (with rosemary and basil pesto) is far more subtle than the hearty stew it can sometimes become, and the roasted Atlantic salmon steak with mushrooms and artichoke basil pesto sauce is meaty and filling. Overall, the tone is rustic, and the portion sizes are correspondingly hearty.

Dōng Cháng'ān Jiē 1 (Inside the Grand Hyatt); see map p. 104. ✆ 010/8518-1234. Main courses ¥90–¥195 ($11–$24). AE, DC, MC, V. Daily 10.30am–2.30pm and 5.30–10.30pm.

Jing ★★ FUSION   With the most stylish interior of any restaurant in the capital, Jing has plenty of visual entertainment: wide-open kitchens, wine stacked in transparent temperature-controlled columns, semi-private rooms whose walls are merely circular curtains of chains. A glass staircase leads down into the main dining room, where a Hong Kong artist's video installation plays a perpetual montage of scenes from life in Běijīng. Fusion dishes lean more to the Asian side than those at the Courtyard (see above). The tandoor sampler (lamb, chicken, and swordfish) is a must. Also worthwhile are the Vietnamese king prawns served with spiced nan bread, and the hot smoked salmon with bonito-crusted green beans and citrus-soy dressing. Flavors are juxtaposed well, and nothing is overwrought.

Jīnyú Hútòng 8 (in basement of Palace Hotel); see map p. 104. ✆ 010/6523-0175. Meal for 2 ¥400–¥600 ($50–$75). AE, DC, MC, V. Daily 5:30am–11:30pm.

Noble Court CANTONESE   An elegant circular space downstairs from the Grand Hyatt's lobby, the Noble Court's particular strengths are its Cantonese dim sum and Běijīng-style snacks, which well deserve their "premium" designation, complemented by a comprehensive range of fish and seafood. Among snack offerings, try the shrimp and pork dumplings, the baked seafood in puff pastry and, on the Běijīng side, the particularly piquant sliced goose kidney with preserved vegetable in chili sauce. Steamed garoupa filets with black mushrooms and green vegetables are excellent, the fish at once hot and firm. Hong Kong influence is visible in popular oddities such as fried coffee-flavored lamb chop. Such favorites as almond, chestnut, and bean desserts are available. Set menus include high-end items such as braised shark's fin and simmered lobster. Service is impeccable.

> **Overrated** Imperial Restaurants
>
> Elaborately presented but seldom appetizing, dishes cooked in Běijīng's much-hyped imperial style are one of the city's biggest scams. Famous imperial restaurants **Fǎng Shàn Fànzhuāng** in Běi Hǎi Park and **Lì Jiā Cài (Lì Family Restaurant)** in the Back Lakes area are both set in picturesque surroundings but charge far too much for bad food and are therefore not included in this book. For a better dining experience in either location, pack a picnic. If you really want to drop a hundred bucks on camel paw and soup made from bird saliva, ask the concierge in your hotel to point the way.

Dōng Cháng'ān Jiē 1 (Inside the Grand Hyatt); see map p. 104. ℂ 010/8518-1234. Meal for 2 ¥300–¥500 ($37–$62). Fixed-price lunch ¥380 ($45). AE, DC, MC, V. Daily 10.30am–2pm and 6–10pm.

EXPENSIVE

Green Tiānshí (Lǜsè Tiānshí) VEGETARIAN No longer Běijīng's best vegetarian restaurant, Green Tiānshí is still the most convenient, located just east of the city's main shopping street. Access is through a ground-floor crystal shop and up a flight of stairs lined with photos of famous vegetarians, including a skeptical-looking Paul Newman. Decor is bland but blessedly free of cigarette smoke. The large, slightly overpriced English menu eschews simple vegetables in favor of fake meat dishes. Tofu-based cashew "chicken" is a reasonably good approximation. The kitchen also offers a Běijīng roast (soy) duck and, for the brashest of fake sinners, a vegetarian veal, nicely paired with non-alcoholic beer.

Dēngshìkǒu Dōng Jiē 57–5 (block east of Wángfǔjǐng Dàjiē); see map p. 104. ℂ 010/6524-2476 or 2349. Meal for 2 ¥130–¥150 ($16–$19) AE, DC, MC, V. Daily 10am–10pm.

MODERATE

Be There or Be Square (Bú Jiàn Bú Sàn) HONG KONG This Hong Kong–style cafe chain, with its hip warehouse-style decor, is the city's most fashionable source of the Westernized Cantonese fare commonly found in the former British colony. All the classics are here: BBQ pork with rice, egg foo yung, beef with rice noodles. There's also a selection of vaguely Western breakfast items, including peanut butter–stuffed French toast. Lines form at lunch, but the efficient staff, all equipped with SWAT-style headsets, make sure the wait is never long. Another branch in the Henderson Center (north of Běijīng Zhàn) is open 24 hours a day.

Basement of Oriental Plaza (at far eastern end); see map p. 104. ℂ 010/8518-6518. Main courses: ¥20–¥40 ($3–$5). No credit cards. Daily 9am–9pm. Metro: Wángfǔjǐng (118).

Otto's Restaurant (Rìchāng Chá Cāntīng) 🍴 CANTONESE/HONG KONG Otto's is authentic Hong Kong prole dining, down to the shouts, smoke, and indecipherable wall-mounted menu. The environment may be jarring and the staff too busy to care, but the food is tremendous. The restaurant specializes in *bāozǎi* (clay pot) rice dishes, best of which is the *làwèi huájī bǎozǎifàn*, a mix of rice, salty-sweet sausage, and chicken drizzled in soy. Also good, albeit messy, are the *suànxiāng jǐchì* (paper-wrapped garlic chicken wings). Thick glasses of iced coffee sweetened with condensed milk *(bīng kāfēi)* are the perfect remedy for midsummer malaise. A second sterile branch with limited hours has opened at the west gate of Cháoyáng Gōngyuán.

Dōngdān Dàjiē 72 (just inside small alley past a movie theater on east side of street); see map p. 104. ℂ 010/6525-1783. Meal for 2 ¥60–¥80 ($8–$10). No credit cards. Open 24 hr. Metro: Dōngdān (119); walk north several blocks.

3 Back Lakes & Dōng Chéng

EXPENSIVE

Afunti (Āfántí) *Kids* UIGHUR   Afunti is now more tourist attraction than restaurant, famous for its post-dinner music shows—sometimes Uighur, sometimes Latin—which almost invariably lead to restaurant-wide table dancing. The large hall features an entertainingly over-the-top Muslim motif and the food is still good, although now very overpriced. Try the roasted chicken skewers and any of a number of hearty noodle dishes. Get there early or risk having your food stomped. English menu.

Hòuguǎibàng Hútòng 2A (just off Cháoyáng Mén Nèi Dàjiē, west of Cháoyáng Mén Xiǎo Jiē intersection); see map p. 104. ℂ 010/6527-2288. Reservations recommended on weekends. Meal for 2 ¥200–¥250 ($25–$31). AE, DC, MC, V. Daily 11am–midnight (later on weekends).

Cafe Sambal ✦✦ MALAYSIAN   The race to serve Běijīng's best Malaysian nosh currently has only one contestant, but it will take something extraordinary to top this. Sambal embraces and surpasses all the clichés of a chic Běijīng eatery—a cozy courtyard house decorated with antique and modern furnishings, a sophisticated boss (Cho Chong Gee), relaxed service from a handsome waitstaff, and a well-balanced wine list. And then there's the food, prepared by a charming chef from Kuala Lumpur. You'll need to call a day in advance for the spectacular double-braised Australian lobster in *nyonya* sauce, or the chili curry crab. Try the fried four-sided bean with cashew nut sauce, the divinely creamy king prawn with yellow sauce, or the special lamb curry served in a thick, spicy coconut sauce. Don't miss the signature dish, Kapitan chicken, a mildly spicy dish with a nutty aftertaste, said to have been invented when Chinese migrants reached Penang during the Míng dynasty. Your life won't be the same after sampling the exquisitely marinated deep-fried banana.

Dòufu Chí Hútòng 43 (northwest of the Bell Tower); see map p. 104; Xī Chéng Qū. (Walk south along Jiù Gǔ Lóu Dàjiē and take the 5th street on the left; it's the 1st building on the left.) ℂ 010/6400-4875. Meal for 2 ¥250–¥400 ($31–$50). No credit cards. Daily 12:30pm till late. Metro: Gǔ Lóu (217).

Dào ✦✦ DAOIST   Nestled in half of a defunct Daoist prayer hall at the back of a crumbling residential cluster east of the Back Lakes, Dào is Běijīng's most unique—and most obscure—new restaurant. There's no sign in the *hútòng* outside, only an aged stone archway with the Míng-era temple's name (Guǎngfú Guàn) carved in faded characters at its apex. A narrow path leads from the arch past bemused neighbors to the hall, its beautifully crafted beams and murals brought back to life in early 2003 with help from the people at Nuage (see below). The restaurant's manager, who was born in the building and recalls the false roof that hid it from Cultural Revolution vandals in the 1960s, has hired chefs from Qīng Chéng Shān in Sìchuān, where the Zhèngyī school of Daoism developed recipes for longevity and virility. The set meal includes fresh *jiǎozi*, accompanied by delicate side dishes like goose liver rolls with hoisin sauce (*é'gān juǎn*), deep-fried pork with medicinal herbs (*cùngū shāo*), and sweet gourd-shaped red bean rolls with mountain herbs (*shānyào húlu*). The drink menu features a bracing "immortal's abode" koumiss (*dòngtiān rǔjiǔ*), made with fermented milk, and the somewhat more appetizing Daoist medicinal tea (*gòng chá*). Expect options to expand once the chefs have settled in.

Yāndài Xiéjiē 37, next to the Lotus Bar. (Walking south from Drum Tower on Dì'ānmén Wài Dàjiē, turn onto 1st *hútòng* on right; archway is on northeast side); see map on p. 104. ℭ **010/6404-2778.** Meal for 2 ¥135 ($17). AE, DC, MC, V. Daily 10am–10pm.

Gōng Wángfǔ Sìchuān Fàndiàn SÌCHUĀN   This is the most famous Sìchuān restaurant in Běijīng, known more for its history than its food. Originally located in the former estate of Yuán Shìkǎi (president of the Republic of China, 1912–1916), it was one of the first free-standing restaurants opened in the post-1949 period, established by order of Zhōu Ēnlái in 1959. The restaurant moved here, to the home of a Qīng dynasty court mandarin (see Prince Gōng's Mansion, p. 142), in 1996. The main dining room is a bland space not enhanced by the lackluster food, but those with the foresight to call far ahead and the willingness to pay a 15% surcharge can eat in the stunning garden, where dishes have a way of tasting better. Worthwhile choices are the *guōbā yóuyú* (deep-fried sizzling rice with squid and bamboo shoots) and the bowls of surprisingly subtle *dān dān miàn* (ramen-like noodles).

Liǔyīn Jiē 14A (follow signs to Prince Gōng's Palace); see map on p. 104. ℭ **010/6615–6924.** Meal for 2 ¥160–¥200 ($20–$25). AE, DC, MC, V. Daily 10am–2pm and 5–9pm.

Nuage (Qìng Yún Lóu) ⨂ VIETNAMESE   Lake views from this restaurant's upstairs windows are matched only by its hallucinatory Hanoi-inspired interior. A long silver dragon snakes up the rear staircase to the main dining room, where the low light from red lanterns flickers on reed curtains and finely crafted wooden tables. The first floor has China's most improbably stylish bathrooms, divided by an elaborate cut-glass pool. Food is not quite as impressive—portions are small and prices absurdly inflated—but there are some worthwhile gems. The *xiāngcǎo cuìlà yú* (crispy-skin fish with lemon grass and hot pepper) has to be among the city's best fish dishes; and the *phô* (Vietnamese beef noodles in soup) has a smooth, flavorful broth, but at a price 10 times higher than in Vietnam. Owned by Bái Fēng, the Buddha-like hipster who pioneered the Back Lakes gentrification, this is the closest thing Běijīng has to a "hot" restaurant in the New York City sense, complete with a long-legged hostess who seems to take pleasure in turning people away. (Make reservations well in advance.) An attached dance club is coming soon.

Qián Hǎi Dōng Yán 22 (east of the Yíndìng Bridge, at the intersection of Qián Hǎi and Hòu Hǎi); see map p. 104. ℭ **010/6401-9591.** Reservations required. Meal for 2 ¥200–¥300 ($25–$38). AE, DC, MC, V. Daily noon–2pm and 6–10pm.

MODERATE

Fújiā Lóu BĚIJĪNG   This Old Běijīng eatery is essentially a more stylized copy of the popular Dào Jiā Cháng branch (p. 99) that originally occupied the building. It is more conveniently located and provides a more pleasant atmosphere than its predecessor, with intricate lattice wood screens separating the dining rooms and dish names written on pieces of wood hung from the rafters. Food is high quality and comes quickly. Worth trying are the *zhá qiéhé* (two slices of eggplant deep-fried with pork in the middle) and *kǎo yáng ròu* (thin-sliced roast mutton).

Dōngsì Shítiáo 23 (in gray brick building with fake tile-roof on facade, 3 blocks west of the Cháoyáng Mén metro station); see map p. 104. ℭ **010/8403-7831.** Meal for 2 ¥40–¥80 ($5–$10). No credit cards. Daily 11am–2pm and 5–9:30pm. Metro: Cháoyáng Mén (212).

Hàn Kèjiā ⨂⨂⨂ HAKKA   This sequel to Old Character Hakka (p. 96) is larger and more quaintly located but otherwise identical, with the same artist-owner, stone and rough-wood decor, and heavenly food. English menu.

(**Moments** Dinner on the Lakes, by Candlelight

For roughly ¥400 ($50) plus the cost of food, Běijīng's ancient roast-meat restaurant **Kǎoròujì** now arranges what may be the most charming dining experience in the city: a meal for up to eight people served aboard a narrow **canopied flat-bottom boat,** staffed by a lone oarsman who guides the craft in a gentle arc around the man-made serenity of Qián Hǎi and Hòu Hǎi. The entire trip takes roughly 2 hours. A little extra money buys live traditional music and the opportunity to float candles in the lakes after dark falls—a cliché in the making, but who cares? The restaurant is located next to Nuage (p. 86) at Qián Hǎi Dōng Yán 14 (meal for 2 ¥120– ¥160/$15–$20; daily 11am–2pm and 5–9pm). To make boat arrangements, call ℂ **010/6612-5719** or 010/6404-2554. *Note:* Boat-rental prices vary from season to season and will probably increase as time goes on.

East bank of Qián Hǎi, 50m (165 ft.) north of Běi Hǎi Park north entrance; see map p. 104. ℂ 010/6404-2259. Meal for 2 ¥80–¥100 ($10–$12). AE, DC, MC, V. Daily 11am–2pm and 5–10pm.

Huājiā Yíyuán HOMESTYLE   The chef-owner behind this pair of popular courtyard restaurants claims to have created a new Chinese supercuisine assembled from the best of the country's regional cooking styles. Whether Huācài (his name for the cuisine) will ever spread beyond Běijīng remains to be seen, but his long menu is one of the city's most impressive. Locals still prefer the original branch, a lively gathering spot during the Ghost Street golden era, where they crowd around outdoor tables at night to devour heaping plates of spicy crayfish (*málà lóngxiā*) and drink glasses of green "good for health" beer. The newer branch is less raucous but more charmingly located among the remains of Ghost Street. Try the *làròu dòuyá juǎnbǐng,* a mix of spicy bacon and bean sprouts rolled in pancakes roast duck–style.

Original at Dōng Zhí Mén Nèi Dàjiē 99 (now surrounded by an immense housing project); see map on p. 104. ℂ 010/6403-0677. New location a few blocks west at Dōng Zhí Mén Nèi Dàjiē 235; ℂ 010/6405-1908. Meal for 2 ¥100–¥120 ($12–$15). AE, DC, MC, V. Both open 24 hr.

Hùjiāng Xiāng Mǎn Lóu SHÀNGHǍI   This large eating hall with somewhat cheesy mock-village decor has an extensive range of decently crafted Shànghǎi-style snacks, available in an easy point-to-choose format from a series of stalls that line the back. Both of Shànghǎi's famous pork-and-bread dumplings are here: *xiǎolóng bāozi* (steamed in water) and *shēngjiān bāozi* ("steamed" in oil).

Dōngsì Shí Tiáo 34 (a few blocks east of the East Third Ring Road); see map p. 104. ℂ 010/6403-1368. Meal for 2 ¥60–¥100 ($8–$12). No credit cards. Daily 11am–2pm and 5–9pm. Metro: Dōngsì Shítiáo (213); walk west 3 blocks.

Kǒng Yǐjǐ Jiǔlóu ★★★ HUÁIYÁNG   Named for the alcoholic scholar-bum protagonist of a short story by Lúxùn, the father of modern Chinese literature, this extremely popular restaurant offers one of Běijīng's most thoroughly enjoyable Chinese dining experiences. A small bamboo forest leads to a traditional space pleasingly outfitted with calligraphy scrolls, traditional bookshelves, and other trappings of Chinese scholarship. Tightly packed tables overflow with enthusiastic diners, who shout and shovel their food in the grandest Chinese tradition. The menu, written vertically in the old style, features several hair-raising dishes, including the infamous *zuìxiā* (drunken shrimp), served still squirming in a small glass bowl filled with wine. Less shocking, and highly recommended, are the *mìzhì lúyú,* a whole fish deep-fried then broiled in tin foil with onions in a slightly sweet sauce; and the *yóutiáo niúròu,* savory slices of beef mixed with pieces of fried dough. Nearly everyone orders a small pot of *Dōngpō ròu,* extremely tender braised fatty pork swimming in savory juice. Fans of Lú's story will appreciate the wide selection of *huángjiǔ,* a sweet "yellow" rice wine aged for several years, served in silver pots, and sipped from a special ceramic cup with hot water in the bottom to keep it warm.

Dé Nèi Dàjiē (next to the octagonal Teahouse of Family Fù on the south bank of Hòu Hǎi); see map p. 104. ℂ 010/6618-4917. Reservations strongly recommended. Meal for 2 ¥100–¥140 ($12–$18). AE, DC, MC, V. Daily 10am–2pm and 4:30–10pm.

4 Cháoyáng

VERY EXPENSIVE

Aria (Āliyǎ) ★★★ FUSION This is one of the most thoroughly satisfying dining experiences in Běijīng, from *amuse-bouche* to dessert. The dining room, reached by a spiral staircase from a bustling bar, has a comforting clubby atmosphere, full of woody alcoves and hung with green velvet curtains. All courses come with suggestions for accompanying wines, the bottles creatively stored in wooden slots that run the length of the staircase. Several wines are available by the glass, including a nicely chilled Moët perfectly paired with Harbin caviar. Highly recommended specialties include a melt-in-the-mouth braised pig cheek and a truffle polenta with Turkish fig jam and sherry vinegar *jus.* Seared yellowfin tuna with Sìchuān spices and the salad Niçoise with horseradish emulsion are also fine choices. More than one visit may be necessary.

Jiànguó Mén Wài Dàjiē (inside the China World Hotel); see map p. 115. ℂ 010/6505-2266. Reservations recommended on weekends. Main courses ¥80–¥200 ($10–$250). AE, DC, MC, V. Daily 11am–midnight. Metro: Guómào (122).

Astor Grill ★ AMERICAN You can get anything in Běijīng if you're willing to pay enough. Buried in a quiet corner of the St. Regis Hotel, the Astor Grill charges outrageous prices for its steaks, but they are among the best in the city and are served in one of its most romantic settings. The small space is more midtown Manhattan than eastern Běijīng, unpretentiously elegant with only a handful of tables. Premium cuts of Australian and U.S. beef come with a choice of sauces, including a divine black peppercorn *jus,* and a full range of traditional sides. Appetizers and salads are lackluster for the price and servers tend to hover, making a small space feel even smaller, but the experience is ultimately pleasant. A cigar lounge, stocked with some fine single-malt Scotches, sits across the hall. Spotlights from the deck can be a distraction—choose a table away from the windows.

Jiànguó Mén Wài Dàjiē 21 (on 2nd floor of St. Regis Hotel club building); see map p. 115. ℂ 010/6460-6688, ext. 2714 or 2709. Main courses ¥135–¥300 ($17–$38). AE, DC, MC, V. Mon–Fri 11am–2pm and 6–10pm; weekends 6–10pm. Metro: Jiànguó Mén (120/211); walk east 2 blocks and take left on Rìtán Dōng Lù.

Danieli's (Dānní'àilì) ★★ ITALIAN Tuscan-themed Danieli's is potentially the finest Italian restaurant in the city, with a tremendous wine list; a pleasing, well-lit interior; and an extensive menu that borrows elements from all parts of the boot. The emphasis is on authenticity rather than innovation, part of an attempt not to scare inexperienced Chinese diners, but there is plenty here to satisfy Western epicures. Among the best choices are the tomato and artichoke risotto with a generous sprinkling of truffle oil, and the tender, very flavorful rack of lamb seasoned with fresh thyme. As with the Astor Grill (another St. Regis restaurant), the waitstaff can be overzealous when not busy but is otherwise competent. Quality of food aside, the restaurant seems somewhat uncomfortable in its present guise, and the head chef has toyed with the idea of toning down food presentation and place settings to give it a more casual feel. Danieli's will be even better when it decides what it wants to be.

Jiànguó Mén Wài Dàjiē 21 (on 2nd floor of St. Regis Hotel); see map p. 115. © 010/6460-6688, ext. 2441 or 1440. Main courses ¥100–¥250 ($12–$31). AE, DC, MC, V. Mon–Fri 11:30am–2pm and 6–10pm; weekends 6–10pm. Metro: Jiànguó Mén (120/211); walk east 2 blocks and take left on Rìtán Dōng Lù.

Justine's (Jiésītīng) ★★ FRENCH   There is an inverse relationship between age and quality in most Běijīng restaurants, with tradition too often cited as a cover for sub-par food. Such is resolutely not the case with this, the city's oldest and most elegant French restaurant. Little about Justine's has changed in the 20 years since it opened. Fully set tables still glitter just so in the soft light of low-hanging chandeliers, service is still impeccable, and though a few head chefs have come and gone, the extensive menu still offers some of the finest and most consistent French food in the country. The best choice these days is the fricassée of Bresse chicken with wild rice, improbably tender and flavorful in a sauce made of morel mushrooms from Yúnnán Province. There's a generously stocked by-the-glass wine cart, and the Chinese staff has been well trained in suggesting the right pairings of food and drink, like a cool sauterne with the silky smooth goose liver terrine. Prices are high, but not absurdly so. The set-menu "business lunch" is an incredible steal at ¥138 ($17).

Jiànguó Mén Wài Dàjiē 5 (inside the Jiànguó Hotel); see map p. 115. © 010/6500-2233, ext. 8039. Main courses ¥120–¥230 ($15–$29). AE, DC, MC, V. Daily 6:30–9:30am, noon–2:30pm, and 6–10:30pm. Metro: Yǒng'ānlǐ (121).

Shànghǎi Fēngwèi Cāntīng ★★ SHÀNGHǍI   When members of former president Jiāng Zémín's powerful Shànghǎi Clique come to Běijīng, this is where they dine. Set inside an elaborate and truly breathtaking fake forest, with rounded stone pathways that wind past misty waterfalls and plant-shielded private dining nooks, it may be Běijīng's most authentic Shànghǎi restaurant, and is certainly its most lavish. The central dining room is sumptuously furnished with Míng-style tables and chairs, dark polished wood floors, delicately latticed windows looking out onto the forest, and an elaborate gilded dragon set in the ceiling. The chef specializes in hairy crab (available July–Dec) and light, flavorful, stir-fried vegetables cooked with a spoonful of reduced soup. Dishes aren't really worth the prices, but the setting is. The gold and cream decor of the upstairs dining area is nice but not nearly as impressive. Book a table downstairs well in advance.

Xīnyuán Nán Lù 2 (inside the Kūnlún Hotel, block west of East Third Ring Road); see map p. 115. © 010/6590-3388. Reservations absolutely required. Meal for 2 ¥400–¥480 ($50–$60). AE, DC, MC, V. Daily 11:30am–2pm and 5:30–9:30pm.

EXPENSIVE

Chingari (Xīngélì) INDIAN   If it weren't for the half-hearted decor and dance-club pretensions, Chingari would easily be the best Indian restaurant in Běijīng. Portions are a bit small for the price but service is friendly and flavors are authentic: This is where Běijīng's Indian residents come to eat. The tandoori chicken, tender and flavorful, is as good as it comes this far north of the border; *mutton do piazza* (lamb pieces in spicy coconut sauce) and *palak paneer* (spinach curry) are also highly recommended. The band starts playing Bollywood covers of 1980s American pop at 8:30pm. Get there well beforehand. The business lunch (11am–1:30pm) is a tremendous deal: ¥38 ($5) for choice of curry, rice or nan, and a drink.

Dōng Zhí Mén Wài Dàjiē 27 (at intersection with Liàngmǎ Hé Nán Lù; on 4th floor, above Pizza Hut); see map p. 115. ⓒ **010/8448-3690** or 010/8448-3691. Meal for 2 ¥180–¥250 ($23–$31). AE, DC, MC, V. Daily 11:30am–2:30pm and 5:30–10:30pm (closes at midnight Fri).

Flo (Fú Lóu) ★ *Value* FRENCH   This is a branch of the French restaurant empire described by some Paris foodies as the Starbucks of brasseries, but you can only be so picky in Běijīng. The restaurant occupies the front of a rather flashy building, all balustrades and staircases, with an (inaudible) nightclub at the rear. The menu is straightforward French favorites all done well. Recommended items include the smoked salmon salad with poached egg, pan-fried rib shortloin veal with mushrooms, and the chef's specialty, hot goose liver with apple. Reliability and good value may be why it's one of only a handful of free-standing Western restaurants to have survived more than a few years.

Dōng Sān Huán Běi Lù 12 (south of the Great Wall Sheraton); see map p. 115. ⓒ **010/6595-5139**. Main courses ¥110–¥140 ($11–$14). Fixed-price lunch ¥88 ($11). AE, DC, MC, V. Daily 11am–2.30pm and 5.30–10pm.

Hatsune (Yín Quán) ★★ JAPANESE   Hatsune is sushi sacrilege via Northern California, with a list of innovative rolls long and elaborate enough to drive serious raw fish traditionalists to ritual suicide. The unconventional attitude is also reflected in the stylish space, high-ceilinged and sleek, with a long glass-and-metal entryway and a rock garden path leading to the bathrooms. Nearly every item on the menu is among the best of its kind in the city, but the rolls are what make this place truly special. With the single exception of the Beijing Roll, a roast duck and "special sauce" gimmick, you simply can't go wrong. The 119 Roll, with bright red tuna inside and out topped with a divine spicy-sweet sauce, absolutely should not be missed.

Guānghuá Dōng Lù, Héqiáo Dàshà C (4 blocks east of Kerry Centre, opposite Petro China building); see map p. 115. ⓒ **010/6581-3939**. Meal for 2 ¥200–¥250 ($25–$31); Mon–Fri prix-fixe lunch ¥65 ($8); weekend lunch buffet ¥150 ($19). AE, DC, MC, V. Daily 11:30am–2pm and 5–10pm.

Horizon (Hǎitiān Gé) ★ *Value* CANTONESE   Shangri-La–managed Horizon is one of the finest and more sumptuously decorated Cantonese restaurants in Běijīng—and also one of its most reasonably priced. Cantonese is the subtlest of the Chinese cuisines, and this is the real thing, so don't expect the retina-straining colors or tooth-rotting sweet sauces you find at your neighborhood Chinese takeout joint. The menu features shark's fin, bird's-nest soup, and other classic indulgences designed to show off the fatness of your wallet. If instead you let your taste buds lead the way, then the stewed beef and dry bean curd with XO sauce, and the subtly flavored sweet corn soup with crab, should be among your choices. So should the Mandarin fish, deep-fried in the lightest of batters and prettily presented with a delicate sweet-and-sour sauce. The restaurant has also responded to the current obsession with Sìchuān food, and the sautéed crab with dried chili is a good choice if you're in the mood for more aggressive flavors. The weekend all-you-can-eat lunch, featuring a respectable selection of dim sum, costs only ¥98 ($12) for two.

Guānghuá Lù 1, inside Kerry Centre Mall (near rear entrance of Kerry Centre Hotel); see map p. 115. ℂ 010/ 8529-6999. Meal for 2 ¥200–¥300 ($25–$38). AE, DC, MC, V. Daily 11:30am–2:30pm and 5:30–10pm. Metro: Guómào (122); walk north through China World complex.

Huángchéng Lǎo Mā ℰ HOTPOT   Upmarket hotpot sounds like a contradiction in terms, but Huángchéng Lǎo Mā makes it work—and work well. Set inside a huge multi-storied building with a hyperbolic, tile-eave facade and relatively pleasant decor, the restaurant is almost constantly packed. The reason is their special ingredient, "Lǎo Mā's beef," a magical meat that stays tender no matter how long you boil it. Also popular are the large prawns, thrown live into the pot. The traditional broth is eye-watering spicy; order the split *yuānyang* pot with mild *wǔyútáng* (water world essence) broth in a separate compartment, or risk overheating your tongue. English menu.

Dàběiyáo Nánqíng Fēngzhá Hòu Jiē 39 (south of China World Trade Center and Motorola building; walk south along East Third Ring, take left after crossing river); see map p. 115. ℂ 010/6779-3369. Meal for 2 ¥180–¥200 ($22–$25). AE, DC, MC, V. Daily 10am–11pm.

Makye Ame (Mǎjí Āmī) TIBETAN   The newest of Běijīng's many ethnic theme restaurants combines a folk cabaret with decent but pricey food and surprisingly enjoyable decor. Paper lamps glow in the corners, grimacing wooden masks stare down from the beams, and traditional furniture somehow lends color to the dark lit room. Fare is "Tibetan"—lots of yak and mutton with gourmet accents. Recommended dishes include *tashi-delek* (beef braised in brown sauce with carrots, cheese, and yak marrow) and the chicken with corn and juoma (a vegetable reminiscent of black bean that grows on the Tibetan plateau). Tibetan-style nan bread is good for sopping up sauces. The English menu also features several grain spirits, commonly mixed with yogurt and served in silver goblets. Nightly shows start at 8pm.

Xiùshuǐ Nán Jiē A1 2/F (behind Friendship Store on Jiànguó Mén Wài Dàjiē); see map p. 115. ℂ 010/6506-9616. Meal for 2 ¥100–¥140 ($12–$18). AE, DC, MC, V. Daily noon–2am. Metro: Jiànguó Mén (120/211); walk east 3 blocks, then north half a block.

Matsuko (Sōngzǐ) *Value* JAPANESE   A surprising number of Japanese restaurants in Běijīng offer good lunch buffet deals, but Matsuko's stylish wasabi-green interior makes it a far more pleasant place to dine than its cafeteria-style competitors. The buffet (daily 11am–1:30pm; ¥68/$9) runs the gamut of Japanese favorites from sushi to udon, all with unlimited Asahi beer or soft drinks and a free plate of sashimi. The only complaint is with the tempura shrimp, so good they disappear as soon as they're brought out. Get there early to stake out one of the small tatami rooms, kept semi-separated from the throng by walls of wood and frosted glass. A la carte items are more expensive but nicely done.

In Báijiāzhuāng, on East Third Ring Road (across from T.G.I. Friday's); see map p. 115. ℂ 010/6582-5208. Meal for 2 ¥160–¥180 ($20–23). AE, DC, MC, V. Daily 10:30am–2pm and 5–10:30pm.

Mediterraneo (Dìzhōnghǎi) ℰ ITALIAN/SPANISH   Where most of Běijīng's Western restaurants either lose themselves in Asian clichés or try desperately to re-create the atmosphere of home, Mediterraneo is casually and refreshingly unconventional. The comfortably lit interior is trendy but not overly so, with a long metal tapas bar, curved blue lights flanking the door, and dark stone vases etched with Chinese characters set in the large windows. An umbrella-shaded outdoor seating area is ideal on summer evenings. Expertly managed by a service-savvy Italian expatriate, the waitstaff does an admirable job. Chinese chefs stumble somewhat on the main courses but manage to produce some of the city's best appetizers. The generous antipasto plate is highly recommended—combined with salads and a bottle from the respectable wine list, a fine meal for two.

Sānlǐtún Běi Jiē 1A (in north half of Bar St.; on west side of street, next door to Super 24 convenience store); see map on p. 115. ✆ 010/6415–3691. Main courses ¥50–¥125 ($5–$15). AE, DC, MC, V. Sun–Wed 11:30am–10:30pm; Thurs–Sat 11:30am–11pm (closed Chinese holidays).

Morel's (Mòláolóngxī Xīcāntīng) ★★ BELGIAN

Morel's reputation as the best Western restaurant in the city is probably a holdover from a less competitive era, but this is nevertheless a fine restaurant, with a rare, fanatic devotion to quality. Owned by Belgian Renaat Morel, one of China's most respected European chefs, and run with help from his wife, the restaurant has a casual and cozy feel, its yellow walls and green-and-white checked tablecloths reminiscent of someone's home. The food is simply presented and side dishes are somewhat limp, but main courses are supremely done, particularly the wonderful Flemish beef stew with tender chunks of meat cooked over many hours in a mix of Rodenbach beer, bay leaf, onion, and thyme. Soups change daily and sell out nightly. The restaurant also has an astounding array of Belgian beers, a selection second only to The Hidden Tree's (p. 187). Best of all, however, is the signature Morel's dessert: a near-perfect waffle—save room for it—made in a real waffle iron hand-carried on a plane from Belgium. The restaurant was facing forced relocation at the beginning of 2003; check one of the expatriate magazines or e-mail smorel@263.net to confirm the address.

Xīnzhōng Jiē 5 (opposite Worker's Gymnasium north gate); see map p. 115. ✆ 010/6416-8802 or 138/0131-5794. Reservations recommended for dinner. Main courses ¥40–¥80 ($5–$10). AE, DC, MC, V. Daily 10:30am–2:30pm and 5:30–10:30pm. Metro: Dōngsì Shí Tiáo (213); walk east 3 blocks.

1001 Nights (Yīqiānlíngyī Yè) MIDDLE EASTERN

No longer the only Middle Eastern restaurant in Běijīng, 1001 Nights is still the best. Heaping platefuls of fluffy couscous with lamb or chicken are enough to feed two, baba ghanouj is the city's freshest, and pita bread is baked on-site. On the drinks side, they serve a good range of honey-sweetened fresh-squeezed juices and properly potent cups of "Arabic" coffee. The outdoor seating area is pleasant on summer nights, and puts you out of range of the ear-bursting music played during the nightly belly-dancing shows. Complete the experience with a few puffs offruit or rose tobacco on one of the house hookahs (¥38/$5).

East end of Gōngtǐ Běi Lù, opposite Great Dragon Hotel; see map p. 115. ✆ 010/6532-4050. Meal for 2 ¥200–¥250 ($25–$31). AE, DC, MC, V. Daily 11am–2am.

Red Basil (Zǐ Tiān Jiāo) THAI

Red Basil is probably more expensive than a Thai restaurant in Běijīng should be, but excellent food and a stylish setting make it worth the splurge. The dining room is thoroughly modern, with polished dark wood floors and tall, angular walls. Chefs imported from Thailand produce the city's most authentic *pad thai* (rice noodles with seafood in peanut sauce), and the *tom yum* seafood soup draws consistent raves. Round out a meal for two with the rich green vegetable curry or fresh papaya salad with jumbo shrimp.

Nán Xiǎo Jiē 8 (south side of Sān Yuán Qiáo, opposite Jīngxìn Plaza on North Third Ring Road); see map p. 115. ✆ 010/6460-2339. Meal for 2 ¥200–¥250 ($25–$31). AE, DC, MC, V. Daily 11:30am–2pm and 5:30–10pm.

Taj Pavilion (Tàijī Lóu Yìndù Cāntīng) INDIAN

One of Běijīng's oldest Indian restaurants, the Taj Pavilion is a classier and slightly more expensive alternative to Chingari (p. 89). The small dining room holds only a few tables, nicely

dressed in white linen, with subtle decor refreshingly free of ca
ice are both consistently high quality. Recommended dishes inc
curry (deep-fried vegetables in tomato-based curry sauce), *pe*
curry), *rogan josh* (mutton in spicy tomato curry), and chicker
nated chicken in rich tomato sauce)—all authentic, thick, and

L1-28 West Wing of China World Trade Center, Jiànguó Mén Wài Dàjiē 1; see map p. 115. ℂ 010/6505-5866. Meal for 2 ¥220–¥260 ($27–$33) AE, DC, MC, V. Daily 11:30am–2:30pm and 6:30–10:30pm. Metro: Guómào (122).

Transit (Dùjīnhú) *Finds* FUSION That this place survives despite its obscure location—in a dark spur off an alley north of the Worker's Stadium—is testament to its style. A Sino-foreign joint venture, run by a local Chinese and his European partner, it serves satisfying fusion by way of Sìchuān. The fusion theme runs to the decor as well, the small space outfitted with Chinese furniture arranged according to the Western emphasis on comfort and privacy. Cozy, low lighting and the sound of water in the background finish the job. The menu is small and changes often. There are no appetizers, but there's always a good mix of hot and cold dishes prettily presented, as well as a few simple desserts. Cuban-style mint-heavy *mohitos* are a dangerously good after-dinner drink. You may stay longer than you'd planned.

Xìngfú Yī Cūn 1, next to Black Jack Garden Bar. (Walking west from intersection of Xīndōng Lù and Gōngtǐ Běi Lù, take right at clothing boutique with large windows [opposite Worker's Stadium north gate], walk 60m/ 198 ft., take right; see map p. 115.) ℂ 010/6417-6785. Meal for 2 ¥120–¥160 ($15–$20). AE, DC, MC, V. Daily noon–2am.

MODERATE

Annie's Café (Ānnī Yìdàlì Cāntīng) ★ *Value* ITALIAN A casual, cozy, and tremendously welcoming Italian bistro tucked among the nightspots at the west gate of Cháoyáng Gōngyuán, Annie's is the hands-down favorite for affordable Italian fare in Běijīng. Wood-fired pizzas are the most popular item, but try the baked *gnocchi gratinate* with tomato and broccoli, or the chicken ravioli served with spinach and a fine tomato cream sauce. Appetizers and desserts are just average, the notable exception being the cannoli, a sinful blend of cottage cheese and dried fruit with a touch of brandy in a fresh shell of fried dough. Annie's staff is bend-over-backward friendly, happy to bring as many baskets of free bread (served with small jars of pesto) as you want.

Cháoyáng Gōngyuán Xī Mén (west gate of Cháoyáng Park); see map p. 115. ℂ 010/6591-1931. Main courses ¥40–¥80 ($5–$10). AE, DC, MC, V. Daily 11:30am–11pm.

Ānyuán No. 5 (Ānyuán Wǔ Hào Cāntīng) YÚNNÁN Minimalist name. Artsy interior. Remote location. This is the height (or nadir, depending on your stance) of the minority food trend that has dominated Běijīng of late. Food is a trendy take on Nàxī-influenced cuisine from southern China's Yúnnán Province, inconsistent but beautifully presented. Colorful dishes are a striking contrast to the bare concrete floors, black painted ceilings, and vertical sheets of pale, translucent cloth that make up the award-winning decor. The *mǐ là luófēi yú*—a mix of diced deep-fried fish, green onion, garlic, and Yúnnán red peppers—is worthwhile, but their best offering is the free peanuts, salty-sweet with a hint of numbing peppercorn.

Ānhuì Běilǐ in Yàyùncūn, 2nd floor of Ānyuán 5 (50m/165 ft. north of Huìzhōng Jiē); see map p. 115. ℂ 010/ 6497-9173. Meal for 2 ¥100–¥120 ($12–$15). AE, DC, MC, V. Daily 11am–10pm.

Shi Jí Huǒguō HOTPOT   This hotpot restaurant has become famous for its free post-meal backrubs (*ànmó*), but the food itself is reason enough to come. The hotpot is Sìchuān-style—that is, very spicy—with ingredients (and waitresses) imported from Yúnnán Province. The menu features a few items not found at more common hotpot outlets, including *lǎba jūn* mushrooms from southern China. This place is slightly hard to find, but worth the effort.

South side of alley running east off Jíshìkǒu Dōng Lù (look for a passageway hung with red lanterns), northeast of Jian (Huápú) Hypermarket in Cháowài; see map p. 115. © 010/6551-4119. Meal for 2 ¥90–¥110 ($11–$14). No credit cards. Daily 9am–10pm. Metro: Cháoyáng Mén (212); walk east a block and take a left onto Jíshìkǒu Dōng Lù.

Běijīng Dàdǒng Kǎoyā Diàn ★★ BĚIJĪNG   No hundred years of history or obscure *hútòng* location here, just a crispy-skinned and pleasing roast duck that many say is the best in town. The restaurant claims to use a special method to reduce the amount of fat in its birds, although it seems unlikely that duck this flavorful could possibly be good for you. The birds come in either whole (¥98/$12) or half (¥49/$5) portions and are served in slices with a wide assortment of condiments (garlic, green onion, radish). Place the duck on a pancake with plum sauce and your choice of ingredients, and then roll and eat. An excellent plain broth soup, made from the rest of the duck, is included in the price. The menu, with English and pictures, offers a wide range of other dishes, everything from mustard duck webs to duck tongue in aspic, plus a number of excellent *dòufu* (tofu) dishes with thick, tangy sauces. Every meal comes with a free fruit plate and walnut sago pudding for desert. This is one of the few restaurants in Běijīng with a nonsmoking room.

Tuánjié Hú Běikǒu 3 (on east side of East Third Ring Road, north of Tuánjié Hú Park); see map p. 115. © 010/6582-2892. Meal for 2 (including half-duck) ¥80–¥100 ($10–$12). No credit cards. Daily 8am–noon and 1:30–5pm.

Dīng Dīng Xiāng *Finds* HOTPOT   This Mongolian-style mutton hotpot restaurant is tremendously and justifiably popular for its signature dipping sauce (*jīnpái tiáoliào*), a flavorful sesame sauce so thick they have to dish it out with ice cream scoops. Large plates of fresh sliced lamb (*yàngròu*) are surprisingly cheap; other options include beef (*niúròu*), spinach (*bōcài*), and sliced winter melon (*dōngguā piàn*). Decor is plain, and the place is clean for a local restaurant. You'll probably have to wait at the door.

Dōng Zhí Mén Wài Dōng Jiē 14 (opposite Dōnghuán Guǎngchǎng, in alley across from Guangdong Development Bank); see map p. 115. © 010/6417-2546. Meal for 2 ¥80–¥100 ($10–$12). No credit cards. Daily 11am–10pm.

Grandma's Kitchen (Zǔmǔ de Chúfáng) AMERICAN   An extension of three cafes in Chéngdū, Grandma's has been packed from day one, despite opening in the middle of Běijīng's SARS hysteria. You'll find generous portions of home-cooked fare served up in a Southern homestead atmosphere. The Texas-size hamburgers are as substantial as you'd expect, you can stand your spoon up in the milkshakes, and the apple pies are perfectly caramelized with just the right amount of cinnamon. Located south of the Rìtán diplomatic area, in a city short on Western breakfasts, Grandma has a captive audience in the morning. Booking for breakfast will soon be essential. There are communication problems between the kitchen and the waitstaff—missing orders and cold french fries are common—but hopefully this will be ironed out.

Xiùshuǐ Nán Jiē 11A (behind Friendship Store); see map p. 115. © 010/6503-2893. Reservations recommended on weekends. Main courses ¥20–¥58 ($2.50–$7.20). No credit cards. Daily 8:30am–11:30pm. Metro: Jiànguó Mén (120/211); walk east 3 blocks, then north half a block.

Value   Chinese on the Cheap

Affordable Chinese food is everywhere in Běijīng, and not all of the places that provide it are an offense to Western hygiene standards. As with shopping in this city, high prices don't necessarily guarantee high quality in dining, and cheap restaurants often provide better food than expensive ones. Down-market dining also offers the best chance to connect with the average Běijīng resident.

Most convenient is a stable of adequately clean **Chinese fast-food** restaurants, many of which deliberately try to rip off their Western counterparts. Menus typically offer simple noodles, baked goods, and stir-fries. Top chains include Yŏnghé Dàwáng (with KFC-style sign) and Mǎlán noodle outlets (marked with a Chicago Bulls–style graphic), both with locations throughout the city.

A better option is to visitone of the **point-to-choose food courts** on the top or bottom floor of almost every large shopping center. These typically feature a dozen or so stalls, each selling snacks, noodles, or simple pre-cooked selections from different regions. Prices are reasonable, making it easy to sample a wide range. Just point to what looks good. The food court in the basement of the Oriental Plaza, requiring purchase of a card you use to pay for food at each stall, is the most extensive. Others can be found in the China World Mall, the Yàxiù Clothing Market, and Xī Dān Bǎihuò Shāngchǎng north of the Xī Dān metro stop.

One of the most enjoyable local dining areas in Běijīng, the legendary 24-hour food street on Dōng Zhí Mén Nèi Dàjiē known to most as **Ghost Street (Guǐ Jiē)**, took a severe hit from the wrecking ball in 2001 but is still there in abbreviated form. Beginning around the Dōngsì Běi Dàjiē intersection and running east, dozens of small eateries offer hotpot, *málà lóngxiā* (spicy crayfish), and homestyle fare through the lantern-lit night.

Hóng Jīng Yú *Finds* SÌCHUĀN   This hard-to-find shack of a Sìchuān restaurant is the locals' consensus favorite for *shǔzhǔ yú* (grass carp with numbing black peppercorns and hot peppers), a classic Sìchuān dish rarely found outside China. It comes to the table in a large metal bowl filled with spicy broth and piled high with peppers, which the waitress scoops away to reveal the tender fish underneath. The restaurant uses peppers imported from Chóngqìng, said to be the country's best. This is a heavenly experience, but only for those who can handle their spice. Other Sìchuān standards are available, but in small portions. Look for a small brick building with a wooden roof several blocks northwest of the International Exhibition Center.

In Xībà Hé area 50m (165 ft.) to left of Běijīng Chóngqìng Fàndiàn. (Head northwest on Zuǒjiāzhuāng Dōng Jiē; take 1st left after bridge; see map on p.115.) ℂ **010/6402-4776.** Meal for 2 ¥60–¥80 ($8–$10). No credit cards. Daily 11am–10:30pm.

Lotus in Moonlight (Hétáng Yuèsè Sùshí) ✦ VEGETARIAN   Lotus in Moonlight's well-prepared honest vegetable and tofu dishes mark a nice departure from the imitation meat offerings that previously defined vegetarian Chinese cuisine in the city. Fake chicken and fish, engineered from combinations of soy and taro, are still available here, but with less oil and more flavor than in other meat-free restaurants. Large front windows and skylights brighten the modern blue and yellow interior, suffused with an atmosphere of healthiness. Alcohol is banned, but the menu offers a long list of compelling and colorful herb teas, served in glass pots so you can watch the flowers steep.

Building 12, Liǔfāng Nán Lǐ, in Dōng Zhí Mén Wài area (just outside Second Ring Road); see map p. 115. ℰ 010/6465-3299. Meal for 2 ¥80–¥120 ($10–$15). No credit cards. Daily 11am–2pm and 5–9pm.

Middle 8th (Zhōng Bā Lóu) YÚNNÁN
Another posh Yúnnán restaurant with a number in its name, Middle 8th is less stylish than Ānyuán No. 5 (see above), but more conveniently located in the Sānlǐtún bar district. Again, the name comes from the building's address, and again, the attraction is visual, with spicy red dishes on black glazed plates setting off the green tablecloths. There is a minimum of experimentation here, so quality is steady. The tender braised spare ribs in hot pepper sauce or the stewed chicken and papaya, a pleasant mix of spicy and sour, are both good choices, but most items on the menu will please you. The same cannot be said for the lackluster waitstaff and loud wall-mounted TVs in the corners, the only glitches in an otherwise enjoyable dining experience.

Dōng Sānlǐtún Zhōng Jiē 8 (east off the bar street); see map p. 115. ℰ 010/6413-0629. Meal for 2 ¥80–¥100 ($10–$12). Daily 11am–2pm and 5–10pm.

Noodle Loft (Miàn Kù Shānxī Shíyì) ✦ SHĀNXĪ
Unheard of outside China and rarely found in such stylish surroundings, Shānxī cuisine is noted for its vinegary flavors, liberal use of tomatoes, and large variety of interesting noodles. The Noodle Loft's interior is ultra-modern in orange and gray, with a large open kitchen featuring giant woks and steamers. An English menu makes ordering easy. Highlights include *yì bǎ zhuā* (fried wheat cakes with chives), *qiāo miàn māo ěrduo* (cat's ear–shaped pasta stir-fried with chopped meat), and *suāncài tǔdòu* (vinegared potato slices).

Dàwàng Lù 20 (in the new Soho district, east of China World Trade Center); see map p. 115. ℰ 010/6774-9950. Meal for 2 ¥80–¥100 ($10–$12). Daily 11am–2:30pm and 5:30–10:30pm. Metro: Dàwàng Lù (123).

Old Character Hakka (Lǎo Hànzì Kèjiā Càiguǎn) ✦✦✦ HAKKA
The Hakka, or "guest people" (Kèjiārén), are Hàn from central China who migrated southeast generations ago but never managed to integrate. Forced by discrimination to live in isolated communities in the poor mountainous regions, they kept to their separate culture—and cooking traditions. A historically marginal cuisine, Hakka food has over the past 2 years become the center of epicurean fashion in Běijīng, largely because of this restaurant. The owner, a local artist, designed the space with a rustic motif: thick wood tables, stone floors, crinkled character-laden wallpaper next to patches of exposed brick, and waitresses in peasant garb. Enjoyable as the dining rooms are, it is the kitchen that keeps lines of customers winding out the door. The cooking style is hard to define vis-à-vis other cuisines available in the city, but ask regular patrons to explain the difference and most will give a quick answer: It's better. The *yánjú xiā* (shrimp skewers served in rock salt) and *láncài sìjìdòu* (diced green beans with ground pork) are both divine. The one dish you'll find on every table is *mìzhì zhǐbāo lúyú*, a "secret recipe paper-wrapped fish"—tender and nearly boneless, in a sweet sauce you'll want to drink.

(*Tips*) **Where to Buy Picnic Supplies**

Picnicking is perhaps the most neglected tradition among travelers in Běijīng considering the city's wealth of picturesque parks and scenic areas. In the past, this was due to a paucity of the necessary components, but the availability of nearly any food item from nearly anywhere now means there is no excuse.

You can purchase basic **groceries** and Chinese-style **snacks** at local markets and the *xiǎomàibù* (little-things-to-buy units) found nearly everywhere. Several fully stocked **supermarkets** and a handful of smaller grocers now carry imported wine and cheese, pesto sauce, Frito-Lay junk food, Newcastle Brown Ale, and just about anything else you could want, albeit at inflated prices. Supermarkets include one in the basement of the Lufthansa Center, and the CRC in the basement of the China World Trade Center. The Hépíng Market, in the first major alley on the left as you walk up Sānlǐtún bar street, has sliced meats, rare Western vegetables, and a full selection of familiar breakfast cereals. Much the same can be found at Jenny Lou's just east of the northeast corner of Rìtán Gōngyuán.

Among **delis and bakeries,** the best is the Kempi Deli (inside the Lufthansa Centre; ℰ **010/6465-3388,** ext. 5741). It offers satisfying crusty-bread sandwiches and a tremendous pastry and fresh baked bread selection that goes for half-price after 9pm. Charlotte's Butchery and Delicatessen (ℰ **010/6508-3884**), next to Annie's at the west gate of Cháoyáng Park, serves sandwiches at lower prices that are almost as good and offers a wider selection of other Western food items.

Recommended picnic spots in the city proper include the Summer Palace, the "Old" Summer Palace (Yuánmíng Yuán), and Rìtán Park in central Cháoyáng, as well as Cháoyáng and Tuánjié Hú parks, also in Cháoyáng. Outside Běijīng, the Sīmǎtái and Huánghuā sections of the Great Wall provide dramatic backdrops for an outdoor meal, as do Fragrant Hills Park (Xiāng Shān Gōngyuán), the Míng and Qīng tombs, and the Tánzhè and Jiètái temples in the western suburbs.

Sānlǐtún Běi Jiē (walking north on bar street, take 2nd left, then 1st right); see map p. 115. ℰ **010/6415 3376.** Meal for 2 ¥80–¥100 ($10–$12). No credit cards. Daily 11:30am–2pm and 5:30–11pm.

Pure Lotus (Jìngxīn Lián) VEGETARIAN   Běijīng's most outwardly Buddhist vegetarian restaurant has the atmosphere of an overstuffed meditation pillow. Low, softly lit tables sit generously draped in bright orange cloth, immense flower-filled vases flank statues of Guānyīn (the Bodhisattva of Compassion) in the corners, and conversation is kept quiet against the whispered backdrop of a mantra pop soundtrack. It all feels a bit silly at first, and the waitstaff is gentle often to the point of being annoying, but few other eateries in Běijīng leave you feeling more relaxed than when you entered. Simple dishes mirror the decor. Fans of fake meat will want to try the *tiěbǎn hēijiāo yuánpái* (pork-like tofu patties served on a sizzling plate with black bean sauce), but the just plain vegetable dishes are better. Don't miss the *láncài ròusōng sìjìdòu,* diced green beans lightly stir-fried with a salty Chinese vegetable and wrapped taco-style in fresh lettuce leaves.

Nóngzhǎn Nánlǐ 10 (just off East Third Ring Road, behind the Dance Agogo building, marked by a purple neon sign with an arrow); see map on p. 115. ℂ 010/6592-3627. Meal for 2 ¥100–¥120 ($12–$15). No credit cards. Daily 11am–10pm.

Sǎn Gè Guìzhōurén GUÌZHŌU   Southern China's Guìzhōu Province is one of the country's poorest regions, which lends a certain irony to this restaurant's hip minimalist setting and rich artist clientele. The menu offers a stylish take on the province's Miáo minority food with dishes that tend to be spicy, colorful, and slightly rough. Both table-top hotpots—the Miáo-style peppermint lamb and the cilantro-heavy dry beef—are highly recommended, as is the "sour and wot meat luinere vegerable [sic]," a mix of jalapeño-like peppers and dried chilies stir-fried with sliced pork—not as spicy as it sounds. *Note:* Items listed on the menu as "vegetarian" are not.

Guānghuá Xī Lù 3 (take left down alley north of Mexican Wave, look for blue sign); see map p. 115. ℂ 010/6507-4761. Meal for 2 ¥80–¥100 ($10–$12). AE, DC, MC, V. Daily 10:30am–2:30pm and 5:30–10:30pm. Metro: Yǒng'ānlǐ (121); walk north on Dōng Dà Qiáo Lù.

Sìhéxuān BĚIJĪNG   A cluttered little restaurant with slightly more than token Old Běijīng interior, this longtime favorite is famous for its constantly changing range of typical Běijīng snacks. Some items are listed on the English menu, while others are rolled through dim sum–style on a cart. This is the best way to sample street food without fretting over hygiene.

Jiànguó Mén Wài Dàjiē 3 (4th floor of Jīnglún Hotel); see map p. 115. ℂ 010/6500-2266, ext. 8116. Meal for 2 ¥50–¥100 ($6–$12). AE, DC, MC, V. Daily 11:30am–2pm and 5:30–10pm. Metro: Yǒng'ānlǐ (121).

Yúxiāng Rénjiā ✿ SÌCHUĀN   Franchise food in the Chinese capital doesn't carry the same connotations of blandness it does in the United States. Yúxiāng Rénjiā, a constantly crowded chain of restaurants with bright mock-village decor and a talent for producing authentic Sìchuān fare, is a case in point. Dishes are slightly heavy on the oil but as flavorful as anything found outside Sìchuān itself. The spicy familiar *gōngbào jīdīng* (diced chicken with peanuts and hot peppers) is superb, putting American versions of "kung pao chicken" to shame. They also produce several worthwhile signatures you aren't likely to have tried before, including an interesting smoked duck *(zhāngchá yā)* and the "stewed chicken with Grandma's sauce" *(lǎogānmā shāo jī)*. Waitstaff sometimes gets overwhelmed, so prepare to be patient.

Branches: On east side of northeast Third Ring Road, near intersection with Xiāoyún Lù (ℂ 010/8451-0380; daily 11am–3pm and 5:30–10pm); and at Cháoyáng Mén Wài Dàjiē 20, on 5th floor of the Liánhé Dàshà, behind Foreign Ministry Building just off Third Ring Road (ℂ 010/6588-3841; daily 11am–10:30pm). Meal for 2 ¥80–¥100 ($10–$12). No credit cards.

INEXPENSIVE

Ǎndiē Ānniáng *Finds* HOMESTYLE   One local, eating here for the first time, described it as truly homestyle—the kind of place that recalled family meals in her parents' house. The atmosphere is casual, with diners on simple benches crowded around wooden tables in a clean, cozy space the size of a living room. The restaurant's immense *bāozi* (stuffed buns) are justifiably famous, best with the traditional *zhūròu báicài* (pork and cabbage) filling. Stuffed meat pies *(ròudīng báicài xiànbǐng)* are also worth a try. Shelves line the walls, stacked year-round with jars of preserved garlic traditionally only available around Chinese New Year. Vinegar from the jars, known as *làbā cù*, makes a perfect dipping sauce for the *bāozi*. A small glass-enclosed kitchen in the corner provides entertainment while you wait.

Moments Night Market Nosh

Late-night dining is a favorite Běijīng pastime, and the most convenient way to experience it is to visit one of several night markets scattered about the city. This is street food, government regulated but not guaranteed to be clean, so the weak in stomach or courage may want to pass. Gastrointestinal gamble aside, the markets are a vivid and often delicious way to spend an evening.

The markets are typically made up of stalls, jammed side by side, selling all manner of snacks that cost anywhere from ¥0.50 (6¢) to ¥5 (60¢). Most legendary are the little animals on sticks, a veritable zoo of skewers that includes baby birds and scorpions. There are popular markets on **Lóngfú Sì Jiē** (north of Wángfǔjǐng Dàjiē next to the Airlines Ticketing Hall) and **west of the Běijīng Zoo** (at the Dōngyuán Yèshì), but the most celebrated is the **Dōnghuá Mén** night market, just off Wángfǔjǐng Dàjiē opposite the Xīn Dōng Ān Plaza.

In a year of citywide cosmetic overhauls, even the Dōnghuá Mén has received a face-lift. With a history supposedly dating back to 1655, it was closed during the Cultural Revolution and finally reopened in 1984. Previously a charming mish-mash of independent operators each in their own battered tin shacks, it was "reorganized" in 2000. The stalls are all now a uniform red and white, each with identical twin gas burners. Prices have risen into the ¥10 ($1) range and the food has fallen a bit in quality, but the payoff is a rise in cleanliness and an increase in revenues from foreign tourists.

Below are some of the most common items you'll find for sale at the stalls.

- **Bāozi:** Steamed buns typically filled with mixtures of pork and vegetable, but occasionally available with just vegetables (around ¥3/ 40¢ for a basket of five).
- **Jiānbǐng:** Large crepe with egg, folded around fried dough with cilantro and with plum and hot sauces (¥2/30¢).
- **Jiǎozi:** Pork and vegetable filling with doughy wrapper, commonly boiled (¥2–¥4/30¢–50¢ for 12).
- **Miàntiáo:** Noodles, commonly stir-fried with vegetables or boiled in beef broth with cilantro (¥1–¥3/10¢–20¢).
- **Xiànbǐng:** Stuffed pancakes, usually filled with meat or vegetables, fried golden brown (around ¥2/30¢).
- **Yáng ròu chuàn:** Lamb skewers with cumin and chili powder, either fried or roasted; also available in a chicken (*jīròu*) version (¥1/10¢).

Cháoyáng Gōngyuán Xī Mén (next to Cháoyáng Park ticket booth); see map p. 115. ✆ 010/6591-0231. Meal for 2 ¥40–¥60 ($5–$8). No credit cards. Daily 10am–2am.

Dào Jiā Cháng ✿ BĚIJĪNG   Chaos. The clanging dishes and shouting staff are a bit too theatrical for this to be called authentic Běijīng dining, but it's as close as you're likely to get. Decor is a cheap attempt to re-create the feel of Old Běijīng, with cut red paper substituting for real lanterns and eaves covered in cardboard tile, but cheapness is part of the atmosphere. Best by far are the servers, who rush about like madmen, pouring tea and clearing tables with a controlled, smiling fury. The kitchen produces the city's choicest version of local favorite *jīngjiàng ròusī* (shredded pork rolled in tofu skin with scallion) and a respectable *jiàngshāo qiézi* (diced eggplant in soy-based sauce). They also serve some of the *real* stuff, traditional dishes only the oldest of natives still eat, like the pungent *yángròu mádòufu,* a mound of mashed tofu and whole soybeans drizzled in "lamb oil."

Guāngxī Mén Běilǐ 20, in Xībà Hé area northeast of the Chóngqìng Fàndiàn (look for plaster Old Běijīng couple in window); see map p. 115. ✆ **010/6422-1078.** Meal for 2 ¥40–¥60 ($5–$8). No credit cards. Daily 10:30am–2pm and 4:30–9pm.

5 Běijīng South

EXPENSIVE

Quánjùdé Kǎoyā Diàn *Overrated* BĚIJĪNG Běijīng's most famous purveyor of roast duck opened in 1864, and it must have been good at one time to have survived so long. Every important state guest from Castro to Yanni has been dragged here, but regular visitors can find better, cheaper duck elsewhere (see the Běijīng Dàdǒng Kǎoyā Diàn on p. 94). Quality and price climb with each floor. Whatever you do, avoid the awful carry-out fast-food duck now dispensed out the front.

Qián Mén Dàjiē 32 (north of Dà Zhàlán); see map p. 108. ✆ **010/6511-2418.** Prix-fixe duck ¥168 ($20) and up. AE, DC, MC, V. Daily 11am–1:30pm and 4:45–8pm.

MODERATE

Pamer (Pàmǐ'ěr Shífǔ) ★ *Finds* UIGHUR Běijīng's best Uighur restaurant isn't much to look at, but it is far cleaner than other Muslim eateries, and the food it serves is cheaper and better than anything at the more famous Afunti (p. 85). Cumin-spiced lamb skewers *(yang ròu chuàn)* are immense and surprisingly low on fat. Also not to be missed are the *dà pán jī* (diced chicken, peppers, potatoes, and thick noodles in tomato sauce) and *shǒubā fàn* (rice with lamb and raisins).

Liánhuā Chí Dōng Lù 3 (north side of Báiyún Qiáo; large sign depicts dancing silhouettes); see map p. 108. ✆ **010/6326-3635.** Meal for 2 ¥60–¥100 ($8–$12). AE, DC, MC, V. Daily 11am–2pm and 5–9:30pm.

Tàipó Tiānfū Shānzhēn ★★ HOTPOT To make the broth for their divine hotpot, this restaurant stews a whole black-skinned chicken with 32 different kinds of mushrooms and lets the mixture reduce for hours. The mushrooms are strained but the chicken stays, served with the by-now vibrant broth in a heavy clay pot kept boiling at your table. Already a fine meal on its own, it gets even better as you add ingredients—lamb *(yang ròu),* beef *(niúròu),* lotus root *(ǒu piàn),* spinach *(bōcài)* or, best of all, more mushrooms *(shānjūn).* Many of the mushrooms, shown in their uncooked form on a series of posters hung along the walls, are imported from the southern provinces. Good enough to make coverts of fungus haters.

At south end of Èr Qī Jùchǎng Lù, behind the east side of the Cháng'ān Shāngchǎng (4 blocks west of the Fùxīng Mén metro stop); see map p. 108. ✆ **010/6801-9641.** Meal for 2 ¥120–¥140 ($15–$18). No credit cards. Daily 11am–11pm. Metro: Fùxīng Mén (114/204).

INEXPENSIVE

Gǒubùlǐ Bāozi Diàn HOMESTYLE The most common explanation for *gǒubùlǐ bāozi* (dogs-won't-touch dumplings) is that they were named after their inventor, a man born when Chinese infant-mortality rates were still high and mothers named their children with a mind to protecting them from beasts and evil spirits. Other stories abound, but these addictive morsels of pork-stuffed bread remain popular despite the debate, and are a cheap, satisfying way to refuel during a long day of shopping south of Qiánmén. A plaster empress dowager sits eating *bāozi* just outside the entrance.

Dà Zhàlán Jiē 21 (at west end of pedestrian section); see map p. 108. Ⓒ 010/6315-2389. Meal for 2 ¥20–¥35 ($3–$4). No credit cards. Daily 9am–10pm. Metro: Qián Mén (208).

Tiānjīn Bǎi Jiǎo Yuán JIǍOZI   No restaurant has managed to fill the vacuum left by the inexplicable closing of Gold Cat, once Běijīng's most charming outlet for *jiǎozi* (ravioli-like dumplings), but Tiānjīn Bǎi Jiǎo Yuán comes closest. Staff are given to occasional catatonia, and the clichéd red-and-gold interior can't match Gold Cat's old courtyard setting, but the *jiǎozi* are just as delicious. The *xièsānxiān shuǐjiǎo* (dumplings with shrimp, crab, and mushroom filling) are a treasure. There's also a respectable range of Sìchuān dishes, pictured on the menu.

Xīn Wénhuà Jiē 12A (in alley opposite the Marco Polo); see map p. 108. Ⓒ 010/6605-9371. Meal for 2 ¥30–¥60 ($4–$8). No credit cards. Daily 10am–2:30pm and 4:30–9:30pm.

6 Běijīng West & Hǎidiàn

MODERATE

Jiǔhuā Shān ⭑ BĚIJĪNG   Another fine roast duck eatery, Jiǔhuā Shān is larger and not quite as pleasant as the Běijīng Dàdǒng Kǎoyā Diàn (see above), but it's more conveniently located for people staying on the west side of the city. Whole ducks, relatively low on fat and crispy, are reasonable at ¥88 ($11). Sesame buns make a nice alternative to traditional pancakes. They only roast 200 birds a day, so get there early.

Zhèngguāng Lù 55 (behind the Zǐyù Hotel); see map p. 112. Ⓒ 010/6848-3481. Meal for 2 (including half duck) ¥100–¥140 ($12–$18). AE, DC, MC, V. Daily 11am–2pm and 5–9pm.

Yúnnán Jīn Kǒngquè Déhóng Dǎiwèi Cānguǎn ⭑ (Value) YÚNNÁN   The street north of the Minorities University (Mínzú Dàxué) was once a claustrophobic *hútòng* packed with Uighur, Korean, and Dǎi restaurants. The seedy chaps from Kashgar who addressed you as "Hashish" are gone, along with most of the restaurants. But this holy grail of Dǎi cuisine remains, offering a superb synthesis of Thai and Chinese fare. Mirrors, tiled floors, and predictable bamboo furnishings lend it a sterile feel, but the gracious waitstaff more than compensates. Must-devour dishes include crispy *tǔdòu qiú* (deep-fried potato balls with chili sauce), delectable *bōluó fàn* (pineapple rice), *zhútǒng zhūròu* (steamed pork with coriander), *zhútǒng jī* (chicken soup), and *zhá xiāngjiāo* (deep-fried banana) for dessert. Wash it all down with a cup of sweet rice wine *(mǐ jiǔ)*, served in a bamboo cup.

Mínzú Dàxué Běi Lù 1 (cross footbridge, head right, take the 1st street on your left), Hǎidiàn Qū; see map p. 112. Ⓒ 010/6893-2030. Meal for 2 ¥60–¥120. No credit cards. Daily 11am–10pm.

INEXPENSIVE

Xiàngyáng Tún HOMESTYLE/NORTHEASTERN   Set in new courtyard-style complex in northwestern Běijīng, this nostalgia restaurant is one of the only venues in the city for *èrrénzhuàn*, a raunchily entertaining style of opera rarely performed outside the frigid northeast. The opera stage sits at one end of the cavernous main hall, decorated in an exaggerated Cultural Revolution–era countryside theme with bright red tables and propaganda-heavy newspapers from the 1960s plastered on the walls. Dishes are large and simple in the northeastern tradition. Good choices are the *Dōngběi fēngwèi dàpái* (northeast-style braised ribs) and the *nóngjiā xiǎochǎo*, an authentically rural combination of soybeans, green onion, Chinese chive, and bell peppers in a clay pot. Combine a stop here with an afternoon visit to the Summer Palace.

Wànquán Hé Lù 26 (in Hǎidiàn, across from the Zhōngyī Yīyuàn [Chinese Traditional Medicine Hospital]); see map p. 112. ℂ **010/6264-5522** or 010/6264-2907. Meal for 2 ¥40–¥80 ($5–$10). No credit cards. Daily 9am–9pm.

6

Exploring Běijīng

by Graeme Smith

This is an overwhelming prospect. No other city in China, and few other cities in the world, offer so many must-see attractions, or such a likelihood of missed opportunity. It is technically possible to see the big names—the **Forbidden City, Temple of Heaven, Summer Palace,** and **Great Wall**—in as little as 3 days, but you'll need at least a week to get any sort of feel for the city. People spend years here and still fail to see everything they should.

Sights outside of Běijīng require at least half a day. However, the Great Wall requires a full day. (See chapter 10 for details on these.)

Note: Most major sights now charge different prices for admission in summer and winter. The summer high season officially runs from April 1 to October 31 and the winter low season from November 1 to March 31.

HOW TO SEE BĚIJĪNG

Běijīng's traffic is appalling. Do *not* plan to see too many sights that are far apart, unless you want your memories of the capital to consist mainly of staring helplessly out of a taxicab window. Regardless of whether you choose to get around by taxi, metro, bus, bike, or foot, plan each day to see sights that are close together.

The best option for reaching sights within Běijīng is to take the metro to the stop nearest the attraction you plan on seeing, and duck into one of the many waiting taxis. As an example, the **Summer Palace** is a short ¥15 ($2) cab ride from the new light rail station at Wǔdàokǒu. Buses are slow but plentiful and relatively safe, especially if you choose the air-conditioned 800-series buses. Maximum freedom (and usually speed) is realized by hiring a bike for the day. More convenient still is to hire a normal taxi for the day (see section 2, "Getting Around" in chapter 3).

The standard of organized tours in Běijīng leaves much to be desired. But if this is your preference, most hotels have offices of Panda Tours and Dragon Tours, which offer overpriced tours to the major attractions (see section 11, "Organized Tours" in this chapter). The advantage is that transport and language barriers are removed, but the freedom to visit smaller attractions and meet locals is sacrificed. The pace of these tours can leave you giddy.

The last and least recommended option is to hire a car through your hotel. You will be charged up to five times what you should pay. Aside from convenience, the only conceivable plus is that if you are staying at a foreign-run, luxury hotel, they have a reputation for good service to protect. Organizations such as Panda Tours, which are run by the China International Travel Service, do not.

Běijīng City Center

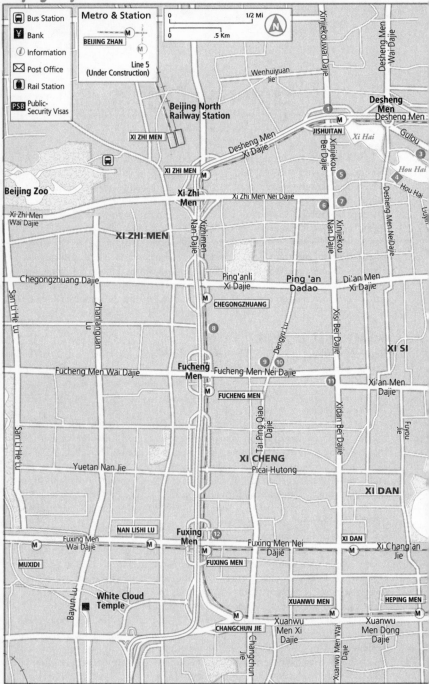

Bus Station
Bank
Information
Post Office
Rail Station
PSB Public-Security Visas

Metro & Station
M
BEIJING ZHAN
M
Line 5
(Under Construction)

0   1/2 Mi
0   .5 Km

XINJIEKOUWAI DAJIE

Desheng Men Wai Dajie

Wenhuiyuan Jie

Desheng Men
Desheng Men

XI ZHI MEN

Beijing North Railway Station

Desheng Men Xi Dajie

JISHUITAN

Xi Hai

Gulou

Hou Hai

XI ZHI MEN

Xinjiekou Bei Dajie

Hou Hai Luyin

Xi Zhi Men

Xi Zhi Men Nei Dajie

Desheng Men Nei Dajie

Beijing Zoo

Xi Zhi Men Wai Dajie

XI ZHI MEN

Xinjiekou Nan Dajie

Xizhimen Nan Dajie

Chegongzhuang Dajie

San'Li He Lu

Zhanlanguan Lu

Ping'anli Xi Dajie

Ping 'an Dadao

Di'an Men Xi Dajie

CHEGONGZHUANG

Xisi Bei Dajie

XI SI

Dengru Lu

Fucheng Men Wai Dajie

Fucheng Men

Fucheng Men Nei Dajie

Xi'an Men Dajie

FUCHENG MEN

San'Li He Lu

Tai Ping Qiao Dajie

Xidan Bei Dajie

Fuyou Jie

XI CHENG

Yuetan Nan Jie

Picai Hutong

XI DAN

NAN LISHI LU

Fuxing Men

Fuxing Men Nei Dajie

XI DAN

MUXIDI

M

Fuxing Men Wai Dajie

M

M

FUXING MEN

Xi Chang'an Jie

Bayun Lu

White Cloud Temple

XUANWU MEN

HEPING MEN

M

M

M

CHANGCHUN JIE

Xuanwu Men Xi Dajie

Xuanwu Men Dong Dajie

Xuanwu Men Xi Dajie

Changchun Jie

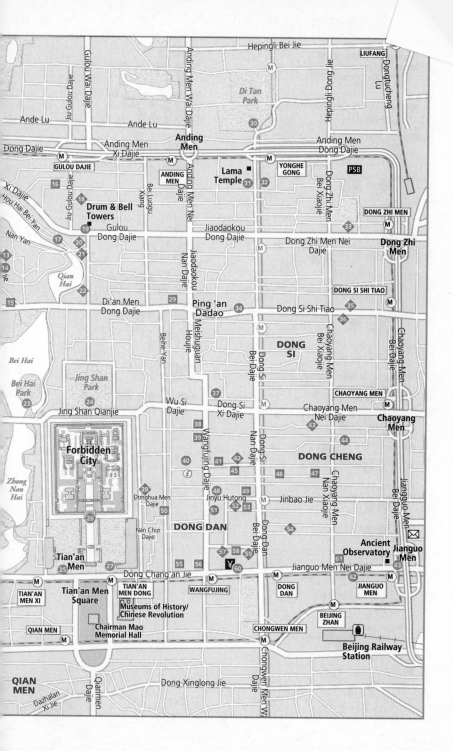

Hepingli Bei Jie

LIUFANG

Dongtucheng Lu

Di Tan
Park

Ande Lu

Gulou Wai Dajie

Ande Lu

Anding Men
Xi Dajie

Anding
Men

Anding Men
Dong Dajie

30

Dong Dajie

GULOU DAJIE

ANDING
MEN

Lama
Temple

YONGHE
GONG

PSB

DONG ZHI MEN

Xi Dajie

16

Hepingli Dong Jie

Anding Men Wai Dajie

Anding Men Nei Dajie

Bei Luogu Xiang

31

32

Dong Zhi Men
Bei Xiaojie

Jiu Gulou Dajie

18

Drum & Bell
Towers

Gulou
Dong Dajie

Jiaodaokou
Dong Dajie

33

Dong Zhi Men Nei
Dajie

Dong Zhi
Men

Hou Hai Bei Yan

19

Nan Yan

17

20

21

Jiaodaokou Nan Dajie

DONG SI SHI TIAO

Qian
Hai

22

Di'an Men
Dong Dajie

29

Ping 'an
Dadao

34

Dong Si Shi Tiao

35

36

Chaoyang Men
Bei Xiaojie

Chaoyang Men
Bei Dajie

13

14

15

Meishuguan Houjie

Beihe Yan

DONG
SI

Dong Si Bei Dajie

Bei Hai

Bei Hai
Park

Jing Shan
Park

23

Jing Shan Qianjie

24

Wu Si
Dajie

37

Dong Si
Xi Dajie

CHAOYANG MEN

Chaoyang Men
Nei Dajie

Chaoyang
Men

38

43

39

Zhong
Nan
Hai

Forbidden
City

Wangfujing Dajie

Dong Si Nan Dajie

DONG CHENG

40

41

42

44

i

45

46

47

Chaoyang Men
Nan Xiaojie

Jianguo Men Bei Dajie

28

Donghua Men
Dajie

48

49

Jinyu Hutong

Jinbao Jie

50

52

53

26

Nan Chizi
Dajie

51

DONG DAN

Dong Dan Bei Dajie

54

Tian'an
Men

25

27

57

58

59

Jianguo
Men

55

56

60

61

Ancient
Observatory

Jianguo Men Nei Dajie

62

63

Dong Chang'an Jie

TIAN'AN
MEN XI

Tian'an Men
Square

TIAN'AN
MEN DONG

WANGFUJING

DONG
DAN

JIANGUO
MEN

QIAN MEN

Museums of History/
Chinese Revolution

CHONGWEN MEN

BEIJING
ZHAN

Chairman Mao
Memorial Hall

Beijing Railway
Station

QIAN
MEN

Qianmen Dajie

Dong Xinglong Jie

Chongwen Men Wai Dajie

Dazhalan
Xi Jie

Key for Běijīng City Center

ACCOMMODATIONS ■

Bamboo Garden Hotel
(Zhú Yuán Bīnguǎn) **16**
竹园宾馆

Běijīng Hotel (Běijīng Fàndiàn) **56**
北京饭店

Crowne Plaza Hotel
(Guójì Yìyuàn Huángguān Fàndiàn) **41**
国际艺苑皇冠饭店

Cuìmíng Zhuāng Bīnguǎn **50**
翠明庄宾馆

Fùháo Bīnguǎn **38**
富豪宾馆

Grand Hotel
(Běijīng Guìbīnlóu Fàndiàn) **55**
北京贵宾楼饭店

Grand Hyatt Běijīng
(Běijīng Dōngfāng Jūnyuè) **58**
东方君悦大酒店

Hǎoyuán Bīnguǎn **46**
好园宾馆

Héjìng Fǔ Bīnguǎn **34**
和敬府宾馆

International Youth Hostel
(Guójì Qīngnián Lǚ xíngshè) **61**
国际青年旅行舍

Lǚ sōng Yuán Bīnguǎn **29**
吕松园宾馆

Novotel Peace Běijīng
(Běijīng Nuòfùtè Hépíng Bīnguǎn) **49**
诺富特和平宾馆

The Peninsula Palace Běijīng
(Wángfǔ Fàndiàn) **53**
王府饭店

Qílǔ Fàndiàn **15**
齐鲁饭店

Saga Youth Hostel
(Shǐjiā Guójì Qīngnián Lǚ xíngshè) **47**
史家国际青年旅行舍

Sōnghè Dàjiǔdiàn **45**
松鹤大酒店

Wángfǔjǐng Grand
(Wángfǔjǐng Dàjiǔdiàn) **39**
王府井大酒店

DINING ◆

Afunti (Āfǔántí) **43**
阿凡提

Be There or Be Square
(Bú Jiàn Bú Sàn) **59**
不见不散

Cafe Sambal **18**
豆腐池胡同４３号

The Courtyard (Sìhéyuàn) **28**
四合院

Da Giorgio **57**

Dào **20**
道

Fújiā Lóu **35**
福家楼

Gōng Wángfǔ Sìchuān Fàndiàn **13**
恭王府四川饭店

Green Tiānshí (Lǜ sè Tiānshí) **42**
绿色天食

Hàn Kèjiā **22**
汉客家

Huājiā Yíyuán **33**
花家怡园

Hùjiāng Xiāng Mǎn Lóu **36**
沪江香满楼

Jing **52**
京

Kǒng Yǐjǐ Jiǔlóu **4**
孔乙己酒楼

Noble Court **57**

Nuage (Qìng Yún Lóu) **21**
庆云楼

Otto's Restaurant
(Rìchāng Chá Cāntīng) **54**
日昌茶餐厅

Běijīng South

Bus Station
Bank
Information
Post Office
Rail Station
Public-Security Visas

Metro & Station

BEIJING ZHAN

Line 5
(Under Construction)

XI ZHI MEN

Xi Zhi Men Nei Dajie

XI ZHI MEN

Ping'anli
Xi Dajie

Ping 'an
Dadao

Di'an Men
Xi Dajie

XI SI

Fucheng Lu

CHEGONGZHUANG

Fucheng Men Wai Dajie

Fucheng Men Nei Dajie

Xi'an Men
Dajie

Fuyou
Jie

FUCHENG MEN

Yuyuan Tan Park
Yuyuan Tan

Yuetan Nan Jie

XI CHENG
Picai Hutong

XI DAN

JUNSHI
BOWUGUAN

Fuxing Lu

FUXING MEN

Fuxing Men
Wai Dajie

Fuxing Men Nei
Dajie

XI DAN

Xi Chang'an
Jie

MUXIDI

NAN LISHI LU

White Cloud
Temple

Xibian
Men

XUANWU MEN
Xuanwu Men
Xi Dajie

HEPING
MEN

Xuanwu Men
Dong Dajie

CHANGCHUN JIE

Lianhuachi Dong Lu

Beijing West
Railway Station

Guang'an Men Wai Dajie

Guang'an Men Nei Dajie

Guang'an
Dajie

Luomashi
Dajie

Maliandao
Lu

Maliandao Nan Jie

Zaolin Qian Jie

Nanheng
Dong Jie

Third Ring
Road

Second Ring Road

Baizhifang
Xi Jie

Baizhifang
Dong Jie

Taoranting Lu

Taiping
Qiao Lu

XUANWU

Tong Hui

Taoranting
Park

Lize Lu

You'an Men
Xi Bin He Lu

You'an Men
Dong Bin He Lu

Beijing South
Railway Station

FENGTAI

Nan San Huan
Xi Lu

0   1 Mi
0   1 Km

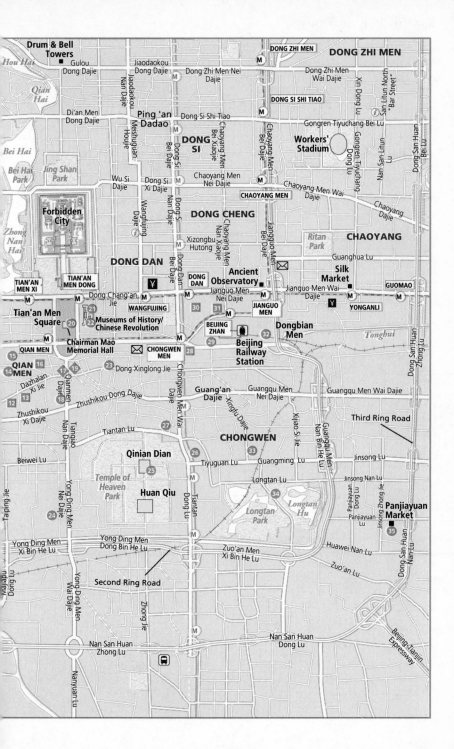

Drum & Bell
Towers
■ Gulou
Hou Hai
Jiaodaokou
Dong Dajie
Dong Zhi Men Nei
Dajie
DONG ZHI MEN
DONG ZHI MEN

Qian
Hai
Jiaodaokou
Nan Dajie
Dong Zhi Men
Wai Dajie
Xin Dong Lu
San Litun North
"Bar Street"

Di'an Men
Dong Dajie
Ping 'an
Dadao
Dong Si Shi Tiao
DONG SI SHI TIAO

Bei Hai
Meishuguan
Houjie
**DONG
SI**
Chaoyang Men
Bei Xiaojie
Chaoyang Men
Bei Dajie
Gongren Tiyuchang Bei Lu
**Workers'
Stadium**
Gongren Tiyuchang
Dong Lu
Nan San Litun

Bei Hai
Park
Jing Shan
Park
Wu Si
Dajie
Dong Si
Xi Dajie
Chaoyang Men
Nei Dajie
Chaoyang Men Wai
Dajie
Chaoyang
Dajie

Zhong
Nan
Hai
**Forbidden
City**
Wangfujing
Dajie
Nan Dajie
DONG CHENG
CHAOYANG MEN
Ritan
Park
CHAOYANG
Guanghua Lu

DONG DAN
Xizongbu
Hutong
Chaoyang Men
Nan Xiaojie
Chaoyang Men
Bei Dajie
Jianguo Men Bei Dajie
✉
**Silk
Market**
GUOMAO

**TIAN'AN
MEN XI**
**TIAN'AN
MEN DONG**
**DONG
DAN**
**Ancient
Observatory**
Jianguo Men
Nei Dajie
Jianguo Men Wai
Dajie
YONGANLI

**Tian'an Men
Square**
20
21
22
Dong Chang'an
Jie
¥
WANGFUJING
30
31
M
**JIANGUO
MEN**
¥
**Dongbian
Men**

15
QIAN MEN
**Chairman Mao
Memorial Hall**
✉
29
**BEIJING
ZHAN**
🏛
32
**Beijing
Railway
Station**
Tonghui
Dong San Huan Zhong Lu

**QIAN
MEN**
15
16
17
23
Dong Xinglong Jie
**CHONGWEN
MEN**
28

Dazhalan
Xi Jie
12
13
18
Zhushikou Dong Dajie
Chongwen Men Wai
Dajie
**Guang'an
Dajie**
Guangqu Men
Nei Dajie
Guangqu Men Wai Dajie

Zhushikou
Xi Dajie
Tianqiao
Nan Dajie
Yingtu Dajie
Xijiao Si Jie
Guangqu Men
Nan Bin He Lu
Third Ring Road

Beiwei Lu
Yong Ding Men
Nei Dajie
27
Tiantan Lu
CHONGWEN
33
Guangming Lu
Jinsong Lu
Panjiayuan Lu
Jinsong Zhong Jie

Qinian Dian
26
Tiyuguan Lu
Jinsong Nan Lu
**Panjiayuan
Market**

**Temple of
Heaven
Park**
25
Longtan Lu
34
Longtan
Hu
Panjiayuan
Lu
35

Huan Qiu
Tiantan
Dong Lu
Longtan
Park
Huawei Nan Lu

24
Yong Ding Men
Dong Bin He Lu
Yong Ding Men
Xi Bin He Lu
Zuo'an Men
Xi Bin He Lu
Zuo'an Lu

Second Ring Road
Zhong Jie
Yong Ding Men
Wai Dajie

Nan San Huan
Zhong Lu
Nan San Huan
Dong Lu
Beijing-Tianjin
Expressway

Nanyuan Lu

Key for Běijīng South

ACCOMMODATIONS ■

Far East Youth Hostel
(Yuǎn Dōng Qīngnián Lǚshè) **12**
远东青年旅舍

Fēiyīng Bīnguǎn 7
飞鹰宾馆

Hademen Hotel
(Hādé Mén Fàndiàn) **28**
哈德门饭店

Harmony Hotel
(Huáměilún Jiǔdiàn) **30**
华美伦酒店

Howard Johnson Paragon Hotel
(Bǎochén Fàndiàn) **31**
宝辰饭店

The Marco Polo
(Mǎgē Bóluó Jiǔdiàn) **10**
马哥勃罗酒店

Qián Mén Chánggōng Fàndiàn 16
前门长宫饭店

Shǎnxī Xiàng Dì'èr Bīnguǎn 13
陕西巷第二宾馆

DINING ◆

Gǒubùlǐ Bāozi Diàn 17
狗不理包子店

Pamer
(Pàmǐ'ěr Shífǔ) **2**
帕米尔食府

Quánjùdé Kǎoyā Diàn 19
全聚德烤鸭店

Tàipó Tiānfǔ Shānzhēn 4
太婆天府山珍

Tiānjīn Bǎi Jiǎo Yuán 8
天津百饺园

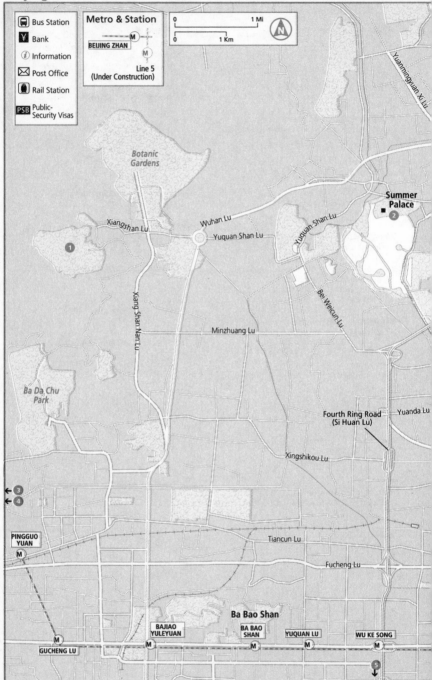

Bus Station

¥ Bank

i **Information**

⊠ **Post Office**

Rail Station

PSB Public-Security Visas

Metro & Station

Ⓜ **BEIJING ZHAN**

Ⓜ Line 5 (Under Construction)

0 .... 1 Mi
0 .... 1 Km

Botanic Gardens

Summer Palace ■ ②

Xiangshan Lu

Wuhan Lu

Yuquan Shan Lu

Yuquan Shan Lu

Xiang Shan Nan Lu

Bei Weicun Lu

①

Minzhuang Lu

Ba Da Chu Park

Fourth Ring Road (Si Huan Lu)

Yuanda Lu

Xingshikou Lu

③
④

PINGGUO YUAN
Ⓜ

Tiancun Lu

Fucheng Lu

Ba Bao Shan

BAJIAO YULEYUAN
Ⓜ

BA BAO SHAN
Ⓜ

YUQUAN LU
Ⓜ

WU KE SONG
Ⓜ

Ⓜ
GUCHENG LU

⑤

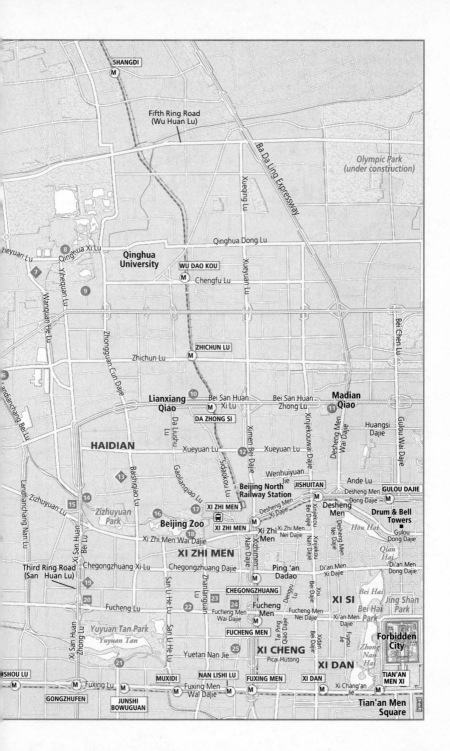

SHANGDI

Fifth Ring Road
(Wu Huan Lu)

Olympic Park
(under construction)

Xueqing Lu

Ba Da Ling Expressway

Qinghua Dong Lu

heyuan Lu

Qinghua Xi Lu

Qinghua
University

WU DAO KOU

Chengfu Lu

Xueyuan Lu

Yihequan Lu

Wanquan He Lu

Bei Chen Lu

ZHICHUN LU

Zhichun Lu

Zhongguan Cun Dajie

andianchang Bei Lu

Lianxiang
Qiao

Bei San Huan
Xi Lu

Bei San Huan
Zhong Lu

Madian
Qiao

DA ZHONG SI

Xinjiekouwai Dajie

Huangsi
Dajie

Gulou Wai Dajie

HAIDIAN

Da Liushu
Lu

Xueyuan Lu

Ximen Bei Dajie

Xueyuan Lu

Desheng Men
Wai Dajie

Baishiqiao Lu

Gaoliangqiao Lu

Sidaokou Lu

Wenhuiyuan
Jie

JISHUITAN

Ande Lu

Landianchang Nan Lu

Zizhuyuan Lu

Beijing North
Railway Station

Desheng Men

Desheng Men
Nei Dajie

Dong Dajie

GULOU DAJIE

Drum & Bell
Towers

Zizhuyuan
Park

Bei Lu

Xi Zhi Men
Wai Dajie

XI ZHI MEN

XI ZHI MEN

Desheng Men
Xi Dajie

Xi Zhi Men
Nei Dajie

Desheng
Men

Xinjiekou
Bei Dajie

Gulou
Dong Dajie

Hou Hai

Beijing Zoo

Xi Zhi Men
Wai Dajie

XI ZHI MEN

Xizhimen
Nan Dajie

Xi Zhi
Men

Qian
Hai

Xi San Huan
Zhong Lu

Chegongzhuang Xi Lu

Chegongzhuang Dajie

Ping 'an
Dadao

Di'an Men
Xi Dajie

Bei Hai

Di'an Men
Dong Dajie

Third Ring Road
(San Huan Lu)

Zhanlanguan
Lu

CHEGONGZHUANG

Dengshi
kou

XI SI

Jing Shan
Park

Fucheng Lu

San Li He Lu

Fucheng
Men

Fucheng Men
Nei Dajie

Bei Hai
Park

Xi'an Men
Dajie

Fuyou

Forbidden
City

Yuyuan Tan Park

Yuyuan Tan

Fucheng Men
Wai Dajie

FUCHENG MEN

Tai Ping
Qiao Dajie

Xidan
Bei Dajie

Zhong
Nan Hai

Xi San Huan
Zhong Lu

Yuetan Nan Jie

XI CHENG

Picai Hutong

XI DAN

TIAN'AN
MEN XI

SHOU LU

Fuxing Lu

MUXIDI

NAN LISHI LU

FUXING MEN

XI DAN

Xi Chang'an

Tian'an Men
Square

GONGZHUFEN

JUNSHI
BOWUGUAN

Fuxing Men
Wai Dajie

113

Key for Běijīng West & Hǎidiàn

Cháoyáng

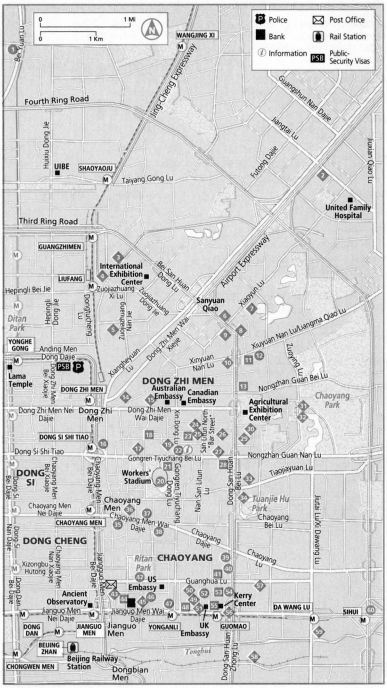

Police — P
Bank — ■
Information — ⓘ
Post Office — ⊠
Rail Station — 🏛
Public-Security Visas — PSB

WANGJING XI

Guangshun Nan Dajie

Jing-Cheng Expressway

Fourth Ring Road

Jiangtai Lu

Hun Dong Jie

Jiuxian Qiao Lu

UIBE   SHAOYAOJU

Taiyang Gong Lu

Futong Dajie

United Family Hospital

Third Ring Road

GUANGZHIMEN

Airport Expressway

Hepingli Bei Jie

LIUFANG

International Exhibition Center

Bei San Huan Dong Lu

Xiaoyun Lu

Dongtucheng Lu

Zuojiazhuang Xi Lu

Zuojiazhuang Dong Jie

Sanyuan Qiao

Ditan Park

Dong Zhi Men Wai Xiejie

Xinyuan Nan Lu

Xiuyuan Nan Lu/Liangma Qiao Lu

YONGHE GONG

Anding Men Dong Dajie

Xiangheyuan Lu

Zhuojiayuan Nan Jie

Xinyuan Nan Lu

Zuoying Lu

Lama Temple

PSB P

Dong Zhi Men Bei Xiaojie

DONG ZHI MEN

Nongzhan Guan Bei Lu

Chaoyang Park

DONG ZHI MEN

Dong Zhi Men Nei Dajie

Dong Zhi Men

Australian Embassy

Canadian Embassy

Agricultural Exhibition Center

Dong Zhi Men Wai Dajie

San Litun North "Bar Street"

Nongzhan Guan Nan Lu

DONG SI SHI TIAO

Dong Si Shi Tiao

San Dong Lu

DONG SI

Chaoyang Men Bei Xiaojie

Chaoyang Men Bei Dajie

Gongren Tiyuchang Bei Lu

Nan San Litun

Dong San Huan

Tiaojiayuan Lu

Workers' Stadium

Gongren Tiyuchang Nan Lu

Gongren Tiyuchang Dong Lu

Chaoyang Men Nei Dajie

Chaoyang Men

Tuanjie Hu Park

CHAOYANG MEN

Chaoyang Men Wai Dajie

Chaoyang Bei Lu

Jiutai Lu/Xi Dawang Lu

DONG CHENG

Dong Si Nan Dajie

Xizongbu Hutong

Chaoyang Men Nan Xiaojie

Jianguo Men Bei Dajie

Ritan Park

CHAOYANG

Chaoyang Dajie

Chaoyang Lu

Ancient Observatory

US Embassy

Guanghua Lu

Kerry Center

DA WANG LU

SIHUI

DONG DAN

JIANGUO MEN

Jianguo Men Wai Dajie

Jianguo Men

YONGANLI

UK Embassy

GUOMAO

Dong San Huan Zhong Lu

BEIJING ZHAN

Beijing Railway Station

Jianguo Men Nei Dajie

Tongbui

CHONGWEN MEN

Dongbian Men

115

Key for Cháoyáng

ACCOMMODATIONS ■

China World Hotel
(Zhōngguó Dàfàndiàn) **55**
中国大饭店

Gōngtǐ Youth Hostel
(Guójì Qīngnián Lǚxíngshè) **21**
工体青年旅行社

Great Wall Sheraton
(Cháng Chéng Fàndiàn) **13**
长城饭店

Hilton Běijīng
(Běijīng Xīěrdùn Fàndiàn) **8**
北京希尔顿饭店

Holiday Inn Lido
(Lìdū Jiàrì Fàndiàn) **2**
丽都假日饭店

Jiànguó Hotel (Jiànguó Fàndiàn) **48**
建国饭店

Kempinski Hotel (Kǎibīnsījī Fàndiàn) **11**
凯宾斯基饭店

Kerry Centre Hotel
(Běijīng Jiālǐ Zhōngxīn Fàndiàn) **41**
北京嘉里中心饭店

Poacher's Inn Youth Hostel
(Yǒuyì Qīngnián Jiǔdiàn) **23**
友谊青年酒店

Red House (Ruìxiù Bīnguǎn) **18**
瑞秀宾馆

Renaissance Běijīng
(Guóháng Wànlǐ Jiǔdiàn) **7**
国航万丽酒店

St. Regis Běijīng
(Běijīng Guójì Jùlèbù Fàndiàn) **44**
北京国际俱乐部饭店

Traders Hotel Běijīng (Guómào Fàndiàn) **53**
国贸饭店

Zhàolóng Qīngnián Lǚguǎn **28**
兆龙青年旅馆

DINING ◆

Ǎndiē Ǎnniáng **31**
俺爹俺娘

Annie's Café (Ānnī Yìdàlì Cāntīng) **32**
安妮意大利餐厅

Ānyuán No. 5
(Ānyuán Wǔ Hào Cāntīng) **1**
安园五号餐厅

Aria (Ālìyǎ) **56**

Astor Grill **43**

Bǎi Shì Jí Huǒguō **36**
百事吉火锅

Běijīng Dàdǒng Kǎoyā Diàn **33**
北京大董烤鸭店

Chingari (Xíngéi) **15**
鑫格里

Danieli's (Dānní'àilì) **43**
丹尼艾丽

Dào Jiā Cháng **3**
到家尝

Dǐng Dǐng Xiāng **14**
鼎鼎香

Flo (Fú Lóu) **29**
福楼

Grandma's Kitchen
(Zǔmuǔ de Chúfáng) **45**
祖母的厨房

Hatsune (Yǐn Qhuán) **57**
隐泉

Hóng Jīng Yú **4**
红京鱼

Horizon (Hǎitiān Gé) **40**
海天阁

Huángchéng Lǎo Mā **58**
皇城老妈

Justine's (Jiésītīng) **49**
杰斯汀

Lotus in Moonlight
(Hétáng Yuèsè Sùshí) **5**
荷塘月色素食

Makye Ame (Mǎjí Āmǐ) **45**
玛吉阿米

SUGGESTED ITINERARIES

If You Have 1 Day

Máo's oft-quoted dictum states that anyone who fails to visit the **Great Wall** comes up short as a human being *(bú dào Cháng Chéng fēi hǎo Hàn)*. The price of self-improvement is the best part of a day's touring. If you hire your own cab, start early, and visit the easily accessed **Bā Dá Lǐng** (p. 194) or **Jūyōng Guān** (p. 195) sections of the Wall. Stopping briefly at the **Summer Palace** on the way back is possible.

If you skip the Wall, start early with **Tiān Tán Gōngyuán (Temple of Heaven).** Head north to **Tiān'ān Mén Square,** but instead of following the crowds, approach the **Forbidden City** through **Tài Miào.** Allow at least 3 hours for exploring the remoter corners of the **Forbidden City.** The **Back Lakes** area, with a plethora of dining options, lies to the north. Enjoy the cool of evening with a stroll through Běijīng's remaining *hútòng* (narrow lanes).

If You Have 2 Days

Spend your first day visiting a remoter section of the Wall, such as **Jīn Shān Lǐng** (p. 197) or **Sīmǎtái** (p. 197). Better yet, hike from one to the other. Then round off the day watching a performance of Běijīng opera at **Zhèngyǐcí Xìlóu** (p. 181) or **Húguǎng Guild Hall** (p. 180). Spend the next day exploring the center of town as described under "If You Have 1 Day."

If You Have 3 Days

Three days is the minimum time to realistically fit in all of Běijīng's big sights—the **Great Wall,** the **Forbidden City, Tiān Tán Gōngyuán,** and the **Summer Palace.** The latter requires around 4 hours; it's possible to round out the day with a visit to nearby **Yuán Míng Yuán (Old Summer Palace)** or to one of Běijīng's more interesting temples such as **Lama Temple, Kǒng Miào,** or **Dōng Yuè Miào,** depending on whether Buddhism, Confucianism, or Daoism attracts you. An evening performance of acrobatics at **Wàn-shèng Jùchǎng** will help you forget about your aching limbs.

If You Have 4 Days or More

Realistically, even 2 weeks isn't enough to see all Běijīng has to offer, but after making your pilgrimage to the Great Wall, you will have time to group the attractions you plan to see by area, and spend less time dashing about. For example, if you're visiting **Tiān Tán Gōngyuán (Temple of Heaven)** in the south of town, it's possible to first visit the fascinating **Gǔdài Jiànzhù Bówùguǎn (Museum of Ancient Architecture),** then continue east to the shopping delights of **Hóng Qiáo** and **Yuánlóng Silk,** before taking a short cab or bus ride to the **Gǔ Guānxiàng Tái (Ancient Observatory)** or **Míng City Wall Park** to watch the sunset. In the north, **Lama Temple, Kǒng Miào,** and **Guó Zǐ Jiàn** are all within strolling distance, as are the attractions described in the walking tours in chapter 7.

1 Tiān'ān Mén Square (Tiān'ān Mén Guǎngchǎng)

This is the world's largest public square, the size of 90 American football fields (40 hectares/99 acres), with standing room for 300,000 people. It is surrounded by the Forbidden City in the north, the Great Hall of the People in the west, and the museums of Chinese History and Chinese Revolution in the east. In the center of the square stands the Monument to the People's Heroes (Rénmín

Travel Tip: He who finds the best hotel deal has more to spend on facials involving knobbly vegetables.

Hello, the Roaming Gnome here. I've been nabbed from the garden and taken round the world. The people who took me are so terribly clever. They find the best offerings on Travelocity. For very little cha-ching. And that means I get to be pampered and exfoliated till I'm pink as a bunny's doodah.

travelocity®

1-888-TRAVELOCITY / travelocity.com / America Online Keyword: Travel

Plan your vacation

- flights, hotels, car rentals
- cruises & vacation packages
- destination guides
- fare alerts
- go to yahoo.com, click travel

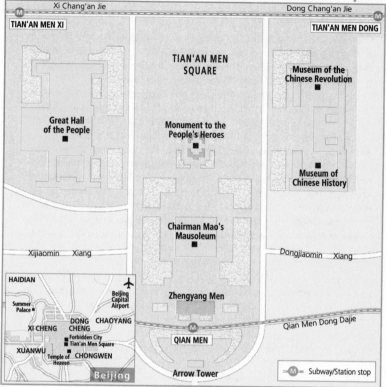

Yīngxióng Jìniàn Bēi), a 37m (124-ft.) granite obelisk erected in 1958, engraved with scenes from famous uprisings and bearing a central inscription (in Máo's handwriting): THE PEOPLE'S HEROES ARE IMMORTAL. The twin-tiered dais is said to be an intentional contrast to the imperial preference for three-tiered platforms; the *yīn* of the people's martyrs contrasted with the *yáng* of the emperors (see the "Lucky Numbers" box on p. 125).

The area on which the square stands was originally occupied by the **Imperial Way**—a central road that stretched from inside the Forbidden City, through Tiān'ān Mén, and south to Dà Qīng Mén (known as Zhōnghuá Mén during the Nationalist era), which was demolished to make way for Máo's corpse in 1976 (see the review for Chairman Máo's Mausoleum, below). This road, lined on either side with imperial government ministries, was the site of the pivotal May Fourth movement (1919), in which thousands of university students gathered to protest the weakness and corruption of China's then-Republican government. Máo ordered destruction of the old ministries. The vast but largely empty **Great Hall of the People** rose from the rubble to the west, and equally vast but unimpressive **museums** were erected to the east, as part of a spate of construction to celebrate 10 years of Communist rule. But the site has remained a magnet for politically charged assemblies; the most famous was the gathering of **student protestors** in late spring of 1989. That movement, and the government's violent suppression of it, still define Tiān'ān Mén Square in most minds. You'll search

---

Fun Fact **One Picture, Two Stories**

Everyone knows the image: a lone protestor, wearing a white shirt and holding a plastic shopping bag, moving to and fro to block the path of a long column of tanks. His whereabouts and identity are still unknown, but by virtue of this act he became one of only two Chinese who made *Time* magazine's list of the major figures of the 20th century, alongside Máo. Presented by CNN and other Western agencies as an image of an individual bravely resisting a monstrous totalitarian regime, this is one picture you would never expect ordinary Chinese to see. But the official media were happy to run it—with a different slant. The protestor is shown clambering onto the tank, and the indignant narrator praises the tremendous restraint employed by the armed forces when faced by such an unreasonable foe. The government, when forced to mention the matter at all, maintains that no civilians were killed *in the square*. The matter is still sensitive. A dissident who founded a website with the provocative URL www. 6-4tianwang.com (6-4 is shorthand for June 4, the date of the massacre) was recently sentenced to 5 years in prison for subversion.

---

in vain for bullet holes and bloodstains. The killing took place elsewhere. Brutal scenes were witnessed near Fùxīng Mén and Xī Dān (west of the square), as workers and students were shot in the back by a cowardly regime that showed its true colors, bringing a halt to a decade of intermittent political reform. Today, stiff-backed soldiers, video cameras, and plain-clothed police still keep a close watch on the square.

Other than flying a kite and playing "spot the plain-clothed policeman," there isn't much to do in the square, but early risers can line up in front of Tiān'ān Mén at dawn to watch the **flag-raising ceremony,** a unique suffocation-in-the-throng experience on National Day (Oct 1), when what seems like the entire Chinese population arrives to jostle for the best view.

Chairman Máo's Mausoleum (Máo Zhǔxí Jìniàn Guǎn)   This is one of the eeriest experiences in Běijīng. The decision to preserve Máo's body was made hours after his death in 1976. Panicked and inexperienced, his doctors reportedly pumped him so full of formaldehyde his face and body swelled almost beyond recognition. They drained the corpse and managed to get it back into acceptable shape, but they also created a wax model of the Great Helmsman just in case. There's no telling which version—the real or the waxen—is on display at any given time. The mausoleum itself was built in 1977, near the center of Tiān'ān Mén Square. However much Máo may be mocked outside his tomb (earnest arguments about whether he was 70% right or 60% right are perhaps the biggest joke), he still commands a terrifying sort of respect inside it. Not quite the kitsch experience some expect. The tour is free and fast, with no stopping, photos, or bags allowed inside.

South end of Tiān'ān Mén Sq.; map p. 119. Free admission. Mon–Sat 8–11:30am; sometimes also 2–4pm (usually Mon, Wed, Fri). Bag storage in building across the street, directly west: ¥10 ($1) per piece. Metro: Qián Mén (208).

Qián Mén (Front Gate)   The phrase Qián Mén is actually a reference to two separate towers on the south side of the square which together formed the main entrance to the Tartar (or Inner) City. The southernmost Arrow Tower (Jiàn

Lóu) is no longer open to the public. You can, however, still climb up inside the rear building, called the Zhèngyáng Mén, where a fairly enjoyable photo exhibition depicts life in Běijīng's pre-1949 markets, temples, and *hútòng*.

South end of Tiān'ān Mén Sq.; map p. 119. Admission ¥10 ($1.25). Daily 8:30am–4pm. Metro: Qián Mén (208).

2 Forbidden City (Gù Gōng)

The universally accepted symbol for the length and grandeur of Chinese civilization is undoubtedly the Great Wall, but the Forbidden City is more immediately impressive. A 720,000-sq.-m (864,000-sq.-yard) complex of red-walled buildings and pavilions topped by a sea of glazed vermilion tile, it dwarfs nearby Tiān'ān Mén Square and is by far the largest and most intricate imperial palace in China. The palace receives more visitors than any other attraction in the country (over seven million a year, the government says), and has been praised in Western travel literature ever since the first Europeans laid eyes on it in the late 1500s. Yet despite the flood of superlatives and exaggerated statistics that inevitably go into its description, it is impervious to an excess of hype, and it is large and compelling enough to draw repeat visits from even the most jaded travelers. Make more time for it than you think you'll need.

> **Map of the Forbidden City**
>
> For a map of the palace, see the inside back cover of this book.

The palace, most commonly referred to in Chinese as Gù Gōng (Former Palace), is on the north side of Tiān'ān Mén Square across Cháng'ān Dàjiē (© **010/6513-2255,** ext. 615). It is best approached on foot or via metro (Tiān'ān Mén Dōng, 117), as taxis are not allowed to stop in front. The palace is open daily from 8:30am to 5pm during summer and from 8:30am to 4:30pm in winter. Regular admission *(mén piào)* in summer costs ¥60 ($8), dropping to ¥40 ($5) in winter; last tickets are sold an hour before the doors close. Various exhibition halls and gardens inside the palace charge an additional ¥10 ($1). All-inclusive tickets *(lián piào)* had been discontinued at press time, perhaps in an effort to increase revenues (see the box "The Big Makeover" below), but it's always possible these will be reinstated. *Tip:* If you have a little more time, it is highly recommended that you approach the entrance at **Wǔ Mén (Meridian Gate)** via **Tài Miào** (p. 134) to the east, and avoid the gauntlet of tiresome touts and tacky souvenir stalls.

Ticket counters are clearly marked on either side as you approach. **Audio tours** in several languages (¥40/$5 plus ¥500/$63 deposit; the English version is narrated by ex-007 Roger Moore) are available at the gate itself, through the door to the right. Those looking to spend more money can hire **"English"-speaking tour guides** on the other side of the gate (¥200–¥350/$25–$44 per person, depending on tour length). The tour guide booth also rents **wheelchairs** and **strollers** at reasonable rates. *Note:* Only the central route through the palace is wheelchair-accessible, and steeply so.

BACKGROUND & LAYOUT

Construction of the original palace buildings began in 1406, during the reign of the Yǒnglè emperor, and took an army of workers 14 years to complete. A single moat, 52m (171 ft.) wide and nearly 4km (2½ miles) long, surrounds it. Between 1420 and 1923, the palace was home to 24 emperors of the Míng and

The Big Makeover

Běijīng recently launched an immense **$75-million renovation of the Forbidden City,** the largest in 90 years, to be completed in two phases (the first by 2008, the second by 2020). Work started on halls and gardens in the closed **western sections of the palace** in 2002, with the most effort concentrated on opening the Wǔyīng Diàn (Hall of Valiance and Heroism) in the southwest corner of the palace, followed by Cíníng Huāyuán (Garden of Love and Tranquillity) next to the Tàihé Diàn. No one can say exactly when visitors will be allowed in; all you can do now is peer through door cracks on the left side of the outer court. Plans also call for the construction of new temperature-controlled buildings to house and exhibit what is claimed to be a collection of **930,000 Míng and Qīng imperial relics,** most now stored underground.

Welcome as the project is, China's track record of tacky restorations has made many people nervous. Shortly after the plans were announced, the *China Youth Daily* launched a **call for public hearings** to approve the details, claiming in typical language that any changes to the complex "will have psychological influences on all Chinese people." The suggestion was politely rejected, but an incongruous coat of bright red paint recently slapped over parts of the palace's Gate of Heavenly Purity indicates that more input might not be a bad thing.

Qīng dynasties. The last of these was Aisin-Gioro Pǔyí, who was forced to abdicate in 1912 but was allowed to remain in the palace for several years afterward.

The Forbidden City is arranged along a north-south meridian, aligned on the Pole Star. The Qīng court was unimpressed when the barbarians designated Greenwich Royal Observatory as the source of the prime meridian in 1885; they believed the Imperial Way marked the center of the temporal world. Major halls open to the south. Furthest south and in the center is the symmetrical **outer court,** dominated by immense ceremonial halls where the emperor conducted official business. Beyond the outer court and surrounding it on both sides is the **inner court,** a series of smaller buildings and gardens that served as living quarters.

The palace has been ransacked and parts destroyed by fire several times over the centuries, so most of the existing buildings date from the Qīng rather than the Míng. The original complex was said to contain 9,999 rooms, testament to the Chinese love of the number nine (see the box "Lucky Numbers," p. 125), and also to an unusual counting method. The square space between columns is counted as a room *(jiān)*, so the largest building, **Tàihé Diàn,** counts as 55 rooms. Using the Western method of counting, there are now 980 rooms. Only half of the complex is open to visitors (expected to increase to 70% after repairs are completed in 2020; see the box, "The Big Makeover" above), but this still leaves plenty to see.

THE ENTRANCE GATES

Tiān'ān Mén (Gate of Heavenly Peace) ★★   This gate is the largest in what was once known as the Imperial City and the most emblematic of Chinese government grandeur. Above the central door, once reserved almost exclusively for the emperor, now hangs the famous **portrait of Máo,** flanked by inscriptions that read: LONG LIVE THE PEOPLE'S REPUBLIC OF CHINA (left) and LONG LIVE THE GREAT UNITY OF THE PEOPLES OF THE WORLD (right). Máo declared the founding of the People's Republic from atop the gate on October 1, 1949. There is no charge to walk through, but tickets are required if you want to ascend to the **upper platform** for worthwhile views of Tiān'ān Mén Square. Pretend to be the Great Helmsman addressing a sea of Red Guards, all struggling to understand your thick Húnán accent and waving your little red book. Note the pair of *huábiǎo* (ornamental columns) topped with lions, wreathed in dragons and clouds, and facing the square. In their original form, *huábiǎo* were wooden posts in the shapes of a battle-axes, upon which subjects would attach petitions or scrawl their grievances to the king. Over time, their function was reversed. Turned to stone and wreathed in the ultimate symbol of the emperor's mandate—the dragon—they became a warning to the ruled to keep out.

North of Tiān'ān Mén Sq.; ticket office to left as you enter. Admission ¥20 ($3) in summer, ¥15 ($2) in winter. Daily, 8am–4:30pm in summer; 8:30am–4pm in winter. Mandatory bag storage (¥2–¥6/30¢–75¢) behind and to left of ticket booth; cameras allowed.

Wǔ Mén (Meridian Gate)   The trees leading up to this gate are recent additions. Originally no trees were planted along the Imperial Way, stretching over 2km (1¼ miles) from **Dà Qīng Mén** (now demolished) to **Qiánqīng Mén (Gate of Heavenly Purity)** in the Inner Court, as according to the "five processes" *(wǔ xíng)*, wood (green) subdues earth (yellow), the element associated with the emperor (hence the yellow glazed tiles). The **Outer Court** is also free of trees. Built in 1420 and last restored in 1801, Wǔ Mén is the actual entrance to the Forbidden City. The emperor would sit atop the gate to receive prisoners of war, flanked by a battalion of imperial guards clad in full battle armor. The prisoners, clad in chains and red cloth, kneeled in the courtyard while charges were read before the emperor confirmed they would be taken to the marketplace for execution. The order would be repeated first by two, then four, then eight officers, until the entire battalion was thundering the edict in unison. The watchtowers extending out either side of the gate *(què)* are an expression of imperial power. This style was prevalent during the Hàn dynasty (206 B.C.–220 A.D.); this is the only example from the Míng and Qīng.

Tàihé Mén (Gate of Great Harmony)   Immediately inside the Meridian Gate entrance is a wide courtyard with five marble bridges spanning the Jīn Hé (Golden River), followed by Tàihé Mén. Míng emperors came here to consult with their ministers; this function moved further inside under the Qīng.

THE OUTER COURT (QIÁN CHÁO)

Tàihé Diàn (Hall of Great Harmony) ★★   Located beyond Tàihé Mén, and across an even grander stone courtyard, is an imposing double-roofed structure mounted atop a three-tiered marble terrace with elaborately carved balustrades. This is the largest wooden hall in China, and the most elaborate and prestigious of the palaces' throne halls; it was therefore rarely used. Emperors came here to mark the New Year and winter solstice. Note the row of ceramic figurines on the roof, led by a man on a chicken (a despotic and despised prince) fleeing a terrible dragon that heads a group of nine animal figures. The number of figures reflects the importance of the building.

Zhōnghé Diàn (Hall of Middle Harmony)   The second great hall of the outer court houses a smaller imperial throne. The emperor would prepare for various annual rites, such as sowing the fields at the Altar of Agriculture (Xiān Nóng Tán; see Gǔdài Jiànzhù Bówùguǎn, p. 139) in spring, by examining the appropriate manuals here.

Bǎohé Diàn (Hall of Preserving Harmony) This last hall, supported by only a few columns, is where the highest level of imperial examinations was held until the exams were suspended in 1901 and abolished in 1905. To the southwest, you can spy **Wényuán Gé** (the former Imperial Archive), easily recognized by its black-tiled roof with green trim. (Black is associated with water which, it was hoped, would protect the building from fire.) At the rear of Bǎo Hé Diàn is an impressive carved marble slab weighing over 200 tons; 20,000 men supposedly spent 28 days dragging it to this position from a mountain roughly 50km (31 miles) away.

THE INNER COURT (NÈI TÍNG)

Only the emperor, his family, his concubines, and the palace eunuchs (who numbered 1,500 at the end of the Qīng dynasty) were allowed in this section, sometimes described as the truly forbidden city. It begins with the **Qiánqīng Mén (Gate of Heavenly Purity)**, directly north of the Bǎohé Diàn, fronted by a magnificent pair of **bronze lions** and flanked by a **Bā Zì Yǐngbì** (a screen wall in the shape of the character for "eight"), both warning non-royals not to stray inside. Beyond are three palaces designed to mirror the three halls of the Outer Court.

The first of these is the **Qiánqīng Gōng (Palace of Heavenly Purity)**, where the emperors lived until Yǒngzhèng decided to move to the western side of the palace in the 1720s. Beyond is **Jiāotài Diàn (Hall of Union)**, containing the throne of the empress and 25 boxes that once contained the Qīng imperial seals. A considerable expansion on eight seals used during the Qín dynasty, the number 25 was chosen because it is the sum of all single-digit odd numbers (see the box "Lucky Numbers," p. 125). Next is the more interesting **Kūnníng Gōng (Palace of Earthly Tranquility)**, a Manchu-style bedchamber where a nervous Pǔyí was expected to spend his wedding night before he fled to more comfortable rooms elsewhere.

At the rear of the inner court is the elaborate **Yù Huāyuán (Imperial Garden)**, a marvelous scattering of ancient conifers, rockeries, and pavilions said to be largely unchanged since it was built in the Míng dynasty. Pǔyí's British tutor, Reginald Fleming Johnston, lived in the **Yǎngxīn Zhāi,** the first building on the west side of the garden (now a tea shop).

From behind the mountain, you can exit the palace through the **Shénwǔ Mén (Gate of Martial Spirit)** and continue on to Jǐng Shān and/or Běi Hǎi Park. Those with time to spare, however, should take the opportunity to explore less-visited sections on either side of the central path.

WESTERN AXIS

Most of this area is in a state of heavy disrepair, but a few buildings have been restored and are open to visitors. Most notable among these is the **Yǎngxīn Diàn (Hall of Mental Cultivation)**, southwest of the Imperial Garden. The reviled Empress Dowager Cíxǐ, who ruled China for much of the late Qīng period, made decisions on behalf of her infant nephew, the Guāngxù emperor, from behind a screen in the east room. This is also where emperors lived after Yǒngzhèng moved out of the Qiánqīng Gōng.

EASTERN AXIS

This side tends to be peaceful and quiet even when other sections are teeming. Entrance costs ¥10 ($1.25) and requires purchase of useless over-shoe slippers which quickly disintegrate (¥2/30¢). The most convenient ticket booth is 5 minutes' walk southwest of the Qiánqīng Mén, opposite **Jiǔlóng Bì (Nine Dragon Screen)**, a 3.5m (11½-ft.) -high wall covered in striking glazed-tile

(**Fun Fact** Lucky Numbers

The layout of imperial Běijīng is based on an ancient system of numerology that still resonates today. Odd numbers are seen as *yáng* (male, positive, light) and are more auspicious than even numbers, which are viewed as *yīn* (female, negative, dark). **Three** is a positive number, as seen in the three-tiered platforms that are reserved for Běijīng's most sacred structures—Tàihé Diàn in the Forbidden City; Tài Miào, the Hall of Prayer for Good Harvests at Tiān Tán; and Cháng Líng at the Míng Tombs. It's also the number chosen for China's latest political theory, the Three Represents, which explains how a Communist party can be staffed by capitalists. **Four** *(sì)*, as a *yīn* number, signifies submission. When the emperor carried out sacrifices at the Temple of Heaven, he would face north and bow four times. It's also faintly homophonous with death *(sǐ)*, and is the most inauspicious number in present-day China. Máo, the Communist Party, and the Chinese people all escaped blame for the horror of the Cultural Revolution because it was blamed on four naughty people—the Gang of Four *(sì rén bāng)*. **Five** is revered as the center of the Luò Diagram (which allows single-digit numbers arranged in noughts-and-crosses formation to add up to 15), and for signifying the "five processes" *(wǔ xíng)*—metal, wood, water, fire, and earth, which also correspond to the five points of the Chinese compass and to the five colors. Significant imperial buildings are five rooms *(jiān)* deep; five openings welcome you into Tiān'ān Mén; and until Zhōnghuá Mén was razed to make way for Máo's corpse, the Imperial Way had five gates. **Eight** has gained popularity because it is homophonous with "get rich" in Cantonese. **Nine**, situated at the top of the Luò Diagram and the largest single-digit odd number, was reserved for the imperial house, with grand buildings measuring nine rooms across.

dragons depicted frolicking above a frothing sea, built to protect the Qiánlóng emperor from prying eyes and malevolent spirits (that are only able to move in straight lines). The Qiánlóng emperor (reign 1736–1795) abdicated at the age of 85 in favor of his son (so as not to rule for longer than his grandfather, the Kāngxī emperor) and lived here in seclusion for 4 years while his favorite official, Heshen, set about plundering the imperial coffers. Empress Dowager Cíxǐ also took up residence here in 1894.

Zhēnbǎo Guǎn (Hall of Jewelry) ✵, just north of the ticket booth, has all 25 of the Qīng imperial seals, ornate swords, and bejeweled mini-pagodas—evidence that the Qīng emperors were devoted to Tibetan Buddhism. In a piece of creative history, one caption claims that this was a ruse to maintain their "rule" over the Tibetans. One of the highlights is the secluded **Níngshòu Gōng Huāyuán** ✵✵✵, where the Qiánlóng emperor spent his retirement. Water was directed along a snake-like trough carved in the floor of the main pavilion. A cup of wine would be floated down the miniature stream, and the person nearest wherever it stopped would have to compose a poem, or drink the wine. The Qiánlóng emperor, whose personal compendium of verse ran to a modest 50,000 poems, was rarely short of words.

East of the garden is the **Chàngyīn Gé,** sometimes called Cíxǐ's Theater, an elaborate green-tiled three-tiered structure with trap doors and hidden passageways to allow movement between stages. Further north is sumptuous **Lèshòu Táng** ★★, built entirely from sandalwood, where the Qiánlóng emperor would read, surrounded by poems and paintings composed by loyal ministers set into the walls and framed by blue cloisonné tablets. Cíxǐ slept in the room to the west. The following hall, **Yíhé Xuān,** is not a good place to bring friends from Mongolia or Xīnjiāng. The west wall has an essay justifying the Qiánlóng emperor's decision to colonize the latter, while the east wall has a poem celebrating the invasion of Mongolia. In the far northeastern corner is **Zhēn Fēi Jǐng (Well of the Pearl Concubine),** a surprisingly narrow hole covered by a large circle of stone. The Pearl Concubine, one of the Guāngxù emperor's favorites, was 25 when Cíxǐ had her stuffed down the well by a eunuch as they were fleeing in the aftermath of the Boxer Rebellion. According to most accounts, Cíxǐ was miffed at the girl's insistence that Guāngxù stay and take responsibility for the imperial family's support of the Boxers.

Also worth seeing is the **Hall of Clocks (Zhōngbiǎo Guǎn),** a collection of elaborate timepieces, many of them gifts to the emperors from European envoys. Entrance to the exhibit costs ¥10 ($1.25). At press time it had been temporarily relocated in a hall to the right (east) of the Bǎohé Diàn, while the original Hall of Clocks was being restored.

3 Temple of Heaven (Tiān Tán Gōngyuán)

At the same time that the Yónglè emperor built the Forbidden City, he also oversaw construction of this enormous park and altar to Heaven directly to the south. Each winter solstice, the Míng and Qīng emperors would lead a procession here to perform rites and make sacrifices designed to promote the next year's crops and curry favor with Heaven for the general health of the empire. It was last used for this purpose by the president of the Republic, Yuán Shìkǎi, on the winter solstice of December 23, 1914, updated with photographers, electric lights (the height of modernity at the time), and a bulletproof car for the entrance of the increasingly unpopular president. This effectively announced his intent to promote himself as the new emperor, but few of the onlookers shared his enthusiasm. Formerly known as the Temple of Heaven and Earth, the park is square (symbolizing Earth) in the south and rounded (symbolizing Heaven) in the north.

ESSENTIALS

Temple of Heaven Park (Tiāntán Gōngyuán; ✆ 010/6702-8866) is south of Tiān'ān Mén Square, on the east side of Qián Mén Dàjiē. It's open daily from 5am to 9:30pm (6am–8pm in winter), but the ticket offices and major sights are only open from 8:30am to 4:30pm. All-inclusive tickets *(lián piào)* cost ¥35 ($4.50) (¥30/$4 in winter); simple park admission costs ¥15 ($2). The east gate *(dōng mén)* is easily accessed by public transport; take the no. 807 or no. 812 bus from just north of the Chóngwén Mén metro stop (209, exit B) to Fǎhuá Sì. However, the best approach is from the south gate *(nán mén),* the natural starting point for a walk that culminates in the magnificent Hall of Prayer for Good Harvests.

SEEING THE HIGHLIGHTS

During the Cultural Revolution, Tiān Tán lost its perfect symmetry as large bites were taken out of the southwest and southeast corners. There's no sign that the land will be returned, with massive apartment blocks ready to sprout on

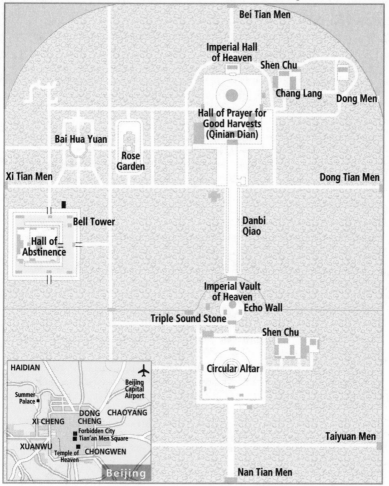

Bei Tian Men

Imperial Hall
of Heaven

Shen Chu

Chang Lang

Dong Men

Hall of Prayer for
Good Harvests
(Qinian Dian)

Bai Hua Yuan

Rose
Garden

Xi Tian Men

Dong Tian Men

Bell Tower

Danbi
Qiao

Hall of
Abstinence

Imperial Vault
of Heaven

Echo Wall

Triple Sound Stone

Shen Chu

Circular Altar

HAIDIAN

Beijing
Capital
Airport

Summer
Palace

DONG   CHAOYANG
CHENG

XI CHENG

Forbidden City
Tian'an Men Square

XUANWU   Temple of   CHONGWEN
Heaven

Beijing

Taiyuan Men

Nan Tian Men

both corners, but it's still a vast park taking at least 2 hours to see in any depth. The west gate is convenient to the Altar of Agriculture (see Gǔdài Jiànzhù Bówùguǎn, p. 139), Tiānqiáo Happy Tea House (p. 182), and Wànshèng Jùchǎng (see section 1, "Performing Arts" in chapter 9). At the northeast corner lie the shopping delights of Yuánlóng Silk Co. Ltd. (p. 176) and Hóng Qiáo Shìchǎng (see section 2, "Markets & Bazaars" in chapter 8).

Circular Altar (Yuán Qiū)   This three-tiered marble terrace is the first major structure you'll see if you enter from the south gate *(nán mén)*. It was built in 1530 and enlarged in 1749, with all of its stones and balustrades organized in multiples of nine (see the box "Lucky Numbers," p. 125). Here, a slaughtered bull would be set ablaze, the culmination of an elaborate ceremonial entreaty to the gods.

Imperial Vault of Heaven (Huáng Qióng Yǔ)   Directly north of the Circular Altar, this smaller version of the Hall of Prayer (see below) was built to store ceremonial stone tablets. The vault is surrounded by the circular **Echo**

> **Fun Fact** Imperial Gridiron
>
> British forces camped in the grounds of Tiān Tán following the suppres-
> sion of the Boxer Rebellion of 1900 but, in theory, the grounds were as
> much off-limits to common folk as the Inner Court of the Forbidden City
> or the Imperial Tombs. In 1913, Tiān Tán was opened to foreigners from
> the old **Legation Quarter,** to the north of Tiān Tán, and became a popular
> picnic spot. Yuán Shìkǎi, already dreaming of reviving the imperial rites,
> had ordered that the park remain closed to the public. But he was pow-
> erless to stop a handful of profit-minded park wardens. British troops
> enjoyed games of cricket here, and Yuán penned a furious letter to the
> American government, complaining that their troops were damaging the
> temples and the "old trees" with their "rough" games of football.

Wall (Huíyīn Bì). In years past, when crowds were smaller and before the railing was installed, it was possible for two people on opposite sides of the enclosure to send whispered messages to each other along the wall with remarkable
clarity. You can still experience this magical acoustic effect at the Western Qīng
Tombs (see section 4 in chapter 10), but unless there's another outbreak of
SARS, there's little hope of enjoying it here.

Hall of Prayer for Good Harvests (Qīnián Diàn) ★★   Undoubtedly the
most stunning building in Běijīng, this circular wooden hall, with its triple-
eaved cylindrical blue-tiled roof, is perhaps the most recognizable emblem of
Chinese imperial architecture outside of the Forbidden City. Completed in
1420, the original hall was struck by lightning and burned to the ground in
1889 (not a good omen for the dynasty), but a near-perfect replica was built the
following year. Measuring 38m (125 ft.) high and 30m (98 ft.) in diameter, it
was constructed without a single nail. The 28 massive pillars inside, made of fir
imported from Oregon, are arranged to symbolize divisions of time: The central
four represent the seasons, the next 12 represent the months of the year, and the
outer 12 represent traditional divisions of a single day. The hall's most striking
feature is its ceiling, a kaleidoscope of painted brackets and gilded panels as intricate as anything in the country. Don't skip the **Imperial Hall of Heaven
(Huángqián Diàn),** a smaller building to the north where the emperor would
pray before the wooden tablets of his ancestors. Although Red Guards ruined
the tablets, the balustrades surrounding this prayer hall are elegantly carved.

Hall of Abstinence (Zhāi Gōng)   Yuán Shìkǎi fasted for 3 days in his own
residence rather than here, as tradition dictated. Perhaps this was his undoing
(he died 1½ years later). Real emperors would fast and pray for 5 days, spending their final night in the **Living Hall (Qǐn Diàn)** at the rear of this compound. Note the rare swastika emblems, a symbol of longevity in China, on the
door piers. This green-tiled double-moated compound faces east, the best side
at which to enter. The grounds are agreeably dilapidated, and are on a much
more human scale than the rest of the compound.

4 Summer Palace (Yíhé Yuán)

This expanse of elaborate Qīng-style pavilions, bridges, walkways, and gardens,
scattered along the shores of immense Kūnmíng Lake, is the grandest imperial
playground in China, constructed from 1749 to 1764. Between 1860 and 1903,

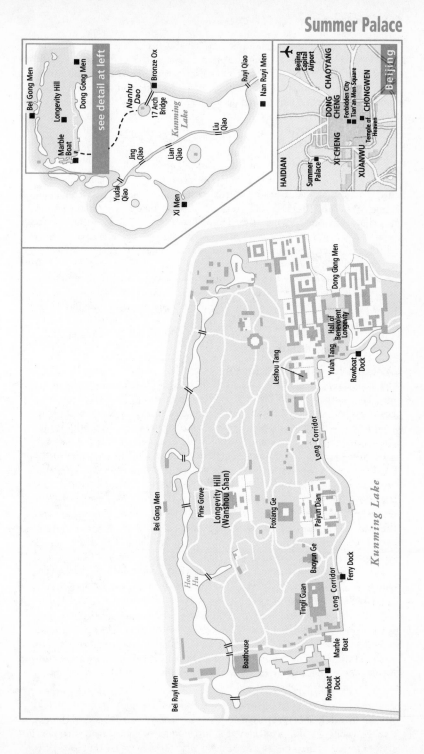

Beijing

Beijing Capital Airport

CHAOYANG

DONG CHENG

XI CHENG

Forbidden City

Tian'an Men Square

Temple of Heaven

CHONGWEN

XUANWU

HAIDIAN

Summer Palace

Bei Gong Men

Longevity Hill

Dong Gong Men

Bronze Ox

Nanhu Dao

17 Arch Bridge

Ruyi Qiao

Nan Ruyi Qiao

see detail at left

Kunming Lake

Liu Qiao

Marble Boat

Lian Qiao

Jing Qiao

Yudai Qiao

Xi Men

Dong Gong Men

Hall of Benevolent Longevity

Yulan Tang

Rowboat Dock

Leshou Tang

Long Corridor

Bei Gong Men

Pine Grove

Longevity Hill (Wanshou Shan)

Foxiang Ge

Paiyun Dian

Hou Hu

Baoyun Ge

Ferry Dock

Tingli Guan

Long Corridor

Kunming Lake

Boathouse

Marble Boat

Bei Ruyi Men

Rowboat Dock

it was twice leveled by foreign armies and rebuilt; hence it is often called the New Summer Palace, even though it pre-dates the ruined Old Summer Palace (Yuán Míng Yuán, p. 138). The palace is most often associated with the Empress Dowager Cíxǐ, who made it her full-time residence. The grounds were declared a public park in 1924 and spruced up in 1949.

ESSENTIALS

The **Summer Palace** (© **010/6288-1144**) is located 12km (7 miles) northwest of the city center in Hǎidiàn. Take **bus no. 726** from just west of Wǔdàokǒu light rail station (1304, exit A); or take a 30- to 40-minute **taxi** ride (¥60/$8) from the center of town. A more pleasant option is to travel there by **boat** along the reno-vated canal system; slightly rusty "imperial yachts" leave from the Běizhǎn Hòuhú Mǎtóu (© **010/8836-3576**), behind the Běijīng Exhibition Center just south of the Běijīng Aquarium (50-min. trip; ¥40/$5 one-way, ¥70/$9 round-trip), dock-ing at Nán Rúyì Mén in the south of the park. The gates open daily at 7am; no tickets are sold after 5pm in summer and 4pm in winter. Admission is ¥30 ($4) for entry to the grounds or ¥50 ($6) for the all-inclusive *lián piào*, reduced to ¥20 ($2.50) and ¥40 ($5) respectively in winter (Nov–Mar). The most convenient entrance is Dōng Gōng Mén (East Gate). Go early and allow at least 4 hours for touring the major sites on your own. Overpriced **imperial-style food** in a pleas-ant setting is available at the Tīnglí Guǎn Restaurant, at the western end of the Long Corridor. Spots around the lake are perfect for picnics, and Kūnmíng Lake is ideal for skating in the depths of winter.

EXPLORING THE SUMMER PALACE

This park covers roughly 290 hectares (716 acres), with **Kūnmíng Lake** in the south and **Longevity Hill (Wànshòu Shān)** in the north. The lake's northern shore boasts most of the buildings and other attractions and is the most popu-lar area for strolls, although walking around the smaller lakes (Hòu Hú) behind Longevity Hill is more pleasant. The hill itself has a number of temples as well as **Bǎoyún Gé (Precious Clouds Pavilion),** one of the few structures in the palace to escape destruction by foreign forces. There are literally dozens of pavil-ions and a number of bridges to be found on all sides of the lake, enough to make for a full day of exploration. Rather slow electric-powered boats may be rented; they are an appealing option on muggy summer days.

Rénshòu Diàn (Hall of Benevolence and Longevity)   Located directly across the courtyard from the east gate entrance, Rénshòu Diàn is the palace's main hall. This is where the Empress Dowager received members of the court, first from behind a screen and later, all pretenses dropped, from the Dragon Throne itself. North of the hall is Cíxǐ's private theater, now a museum that con-tains an old Mercedes-Benz—the first car imported into China.

Long Corridor (Cháng Láng) ✦   Among the more memorable attractions in Běijīng, this covered wooden promenade stretches 700m (nearly half a mile) along the northern shore of Kūnmíng Lake. Each crossbeam, ceiling, and pillar is painted with a different scene (roughly 10,000 in all) taken from Chinese his-tory, literature, myth, or geography. Politely rebuff the "students" who offer to show you their "original art" at this spot.

Marble Boat (Shí Fǎng)   Docked at the end of the Long Corridor is an odd structure which is "neither marble nor a boat," as one novelist observed. Locals, keen to blame the Empress Dowager for China's decline during the Qīng dynasty, wring their hands and cite it as the symbol of China's demise. Cíxǐ funded a general restoration of the palace using money intended for the Chinese navy, and the (completely frivolous) boat is said to be Cíxǐ's backhanded reference to the source of the funds. Shortly after the restoration was completed in 1888, China's paltry fleet was destroyed in a skirmish with Japan, the loudest evidence yet of China's weakness in the modern era. But as writer John Blofeld's redoubtable companion, Professor Ch'eng, pointed out in the 1930s (as quoted in Blofeld's *City of Lingering Splendour*, 1961): "Most people hate the Old Buddha (Cíxǐ) for diverting the naval funds. How unjust! Any navy we built in those days would have been destroyed in the first battle. Which of our enemies would have helped us build a fleet capable of destroying a single ship of theirs? They would have sent our fleet to the bottom of the sea and then charged us with the costs of the action, as they always did! As it is, the Old Buddha's palace still stands—they say there is nothing equal to it in the world! Could anyone, Chinese or foreign, of our generation duplicate it?"

Seventeen-Arch Bridge (Shíqī Kǒng Qiáo) ★   This marble bridge, 150m (490 ft.) long, connects South Lake Island (Nán Hú Dǎo) to the east shore of Kūnmíng Lake. There is a rather striking life-size bronze ox near the eastern foot of the bridge.

5 Temples, Mosques & Churches

While signs around Běijīng whip up indignation at the destruction of Chinese temples by foreign forces in 1860 and 1900, most destruction was carried out by the Chinese themselves, particularly after 1949. Medium-size houses of worship— Buddhist, Christian, Confucian, Daoist, and Muslim alike—fared badly; many were torn down straight away, while others were converted to factories, hospitals, schools, or police stations. With the realization by the Chinese authorities that tourists are willing to pay money to inspect them, some have been converted back to a semblance of their original form, if not function.

Bái Tǎ Sì (White Dagoba Temple)   Renovated in 1998 and again in 2003, this Liáo dynasty temple features the largest Tibetan pagoda (also called *chorten, dagoba* or *stupa*) in China, towering over the neighborhood at 51m (167 ft.) tall. A Nepali architect built it over 700 years ago (completed 1279) by order of Kublai Khan, one of the first Mongols to convert to Tibetan Buddhism. Originally known as Miào Yīng Sì, the temple has undergone numerous reconstructions, usually as a result of fire. The Dàjué Diàn (Hall of the Great Enlightened Ones), the first building, contains thousands of little Buddhas in glass cases, set into the columns. An earthquake in 1976 turned up numerous artifacts, some of which are now on display in the museum. You'll find Buddhist statuary demonstrating ritualistic hand positions *(mudra)*, a sutra copied out by the Qiánlóng emperor, and vivid *thangka* (silk hangings depicting Buddhist images). Just to the east is a potentially fascinating temple, **Lìdài Dìwáng Miào (Temple for Emperors of Past Dynasties)**, which should open in October 2004. Constructed during the 1530s to house the ancestral tablets of the emperors of "Chinese" dynasties—the Hàn, Táng, and Sòng, it was expanded by Qīng emperors to include not only their Míng predecessors, but also the "barbarian" rulers of the Liáo, Jīn, and Yuán.

Fùchéng Mén Nèi Dàjiē 171, Xī Chéng Qū (a 10-min. walk east from the metro stop); map p. 104. © **010/ 6616-0023.** Admission ¥10 ($1.25). Daily 9am–4:30pm. Metro: Fùchéng Mén (203, exit B).

Báiyún Guàn ⭐⭐ If the incense here somehow smells more authentic, it's because this sprawling complex, said to have been built in 739, is the most active of Běijīng's Daoist temples. Chinese visitors seem intent on actual worship rather than smug tourism, and the blue-frocked monks wear their hair in the rarely seen traditional manner—long and tied in a bun at the top of the head. The temple acts as headquarters for the Chinese Daoist Association. Although the texts of Daoism (China's only native religion) decry the pursuit of wealth and honors as empty, the gods of wealth attract the most devotees. One notable structure is the Láolù Táng, a large cushion-filled hall in the third courtyard originally built in 1228, now used for teaching and ceremonies.

On Báiyún Guàn Lù, east of the intersection with Báiyún Lù (1st right north of Báiyún Qiáo, directly across from Báiyún Guàn bus stop), Hǎidiàn Qū; map p. 108. ℂ 010/6327-2151. Admission ¥10 ($1.25). Daily 8:30am–4:30pm. Bus: 717 or 727 from Mùxīdì metro (112) to Báiyún Guàn.

Dōng Táng (East Church or St. Joseph's Cathedral) This gray Gothic structure has endured torrid history. Built on ground donated by the Shùnzhì emperor in 1655, this Jesuit church was toppled by an earthquake in 1720, then gutted by fire in 1812, after which it was leveled by an increasingly anti-foreign regime. It was rebuilt after foreigners forced their way into Běijīng in 1860, and was razed again during the Boxer Rebellion of 1900. Chinese Christians were the first targets of the xenophobic Boxers, who disparagingly referred to them as "lesser hairy ones." Local converts were slaughtered in the hundreds before the Boxers (who also murdered women with unbound feet) worked up the courage to kill a real foreigner. Yet they are usually portrayed as a "patriotic" movement in China's history books. After a major renovation in 2000, Dōng Táng is notable for its wide, tree-lined forecourt, a favorite spot for Běijīng's skateboarders. Its counterpart in the south of town, **Nán Táng (South Church)** is just northeast of the Xuānwǔ Mén metro stop, and has services in English. Call ℂ **010/6602-5221** to check times. *Note:* Catholic churches in Běijīng are not recognized by the Roman Catholic Church.

Wángfǔjǐng Dàjiē 74 (walk north for 10 min.), Dōg Chéng Qū; map p. 104. ℂ **010/6524-0634.** Sunday services in Chinese and Latin at 6:15am, 7am, and 8am. Metro: Wángfǔjǐng (118, exit A).

Dōng Yuè Miào ⭐⭐ *Finds* Reopened to the public in 1999, one of Běijīng's most captivating Daoist temples stands largely disregarded. Founded in 1322 by the devotees of the Zhèngyī sect, the temple is dedicated to the god Dōng Yuè, who resides in the sacred mountain of Tài Shān. Aside from coping with the hordes of tourists who now visit his abode, Dōng Yuè is charged with supervising the 18 layers of Hell and the 76 departments (*sī*).

The garishly represented emissaries of these departments may be conveniently found in the 72 halls that ring the main courtyard of the temple. Worshippers present themselves at the relevant hall, with offerings of money, incense, and red tokens inscribed with their names (*fúpái*). With 76 departments (some are forced to share a cubicle), there are emissaries for every conceivable aspiration, and if viewed as a straw poll of China's preoccupations, the results are not encouraging. The Department for Accumulating Wealth ("justifiable" is added in the translation) is the busiest, while the Department of Pity and Sympathy, depicting beggars, awaits its first petition. The Deep-Rooted Disease Department was kept busy during the SARS hysteria, but there were still an alarming number of donations for the Department for Implementing 15 Kinds of Violent Death. This may or may not be related to the ongoing popularity of the Department of Official Morality, which rails against corrupt government.

A glassed-in stele at the northeast corner of the courtyard is written in the fine hand of Zhào Mèngfǔ, recording the building of the temple and the life of its founder, Zhāng Liúsūn, who died soon after purchasing the land. At the north of the complex stands the two-story Mínsú Bówùguǎn (Folk Museum). This hosts exhibitions to remind Beijingers of their marvelous but largely forgotten traditions. Admission is free during traditional Chinese festivals.

Cháoyáng Mén Wài Dàjiē 141, Cháoyáng Qū (10-min. walk east on the north side); map p. 115. 𝒞 010/6551-0151. Admission ¥10 ($1.25). Tues–Sun 8am–4:30pm. Metro: Cháoyáng Mén (212, exit B).

Fǎhǎi Sì   Located in the far west of Běijīng, this early Míng temple is not worth a trip in itself, but it is easily combined with a visit to the cemetery for eunuchs, **Tiányì Mù** (p. 143). This temple was funded by a wealthy eunuch who attracted artisans from all over China to produce stunning murals and statuary, under the close eye of artists from the imperial court. The statues didn't survive the Cultural Revolution, but several exquisite Buddhist murals in the main hall remain untouched. A 2m (7-ft.) mural of Guānyīn (the Goddess of Compassion), clad in white gauze, is striking, as are murals of the fierce four heavenly kings which guard the entrance. These murals were modeled on the art of the Táng, and show Central Asian influences. The hall is dimly lit, so take a torch.

Móshì Kǒu Dàjiē, Shíjīng Shān Qū. (From bus stop, continue up the rise and take a right after 5 min. Pass Tiányì Mù, take a left turn, and continue uphill to a T-junction. Take a right turn; the temple is immediately ahead.) Map p. 112. 𝒞 010/8871-5776. Admission ¥20 ($2.50). Tues–Sun 9am–4pm. Bus: 959 or 746 from left of Píngguǒ Yuán metro stop (103, exit D) to Shǒugāng Xiǎoqū.

Guǎnghuà Sì   The only one to survive on the eastern shores of the Back Lakes, the "Great Transformation" temple is named for a wandering monk who ate only half the rice he received from the people and used the other portion to help pay for (or be "transformed" into) this temple. Guǎnghuà Sì is best visited on the 1st and 15th days of the month, when believers praying for the success of their latest business venture overrun it. In residence are at least 20 monks, many from southern China. China's last known eunuch, Sūn Yàotíng, was caretaker of the temple for 2 decades, and died here in 1996.

On the southeast shore of Hòu Hǎi on Yā'ér Hútòng, west of the Drum Tower, Xī Chéng Qū; map p. 104. 𝒞 010/6403-5032. Free admission. Daily 8am–5pm. Metro: Gǔ Lóu (217).

Guó Zǐ Jiàn and Kǒng Miào ⚔   This classic temple-school compound, buried down a tree-shaded street west of the Lama Temple (see below), is still in use. **Kǒng Miào,** China's second largest Confucian temple, is on the right, and **Guó Zǐ Jiàn (Directorate of Education)** is on the left; both were originally built in 1306. Two stelae at the front *(xià mǎ bēi)* instruct you to park your horse in six different languages. The front courtyard of the temple contains 198 stelae inscribed with the names of successful candidates in the *jìnshì* (highest level) imperial examinations during the Yuán, Míng, and Qīng dynasties. To the right of the second courtyard is **Shǒudū Bówùguǎn** ⚔, a well-displayed history of Běijīng, due to be relocated to a new museum in 2005. Noteworthy exhibits include a terra-cotta duck and a white jade statue of Guān Yīn, looking casual with her leg up. Staff admit they see few local visitors, except during the weekend before the university entrance examinations, when students and their parents descend in droves to ask for the Great Sage's assistance. The main hall, **Dàchéng Diàn,** is the focus for students, who must throw their incense on the shrine rather than burn it, because of fire regulations. Ancient musical instruments, which

Confucius saw as essential to self-cultivation, are the main point of interest. Behind the hall and to the left are 189 stelae, which contain the 630,000 characters that make up the Thirteen Confucian Classics—incredibly, copied by one man over a 12-year period. The attendant enhances the mood of antiquity by earnestly reciting old texts.

Success in the imperial examination was the key to social advancement, so **Guó Zǐ Jiàn** wielded immense power. It was originally joined to Kǒng Miào by Chíjìng Mén, to the right as you enter. They will be reunited in 2005, if the Ministry of Culture (housed in Guó Zǐ Jiàn) and the Ministry of Cultural Relics (housed in Kǒng Miào) can sort out their differences. A striking yellow glazed-tile *páilou* with elaborately carved stone arches leads to **Bì Yōng Dàdiàn** ⭐, a square wooden hall encircled by a moat. The emperor would deliver a lecture on the classics here at the start of his reign, although the irrepressible Qiánlóng visited three times—after assuming the throne, after renovations were completed to mark the 50th anniversary of his reign, and when handing the throne over to his son, the Jiāqìng emperor. He even wrote poems to decorate the sandalwood screen behind the throne. Ministers and the royal family were permitted inside, while three criers (to the west, south, and east) would repeat the emperor's words to students and minor officials kneeling outside.

Kǒng Miào at Guó Zǐ Jiàn Jiē 13 (walk south from station along west side of Lama Temple, turn right onto street marked with arch), Dōg Chéng Qū; map p. 104. ☎ 010/8401-1977. Admission ¥10 ($1.25). Daily 8:30am–4:30pm. Guó Zǐ Jiàn next door: admission ¥6 (75¢); daily 9am–5pm. Metro: Yōnghé Gōng/Lama Temple (215, exit C).

Niú Jiē Lǐbài Sì (Niú Jiē Mosque)

This is Běijīng's largest mosque and the spiritual center for the city's estimated 200,000 Muslims. Built in 996, the complex looks more Eastern than Middle Eastern, with sloping tile roofs similar to those found in Buddhist temples. Halls are noticeably free of idols, however. A small courtyard on the south side contains the tombs and original gravestones of two Arab imams who lived here in the late 13th century. The main prayer hall is ghostly quiet except on Friday, the traditional day of worship.

Niú Jiē 88 (on east side of street), Xuānwǔ Qū; map p. 108. ☎ 010/6353-2564. Admission ¥10 ($1.25) for non-Muslims. Daily 8am–7pm. Bus: 61 to Lǐbài Sì from Chángchūn Jiē metro stop (205, exit D).

Tài Miào ⭐⭐ *Finds*

Sometimes the biggest surprises are under your nose. Just east of Tiān'ān Mén stands the only example of an imperial ancestral hall *(zǔ miào)* remaining in China; here are grand imperial edifices in a sleepy, atmospheric setting. Laid out in accordance with the ancient principle from the Rites of Zhōu, "Ancestors to the left, land to the right" *(zuǒ zǔ yòu shè)*, the wooden tablets *(páiwèi)* that represented the ancestors of the imperial house were housed to the left of the Forbidden City (the land was offered its due at the Altar of Land and Grain, housed in Zhōngshān Gōngyuán to the west). Beyond the Halberd Gate (Jǐ Mén), untouched since it was constructed in 1420, the three main buildings are lined up on a central axis. Sacrifices to the ancestors took place in the southernmost building (Xiǎng Diàn), which now houses an exhibit of bronze bells. This is one of only four buildings in Běijīng to stand on a three-tiered platform, a hint that it was the most sacred site in imperial Běijīng. Máo renamed it the Workers' Cultural Palace (Láodòng Rénmín Wénhuà Gōng), and the wooden tablets were pilfered during the Cultural Revolution. The workers have moved on, and the complex is largely deserted. Once you reach the moat at the northern end of the complex, turn left. Immediately opposite is **Zhōngshān Gōngyuán;** to the right stands **Wǔ Mén** and the Forbidden City. Infinitely preferable to running the souvenir vendor gauntlet north from Tiān'ān Mén, entering the Forbidden City from Tài Miào may be the best ¥2 you'll ever spend.

East of Tiān'ān Mén, Dōg Chéng Qū; map p. 104. 🅒 010/6525-2189. June–Sept 6am–10pm; Oct–May 6am–9pm. Admission ¥2 (25¢), admission to bell exhibit ¥15 ($2). Metro: Tiān'ān Mén Dōng (117, exit A).

Wànshòu Sì 🅐

The Longevity Temple, now home to the **Běijīng Art Museum (Běijīng Yìshù Bówùguǎn),** was funded by a eunuch and was originally constructed in 1557. It later became a stopping point for the Qiánlóng emperor and his successors (particularly the Empress Dowager Cíxǐ) on their way to the Summer Palace by boat, a route now followed by tour boats departing from just north of the zoo. The long sequence of heavily restored but low-key halls now houses an odd set of exhibitions, featuring everything from early ceramics, iron, and copperware, to late and very intricate lacquerware and carved ivory. Perhaps best of all is an exhibition of highly decorated and ancient seals, wrought from a variety of precious and semiprecious materials. At the rear of the complex is a rock garden from whose top Cíxǐ is supposed to have admired the surrounding countryside, now long built over.

Xī Sān Huán Běi Lù 18 (on north side of Cháng Hé, east side of the West Third Ring Road), Hǎidiàn Qū; map p. 112. 🅒 010/6841-3380. Admission ¥10 ($1.25). Tues–Sun 9am–5:30pm. Bus: 811 from Gōngzhǔ Fén metro stop (110) to Wànshòu Sì.

Wǔ Tǎ Sì (Five Pagoda Temple)

More correctly known as Zhēnjué Sì (Temple of True Awakening), the one ancient building remaining on this site is a massive stone block with magnificently preserved Indian Buddhist motifs carved out of the bare rock. Peacocks, elephants, and dharma wheels adorn the base, which is also decorated with sutras copied out in Sanskrit (the large script) and Tibetan (the small script). The central pagoda has an image of two feet, harking back to an age where artisans could only hint at the presence of Buddha through symbols. The surrounding courtyard is gradually filling up with stone tombstones, spirit-way figures, and stelae commemorating the construction or renovation of temples; most are refugees from construction and road-widening projects around the capital. The well-lit **Shíkè Yìshù Bówùguǎn (Stone Carving Museum)** 🅐 has finally opened at the rear of the complex, but most of the renovation money has gone toward building offices for the surly staff. The Běijīng Aquarium is a 15-minute walk to the northeast.

Wǔ Tǎ Sì Cūn 24 (from Běijīng Túshūguǎn walk south and turn left at the Náncháng Canal; the walk takes 10-min.), Hǎidiàn Qū; map p. 112. 🅒 010/6217-3836. Admission ¥10 ($1.25); climbing the pagoda ¥5 (60¢) extra. Daily 8:30am–4pm. Bus: 808 from just east of Xī Zhí Mén metro stop (201, exit B) to Běijīng Túshūguǎn.

Yōnghé Gōng (Lama Temple) 🅐🅐🅐

If you only visit one temple after the Temple of Heaven, this should be it. A complex of progressively larger buildings topped with ornate yellow-tiled roofs, Yōnghé Gōng was built in 1694 and originally belonged to the Qīng prince who would become the Yōngzhèng emperor. As was the custom, the complex was converted to a temple after Yōngzhèng's move to the Forbidden City in 1744. The temple is home to several rather beautiful **incense burners,** including a particularly ornate one in the second courtyard that dates back to 1746. The Fǎlún Diàn (Hall of the Wheel of Law), second to last of the major buildings, contains a 6m (20-ft.) bronze statue of Tsongkapa (1357–1419), the founder of the reformist Yellow Hat (Geluk) sect of Tibetan Buddhism, which is now the dominant school of Tibetan Buddhism. He's easily recognized by his pointed cap with long earflaps. The last of the five central halls, the Wànfú Gé (Tower of Ten Thousand Happinesses), houses the temple's prize possession—an ominous Tibetan-style **statue of Maitreya** (the future Buddha), 18m (60 ft.) tall, carved from a single piece of white sandalwood. Once something of a circus, the site is slowly starting to feel like a place of worship now that there is a large number of Chinese followers of Tibetan Buddhism.

Yōnghé Gōng Dàjiē 12, south of the North Second Ring Road (entrance on the south end of the complex); map p. 104. ℂ 010/6404-3769. Daily 9am–4pm. Admission ¥25 ($3); audio tours in English additional ¥25 ($3). Metro: Yōnghé Gōng/Lama Temple (215, exit C).

6 Parks & Gardens

Imperial parks, used either for sacrifices to the gods or for leisure activities, were off-limits to the common folk. Now they are overrun with them, particularly just after dawn, when the older generation turns out in force to practice *tàijíquán* and ballroom dancing, or to chat and show off their caged birds *(zǒu niǎo)*.

Běi Hǎi Gōngyuán (Běihǎi Park) ★ An imperial playground dating back to the Tartar Jīn dynasty (1115–1234), Běi Hǎi lies to the north of Zhōng Hǎi and Nán Hǎi, which were also opened to the public in 1925. In the best tradition of *Animal Farm*, the Communist leaders created a new Forbidden City and named it Zhōng Nán Hǎi. Běi Hǎi was left to the masses. Although it's a convenient way to combine a morning visit to the Forbidden City with a more relaxing afternoon in the Back Lakes area, most visitors have a quick peek at the southern half and then disappear. But the north side of the park is more interesting.

Entering from the south, you come to **Tuán Chéng (Round City),** a small citadel on a raised platform whose most notable structure, **Chéngguāng Diàn,** houses a 1.5m (5-ft.) tall statue of a feminine-looking Buddha, crafted from Burmese white jade. Crossing the Yǒng'ān Bridge to **Qióng Dǎo (Qióng Islet),** you pass the remains of a KFC on your left (deemed "inappropriate"— Starbucks in the Forbidden City must be nervous). Ahead is **Yǒng'ān Sì,** which provides further evidence of the Qīng emperors' devotion to Tibetan Buddhism. The founder of the prominent Geluk sect, Tsongkapa, is the focus of devotion. He is portrayed as a Chinese reformer of corrupt Tibetan Buddhism, on the grounds that he was born in Qīnghǎi rather than "autonomous" Tibet. Beyond the conspicuous white pagoda, the north part of the island houses the renowned but overrated imperial restaurant, **Fǎng Shàn Fànzhuāng** (p. 84). From here, boats run to the north side of the park (¥5/60¢), or you can walk around the east side, passing calligraphers wielding enormous sponge-tipped brushes to compose rapidly-evaporating poems on the flagstones.

Boats pull in to the east of **Wǔ Lóng Tīng (Five Dragon Pavilion),** where aspiring singers treat the public to revolutionary airs popular in the 1950s. Off to the left is an impressive green-tiled *páilou* (memorial arch; the green tiles signify a religious purpose, in contrast to the yellow imperial tiles of the Forbidden City and Guó Zǐ Jiàn). Continue on to the square-shaped **Jílè Shìjiè Diàn** ★, encircled by a dry moat. Built by the Qiánlóng emperor to honor his mother, the sandalwood structure is exquisite, topped with a priceless gold dome (apparently too high for either foreign troops or local warlords to reach). The gaudy fiberglass statuary inside brings you back to the present. Back to the west stands an impressive **Nine Dragon Screen,** which guarded the entrance of a now-vanished temple. Further east is the striking **Dàcí Zhēnrú Bǎo Diàn** ★★, an atmospheric Buddhist hall built during the late Míng dynasty from unpainted cedar; topped with a black roof (to protect the precious wood from fire), it has a cool slate floor. Continue east to the northern exit onto Píng'ān Dàdào, which marks the southern end of the Back Lakes (Shíchà Hăi) area.

Wénjīn Jiē 1, Xī Chéng Qū; map p. 104. (South entrance is just west of the north gate of the Forbidden City; east entrance is opposite the west entrance of Jǐng Shān Park.) ℂ 010/6404-0610. Admission: Summer ¥10 ($1.25); winter ¥5 (60¢); ¥10 ($1.25) extra for Yŏng'ān Sì; ¥1 (10¢) extra for Tuánchéng. Daily 6am–9pm. Bus: 812 from Dōng Dān metro stop (119, exit A) to Bĕi Hăi.

Jǐng Shān Gōngyuán (Jǐng Shān Park)   If you want a clear aerial view of the Forbidden City, you'll find it here. The park's central hill—known both as Jǐng Shān (Prospect Hill) and Méi Shān (Coal Hill)—was created using earth left over from the digging of the imperial moat and was the highest point in the city during the Míng dynasty. It was designed to enhance the *fēngshuǐ* of the Forbidden City, both by blocking the harsh northern wind and by providing a cosmic link with the ancestral mountains of the Míng Tombs. A hint at this purpose is the crescent-shaped layout of the five pavilions, mirroring the curvature of the moat south of the Forbidden City. A tree on the east side of the hill marks the spot where the last Míng emperor, Chóngzhēn, hanged himself in 1644, just before Manchu and rebel armies overran the city. The original tree, derided as the "guilty sophora" during the Qīng, was hacked down by Red Guards who failed to recognize a fellow anti-imperialist.

Jǐng Shān Qián Jiē 1 (opposite Forbidden City north gate), Dōg Chéng Qū; map p. 104. Admission ¥2 (20¢).Summer daily 6am–10pm; winter daily 6:30am–8pm. Bus: 812 from Dōng Dān metro stop (119, exit A) to Gù Gōng.

Míng Chéngqiáng Gōngyuán (Míng City Wall Park) ⚘   The section of wall presented here, running a mile east-to-west from Dōngbiàn Mén to Chóng-wén Mén, was originally built in the Yuán dynasty (1279–1368) and reconstructed in the mid-1500s by the Míng. Modern restoration work on the section began in 2002 and is still in progress, using bricks from the original Míng reconstruction collected from nearby residents (some of whom employed them to build toilets after the wall was demolished in the 1950s). A pleasant park runs east along the length of the wall to the dramatic Dōngnán Jiǎolóu (Southeast Corner Tower; daily 9am–5pm; ¥10/$1), with its dozens of arrow slots; a contemporary art gallery and interesting exhibition on the history of Chóngwén can be found inside. A similar park, featuring the ancient rammed-earth **Yuán City Wall (Yuán Tǔchéng Yíshù Gōngyuán),** will be open soon at a site near Jì Mén Qiáo, about a mile north of the Xī Zhí Mén metro stop.

East of metro stop; map p. 108. Open 24 hr. Metro: Chóngwén Mén (209, exit B).

Rì Tán Gōngyuán (Rì Tán Park)   The Temple of the Sun (Rì Tán) served as an altar where the emperor conducted annual rites. Built in 1530, Rì Tán is a pleasant park with a delightful outdoor **teahouse** ⚘ and a **rock-climbing wall** at its heart. Fishponds, a pedal-powered monorail, kites, and a bonsai market also keep the locals amused.

The other imperial altars are located in similar city parks, roughly marking the five points of the Chinese compass. To the north is **Dì Tán Gōngyuán (Temple of Earth),** just north of the Lama Temple; to the west is **Yuè Tán Gōngyuán (Temple of the Moon);** the much grander **Tiān Tán Gōngyuán (Temple of Heaven)** marks the southern point. **Shè Jì Tán (Altar of Land and Grain)** in Zhōngshān Gōngyuán southwest of the Forbidden City, pre-dates them all by several centuries, and marks that peculiarly Chinese compass point, the center.

Impressions

You can scarcely imagine the beauty and magnificence of the palaces we burnt. It made one's heart sore to burn them; in fact, these palaces were so large, and we were so pressed for time, that we could not plunder them carefully. Quantities of gold ornaments were burnt, considered as brass. It was wretchedly demoralising work for an army. Everybody was wild for plunder.

—Captain Charles Gordon, *Letter*, October 1860

Rì Tán Lù 6, Cháoyáng Qū; map p. 115. © 010/8561-3971. Admission ¥1 (5¢). Daily 6:30am–9:30pm. Metro: Yǒng'ān Lǐ (121, exit A).

Yuán Míng Yuán (Old Summer Palace) ⭐ *Kids*   This imperial garden, established by the redoubtable Kāngxī emperor in 1707, is a more recent construction than the New Summer Palace to the west, but it is usually called the Old Summer Palace because it was never rebuilt after French and British troops looted and burned it down during the Second Opium War of 1860. Ironically, many of the buildings were Western-style and filled with European furnishings. Two Jesuit priests, Castiglione and Benoist, were commissioned by the Qiánlóng emperor to design buildings and gardens for the northeast section of the park. An amalgamation of three separate imperial gardens, the ruins create a ghostly and oddly enjoyable scene, beloved for years as a picnic spot. Plans to restore Yuán Míng Yuán have met with fierce protest from locals who've grown to appreciate its overgrown, mangled state. A few restorations have nevertheless begun, starting with the **Wànhuā Zhèn (10,000 Flowers Maze),** a rather nicely reconstructed labyrinth in the **Chángchūn Yuán (Garden of Eternal Spring)** in the northwest section.

Qīnghuá Xī Lù 28 (north of Peking University), Hǎidiàn Qū; map p. 112. © 010/6262-8501. Summer daily 7am–6pm; winter daily 7am–5pm. Admission ¥10 ($1.25). Bus: 810 from south of Jīshuǐ Tán metro stop (218, exit C) to Yuán Míng Yuán.

7 Museums

In keeping with the Communist (and Confucian) passion for naming and quantification, Běijīng has a museum for everything—police, bees, even the humble watermelon. If you share this passion and plan on spending a week or more in the capital, invest in a *bówùguǎn tōng piào* (¥60/$7.50), which grants you free (or half price) admission to over 70 sites in and around Běijīng.

Dà Zhōng Sì (Great Bell Temple)   An attraction to bring out the hunchback in anyone, this Qīng temple now houses the **Ancient Bell Museum (Gǔ Zhōng Bówùguǎn),** best visited on the way to the **Summer Palace** or in conjunction with **Wànshòu Sì,** which lies to the southwest along the Third Ring Road. The temple was known as Juéshēng Sì (Awakened Life Temple), but clearly there wasn't enough awakening going on, so a 46½-ton bell was transported here on ice sleds in 1743. The third hall on the right houses clangers garnered from around Běijīng. Some were donated by eunuchs wishing the relevant emperor long life, with hundreds of donors' names scrawled on their sides. But none of this is fleshed out; captions are of the "China is a great country with an ancient civilization" variety. The main attraction is housed in the rear hall, carved inside and out with 230,000 Chinese and Sanskrit characters. The big bell tolls but once a year, on New Year's Eve. Visitors rub the handles of Qiánlóng's old washbasin, and scramble up narrow steps to play "Chinese golf" by making a wish and throwing coins through a hole in the top of the monster. But it is no longer the "King of Bells"—that honor now goes to the 50-ton bell housed in the **Altar to the Century (Zhōnghuá Shìjì Tán),** constructed in 1999 to prove that China could waste money on the millennium, too.

Běi Sān Huán Xī Lù 31A (west of metro stop, north of Liánxiǎng Qiáo on the northwest side of the Third Ring Road), Hǎidiàn Qū; map p. 112. ℭ 010/6255-0819. Admission ¥10 ($1.25); ¥2 (15¢) extra to climb the Bell Tower. Tues–Sun 8:30am–4pm. Metro: Dà Zhōng Sì (1302, exit A).

Guānfù Gǔdiǎn Yìshù Bówùguǎn (Guānfù Classical Art Museum) ✦

Here you'll find a friendly and knowledgeable staff, well-lit and well-displayed exhibits, piped instrumental music, and comprehensive English explanations. Something is wrong. Relax. This is a private museum, one of a handful in the capital. For those with an interest in antique furniture, particularly those contemplating making a purchase, this museum provides useful background information, explaining the history and properties of the wood grains you'll encounter. The cheap, sturdy wood common in the north is euphemistically renamed "country style" (locals call it *cháimù,* or firewood), but otherwise you'll read nothing but the facts. Oddities include short-backed meditation chairs, a folding chair for imperial hunting expeditions, and an intricate mirror stand. This museum has an outlet near the airport, but you practically have to beg staff to tell you where it is.

For those with an interest in exotic hardwood furniture, the **Red Sandalwood Museum (Zǐtán Bówùguǎn,** ℭ **010/8575-2818;** Tues–Sun 9am–5pm) is also recommended. Founded by Chén Lìhuá, China's wealthiest woman, re-creations of rooms within the Forbidden City reveal her penchant for the tastes and excesses of her Manchu forebears. The three-story museum is a 10-minute walk east from the Sì Huì Dōng metro stop, north of Gāobèidiàn.

Nán Zhúgān Hútòng (in the basement of Huázhì Shāngwù Dàshà), Dōg Chéng Qū; map p. 104. (Walk a block west, turn left into Xiǎo Jiē, then take the 2nd left.) ℭ 010/6526-5566, ext. 111. Admission ¥20 ($2.50). Daily 9am–4:30pm. Metro: Cháoyáng Mén (212, exit C).

Gǔdài Jiànzhù Bówùguǎn (Museum of Ancient Architecture) ✦✦

This exhibition, a mixture of models of China's most famous architecture and fragments of buildings long disappeared, is housed in halls as dramatic as those on the central axis of the Forbidden City. These were once part of the **Xiān Nóng Tán,** or Altar of Agriculture, now as obscure as its neighbor, Tiān Tán, the Temple (properly Altar) of Heaven, is famous. From about 1410, emperors came to this once-extensive site to perform rituals in which they started the agricultural cycle by playing farmer and plowing the first furrows.

The exhibition in the surviving halls is striking in its extensive English explanations of everything from the construction of the complicated bracket sets, which support temple roofs, to the role of geomancy in Chinese architectural thinking. The English-speaking volunteer guides are mostly cheerful students. Models of significant buildings around Běijīng can help you select what to see in the capital during the remainder of your trip.

The rearmost **Tàisuì Diàn (Hall of Jupiter)** of 1532, with its vast, sweeping roof, is only exceeded in magnificence by the Forbidden City's Hall of Supreme Harmony.

Dōng Jīng Lù 21, Xuānwǔ Qū; map p. 108. ℭ 010/6301-7620. Admission ¥15 ($2). Tues–Sun 9am–4pm. Bus: 803 from just south of Wángfǔjǐng (118) or Qián Mén (208) metro stops to Xiān Nóng Tán.

Museum of Chinese History (Zhōngguó Lìshǐ Bówùguǎn) ⭐ The southern wing of the massive building that also houses the Museum of the Chinese Revolution, this poorly lit but still impressive museum contains China's largest collection of historical artifacts although, as at all museums in China, many are copies. Some effort has been made to spruce things up, and English captions have been added to a number of the displays. Exhibits have also been reorganized and now require separate tickets. There is a *tōng piào* (all-in-one ticket) that allows access to all exhibits for a single price. Audio tours in English cost ¥30 ($4).

East side of Tiān'ān Mén Sq., Dōng Chéng Qū; map p. 108. ℂ 010/6512-8901. Admission ¥30 ($4) for *tōng piào*, or ¥10–¥20 ($1–$3) for each exhibit. Daily 9am–4:30pm. Last ticket sold at 3:30pm; ticket booth at top of far right stairs. Metro: Tiān'ān Mén E. (117).

Museum of the Chinese Revolution (Zhōnguó Gémìng Bówùguǎn) On the north side of the Museum of Chinese History, this museum (no surprise) is quite a bit less interesting. The main exhibition covers an idealized history of the Chinese Communist Party from 1919 to 1949. Other exhibits on completely unrelated subjects sometimes appear as well.

East side of Tiān'ān Mén Sq., Dōng Chéng Qū; map p. 108. ℂ 010/6512-9347. Admission ¥30 ($4) for *tào piào*, or ¥5–¥20 ($1–$3) for individual exhibits. Tues–Sun 8:30am–4:30pm. Last tickets sold before 3:30pm; ticket office at top of far left stairs. Metro: Tiān'ān Mén E. (117).

Zhōngguó Gōngyì Měishùguǎn (National Arts & Crafts Museum) Located on the fifth floor of Parkson Department Store (Bǎishèng Gòuwù Zhōngxīn), you'll find no ancient, dusty treasures here. This is a museum to prove that contemporary Chinese craftsmanship is every bit as good as it was during the Táng dynasty. Many items suggest otherwise, particularly large chunks of jade painstakingly carved into monuments to bad taste, and ceramic statues of arhats picking the wax from their ears. But it's a good introduction to traditional crafts and where they are produced in China. Striking exhibits include clay figurines from Jiāngsū, cloisonné from Běijīng, lacquerware from Fújiàn, and ceramics from Jǐngdézhèn, which predictably steal the show.

Fùxīng Mén Nèi Dàjiē 101, Xī Chéng Qū; map p. 104. ℂ 010/6605-3476. Admission ¥8 ($1). Tues–Sun 9:30am–4pm. Metro: Fùxīng Mén (114/204, exit B).

8 Former Residences & Other Curiosities

Constructing memorial halls to the heroes of past and present dynasties has a long history, and the communists have adopted this tradition with élan. As before, historical accuracy matters little; cultivating patriotic subjects is the goal.

Ancient Observatory (Gǔ Guānxiàng Tái) Most of the observatory's large bronze astronomical instruments—mystifying combinations of hoops, slides, and rulers stylishly embellished with dragons and clouds—were built by the Jesuits in the 17th and 18th centuries. You can play with reproductions of the Chinese-designed instruments they superseded (the originals were moved to Nánjīng in 1933 and, for unexplained reasons, haven't been returned) in the grassy courtyard below. At the back of the garden, there's a crude "we-invented-it-first" display outlining the achievements of Sòng dynasty astronomer Guō Shǒujìng, who also has his own memorial hall on the northern tip of Xī Hǎi. To the right of the entrance there's a more useful exhibition, which houses a photo of a bone from 1300 B.C. on which China's first astronomers etched a record of solar eclipses, details which are still used in present-day astronomy.

(**Fun Fact** Happy Boys

The rickshaw boys made famous by **Lǎo Shě** can still be found in the capital, most commonly around metro stations, where the muddle of one-way streets and construction sites makes them a handy alternative to a taxi for locals. They don't slog along on foot like the hero of the novel *Rickshaw,* and they are more likely to have a provincial brogue than the Běijīng dialect of their literary forebears, but they still live a precarious existence. Most are from poorer provinces, and as nonresidents they are easy prey for police; news bulletins frequently show police jumping out of vans and confiscating rickshaws to "clean up" the capital. While this is for show (after paying a "fine" of up to ¥200/$25, they get their rickshaw back), most live by the adage "When the police clock off (at 4:30pm), we clock on."

Jiànguó Mén Dōng Biǎobèi 2 (southwest side of Jiànguó Mén intersection, just south of metro), Dōng Chéng Qū; map p. 104. ℭ 010/6512-8923. Admission ¥10 ($1.25). Wed–Sun 9am–5pm. Metro: Jiànguó Mén (120/211, exit C).

Dixià Chéng (Underground City) ⚲ *Kids*   A sign near the entrance proclaims this seldom-visited attraction a "human fairyland and underground paradise." Far from it. Aside from odd recent additions, such as a silk factory, these tunnels are dark, damp, and genuinely eerie. A portrait of Máo stands amid murals of ordinary folk "volunteering" to dig tunnels, and fading but catchy slogans (DIG THE TUNNELS DEEP, ACCUMULATE GRAIN, OPPOSE HEGEMONY, and FOR THE PEOPLE: PREPARE FOR WAR, PREPARE FOR FAMINE). Built during the 1960s, with border skirmishes with the USSR as the pretext, the tunnels could accommodate all of Běijīng's six million inhabitants upon its completion—or so it was boasted. Army engineers were said to have built a secret network of tunnels connecting the residences of Party leaders at Zhōng Nán Hǎi to the Great Hall of the People and the numerous military bases near Bā Dà Chù to the west of town. Suspicions were confirmed in 1976 and 1989 when large numbers of troops emerged from the Great Hall of the People to keep the people in check. The recent construction boom means that this is the only remaining entrance to the non-secret tunnels, and it may disappear soon. Take a flashlight to explore unlit nooks and side tunnels, but watch out for broken glass, slippery floors, and rusty wires.

Xī Dǎmóchǎng Jiē 64, Chóngwén Qū; map p. 108. (From metro stop, walk west; take the 1st left into Qián Mén Dōng Dàjiē, then the 2nd right. Entrance is on south side, just past Qián Mén Xiǎoxué.) ℭ 010/6702-2657. Admission ¥20 ($2.50). Daily 8:30am–5pm. Metro: Chóngwén Mén (209, exit D).

Lǎo Shě Jìniànguǎn (Former Residence of Lǎo Shě)   The courtyard home of one of Běijīng's best-loved writers, Lǎo Shě (1899–1966), is the most charming of many converted homes scattered around Běijīng's *hútòng.* Despite being granted this home by Zhōu Ēnlái in 1950, the writer refused to become a cheerleader for the regime, and his post-revolution years were remarkably quiet for such a prolific writer. He recently came in at no. 5 in an online survey of "China's leading cultural icons," ahead of pop diva Wang Faye but well behind the no. 1 choice, the iconoclastic writer Lǔ Xùn (who has a less interesting memorial hall in the west of town, near Báitǎ Sì). Lǎo Shě is renowned for the novel *Rickshaw (Luòtuo Xiángzi),* a darkly humorous tale of a hardworking rickshaw puller, Happy Boy.

Start in Hall 3, to the right, which records his early years in London, the United States, and Shāndōng Province. Hall 2 is an attempt to re-create the mood of his original study and sitting room, with his personal library untouched and his desk calendar left open at the day of his disappearance—August 24, 1966. While the date of his death is certain, the details are murky. The official line has him committing a poetic suicide in nearby Tàipíng Hú (Peace Lake, pictured in Hall 1) after being subjected to a "struggle session" at Kǒng Miào along with other intellectuals. It's possible that he was simply murdered by Red Guards.

Fēngfù Hútòng 19, Dōng Chéng Qū; map p. 104. (From Wángfǔjǐng Dàjiē, go west at the Crowne Plaza along Dēngshìkǒu Xī Jiē to the 2nd *hútòng* on your right.) ℃ 010/6514-2612. Admission ¥5 (60¢). Tues–Sun 9am–5pm. Metro: Wángfǔjǐng (118, exit A).

Prince Gōng's Mansion (Gōng Wáng Fǔ) ★

This splendid imperial residence belonged to several people, including the sixth son of the Guāngxù emperor (Prince Gōng) who, at the age of 27, was left to sign the Convention of Peking in 1860, after the Qīng royal family took an early summer holiday when British and French forces advanced on the capital. The convention (which ratified the ill-enforced Treaty of Tiānjīn) is reproduced in an exhibition hall. But other than one picture, there's little information on an earlier owner, Heshen (1750–1799), the infamous Manchu official. Thought to have been the Qiánlóng emperor's lover, he ruled China for his own gain when Qiánlóng abdicated in 1796, but his demise was swift. While he was mourning Qiánlóng in the Forbidden City, officials were dispatched to this mansion. Though the extent of his graft was widely known, officials were shocked by the piles of gold and silver ingots they uncovered. His remaining friends at court managed to persuade the Qiánlóng emperor's son to spare him from "death by a thousand cuts," but he was soon hanged. His most lavish building—constructed entirely from cedarwood—is housed in the China Arts Research College next door. While the curators aren't game to mention it, the shop is doing brisk trade in the lurid *Secrets of Heshen*. The labyrinthine combination of rockeries and pavilions here offers plenty to see. Short but sweet performances of opera and acrobatics are served up to tour groups in the three-story "Grand Opera House."

Liǔyīn Jiē 17; map p. 104. (Signposted in English at top of Qián Hǎi Xī Dàjiē running north off Píng'ān Dàdào opposite north gate of Běi Hǎi Park; turn left at sign and follow alley past large parking lot. Entrance marked with huge red lanterns.) ℃ 010/6616-8149. Admission ¥5 (60¢). Daily 8:30am–4:30pm. Metro: Jīshuǐ Tán (218, exit C).

Sòng Qìnglíng Gùjū (Former Residence of Soong Ching Ling)

Sòng Qìnglíng is as close as you'll get to a modern Chinese Communist saint— wealthy, obsessed with children, and a friend of Máo to boot. She married Sun Yat-sen, 30 years her senior, a diminutive man acknowledged as the "father of modern China" on both sides of the Táiwān Strait (even though he was in Denver during the 1911 Revolution). Qìnglíng showed some sympathy to the Communist cause only after her husband's death in 1925. Her younger sister married Chiang Kai-shek (leader of the Nationalist Party and China's public enemy no. 1 until his death in 1975), while Qìnglíng nearly died during the "white terror" of 1927 when the Nationalist Party was purged of Communist sympathizers. Máo rewarded Qìnglíng for her loyalty by granting her this mansion in 1963, and she lived here until her death in 1981, devoting much time to education. The grounds are well-kept, making them the most popular spot in Běijīng for soon-to-be-weds to be photographed. The exhibition on her life seems to contain nearly every article of clothing she wore and every letter she wrote. It's all a little too perfect.

Hòu Hǎi Běi Yán 46 (northeast shore of Hòu Hǎi), Xī Chéng Qū; map p. 104. ℰ 010/6404-4205. Admission ¥20 ($2.50). Daily 9am–4:30pm. Metro: Jīshuǐtán (218, exit B).

Tiānyì Mù ⭑ *Finds*   Upon the accession of the Wànlì emperor (reign 1573–1620), the Imperial City housed nearly 20,000 eunuchs (*huànguān*, later *tàijiān*), from powerful bureaucrats enjoying their own mansions, down to junior eunuchs scraping by through petty graft. Yet the Forbidden City currently provides no glimpse of their living quarters, and little mention of them at all. This cemetery for eunuchs dates from 1605 and opened to the public in 1996, immediately after the death of China's last eunuch. It's a fair hike from the city center, and is best combined with a visit to Tánzhè Sì or Chuàn Dǐ Xià (see chapter 10 for both) and to Fǎhǎi Sì (p. 133), which is a 5-minute walk to the northeast. Unlike its occupants, the cemetery has survived almost intact, and provides insight into the desperate spirituality of eunuchs. Most intriguing are rounded burial chambers at the rear, where the good deeds of eunuchs—fanning the emperor, serving food, playing music—are carved onto the tombs, standing as plaintive reminders to the gods. There are no images of them plotting against the emperor, extracting bribes, or burning down palaces, activities for which they were better known.

A small exhibition hall is set to the left of the entrance, but all captions are in Chinese. The last eunuch, Sūn Yàotíng (1902–1996), is pictured making a visit to the Forbidden City in 1993, his first since Pǔyí was driven out by a warlord in 1924. He is said to have taken issue with the accuracy of many of the captions there. On the right a naïve letter describes his years in service. Castrated at the age of 8, he was devastated when the emperor abdicated months later, although he continued to serve Pǔyí until 1924. He earned enough money to

The Unkindest Cut

The practice that created eunuchs is said to date back 4,000 years, when it was an alternative to the death penalty, often used in the case of political crimes. By the Míng dynasty, most eunuchs submitted to this operation voluntarily, usually as a way out of poverty. The eunuch's abdomen and upper thighs were bound tightly with coarse rope or bandages; his penis was anesthetized with hot pepper water. He was then seated in a semi-reclining chair, with waist and legs held down by three assistants. At this point, he was asked if he would have any regrets. Those who hesitated would be asked to leave. Consent given, the small curved blade flashed and "fountains of red, white, and yellow liquid spouted from the wound" as both the testes and penis were removed. A goose quill would then quickly be inserted into the urethra to prevent it from closing, and the wound plugged with cloth previously dipped in wax, sesame oil, and pepper. The surplus organs (or "treasure") were plopped in a jar and jealously guarded, as they were necessary to establish a eunuch's credentials for future promotions, and to pass into the next life as complete men. After the often unconscious patient had endured 3 days without food or drink, the plug was removed. If urine gushed out, the operation was a success, and a lifetime in service awaited. If not, a horrible, lingering death awaited.

adopt a son, but lost his "treasure" during the Cultural Revolution (see the box, "The Unkindest Cut" above).

Cíxǐ is photographed with a large entourage of eunuchs at the Summer Palace, and the temples pictured indicate that a large number of Běijīng's shrines, such as nearby Fǎhǎi Sì, were sponsored by eunuchs. Buddhism, with its emphasis on celibacy and renunciation, had more appeal for eunuchs than Confucianism. Wealthier eunuchs could adopt sons, but most relied on Buddhist monks to tend their graves. A second eunuch museum will be opening soon inside a late Qīng temple, **Lìmǎ Guāndì Miào.** Built for one of Cíxǐ's most trusted eunuchs, Liú Chéngyìn, the keeper of the imperial seals, it stands just south of the Summer Palace in an area that was akin to a eunuch retirement village.

Móshì Kǒu Dàjiē 80, Shíjīng Shān Qū; map p. 112. (From bus stop, continue up the rise; take a right after 5 min. The cemetery is on the left.) ② 010/8872-4148. Admission ¥8 ($1). Daily 8am–6pm. Bus: 959 or 746 from left of Píngguǒ Yuán metro stop (103, exit D) to Shǒu Gāng Xiǎoqū.

9 Hútòng & Sìhéyuàn (Lanes & Courtyard Compounds)

As distinct as Běijīng's palaces, temples, and parks may be, it is the *hútòng* that ultimately set the city apart. Prior to the 20th century, when cars and the Communist love of grandeur made them impracticable, these narrow and often winding lanes were the city's dominant passageways. Old maps of Běijīng show the city to be an immense and intricate maze composed almost entirely of *hútòng,* most no wider than 10m (30 ft.) and some as narrow as 50cm (20 in.).

Běijīng's other famous feature is the *sìhéyuàn* (courtyard house)—traditional dwellings typically composed of four single-story rectangular buildings arranged around a central courtyard with a door at one corner (ideally facing south). Originally designed to house a single family, they now house up to five or six. Until recently, as much as half of Běijīng's people lived in some form of *sìhéyuàn,* but large-scale bulldozing of the *hútòng* has resulted in significant migration into modern apartment buildings. Foreign visitors charmed by the quaintness of the old houses often assume this migration is forced, and it often is. But many move willingly, eager for central heating and indoor plumbing (both of which are rare in the *hútòng* neighborhoods).

The names of these places are a link to the history and humor of the capital. **Sān Bù Lǎo Hútòng,** a couple of blocks west of Prince Gōng's Mansion, is named for its famous former resident, Admiral Zhèng Hé, whose nickname was Sān Bǎo (three jewels). As described in *1421: The Year China Discovered America,* this Huí Muslim eunuch led a vast armada of ships to Southeast Asia, India, Ceylon, the Persian Gulf (where he was able to visit Mecca), and West Africa over seven voyages between 1405 and 1433. Detachments of his fleet probably reached Australia, but the jury is out on the central contention of the book. Other names hint at long-forgotten markets. **Yāndài Xié Jiē (Tobacco Pipe Lane),** east of Yíndìng Qiáo, now harbors the capital's hippest cafes, but it once provided smoking paraphernalia for the capital's numerous opium dens. The meaning of **Xiānyú Kǒu Jiē (Fresh Fish Corner Street)** seems straightforward, but locals swear it's a corruption of *xiányú* (salty fish), a reference to a man who burned down half the street while preparing his favorite meal.

The *hútòng* are being leveled so rapidly the term **"fast-disappearing"** is now a permanent part of their description. With the 2008 Olympics looming, destruction carries the imprimatur of both modernization and house cleaning before the guests arrive. Never mind that visitors prefer quiet lanes to endless

> **Tips Hútòng Etiquette**
>
> Fascinating as *hútòng* neighborhoods may be, always remember that these are people's homes. Sometimes admiring the door piers or lintels is enough to win an invitation inside, and bystanders may mutter, "See, *lǎo wài* (foreigners) appreciate these things," although they're more likely to ask, "What the hell is that *lǎo wài* doing?" Those with some grasp of Mandarin or accompanied by a Chinese friend may be able to flatter their way inside, but never enter a *sìhéyuàn* uninvited. You won't get shot, but you should be.

blocks of identical flats. *China Daily* carries regular sanctimonious articles about the importance of "preserving" *hútòng* that are long on statistics but usually silent on which areas will be spared. But even if it cares, the central government has little control over events. Property developers and local governments are a law unto themselves; the Dōg Chéng government has a well-deserved reputation for ordering brutal evictions and arranging unfavorable resettlement schemes.

Intriguing swathes of *hútòng* still stand south of **Hépíng Mén** and **Qián Mén,** as well as northwest of **Xīsì,** surrounding **Bái Tǎ Sì.** Here you may hear strange humming sounds, produced by pigeons wheeling overhead with small whistles attached to their feathers. For now, the destitution of these areas makes them unattractive to property developers, but their long-term survival is improbable. See them now. The *hútòng* most likely to survive because of their popularity with tourists are in the **Back Lakes (Shíchà Hǎi)** area and in nearby **Dì'ān Mén.** Pedicab tour companies offer to bike you around this area and take you inside a couple of courtyards, but they all charge absurd rates. It's much cheaper, and far more enjoyable, to explore on your own by foot or bicycle (see chapter 7 for suggested routes). If you must, the **Běijīng Hútòng Tourist Agency** (© 010/6615-9097) offers tours in English (¥240/$30).

10 Especially for Kids

Competition for the disposable income of Běijīng's one-child families is intense—advertising ruthlessly targets children. Alas, few of Běijīng's just-for-kids attractions are of a standard that will appeal to Western children, and those few tend to be overcrowded. Some exceptions are noted in this section.

Běijīng Hǎiyángguǎn (Běijīng Aquarium) ✦ "The world's largest inland aquarium" attracted plenty of opposition from local environmental groups when it opened in 1999, and the logic of keeping countless marine animals so far from the sea is questionable. Efforts to compensate are obvious—the environmental message is laid on thickly in the Chinese captions. Introducing Chinese children to the concept that shrimp can exist somewhere other than in a sea of garlic sauce has to be commended, although descriptions of "horrible" sharks show there's a way to go in environmental efforts. **Dolphin shows** at 11am and 3pm pack in the one-child families. **Běijīng Zoo (Běijīng Dòngwùyuán)** lies to the south, and despite improvements to some areas—notably the **Panda House**—the zoo is more likely to traumatize your child than provide entertainment. It is possible to take a boat from the canal south of the aquarium to the Summer Palace (50-min. trip; ¥40/$5 one-way, ¥70/$8.70 round-trip).

Gāoliáng Qiáo Xiéjiē 18B (from Běifāng Jiāo Dà cross road and walk west; north gate of the Běijīng Zoo), Hǎidiàn Qū; map p. 112. ✆ 010/6217-6655. Admission ¥100 ($14) includes admission to Běijīng Zoo; students half price; 2 children free with 1 paid adult ticket. Daily 9am–3:30pm. Bus: 16 (*zhī xiàn*) from Xī Zhí Mén metro stop (201) to Běifāng Jiāo Dà.

Gǔdài Qiánbì Zhǎnlǎnguǎn (Ancient Coin Exhibition Hall) If your child is at the collecting phase, this may or may not be a wise place to visit, although the vast range of shells, coins, and notes is as likely to bewilder as to fascinate. While the tour guides' chant of "5,000 years of history" rings hollow, "5,000 years of retail" rings true. Confucius and Máo both railed in vain against the Chinese mercantile spirit. The exhibition should also impress upon you how simple it is to mint coins; the stalls of the **Ancient Coin Market (Gǔdài Qiánbì Jiāoyì Shìchǎng)** outside are testament to how easy they are to duplicate—*don't* make large purchases. **Déshèng Mén Jiànlóu (Déshèng Mén Arrow Tower),** which houses the exhibition, is akin to an imposing castle, with many dark crannies to explore.

Déshèng Mén Jiànlóu, Běi Ěr Huán Zhōng Lù (north side of North Second Ring Road, just east of metro stop), Xī Chéng Qū; map p. 104. ✆ 010/6201-8073. Admission ¥5 (60¢). Tues–Sun 9am–3:30pm. Metro: Jīshuǐ Tán (218, exit A).

Mílù Yuán (Mílù Park) ★★ Located on the site of the Southern Marshes (Nán Hǎizi) where Yuán, Míng, and Qīng emperors would hunt deer, rabbit, and pheasant, and practice military exercises, this ecological research center is the most humane place to view animals in Běijīng. The main attraction is Père David's deer *(mílù),* a strange deer-like creature that became extinct in China toward the end of the Qīng dynasty. The *mílù* you see today are the descendants of 18 animals that were collected in 1898 by the far-sighted Lord Bedford from zoos around Europe. In 1985, a group of 20 *mílù* was reintroduced to China; they now number about 200, and over 400 animals have returned to the wild. The expansive grounds also house other endangered animals, a maze, plots of land where members can grow vegetables without pesticides (a revelation to most locals), and the chillingly effective World Extinct Wildlife Cemetery, which illustrates the plight of endangered species.

Nán Hǎizi Mílù Yuán, Dàxīng Qū. ✆ 010/8796-2096. Admission ¥10 ($1.25). Annual membership ¥500 ($60). Daily 8am–5:30pm. Bus: 729 from Qián Mén metro stop (208) to Jiù Gōng. Change for minibus no. 4, which will drop you at the signposted turnoff.

Wǔ Sè Tǔ Gōngyìfáng (Five-Color Earth Craft Center) Housed in the old "Eastern Youth Palace" just north of Tiān Dì Jùchǎng (Heaven and Earth Theater), this is a relaxed place to let the kids indulge in tie-dyeing, embroidery, or painting. If they want to try pottery as well, you'll need to call a day in advance so that an instructor can be arranged. The center's main business is recycling Miáo and Dòng minority fabrics into chic clothing, bags, and cushion covers. There will be discreet pressure for you to make a purchase, and exquisite as the designs are, take the American Express sign as fair warning of inflated prices.

Dōg Chéng Shàonián Gōng, Dōng Zhí Mén Nán Lù 10 (east side of East Second Ring Road, green-roofed building north of metro stop), Dōg Chéng Qū; map p. 115. ✆ 010/6415-3839. www.fivecolourearth.com. Admission ¥50 ($6) 1 hr., ¥80 ($10) 2 hr. Minimum 5 children for pottery. Daily 9am–6pm. Metro: Dōngsì Shí Tiáo (213, exit B).

11 Organized Tours

During a visit to Běi Hǎi, writer John Blofeld chanced upon an elderly eunuch, and enquired as to how he was making a living. He touchily replied, "I manage well. I am a guide—not one of those so-called guides who live by inventing history for foreigners and by making commissions on things they purchase. I have not fallen that far yet . . . " Little has changed. In a country where children are taught that South Korea and their American allies started the Korean War when they invaded innocent North Korea, many modern inventions are unintentional. Many visitors assume locals have a unique insight into their own culture. In China, and Běijīng in particular, all-pervasive censorship and a general lack of curiosity ensures this is rarely the case. You *do not* need the services of a local guide.

Several companies offer guided group tours of Běijīng for English speakers, but these are almost always overpriced, often incomplete, and best thought of as an emergency measure when time is short. The most popular operators are **Dragon Bus** (✆ 010/6515-8565) and **Panda Tours** (✆ 010/6525-8372; bjpanda@ public.bta.net.cn), both with offices scattered through the five-star hotels. City highlight tours by air-conditioned bus typically cost around ¥300 ($38) per person for a half day and around ¥500 ($60) for a full day with a mediocre lunch. **China International Travel Service (CITS)** (✆ 010/6515-8566; www.cits.net), offers tours that are more customizable, but at a much higher fee.

The **Chinese Culture Club** (✆ 010/8462-2081; www.chinesecultureclub. org) organizes outings, lectures, and film screenings for expatriates with an interest in Chinese culture. There's usually a weekend half-day or full-day tour. Events are often led by prominent lecturers, and discussions go well beyond the "5,000 years of history" tripe that many guides serve up. There's no membership fee; activities typically cost between ¥40 ($5) and ¥70 ($8.70) per person.

Surrounded by mountains on three sides, the environs of Běijīng provide tremendous scope for 1- or 2-day walks taking in scenery, ancient villages and, of course, the Great Wall. **Běijīng Hikers** (✆ 1370/100-3694; huilin@bjhikers. com) organize day hikes for ¥150 ($19) departing from the Lido Hotel, and are popular with North American expatriates. A cheaper and more interesting alternative is to join a hike organized by **Sanfo Outdoors** (✆ 010/6201-5550; www. sanfo.com.cn). Originally a small club at Peking University, they now have at least four hikes every weekend advertised (in Chinese) on their website. Visit one of their shops (p. 175) to obtain information on the weekend's activities, but take the grading system seriously—difficult hikes are really tough, while outings with all luxuries provided are humorously referred to as "corrupt" *(fǔbài)*.

12 Staying Active

Foreign-run five-star hotels offer the cleanest and best-equipped fitness centers and swimming pools for those desperate to work out. Most locals can't afford this, and head for the parks early in the morning to practice *tàijíquán*, practice ballroom dancing, or walk the bird (walking the dog is prohibited during daylight hours). At night, Běijīng's undersized canines emerge, along with seniors dancing (waddling, really) and beating drums to the rhythm of rice-planting songs *(yāng ge)*. However, if you know where to look, you can find other leisure experiences with a local flavor.

ACTIVITIES A TO Z
BOWLING (BǍOLÍNGQIÚ) With bottles of Johnnie Walker Red Label and French perfume readily traced, and visits to "karaoke" clubs easily photographed, the favorite way to curry favor with a Chinese official is . . . bowling. During the 1990s, more than 15,000 alleys were built, many in Běijīng. The **Běijīng New Century Hotel** at Shǒutǐ Nán Lù 6 has 12 lanes, as well as pool

and table tennis (✆ **010/6849-2001**, ext. 88; daily 10am–2pm, ¥6/75¢ per game; daily 2–7pm, ¥15/$2 per game; daily 7pm–midnight, ¥30/$3.70 per game). The biggest and most fun place to bowl is 24-hour **Gōngtǐ Yībǎi** at Gōngtǐ Xī Lù 6, with 100 lanes, thumping music, and flashing video games to bring in the kids (✆ **010/6552-2688;** daily noon–midnight ¥30/$3.70 per game; daily midnight–noon ¥20/$2.50 per game).

GOLF (GĀO'ĚRFŪQIÚ) If playing golf in a region desperately short of land and water doesn't bother you, the best golf club in town is **Běijīng International Golf Club** (**Běijīng Guójì Gāo'ěrfū Jùlèbù;** ✆ **010/6974-5678**), northwest of town near the Míng Tombs. Eighteen holes will set you back ¥550 ($69) during the week, rising to ¥1,270 ($159) on weekends. Caddy fees are ¥150 ($19).

ICE-SKATING (LIŪBĪNG) Běijīng has superb outdoor ice-skating in the winter at **Běi Hǎi Gōngyuán** and the **Summer Palace.** Skate rental concessions on the shore charge about ¥10 ($1.25) per day, but you might not find boots that fit. Even more popular in winter are "ice cars" (*bīng chē*), box sleds propelled by ski poles that rent for ¥5 (60¢) per hour. Obvious caveats about the thickness of ice sheets apply—global warming makes for a shorter skating season each year. Běijīng's largest skate rink is **Le Cool,** Guómào Liūbīng Chǎng (✆ **010/6505-5776**), in the underground shopping center that connects Traders Hotel to China World Hotel. Open Sunday through Friday from 10am to 10pm and Saturday until midnight, this rink charges ¥30 ($3.70) for 90 minutes from 10am to 6pm, ¥40 ($5) from 6 to 10pm, and ¥50 ($6) after 6pm on Saturday.

KITE-FLYING (FÀNG FĒNGZHENG) Flying in China at least 2,000 years before they were seen in Europe, the humble kite has been used as a communication link in battlefields, a device to frighten enemy troops, and even in the sport of kite fighting. But most locals fly kites peacefully, particularly at **Tiān'ān Mén Square** (where you can rent kites) or in parks such as **Rì Tán Gōngyuán.** You can purchase kites at several markets; good selections are available at Guānyuán Shìchǎng and on the fourth floor of Sānlǐtún Yǎxiù Fúzhuāng Shìchǎng (see section 2, "Markets & Bazaars" in chapter 8).

MASSAGE (ÀNMÓ) Blind massage (*mángrén ànmó*) and foot rubs (*zúdǐ ànmó*) are the ideal treat after pounding the cobblestones and concrete of the capital. **Lèshēng Mángrén Bǎojiàn Ànmó Zhōngxīn,** Dēngshìkǒu Xī Jiē 32 (✆ **010/6525-7532**, ext. 3201), on the second floor of the Dōnghuá Fàndiàn, a long block west of the Crowne Plaza in Wángfǔjǐng, charges ¥88 ($11) for an hour of either treat. It's open from 11am to 11pm. But don't go too far off the beaten track in search of a rubdown or a haircut. . . .

ROCK CLIMBING (PĀNYÁN) The mountains around Běijīng offer spectacular climbing, and the capital also boasts two outdoor climbing walls. The largest is an 18m (59-ft.) wall inside the east gate of **Lóngtán Hú Gōngyuán** (✆ **010/6718-6358**, ext. 9031; ¥10/$1.25 one climb; ¥30/$3.70 per day), with more than 20 routes. A 15m (49-ft.) wall stands in the middle of **Rì Tán Gōngyuán** (✆ **010/8562-3820;** membership ¥60/$7.50; ¥10/$1.25 one climb; ¥30/$3.70 per day), which only has room for four roped climbers.

TÀIJÍQUÁN Tai Chi practitioners can visit any park at daybreak, and enjoy the thrill of practicing with hundreds of others. The **Chinese Culture Club** (✆ **010/8462-2081;** www.chinesecultureclub.org) has a regular course in English.

YOGA (YÚJIĀ) If you need to stretch out, the Yoga Yard, Fāngjiā Yuán Hútòng 11 (✆ **010/8511-5929;** www.yogayard.com) offers Hatha Yoga classes for all levels. From the Cháoyáng Mén metro stop (212), walk west to the first major intersection, turn left down Cháoyáng Mén Nán Xiǎojiē, and turn into the fifth *hútòng* on your left. Yoga Yard is located inside the main hall of Guì Gōng Fǔ Teahouse.

SPECTATOR SPORTS

The **Chinese National Basketball League (CNBL)** has been building a following across China since its inception in 1994. The **Běijīng Ducks** play their home games at **Gōngrén Tǐyùchǎng (Workers' Stadium),** which is also the home of the capital's soccer team. A fanatically loyal green-and-white army of fans follows the soccer team, formerly known as Běijīng Guó Ān. Once the joke of the soccer league, they finished third in 2003. In their new incarnation as **Běijīng Xiàndài** (Modern Běijīng, named for the Hyundai car company), they're hoping to knock perennial champion Dàlián off their perch. Tickets for either team can be purchased at the Workers' Stadium north gate or from Lìshēng Tǐyù Shāngshà, Wángfǔjǐng Dàjiē 74A (© **010/6525-0581;** daily 9am–8:30pm). The basketball season runs November through April; the soccer season, April through November.

7

Běijīng Strolls

by Graeme Smith

Taking a stroll in Běijīng can be hard work. The main boulevard, Cháng'ān Dàjiē, is a soulless and windswept thoroughfare, and the rest of town seems to be a huge construction site choking on dust and car fumes. These strolls will show you a gentler Běijīng, where tallow-faced, rheumy-eyed octogenarians push cane shopping carts through even more ancient tree-lined *hútòng,* where young lovers clasp hands nervously as they gaze across the Back Lakes, and where pot-bellied cab drivers quaff beer while enjoying boisterous games of poker or chess in the middle of the sidewalk.

You'll need your wits about you. No one in Běijīng seems capable of walking in a straight line. Pedestrian crossings are purely decorative, and newly installed crossings with traffic lights are widely ignored by motorists. The car, particularly the four-wheel-drive, dominates both the road and the sidewalk.

Environmentalists, town planners, and doctors all argue that encouraging private car use will be a disaster for Běijīng's residents. But the capital already boasts the highest rate of car ownership in China, and car sales grow by around 20% every year. Foreign car companies and their partners in the Party count the cash, but don't pay the cost.

Renting or purchasing a bike moves you one rung up the traffic food chain and is a less tiring way to get around. Youth hostels rent out bikes for around ¥20 ($2.50) per day, or you can purchase a second-hand bike from a streetside repair stall for less than ¥100 ($12). Bike traffic is orderly, and unlike Guǎngzhōu and Shànghǎi, the capital has yet to block off large numbers of streets to cyclists. Whether you walk or ride a bike, avoid sudden changes of direction, and go with the rather substantial flow around you.

WALKING TOUR 1   LIÚLICHǍNG & DÀ ZHÀLÁN

Start:	Zhèngyǐcí Xìlóu, just south of the metro on Qián Mén Xī Héyàn Jiē (metro: Hépíng Mén, 207).
Finish:	Qián Mén, south end of Tiān'ān Mén Guǎngchǎng (metro: Qián Mén, 208).
Time:	3 hours.
Best times:	Any weekday starting at about 9am or 2pm.
Worst times:	Weekends are crowded. Most shops close about 8:30pm.

This pleasant stroll takes in many of Běijīng's most famous shops. Even if you're not interested in buying anything, it makes an agreeable break from the fumes of the capital's constantly gridlocked streets. **Liúlichǎng,** named for a factory that once turned out the glazed roof tiles that clearly delineated the rank of Běijīng's buildings, was renovated in the 1980s to capture the look and atmosphere of the late Qīng dynasty. Scholars and art connoisseurs once frequented

1 **Zhèngyǐcí Xìlóu**
正乙祠戏楼

2 **Cathay Bookshop (No. 18)**
来薰阁

3 **Róngbaǎo Zhāi (No. 19)**
荣宝斋

4 **Fùshaīn Huácǎi (No. 36)**
富山华彩

5 **Zhōngguó Shūdiàn (No. 115)**
中国书店

6 **Sōngyúngé (No. 106)**
松筠阁

7 **Curio Shops**

8 **Dà Zhàlán**
大栅栏

9 **Nèi Lián Shēng Xiédiàn (No. 34)**
内联升鞋店

10 **Tóngréntáng (No. 24)**
同仁堂

11 **Ruìfúxiáng Chóubù Diàn (No. 5)**
瑞蚨祥绸布店

12 **Liùbìjū Jiàngyuán (No. 3)**
六必居酱园

13 **Bā Dà Hútòng (Eight Great Lanes)**
八大胡同

14 **Lángfáng Èr Tiáo**
廊房二条

15 **Qián Mén (Front Gate)**
前门

Liúlichǎng, and it is still home to the most famous art-supplies store in China, **Róngbǎo Zhāi.** There is a cluster (at times it feels like a gauntlet) of shops selling art books, scrolls, rubbings, handmade paper, paintbrushes, ink sticks, "jade," and antiques (which are nearly all fakes). Liúlichǎng runs about 6 blocks east–west. Southeast of it is **Dà Zhàlán,** an ancient, but more plebeian, shopping street that has been converted into a cobblestoned pedestrian-only mall. There are many ancient shops on Dà Zhàlán, including tailors, shoe stores, and apothecaries selling traditional medicines. North of Dà Zhàlán, the market streets of **Lángfáng Èr Tiáo** and **Lángfáng Tóu Tiáo** wind their ways towards **Qián Mén (Front Gate)** overlooking **Tiān'ān Mén Square.**

Walk south from the Hépíng Mén metro station down Nán Xīnhuá Jiē, and take the first left onto Qián Mén Xī Héyàn Jiē, where you'll find:

❶ Zhèngyǐcí Xìlóu

Dating back more than 340 years, much of the history of Běijīng Opera is tied up with this delightful theater, which began life as a Buddhist temple during the Míng dynasty. It's fairly quiet these days, although there are occasional evening performances (call ✆ **010/6317-7354** to check). During the day, opera fans gather to practice their art, and for a fee of ¥5 (60¢), you will be allowed to view the magnificently restored interior.

Backtrack to the main road and continue south to Liúlichǎng Xī Jiē. On the right-hand side of the road is:

❷ Cathay Bookshop (No. 18)

One of several branches of China Books, this bookshop (south side of street; ✆ **010/6301-7678**) has a great range of art materials—paper, ink stones, chops, brushes, and frames—at far more reasonable prices than you'll find at . . .

❸ Róngbǎo Zhāi (No. 19)

The most renowned art shop in China (north side of street) greets you with what may be the world's largest ink stone. Róngbǎo Zhāi sells woodblock prints, copies of famous calligraphy, historic paintings (reproductions), and art supplies. The handful of workers who are more interested in doing their jobs than in reading the paper are gold mines of information on Běijīng's art scene.

Directly opposite is:

❹ Fùshān Huácǎi (No. 36)

This shop sells a range of Western and traditional Chinese instruments. Upstairs, you'll find classical sheet music at very reasonable prices. The names of the composers are usually written above the scores.

Further west, the street is due to be demolished to make way for a patch of lawn that no one is allowed to sit on. So backtrack to Nán Xīnhuá Jiē and cross the footbridge to Liúlichǎng Dōng Jiē. On the north side is:

❺ Zhōngguó Shūdiàn (No. 115)

Although it's a sprawling, state-run mess, the largest branch of China Books offers a wide range of books on Chinese art, architecture, and literature without the markups that plague arty bookstores.

Continue east to:

❻ Sōngyúngé (No. 106)

This tiny shop, founded in 1903, stocks a marvelous collection of antiquarian books.

❼ Curio Shops

Further east, the street peters out into in a series of bric-a-brac shops. The sea of credit card signs is fair warning of why the vendors are so friendly. But you'll find a fascinating jumble of Buddhist statuary, lacquerware, ceramics, cloisonné, and jewelry, alongside old pipes, clocks, snuffboxes, and general bric-a-brac.

Liúlichăng Dōng Jiē ends at Yánshòu Jiē. Head south before turning onto the second street on your left (Yīngtáo Xié Jiē), which leads to:

⑧ Dà Zhàlán (Dàshílànr in Běijīng dialect)

Known as Lángfáng Sì Tiáo during the Míng dynasty, its name was changed to Dà Zhàlán after a large stockade was built, presumably to give peace of mind to the wealthy retailers who set up shop here. Now, the proletarian answer to Wángfǔjǐng, it's a bustling pedestrian-only street boasting some of Běijīng's oldest retailers.

In the first block on the right side, you'll find:

⑨ Nèi Lián Shēng Xiédiàn (No. 34)

Established in 1853, this famous shoe store (© **010/6301-4863**) still crafts cloth "happy shoes" *(qiāncéng bùxié)* and delicately embroidered women's shoes by hand. Using a little bit of charm, you may get a peek at the workshop out back.

⑩ Tóngréntáng (No. 24)

Established in 1669, Běijīng's most celebrated dispenser of traditional Chinese medicines (© **010/6303-1155**) has been imitated from Shěnyáng to San Francisco. In the building to the west is a clinic where you can have your pulse read and receive a prescription for your deficiencies. Reassuringly, everyone is lacking something. The second floor stocks raw herbs, including a single ginseng root (said to boost male Yáng energy) from Chángbái Shān in the northeast retailing for ¥380,000 ($47,500).

TAKE A BREAK
Now is a good time to stop for a cup of tea and a Chinese steamed pastry on the second floor of **Zhāng Yīyuán Cháyè Diàn**, Dà Zhàlán Jiē 22 (© **010/6303-1082**; open daily 8am–7pm). The shop sells a bewildering range of teas at reasonable prices. If you're feeling peckish, there's a branch of the celebrated dumpling restaurant, **Gǒubùlǐ Bāozi Diàn** (p. 100), diagonally opposite.

You're nearly at the east end of Dà Zhàlán. Don't miss its most famous store, on the left (north) side:

⑪ Ruìfúxiáng Chóubù Diàn (No. 5)

Established in 1893 on the north side of Dà Zhàlán, this fabric store (open daily 9am–8pm) was once the prime outlet for Qīng dynasty royalty and rich merchants. Sadly, the rich, dark wood panels of the original shop have been replaced by chipboard. Expect to bargain 30% to 50% off the marked prices of the vast selection of silks. A tailor-made *qípáo* (cheongsam) will cost upwards of ¥500 ($60). Allow 1 week, with a couple of fittings.

Turn right down Liángshi Diàn Jiē, the last *hútòng* **before Qián Mén Dàjiē. On the right, you'll find:**

⑫ Liùbìjū Jiàngyuán (No. 3)

Pickles and sauces of every imaginable variety sit in glass-covered ceramic vats. Parts of this dimly lit store look like they've been untouched since they opened for business 400 years ago.

To the south lies Běijīng's old red-light district. If time permits, explore the quiet lanes of the area once known as:

⑬ Bā Dà Hútòng (Eight Great Lanes)

This was a major brothel and theater district before the Communists briefly put an end to the world's oldest industry. A 1906 survey found that the capital boasted 308 brothels (more than the number of hotels or restaurants). Many of the former bordellos now offer simple but atmospheric lodgings (see the box "In the Red Lantern District" in chapter 4). Lanes were once graded into three levels, from "lower area" *(xià chǔ)* streets such as Wángpí Hútòng, where prostitutes satisfied the needs of the masses, up to lanes such as Báishùn Hútòng, where "flower girls" versed in classical poetry and music awaited. Money was no guarantee of success; there were various manuals on the etiquette of wooing courtesans. The Tóngzhì emperor (reign 1862–1874) was notorious for creeping out at night to sample the delights of "clouds and rain." He died of syphilis. These days, "hair salons" in nearby alleys are unlikely to house courtesans skilled in the arts of conversation and playing the lute, but the basic needs of the masses are provided for.

North of Dà Zhàlán the *hútòng* becomes Zhūbǎoshì Jiē, a jumble of stands, shops, and carts peddling cheap clothing and bric-a-brac. Take the first left into:

⑭ Lángfáng Èr Tiáo

During the Qīng dynasty, this *hútòng* was renowned for its jade and antiques vendors. Two- and three-story houses with beautifully carved wooden balconies hint at past wealth. To the south

is Lángfáng Sān Tiáo, is the heart of the former banking district.

Head left (north) along Méishì Jiē up to Lángfáng Tóu Tiáo, known as Lantern Street (Dēng Jiē) during the Qīng dynasty. Turn right (east). Ahead looms:

⑮ Qián Mén (Front Gate)

North of Zhūbǎoshì Jiē is the south end of Tiān'ān Mén Square. To the northeast you'll see the old Front Gate (Qián Mén or more correctly Zhèngyáng Mén), a towering remnant of the city wall through which the emperors passed on their annual procession from the Forbidden City to the Temple of Heaven. Ascend the tower for excellent views of Tiān'ān Mén Square to the north and Dà Zhàlán to the southwest. There's also a photographic exhibition of the streets and walls of old Běijīng.

WINDING DOWN
The world's largest **KFC** is a block west on the south side of Qián Mén Xī Dàjiē. Continuing west, you can take in the nightly performance of opera and acrobatics at **Lǎo Shě Teahouse (Lǎo Shě Cháguǎn)**. It's worth paying extra for a seat close to the front. Performances start at 7:50pm and usually run for about 90 minutes. Call to book a spot (✆ 010/6303-6830). Tea and pastries are included.

WALKING TOUR 2   **BACK LAKES RAMBLE**

Start:	Déshèng Mén Jiànlóu (metro: Jīshuǐ Tán, 218).
Finish:	Prince Gōng's Mansion (Gōng Wáng Fǔ), west side of Qián Hǎi (metro: Jīshuǐ Tán, 218).
Time:	4 to 5 hours.
Best times:	Any time between 9am and noon.
Worst times:	Mondays, when some of the museums and sites are closed.

There is, quite simply, no finer place to walk in Běijīng. The Back Lakes area (Shíchà Hǎi) is composed of three idyllic lakes—Qián Hǎi (Front Lake), Hòu Hǎi (Back Lake), and Xī Hǎi (West Lake)—and the tree-shaded neighborhoods that surround them. Combined with other man-made pools to the south, these lakes were once part of a system used to transport grain by barge from the Grand Canal to the Forbidden City. Prior to 1911, this was an exclusive area, and only people with connections to the imperial family were permitted to maintain houses here (a situation that seems destined to return). A profusion of bars and

Point of interest
Ⓜ Subway/Station stop
🍵 Take a Break

JISHUITAN

start here
here

Desheng Men Xi Dajie

Xinkaixyan

Xi Hai

Desheng Men Dong Dajie

Xitao Hutong

Dashiqiao Hutong

Houhai Beiyan

Gulou Xidajie

Guowang Hutong

Doufuchi Hutong

Desheng Men Nei Dajie

Xinjiekou Bei Dajie

Xinjiekou Dongjie

Luo'er Hutong

Hou Hai

Kong Yiji Jiulou

Yangfang Hutong

Bell Tower

Jiugulou

Ya'er Hutong

Houhai Beiyan

Dashihu Hutong

Hongshan Hutong

Sanbulao Hutong

Mianhua Hutong

Liuyin Jie

Houhai Nanyan

Drum Tower

Guanghua Si

Liuhai Hutong

Shangqin Hutong

Yannian Hutong

finish here

Prince Gong's Mansion

Rive Gauche

Xinjiekou Nan Dajie

Deshengmen Neidajie

Dingfu Jie

Qianhai Xijie

Qianhai Beiyan

Huguo Temple

Huguosi Jie

Qianhai Xijie

Qianhaxi Jie

Qian Hai

Qianhai Nanyan

Di'an Men Nei Dajie

Longtouljing Jie

Xishi Beidajie

Xihuangchengen Beijie

Xishiku Dajie

Di'an Men Xi Dajie

Nine Dragon Screen

Di'an Men Wai Dajie

Xisi Nandajie

Five Dragon Pavilion

Bei Hai

Beijing Children's Palace

White Dagoba

JINGSHAN PARK

0   1/4 mi
0   0.25 km

1   Déshèng Mén Jiànlóu
德胜门箭楼

2   Xú Bēihóng Jìniànguǎn
徐悲鸿纪念馆

3   Cáo Shì Fúzhuāng Fúshì
曹氏服装服饰

4   Former Residence of Soong Ching-ling (Sòng Qìnglíng Gùjū)
宋庆龄故居

5   Exercise yard

6   Guǎnghuà Sì
广化寺

7   Drum Tower (Gǔ Lóu)
鼓楼

8   Yíndìng Qiáo (Silver Ingot Bridge)
银锭桥

9   Zen Cat (Chán Māo)
禅猫

10   Prince Gōng's Mansion (Gōng Wáng Fǔ)
恭王府

cafes has sprung up around the lakes in recent years (see chapter 9, "Běijīng After Dark"), providing ample opportunities to take breaks from your walk.

Beyond the lakes, stretching out to the east and west is the city's best-maintained network of *hútòng*. Many families have lived in these lanes for generations, their insular communities a last link to Old Běijīng.

Begin a few blocks east of the Jīshuǐ Tán metro station (exit A) along the north side of the busy Second Ring Road at:

❶ Déshèng Mén Jiànlóu

The "arrow tower" is a massive fragment of the Míng city wall. Impressive as it is, the main tower (one of nine which once granted access to the capital) was deemed unstable and pulled down in the 1920s. Inside the tower are an ancient coin museum (Gǔdài Qiánbì Zhǎnlǎnguǎn; admission ¥5/60¢; open daily 9am–4pm) and an ancient coin market. Upstairs are exhibits on the history of Běijīng's architecture and an art gallery (Yìsēn Huàláng; free admission; open daily 9am–5:30pm) which houses some of Běijīng's best contemporary art. From the balcony, there's a spectacular view across the Back Lakes.

Retrace your steps, cross the Second Ring Road, and head west back toward the metro. Turn left down the lively main street (Xīnjiēkǒu Běi Dàjiē) and cross the road to:

❷ Xú Bēihóng Jìniànguǎn

The work on display in this memorial hall at Xīnjiēkǒu Běi Dàjiē 53 (✆ 010/6225-2265; admission ¥5/60¢; open daily 9am–11:30am and 1–4:30pm) is immediately familiar—copies of the watercolors of Xú Bēihóng are on display at most tourist sites. Xú did much to revive a moribund art, combining traditional Chinese brushwork with Western techniques he assimilated while studying and traveling in Europe and Japan.

Directly opposite is:

❸ Cáo Shì Fúzhuāng Fúshì

Xīnjiēkǒu is renowned for its clothing and CD shops. Despite the demolition of the west side of the street, it's still going strong, and you can easily spend

an hour perusing this strip. This permanently crowded shop, at Xīnjiēkǒu Běi Dàjiē 56 (✆ 010/6615-0568), stocks Western-style women's woolens and some interesting Chinese designs.

Head north along this bustling thoroughfare, pass a KFC, and turn right (east) onto Bǎn Qiáo Tóu Tiáo. Continue straight along the bank of Xī Hǎi (West Lake) until you reach the top of Hòu Hǎi (Back Lake).

TAKE A BREAK
Right on the northwest edge of the lake is **Kǒng Yǐjǐ Jiǔlóu** (p. 87). Named for the drunken hero of one of Lǔ Xùn's best-known short stories, the restaurant serves Huáiyáng cuisine (from the lower reaches of the Yángzǐ River) in a scholarly setting.

If you're not sufficiently rested, hire a rowboat or a "duck boat" *(yāzi chuán)* and go for a paddle around the lake for about ¥30 ($3.70) per hour.

Directly across the lake is the:

❹ Former Residence of Soong Ching-ling (Sòng Qìnglíng Gùjū)

Located at Hòu Hǎi Běi Yàn 46, this former imperial palace is where Soong Ching-ling (1892–1981), middle daughter of famous Bible salesman Charlie Soong and wife of Sun Yat-sen, spent most of her later life. While her family became leading supporters of the Guómíndǎng (Nationalists), Soong Ching-ling steered a more neutral course, displaying some measure of sympathy for the Communists only after her husband's death in 1925. Máo later rewarded her with this house (admission ¥20/$2.50; open daily 9am–4:30pm). China's last emperor, Henry Pǔyí, is said to have been born on this site. On weekends, there's a risk of being trampled by soon-to-be-wed brides in all their finery.

Turn left and continue southeast along Hòu Hǎi Běi Yàn to the:

⑤ Exercise Yard

On the right-hand side of the road, stretch your limbs and meet some locals. There's table tennis on offer, and Běijīng's hardiest swimmers take the plunge from here—year-round! Joining the swimmers is not recommended: There's a reason they wash themselves so quickly when they get out. Just south of here is a picturesque former royal residence, **Chún Qīnwáng Fǔ.** Open to the public during the Nationalist years but now closed, it was sold to a chap with good connections and (apparently) the intent to open a fancy restaurant; it now stands as another monument to greed and cronyism.

Continue along the lakeshore, take the second left, and immediately turn right into Yǎ'ér Hútòng. On your left is:

⑥ Guǎnghuà Sì

A Buddhist temple (admission free; open daily 8am–5pm) dating back to the Yuán dynasty (1279–1368), this complex originally comprised over 20 buildings with 300 rooms. The temple's founder is said to have been a mendicant monk who ate only half the rice he was given and sold the rest to fund its construction. Only a few of the buildings remain, but these have been well maintained by a small group of resident monks. On the 1st and 15th days of the month, the temple is filled with locals praying for the success of their latest business ventures.

At this point you can make an optional detour eastward to the:

⑦ Drum Tower (Gǔ Lóu)

This vaguely trapezoidal building (admission ¥20/$2.50; open daily 9am–4:30pm) with its bright yellow tile roof is the most conspicuous structure north of the old Imperial City. Skip the "free Tibetan Culture Exhibit" on the first floor (essentially an overpriced

fake antiques market) and go around back to the steep set of stairs that leads to the upper chamber. From here you can survey the Back Lakes and take in tremendous views of the old Tartar City, set against the jagged-tooth backdrop of urban Běijīng.

Walk south on Dì'ān Mén Wài Dàjiē and take the first right onto Yāndài Xiéjiē, home to some of Běijīng's trendiest bars and cafes. Bear left until you reach:

⑧ Yíndìng Qiáo (Silver Ingot Bridge)

This white marble bridge, which marks the boundary between Hòu Hǎi and Qián Hǎi, has stood here for centuries, although the latest version is the work of modern masons (1984). Standing on this bridge in the 18th century, the Qiánlóng emperor could see as far as the Western Hills, and he deemed it one of the Eight Great Views of Běijīng. Air quality has dropped since, but there's plenty of entertainment below the bridge, where the rowboats of romantically minded but unskillful oarsmen bump bows.

Cross the bridge and turn right. Take the winding road along the southwest shore of Hòu Hǎi past a jumble of cafes, bars, and shops, and stop for a peek at:

⑨ Zen Cat (Chán Māo)

Among the first to grasp the appeal of Hòu Hǎi, the effervescent Dōng Zi stocks delightful designer pottery in her ever-changing store, found at Hòu Hǎi Yàn 14 (☎ **010/6651-5392**).

Continue northwest as the road leaves the lakeshore, taking a sharp left turn at a wide intersection into Liǔyīn Jiē. Keep to the left side and you'll soon come to:

⑩ Prince Gōng's Mansion (Gōng Wáng Fǔ)

The most lavish of the courtyard residences in the Back Lakes is located at Liǔyīn Jiē 17 (admission ¥10/$1.25; open daily 8:30am–4:30pm). Inside is one of the city's most spectacular gardens, a combination of pavilions and rockeries perfectly arranged to make it all seem larger than it really is. You're

...seeing part of the picture—the original complex, built by the corrupt eunuch Heshen (said to have been Qiánlóng's catamite), was even larger. More extravagant buildings, built entirely from the rare *nánmù* (cedar), are housed in the National Arts Research Institute (Zhōngguó Yìshù Yánjiūyuàn) next door. See p. 142 for a more detailed description of Prince Gōng's Mansion.

WINDING DOWN
Back on the west shore of Qián Hǎi, a short walk up from the Shuàifǔ Restaurant, is **Rive Gauche** (Zuǒ Àn; ② 010/6612-9300; open daily 2pm–2am). This stylish bar/cafe, located inside an unmarked courtyard-style building with tall wooden doors and large windows overlooking the lake, serves a wide range of drinks, which you can enjoy on immensely comfortable couches.

WALKING TOUR 3 — WÁNGFŬJĬNG SHOPPING CIRCLE

Start:	Wángfǔjǐng Palaeolithic Museum (metro: Wángfǔjǐng, 118).
Finish:	Dōngsì Mosque (metro: Dōng Dān).
Time:	3 to 4 hours.
Best times:	Weekday mornings or late afternoons.
Worst times:	Mondays when most attractions are closed. Lunchtime can be crowded.

Wángfǔjǐng (Well of the Prince's Palace) is the commercial heart of Bĕijīng, the modern face that China's leaders desperately want the world to see. But, as you'll find on this tour, duck down alleyways in any direction and the facade melts away. Situated east of the Forbidden City, Wángfǔjǐng was the favorite residential neighborhood of royalty during the Míng and Qīng dynasties. At the end of the Qīng, when the princes fell on hard times, there was plenty of family silver to be sold. Pawnshops sprang up, and the street got its start as a commercial area. By the end of the 19th century, it was attracting foreign residents, including a correspondent of *The Times,* Australian G. E. Morrison. For a time, the area was known among Westerners as "Morrison Street." It also began catering to foreign tastes, not only for Chinese antiques but for imported luxuries. Unsurprisingly, it was one of the first targets of the Boxer Rebellion in 1900.

You wonder what the xenophobic Boxers would make of it now. There is only a handful of traditional Chinese stores left—most of them have been bulldozed to make way for huge mega-malls that could have been shipped straight from the United States. The cathedral razed by the Boxers was soon rebuilt and was fully refurbished in 1999; its forecourt is a magnet for local skaters, talking a talk and walking a walk that owes nothing to the Confucian Classics. But continuing on, the Boxers might find solace in the small remnants of *hútòng,* the gloriously illustrated books of the **Archaeology Bookshop,** and the distinctly Chinese (and more reasonably priced) fashions and street food on offer in the stalls of **Lóngfú Sì Jiē** and **Dōngsì.**

Taking exit A from the metro, you'll soon come to:

❶ Wángfǔjǐng Palaeolithic Museum

The owners of Oriental Plaza were unimpressed when they struck 24,000-year-old bone in the basement of the largest mall in Asia. However, the powers-that-be couldn't resist the urge to build yet another monument to the longevity of Chinese civilization, and forced the Hong Kong developers to build this fancy museum to house their

Walking Tour 3: Wángfǔjǐng Shopping Circle

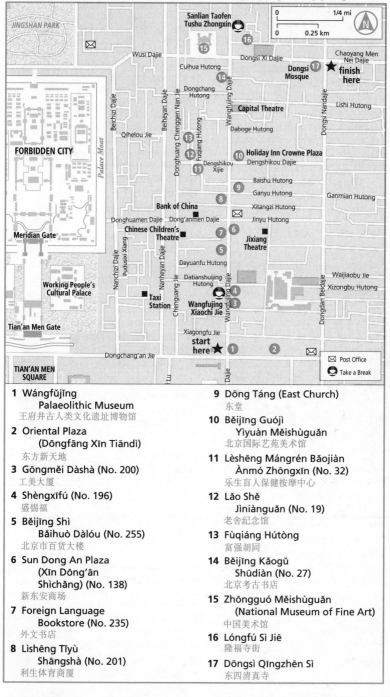

1 Wángfǔjǐng
 Palaeolithic Museum
 王府井古人类文化遗址博物馆

2 Oriental Plaza
 (Dōngfāng Xīn Tiāndì)
 东方新天地

3 Gōngměi Dàshà (No. 200)
 工美大厦

4 Shèngxīfú (No. 196)
 盛锡福

5 Běijīng Shì
 Bǎihuò Dàlóu (No. 255)
 北京市百货大楼

6 Sun Dong An Plaza
 (Xīn Dōng'ān
 Shìchǎng) (No. 138)
 新东安商场

7 Foreign Language
 Bookstore (No. 235)
 外文书店

8 Lìshēng Tǐyù
 Shāngshà (No. 201)
 利生体育商厦

9 Dōng Táng (East Church)
 东堂

10 Běijīng Guójì
 Yìyuàn Měishùguǎn
 北京国际艺苑美术馆

11 Lèshēng Mángrén Bǎojiàn
 Ànmó Zhōngxīn (No. 32)
 乐生盲人保健按摩中心

12 Lǎo Shě
 Jìniànguǎn (No. 19)
 老舍纪念馆

13 Fùqiáng Hútòng
 富强胡同

14 Běijīng Kǎogǔ
 Shūdiàn (No. 27)
 北京考古书店

15 Zhōngguó Měishùguǎn
 (National Museum of Fine Art)
 中国美术馆

16 Lóngfú Sì Jiē
 隆福寺街

17 Dōngsì Qīngzhēn Sì
 东四清真寺

distant ancestors (admission ¥10/ $1.25).

Ascend the escalator to find yourself in the basement of:

➋ Oriental Plaza (Dōngfāng Xīn Tiāndì)

If you don't get enough of this back home, have a poke around Asia's largest shopping center, which stretches east all the way to the next metro station at Dōng Dān. Watson's drugstore, Sony ExploraScience museum, Schlotzsky's Deli, Danesi's Cafe, and the 24-hour restaurant Be There or Be Square (Bú Jiàn Bú Sàn); p. 84) are all here.

Emerging from the west side of the mall, stick to the right (east) side and head north up Wángfǔjǐng Dàjiē, passing the huge but chaotic Wángfǔjǐng Bookstore. Cross the road to:

➌ Gōngměi Dàshà (No. 200)

This is the most reliable shop in town at which to purchase jade rather than the colored glass you'll likely encounter elsewhere. Aim to pay about a third of the marked price. They also stock high-quality tea sets and calligraphy materials, alongside tacky souvenirs. On the fourth floor is a small but interesting craft exhibit (open weekdays 9am–6:30pm, weekends 10am–6:30pm).

Continue along the right-hand side of Wángfǔjǐng Dàjiē to:

➍ Shèngxīfú (No. 196)

Established in 1912, this hat shop was one of the fortunate few to survive. An embarrassing paean to the wisdom of China's leaders on the first floor hints that they're not taking survival for granted. The modern hats are popular with locals, but the shop displays its revolutionary credentials on the second floor, which brims with sturdy Léi Fēng hats (think earflaps, thick tops, shiny red stars) and proletarian Máo caps.

TAKE A BREAK
Wángfǔjǐng Xiǎochī Jiē is about as spruced up as street food gets in Běijīng. Ordering is a cinch—everything is on display, and the vendors are well versed in sign language. In the evening, the **Dōnghuá Mén night market** (p. 99), further north, offers more choices.

Return to Wángfǔjǐng Dàjiē, and continue north along the left (west) side to:

➎ Běijīng Shì Bǎihuò Dàlóu (No. 255)

Despite a recent merger with the fancy Sun Dong An Plaza, the upper floors of Běijīng's premier department store are as chaotic as ever. A branch of China Silk on the third floor offers silk at economical prices.

The east side of the pedestrian mall is dominated by what was just a few years ago China's glitziest shopping center:

➏ Sun Dong An Plaza (Xīn Dōng'ān Shìchǎng) (No. 138)

Rising like a tombstone on the grave of shop-vendors past, this massive emporium holds designer clothing shops and the usual Western and Japanese food chains—Baskin Robbins, Pizza Hut, McDonald's, KFC, Yoshinoya, UCC, Starbucks, and Délifrance. There's also an excellent hotpot restaurant, **Dōng Lái Shùn,** which recently celebrated its 100th anniversary. The old shops that once stood here are mocked by **Old Běijīng Street,** a stupendously tacky re-creation found in the basement.

Directly across Wángfǔjǐng Dàjiē, on the west side, beyond the life-size bronze statues of a Qīng dynasty barber, a musician, and a rickshaw puller, is the:

➐ Foreign Language Bookstore (No. 235)

The Wàiwén Shūdiàn houses Běijīng's largest selection of English-language materials on the first and third floors. The second floor has a surprisingly wide range of CDs featuring local alternative bands, as well as Běijīng opera and soothing instrumental music.

Continue north along the left side, where you'll find:

⑧ Lìshēng Tǐyù Shāngshà (No. 201)

A purveyor of sporting goods since 1921, the store has mountains of sporting clothes and shoes. The basement stocks everything from imported camping gear and skateboards to bizarre, gyrating massage machines and huge shuffleboard tables. **Hóngshēng Musical Instruments,** a highbrow vendor of pianos (grand and otherwise), looks out of place on the third floor.

Diagonally across the road, it's hard to miss:

⑨ Dōng Táng (East Church)

Also known as St. Joseph's Cathedral, this gray Gothic structure has endured a torrid history. Built on ground donated by the Shùnzhì emperor in 1655, this Jesuit church was toppled by an earthquake in 1720, gutted by a fire in 1807, and completely razed during the Boxer Rebellion of 1900. Sunday services are held at 6:15, 7, and 8am. After a major renovation from 1999 to 2000, the church became notable for its wide, tree-lined forecourt, the favorite spot of Běijīng's skaters.

Continuing north up Wángfǔjīng Dàjiē, you come to a second major intersection with Dēngshìkǒu Dàjiē. Cross over and enter the Crowne Plaza Běijīng. To the right-hand side of the lobby you'll find:

⑩ Běijīng Guójì Yìyuàn Měishùguǎn

This art gallery (✆ **010/6513-3388**; open daily 9am–6pm) can be hit-and-miss, and is often clogged with flaccid depictions of rural and *hútòng* life. But their collection of Russian oil paintings, most from the early 1990s, contains some startling and innovative works. You can't go too far wrong—the works are not for sale, admission is free, and staff is exceptionally friendly.

Cross over and follow Dēngshìkǒu Xī Jiē a long block west. If your feet are aching, look for the Dōnghuá Fàndiàn on the left-hand side and pop up to the second floor, where you'll find:

⑪ Lèshēng Mángrén Bǎojiàn Ànmó Zhōngxīn (No. 32)

"Loving Life Massage Center" (open daily 11am–11:30pm) can lift you up with a full body massage (*quán shēn ànmó*) or a foot wash and rub (*zúdǐ ànmó*). ¥88 ($11) buys an hour of bliss. "Hot pot" (*bá huǒ guàn*) won't fill your belly, but the heated glass bowls will leave red welts all over your back.

If you can still walk, there are two narrow lanes opposite. The lane to the left, Fēngfù Hútòng, is the site of:

⑫ Lǎo Shě Jìniànguǎn (No. 19)

The memorial hall to Lǎo Shě, one of China's best-loved writers, is located in a quiet and atmospheric courtyard residence (p. 141). Former premier Zhōu Ēnlái bestowed the house on the writer when he returned from overseas in 1950. While the regime hoped Lǎo Shě would become a cheerleader like fellow scribbler Guō Mòruò, his post-liberation years were relatively unproductive, and his final work (before he drowned himself in a Cultural Revolution–induced suicide) concerned his Manchu ancestors.

Retrace your steps back to the narrow alleyway to the east, and turn left (north). You are now on:

⑬ Fùqiáng Hútòng

The immodestly named "Rich and Powerful" Hútòng still boasts some *sìhéyuàn* courtyard houses that hint at its wealthy past. Note the finely carved roof lintels with swastika motifs and the lotus-emblazoned door piers (*mén dūnr*) at no. 18. While the rectangular door pier indicates the residents weren't officials (whose houses were marked by circular door piers), they must have been well-off to be able to afford skilled stonemasons.

The *hútòng* ends at a T-junction. Turn right to Wángfǔjǐng Dàjiē. To the south you can see Shǒudū Jùchǎng (Capital Theater), but turn left and head north. On your left is:

⑭ Běijīng Kǎogǔ Shūdiàn (No. 27)

Most bookshops near the National Museum of Fine Art are fond of the "stick-up"—a sticker that elevates the price of the book by as much as a factor of eight. Not this shop (open daily 9am–8pm), which houses a staggering range of art and architecture folios. To the right as you enter, you'll find bronze reproductions of drinking vessels, cooking tripods, and the inevitable "flying horse" *(tóng bēn mǎ)*.

Continuing north, you reach the intersection with Wǔsì Dàjiē. Off to the left, it's impossible to miss:

⑮ Zhōngguó Měishùguǎn (National Museum of Fine Art)

Along with musicians and reformist politicians, avant-garde artists took much of the blame for "spiritually polluting" the minds of China's young folks in the 1980s. Once the place to see cutting-edge art, the National Museum of Fine Art (© **010/6401-7076;** open Tues–Sun 9am–4:30pm) gained a conservative director and a well-earned reputation for lackluster exhibitions. After a year-long makeover, the Cultural Bureau promises those days are over. Decide for yourself.

> **TAKE A BREAK**
> Just east of the National Museum of Fine Art is one of Běijīng's most interesting Chinese-language bookstores, **Sānlián Tāofèn Túshū Zhōngxīn**, at Měishùguǎn Dōng Jiē 22 (open daily 9am–9pm). The second floor houses gorgeous pictorials, a music store, and a tranquil cafe.

Backtrack south from the bookstore, and take the next street on your left:

⑯ Lóngfú Sì Jiē

In the early 1990s this was Běijīng's finest pedestrian shopping street. It's slowly slipped down market but is still a lively spot to hunt for cheap clothes, music, and street food. It makes a delightful contrast to its main competitor, Wángfǔjǐng. Halfway down the street, on the south side, is a branch of Běijīng's most renowned vendor of wonton soup *(húntun)*, **Húntun Hóu**, looking much more at home here than the original store does on Wángfǔjǐng.

An archway marks the end of the mall. In front of you is Dōngsì Běi Dàjiē. Turn right and head south to Dōngsì Nán Dàjiē. On the right-hand side, you soon arrive at:

⑰ Dōngsì Qīngzhēn Sì

This is one of Běijīng's earliest mosques (© **010/6262-7824;** admission ¥10/ $1.25 for non-Muslims; open daylight hours). It has enjoyed a peaceful history of worship since the 14th century. The second courtyard is serene, a wonderful break from the mercantile and traffic pandemonium. At press time the mosque was undergoing a full-scale makeover, which should be completed in early 2004. Call to check if they're open.

You can either walk north (or take bus no. 807) to Yōnghé Gōng and Kǒng Miào (20 min.); or cross the road, head south, and take the second street east toward Guānfù Classical Art Museum (15 min.); or you can head south towards the Dōng Dān metro station and the east end of Oriental Plaza (15 min.). In the basement, you'll find:

>
>
> **WINDING DOWN**
> Be There or Be Square (Bú Jiàn Bú Sàn; p. 84), in the basement of Oriental Plaza, offers Hong Kong–style food in a spacious, warehouse-like space. The pork buns, Singapore noodles, and congee are heavenly. If you're in need of a pick-up, try the caffeine-laden milk tea.

8

Shopping

by Graeme Smith

Writer Wáng Shuò memorably observed that there were still devout Communists to be found in China, all of them safely under lock and key in a mental asylum. Consumerism is now the official ideology of China, and shopping is the national sport. Spend, spend, and spend some more is the message drummed into China's bewildered citizens at every turn. To this end, they were granted extra holidays, with the May and October holidays extended from 1 or 2 days to a whole week.

Dusty, empty, and useless state-run department stores are thankfully a thing of the past, though the **Friendship Store** still stands as an amusing reminder of the old days. Mega-malls, shopping streets, and the remaining open-air markets fight for a share of the spoils. Bad times for shopping forays are weekends and evenings, when it can feel as if all of Běijīng's 10 million residents line up at the cash registers to do their bit for the economic miracle.

1 The Shopping Scene

Western-style shopping malls are flexing their muscles in Běijīng, replacing the traditional storefronts, Chinese department stores, and alley markets. Even the new, privately run stores on major shopping streets tend to be versions of the boutiques and specialty outlets familiar to shoppers in the West. But there are still plenty of open-air markets and street-side vendors offering more traditional arts and crafts, collectibles, and clothing, usually at prices far below those in the big plazas and modern stores.

BĚIJĪNG'S BEST BUYS

Stores and markets in Běijīng sell everything from cashmere and silk to knock-off designer-label clothing and athletic wear, antiques, traditional art, cloisonné, lacquerware, Míng furniture, Máo memorabilia, and enough miscellaneous Chinesey doodads to stuff Christmas stockings from now until eternity. Prices are reasonable (certainly lower than in the Asian goods boutiques back home), though increasingly less so. Cheap one-time-use luggage is widely available for hauling your booty if you get carried away.

Before you rush to the ATM, however, it is important to remember that not all that is green and gleams in Běijīng is jade. Indeed, the majority of it is colored glass. The same principle holds for pearls, famous-brand clothing, antiques, and just about everything else. If you plan to make big purchases, you should educate yourself about quality and price well beforehand.

BĚIJĪNG'S TOP SHOPPING AREAS

The grandest shopping area in Běijīng is on and around **Wángfǔjǐng Dàjiē,** east of the Forbidden City. The street was overhauled in 1999, and the south section

---

Tips "Hello, I'm an Art Student"

You should be leery of any English-speaking youngsters who claim to be **art students** and offer to take you to see a special exhibit of their work. This is a **scam**. The art, which you will be compelled to buy, almost always consists of assembly-line reproductions of famous (or not so famous) paintings offered at prices several dozen times higher than their actual value. You are almost sure to encounter this nonsense in the **Wángfǔjǐng** and **Liúlichǎng** areas.

---

was turned into a pedestrian-only commercial avenue lined with clothing outlets, souvenir shops, portrait studios, fast-food restaurants, and the city's top two malls—the Sun (Xīn) Dōng Ān Plaza and Oriental Plaza (Dōngfāng Guǎngchǎng). **Dōng Dān Běi Dàjiē,** a long block east, is a strip of clothing boutiques and CD shops popular among fashionable Běijīng youth. On the western side of town is the mirror image of Dōng Dān, bustling **Xīnjiēkǒu Dàjiē.**

Other major Westernized shopping areas include the section of **Jiànguó Mén Wài Dàjiē** between the Friendship Store and the China World Trade Center, and the neighborhood outside the **Northeast Third Ring Road North,** southeast of Sān Yuán Qiáo around the new embassy district.

Běijīng's liveliest shopping zone, the one most beloved of tourists for its atmosphere and Chinese-style goods, is the centuries-old commercial district southwest of Qián Mén. **Liúlichǎng** is an almost too-quaint collection of art, book, tea, and antiques shops lined up side by side in a polished-for-tourists Old Běijīng–style *hútòng* running east–west 2 blocks south of the Hépíng Mén metro stop. The street is good for window-shopping strolls and small purchases—like the unavoidable **chop** (*túzhāng;* stone or jade stamp), carved with your name—but beware large purchases: Almost everything here is fake and overpriced. In a similar setting but infinitely more raucous, Dà Zhàlán (pronounced Dàshílànr in the Běijīng dialect) is the prole alternative to Wángfǔjǐng Dàjiē. Located in a pedestrian-only *hútòng* 2 blocks due south of Qián Mén, it is jammed on either side with cheap clothing outlets, cheap restaurants, and cheap luggage shops (see "Walking Tour 1: Liúlichǎng & Dà Zhàlán" in chapter 7).

2 Markets & Bazaars

Although malls and shopping centers are becoming more popular, the majority of Běijīng residents still shop in markets. Whether indoors or out, these markets are inexpensive, chaotic and, for the visitor, tremendously interesting. Payment is in cash, bargaining is universal, and pickpockets are plentiful. Perhaps the most common item you'll find in the markets these days is not silk, souvenirs, or crafts, but designer-label clothing, much of it knockoffs with the upscale labels sewn in, although some items are factory seconds or overruns (sometimes smuggled out of legitimate brand-name factories).

The most popular market is **Silk Alley;** the best for clothing and jewelry is **Hóng Qiáo Shìchǎng;** the most interesting is **Pānjiāyuán Jiùhuò Shìchǎng** (also known as "Dirt Market," "Sunday Market," or "Ghost Market"); but there are many others worth browsing.

SILK ALLEY (XIÙSHUǏ JIĒ) ⭐ *Overrated*   This is Běijīng's most famous market among foreign visitors, a crowded maze of stalls selling the city's largest selection of knockoff shoes and clothing—and very little silk. Prices aren't as good as they used to be, and the vendors have learned how to insult your mother in English if you make them lose face. Under no circumstances should you pay more than ¥150 ($20) for a North Face (North Fake, the expats call it) jacket, ¥50 ($6) for a business shirt, or ¥100 ($12) for a pair of jeans. But with Běijīng's outdoor markets being herded inside one by one, Silk Alley would seem to be peddling on borrowed time. It runs north off Jiànguó Mén Wài Dàjiē just west of the Jiànguó Hotel, close to the northwest exit (A) of the Yǒng'ān Lǐ metro stop. It's open daily from 9am to around 5:30pm.

HÓNG QIÁO SHÌCHǍNG ⭐⭐   Also called the **Pearl Market,** Hóng Qiáo Shìchǎng is located at Hóng Qiáo Lù 16 (℃ **010/6713-3354**), just northeast of Tiān Tán Gōngyuán (Temple of Heaven Park) and north of Tìyùguǎn Lù. Hóng Qiáo began life as a fascinating curio market outside Tiān Tán Gōngyuán, but like most outdoor markets it was forced indoors and spruced up. It is now tucked away on the third floor of this four-story market. Popular purchases include reproductions of 1920s Shànghǎi advertisements for "cow soap" and insecticide (where bugs crawl over comely maidens dressed in *qípáo*). Also popular is Cultural Revolution kitsch, such as clocks with Red Guards waving Little Red Books and the book itself in many manifestations (a basic model should cost no more than ¥20/$2.50). On the first floor, look out for flamethrower-like cigarette lighters that play "The East is Red" *("Dōngfāng Hóng")* when you light up. Elsewhere in the store, you'll need to bargain hard for brand-name clothing, footwear, luggage, fake Rolex watches, and pearls (see below), which attract swarms of large, bottle-blonde Russian women. If you get carried away, there's a post office on the fourth floor. The **toy market** *(wánjù shìchǎng),* housed in a separate building at the back, is often overlooked by visitors. Starting prices here are more reasonable, and there are candles, incense, and stationery on the upper floors. From just north of the Chóngwén Mén metro stop, take bus no. 807 to Hóng Qiáo, and cross the footbridge to reach the market. It's open daily from 8:30am to 7pm.

PĀNJIĀYUÁN JIÙHUÒ SHÌCHǍNG ⭐⭐⭐   Eureka! This is the Chinese shopping experience of dreams: row upon crowded row of calligraphy, jewelry, ceramics, teapots, ethnic clothing, Buddha statues, paper lanterns, Cultural

---

Tips **What You Need to Know About Knockoffs & Fakes**

The Customs services of most nations frown on the importation of knockoffs. The U.S. Customs Service allows U.S. residents to return with one trademark-protected item of each type; that is, one counterfeit watch, one knockoff purse, one camera with a questionable trademark, and so on. You are not permitted to bring back a dozen "Polo" shirts as gifts for friends. Even if the brand name is legitimate, you are not a licensed importer. Copyrighted products, such as CD-ROMs and books, must have been manufactured under the copyright owner's authorization; otherwise, tourists may not import even one of these items—they are pirated. The U.S. Customs Service booklet *Know Before You Go* and the U.S. Customs website (www.customs.ustreas.gov) provide further guidelines.

Tips **Buying Pearls**

Most of the pearls on sale at **Hóng Qiáo Shìchǎng** are genuine, although of too low quality to be sold in Western jewelry shops. However, some fakes are floating around. To test if the pearls you want to buy are real, try any one of the following:

- Nick the surface with a sharp blade (the color should be uniform within and without)
- Rub the pearl across your teeth (this should make a grating sound)
- Scrape the pearl on a piece of glass (real pearls leave a mark)
- Pass it through a flame (fake pearls turn black, real ones don't)

Strange as it may feel to do these tests, vendors are generally willing to let you carry them out and might even help, albeit with bemused faces. If you'd rather not bother (and most don't), just assume the worst, shop for fun, and spend modestly.

Revolution memorabilia, PLA belts, little wooden boxes, Míng- and Qīng-style furniture, old pipes, opium scales, and painted human skulls. The market is also known as the Dirt or Ghost Market. There are some real antiques scattered among the junk, but you'd have to be an expert to pick them out. Locals arrive Saturday and Sunday mornings at dawn or shortly after (hence the "Ghost" label) to find the best stuff; vendors start to leave around 4pm. Initial prices given to foreigners are always absurdly high—Máo clocks, for instance, should cost less than ¥40 ($5) rather than the ¥400 ($50) you'll likely be asked to pay. The market is located on the south side of Pānjiāyuán Lù, just inside the southeast corner of the Third Ring Road. It's open Saturday and Sunday from noon until about 4pm.

SĀNLÌTÚN YĀXIÙ FÚZHUĀNG SHÌCHǍNG ★★   Běijīng's clothing vendors have to be nimble—here you'll find refugees from two now-extinct outdoor markets, Yǎbǎo Lù and Sānlìtún. Neither loss will be greatly mourned, particularly the old Yǎbǎo Lù market, a shabby collection of fake fur and bric-a-brac stalls. Opened in May 2002, the new market occupies the old Kylin Plaza building (Qílín Dàshà) and retains at least one feature of the old Kylin—excellent tailors can be found on the third floor. The fourth floor is a fine hunting ground for souvenirs and gifts—there are kites from Wéifāng in Shāndōng, calligraphy materials, army surplus gear, tea sets, and farmer's paintings from Xī'ān (laughably claiming to be originals by Pān Xiǎolíng, the most frequently copied artist). You can even treat yourself to a manicure for just ¥20 ($2.50). The basement and the first two floors house a predictable but comprehensive collection of imitation and pilfered brand-name clothing, shoes, and luggage. Starting prices are only slightly less imaginative than those at the more trammeled Silk Market. The market is just west of Sānlìtún Jiǔbā Jiē, at Gōngtǐ Běi Lù 58 (© **010/6415-1726**), and is open daily from 9:30am to 8pm.

TIĀNYÌ XIǍOSHĀNGPǏN PĪFĀ SHÌCHǍNG ★ *Finds*   Tiānyì is the ultimate "Made in China" shopping experience. You'll find it 4 blocks west of the Fùchéng Mén metro stop (203) at Fùchéng Mén Wài Dàjiē 259 (© **010/6832-7529**), on the north side of the road. It's all here, crammed into hundreds of stalls in a spanking-new five-story building tucked behind the old market. The range of toys, sporting equipment, electronic appliances, and luggage is eye-popping. The market is very much for the locals, so prices are reasonable. But just because the vendor may have never seen a foreigner doesn't mean he or she doesn't know how to fleece one. The market is open daily from 7:30am to 5pm.

MORE MARKETS   Although **Liàngmǎ Qiáo Market,** opposite the Kempinski Hotel in northeast Běijīng, has been leveled by bulldozers (to make way for a new embassy row), and although the popular **Sānlǐtún** clothing and wicker markets have been shut down, too, there are still plenty of markets to explore.

Bàoguó Sì Wénhuà Gōngyìpǐn Shìchǎng (© **010/6303-0976**) is Pānjiāyuán in miniature. Although it's open every day of the week, set on the leafy grounds of a pleasant temple and a 10-minute walk from the metro, this delightful market sees few foreign visitors. It offers mostly bric-a-brac, but vendors aren't pushy, and asking prices are reasonable. Coins, antiquarian books, and Cultural Revolution memorabilia abound. The market is liveliest on Thursday and Saturday mornings. From the Chángchūn Jiē metro stop (205, exit D), walk south along Chángchūn Jiē and take the third right onto a tree-lined avenue that ends at the east gate of Xuānwǔ Yīyuàn. Follow your nose southwest through the *hútòng* to Bàoguó Sì. It's open daily from 8am to 4pm.

Handily located just south of Pānjiāyuán on the west side of Huáwēi Qiáo, **Curio City (Gǔwán Chéng; © 010/6774-7711)** boasts four floors of jewelry (including diamonds and jade), old clocks, cloisonné, furniture, and porcelain, as well as curios and genuine antiques. This establishment sees its share of tour groups; bargaining is essential. There's even a "duty-free" section where you are asked to go through the charade of pulling out your passport and air ticket. Skip this. International shipping is provided. Curio City is open daily from 9:30am to 6:30pm.

Guānyuán Shìchǎng, north of the Fùchéng Mén metro stop (203, exit B) along the east side of the Second Ring Road (Xīchéng) is Běijīng's best bird market. Much of the market has been moved indoors, though it still spills into the crowded *hútòng* to the east. The insect market, in the alley behind the last hall, is not to be missed. Old men select the best grasshoppers for either singing or sport—cricket fighting! The main building houses fishing equipment, "jade," chops, Buddhist statuary, kites, and pet rocks, all of dubious value. The market is open daily from 8:30am to 6:30pm in summer (closes an hour earlier in winter); arrive early for some spectacular photography.

It's hard to imagine anything more chaotic than the original Yǎbǎo Lù Market, but the spanking-new **Lǎo Fān Jiē Fúzhuāng Shìchǎng,** or **Alien's Street** (no, really!) is impossible not to get lost in. The first floor houses shoes, and the second floor is a jumble of fake brand-name clothing. Cheap, expansive, and sometimes nasty, this market is popular with Russian residents. Take the second right as you head east from the Cháoyáng Mén metro stop (212, exit B), and continue south; the market is on the left (east) side.

3 Shopping A to Z

ANTIQUES & CURIOS

The **Pānjiāyuán Jiùhuò Shìchǎng** market (see above) was once *the* place to look for antiques, and it still is for bric-a-brac and oddities. If you're not in town on the weekend, visit **Bàoguó Sì Wénhuà Gōngyìpǐn Shìchǎng** market (see above), which has similar curiosities in a more pleasant setting. Any cracked and dusty treasure you find is almost certainly fake, but you won't have trouble taking it home. Genuine antiques are not allowed out of the country without an official **red wax seal,** and pieces made prior to 1795 cannot be exported at all. "Certified" antiques are available at astronomical prices in the **Friendship Store** (p. 172), at a few hotel gift shops, and in some of the nicer malls. But determined antiques lovers should look elsewhere.

Guǎng Hàn Táng Set in a delightful courtyard house constructed from the ruins of a derelict factory, all of Guǎng Hàn Táng's pieces could be described as partially restored, as they maintain a feeling of antiquity. Prices are serious, but so is the owner, Mr Liáng. No fakes here. Cǎochángdì. (Take the Dà Shānzǐ exit off the airport expressway, follow Jīchǎng Fù Lù northeast, and take the 2nd right onto Nán Gāo Lù. After passing under the railway line, take the left fork in the road and follow the signs.) ⓒ **010/8456-7943.** www.guanghantang.com. Daily 10am–5pm. Bus: 418 from Dōng Zhí Mén metro stop (214/ 1316, exit B) to Cǎochángdì.

Huáyì Classical Furniture (Huáyì Gǔdiǎn Jiājù) With nine halls filled with restored and unfinished antique furniture, Huáyì has an unrivalled range at very reasonable prices. Softwood furniture, such as fir *(shānmù)* and elm *(yúmù),* is disparagingly referred to as "firewood" *(cháimù)* by the locals, though the sturdiness of the latter wood is recognized in the expression for a die-hard traditionalist, *yúmù nǎodai,* literally "elm brain." Hardwood furniture, such as rosewood *(zǐtán* or *hóngmù),* commands a higher price. You'll see sturdy baskets used for carrying a bride's dowry *(gàngxiāng),* and a food cupboard with small holes for ventilation called the "infuriate-the-cat cupboard" *(qì sǐ māo guì).* There's also a showroom on the third floor of Curio City. Packaging and shipping are available. Dōng Wěi Lù, Xiǎo Diàn 89, Cháoyáng Qū. (10-min. drive east of Guǎng Hàn Táng. Take the Dà Shānzǐ exit off the airport expressway, follow Jīchǎng Fù Lù northeast, and turn right at Dōng Wěi Lù.) ⓒ **010/8431-1836.** www.cyjj.com. Daily 9am–6pm. Bus: 418 from Dōng Zhí Mén metro stop (214/1316, exit B) to Dōng Wěi Lù.

Lǔ Bān Gǔdiǎn Jiājù Chéng *Finds* Just east of town, Gāobēidiàn—one of the largest antique furniture markets in China—is one of Běijīng's best-kept secrets. Lǔ Bān was the first shop to open at the location in 1991, but it's remarkable that over a decade later so few locals know of its existence. This outlet is the most reliable of the many furniture stores in Gāobēidiàn. But if you know what you're looking for, the real bargains can be found in small workshops opened by enterprising peasants from Shāndōng, Shānxī, and Ānhuī. At least half of the merchandise is bogus, and any furniture marked with a tag that says TIBETAN should be regarded as counterfeit until proven otherwise. If time permits, visit the **Red Sandalwood Museum** (p. 139) just north of Gāobēidiàn to brush up on your knowledge of Chinese antique furniture. Gāobēidiàn 4 Duì. (from Gāobēidiàn bus stop continue south for around 90m/100 yards; turn left just before the railway tracks). ⓒ **010/ 8575-6516.** Daily 8:30am–6pm. Bus: 363 from Sìhuì Dōng metro stop (125, exit B, cross road) to Gāobēidiàn.

ART SUPPLIES

Liúlichǎng (see "Walking Tour 1: Liúlichǎng & Dà Zhàlán" in chapter 7) has many small shops and stalls selling calligraphy brushes, brush racks, chops, fans, ink stones, paper, and other art supplies. The best bargains are found in the stalls toward the far west end. The most famous outlet is **Róngbǎo Zhāi,** Liúlichǎng Xī Jiē 19 (ⓒ **010/6303-6090**), although its prices are pushed ever higher by

---

Fun Fact The Pigeon Has Landed

Sadly, China's most beloved bicycle, the **Flying Pigeon (Fēigē)**, is no longer with us. The factory in Tiānjīn, which turned out black, steel-framed, one-speed bicycles, recently closed its doors. Designed in 1950, the bike with the FP crest set the standard for millions of proletarian bikes that were to follow. Its maker was keen to show his support for peace during the Korean War, and doubtless meant "Flying Dove" rather than "Flying Pigeon." But the bike looks more like a pigeon.

During the struggle for power during the late 1970s, Dèng Xiǎopíng once promised that "every household would have a Flying Pigeon." Sadly, his promise goes unfulfilled, as the "Four Preconditions" (sì dà jiàn) for a man hoping to find a worthy bride now include a car. Those hoping to purchase a piece of cycling history for around ¥60 ($7.50) should look for a street-side bicycle-repair stall.

---

tour groups. Forgotten your credit card? Not to worry—there's a Bank of China currency exchange in the shop! It's open daily 9am to 5:30pm. Many art-supply shops cluster around the **National Gallery. Bǎihuá Měishù Yòngpǐn,** located diagonally across from the gallery at Wǔsì Dàjiē 12 (© 010/6513-1721), stocks a wide range of modern art supplies and also has a reliable framing service. It's open daily 9am to 6pm. The largest art store in Běijīng is **Gōngměi Dàshà** at Wángfǔjǐng Dàjiē 200 (© 010/6528-8866), although its prices are high. It's open daily from 8am to 6pm.

BIKES

Qián Mén Zìxíngchē Shāngdiàn   One of Běijīng's largest bike stores is handily located a short walk south of Qián Mén. New brands, such as Giant and Strong, dominate. But there are still some old-style Forever (Yǒngjiǔ) bicycles. Sadly, there's not a Flying Pigeon in sight (see "The Pigeon has Landed" box above). Qián Mén Dàjiē 97, Xuānwǔ Qū. © 010/6303-1014. Daily 8:30am–6:30pm. Metro: Qián Mén (208, exit C).

BOARD GAMES

Xīng Qíyì Yuàn Shāngmào Zhōngxīn   Better known in the West by the Japanese name of go, the complex game of strategy, wéiqí, is undergoing a welcome resurgence in its native land, if the number of TV programs dedicated to its exposition are any guide (although it doesn't make for great television). This friendly shop outside the south gate of the National Sports Training Center, where many of China's wéiqí masters work, sells boards and the 361 black-and-white pieces that fill in the spaces. These start at ¥40 ($5) for metal pieces in a wicker basket, and rise to ¥3,600 ($450) for agate stones in a jade bowl. "Traditional" Chinese chess, or xiàngqí, is more commonly seen on the street. Elaborate xiàngqí sets are also sold. Tiān Tán Dōng Lù 80. © 010/6711-4691. Weekdays 9am–5pm; weekends 9am–3pm. Metro: Chóngwén Mén (209), then bus 807 to Dōng Cè Lù; cross bridge and head south, then turn left onto Cháng Qīng Lù.

BOOKS

The bookshop on the first floor of the **Friendship Store** (p. 172) offers a wide range of English-language magazines. Those looking for maps of anyplace in

China should try the first floor of **Wángfǔjǐng Shūdiàn,** Wángfǔjǐng Dàjiē 218 (© **010/6513-2842;** open daily 9am–9pm).

China Bookstore (Zhōngguó Shūdiàn) Liúlichǎng is the place to buy Chinese art books that hotels, museums, and galleries are all fond of marking up. This is the largest of several branches. Liúlichǎng Dōng Jiē 115 (northeast side of the intersection with Nán Xīnhuá Jiē), Xuānwǔ Qū. © 010/6303-5759. Daily 9am–6:30pm (until 6pm in winter). Metro: Hépíng Mén (207, exit C).

Foreign Language Bookstore (Wàiwén Shūdiàn) You'll find a wide selection of maps on the first floor and the largest collection of English-language books in Běijīng on the third floor. Wángfǔjǐng Dàjiē 235, Dōngchéng Qū. © 010/6512-6903. Daily 9am–8:30pm. Metro: Wángfǔjǐng (118, exit A).

Sānlián Tāofèn Túshū Zhōngxīn Come here for the most interesting selection of Chinese-language books in Běijīng, although **Wànshèng Shūdiàn,** south of Qīnghuá University in Hǎidiàn, runs a close second. There's a quiet cafe on the second floor, but most patrons prefer the stairwell. Měishùguǎn Dōng Jiē 22, Dōngchéng Qū. © 010/6400-2710. Daily 9am–9pm. Bus: 803 from north of Wángfǔjǐng metro stop (118, exit A) to Měishùguǎn.

Sānwèi Shūwū Public outrage spared Běijīng's original "dissident bookstore" from being converted into a patch of lawn in 2002. Downstairs is a small bookstore with a few English-language titles. Upstairs is a tranquil, traditional teahouse (p. 184), ideal for a quiet read during the day. Fùxīng Mén Nèi Dàjiē 60 (west of the metro stop, opposite Mínzú Wénhuà Gōng, on the corner of Tónglíngé Lù), Xīchéng Qū. © 010/6601-3204. Daily 9:30am–10:30pm. Metro: Xīdān (115, exit E).

CAMERAS & FILM

Color film and processing are readily arranged, but you're probably better off waiting until you return home or pass through Hong Kong. For black-and-white processing (the only choice for depicting Běijīng in winter), try **Àitúměi Cǎisè Kuòyìn Zhōngxīn,** Xīnjiēkǒu Nán Dàjiē 87 (© **010/6616-0718**), open daily 9am to 9pm. Běijīng is not the place to buy new cameras and accessories, but those looking for secondhand parts for their ancient SLR camera, or wanting to experiment with ancient Russian swing lens cameras, have the two excellent markets listed in this section.

Běijīng Shèyǐng Qìcái Chéng *Finds* Běijīng's largest camera market has a bewildering array of equipment—one shop only sells lens filters! If you're looking for the old, obscure parts they just don't make any more, you'll find them here. Competition between vendors is fierce. Xī Sì Huán Lù 40 (a mile south of the metro stop on the west side), Xīchéng Qū. © 010/8811-9797. Daily 9am–4:30pm. Bus: 748 from south of Wǔkēsōng metro stop (108, exit D) to Zhèngcháng Zhuāng.

Mǎlián Dào Shèyǐng Qìcái Chéng Located on the top floor of Mǎlián Dào Tea City is a cluster of secondhand camera shops. **Hóngshēng Shèyǐng Fúwù Zhōngxīn,** on the north side, has the widest range of gear and the best repair service. Mǎliān Dào 11 (cross road and walk south for 5 min.). © 010/6339-5250. Daily 8:30am–6pm. Bus: 719 from Fùchéng Mén metro stop (203, exit A) to Wānzi.

CARPETS

Gangchen Carpets With an eye to Western tastes provided by their parent company in New York, Gangchen sells exquisite handwoven wool rugs from their factory in Lhasa. If you want to see how well slick advertising and the mystique of Tibet go together, see www.innerasiarugs.com. In the lobby of the

Kempinski Hotel. ⓒ 010/6465-3388. Daily 10am–10pm. Bus: 701 from Dōngsì Shí Tiáo metro stop (213) to Yānshā.

Qián Mén Carpet Factory   Most modern Chinese carpets are testaments to what azo compounds are capable of if they fall into the wrong hands. Fortunately, the carpets in this dusty basement emporium (which was once a bomb shelter) are largely antiques. Rugs from Gānsù and Níngxià in northwest China feature swastikas, dragons, phoenixes, and auspicious symbols, and are free of alarming pinks and oranges. Antiques include Tibetan prayer rugs, Xīnjiāng yurt rugs, and Mongolian saddle rugs, all handmade using natural dyes. The factory also makes antique "reproductions" and Hénán silk carpets. Cleaning and repair services are available. The factory is located at the back of the Chóngwén Worker's Cultural Palace; follow the ANTIQUE CARPETS signs. Xìngfú Dàjiē 44, Chóngwén Qū (opposite the east side of Tiān Tán Fàndiàn). ⓒ 010/6715-1687. Daily 9:30am–5:30pm. Bus: 807 from Chóngwén Mén metro stop (209) to Běijīng Tiyǔguǎn.

COINS & STAMPS

Coin collectors and philatelists rub shoulders in Běijīng. The largest market is **Mǎliǎn Dào Yóu Bì Kǎ Shìchǎng** at Mǎlián Dào 15 (open daily 8:30am–5pm), tucked away behind the tea shops, just south of yet another Carrefour supermarket. Housed in a half-empty building that resembles an aircraft hangar, you'll find stamps and envelopes commemorating great moments in Chinese diplomacy (more than you'd expect), coins and notes of all imaginable vintages, phone cards (popular with locals—there's even a Phone Card Museum), and a large range of Cultural Revolution memorabilia. To get here, take bus no. 719 from the Fùchéng Mén metro stop (203, exit A) to Wānzi, cross the road, and walk south for 5 minutes. Larger post offices also have special sections offering limited-issue stamps. Coin collectors should make the trip to the **Ancient Coin Market** (**Gǔdài Qiánbì Jiāoyì Shìchǎng; ⓒ 010/6201-8073**) at Déshèng Mén (p. 146).

COMPUTERS

In a recent local soap opera, **Zhōngguān Cūn** (touted as China's Silicon Valley), to the northwest of Běijīng, was depicted as innovative, dynamic, and even sexy. Alas, with an education system that stifles creativity and a legal system incapable of enforcing intellectual property laws, copying software remains China's forte. (And software engineers are seldom sexy.) Don't rely on pirated software, but computer games usually work and computer whizzes have been known to build a computer from scratch here. Take bus no. 808 from Xī Zhí Mén.

Bǎi Nǎo Huì   Less dodgy and easier to reach than Zhōngguān Cūn, this four-story amalgam of stores sells computers, digital cameras, and accessories. Software is not sold inside, but a gaggle of gentlemen from Ānhuī loitering outside greet you with a chorus of "Hello. CD-ROM!" Cháowài Dàjiē 10 (10-min. walk east, on the south side of the street). ⓒ 010/6599-5947. Daily 9am–8pm. Metro: Cháoyáng Mén (212, exit B).

CRAFTS

Liú Rèn Papercut House (Liú Rèn Jiǎnzhǐ Wū)   The art of paper cutting might not sound exciting, but self-taught artist Liú Rèn—who's seen her share of tour groups—works up such a good spiel you may be converted. Traditionally, papercuts *(jiǎnzhǐ)* were gifts in rural China, to be stuck on windows, doors, or lanterns. There's nothing subtle about the traditional papercuts—a baby with a large member marks the birth of a boy, and a baby surrounded by protective wolves is appropriate for a girl. Though the charge of ¥5 (60¢) for her "small museum" is cheeky (even in China, a couple of walls in one room doesn't make a museum), Liú Rèn knows her craft. The wrecking ball swings at random; call ahead to see if her quiet courtyard house still stands. Shòu Shuǐ Hé Hútòng 16 (walk south on Xuānwǔ Mén Wài Dàjiē, take the 2nd hútòng on the right, turn left down the 1st lane, then take the 1st right), Xīchéng Qū. ☎ 010/6601-1946. Fri–Sun 9:30am–5pm. Metro: Xīdān (115, exit E).

DEPARTMENT STORES

Although they are gradually being nudged aside by newer mega-malls, a few interesting stores survive.

Friendship Store (Yǒuyì Shāngdiàn)   Friendship Stores were once the only places where locals and foreigners alike could purchase imported goodies. You even needed "foreign exchange currency" to obtain the overpriced goods. Mercifully, this is no longer the case. Largely by dint of its location, one Friendship Store survives: a bizarre throwback to the age when the most plentiful commodity was something called *méiyǒu* (don't have). You can bargain for the overpriced merchandise, but it's really not worth your while. Starbucks, Baskin-Robbins, Délifrance, and Pizza Hut are attached, and the first-floor bookshop stocks a wide range of English-language magazines. Jiànguó Mén Wài Dàjiē 17, Cháoyáng Qū. ☎ 010/ 6500-3311. Daily 9am–8:30pm. Metro: Jiànguó Mén (120/211, exit B).

Pacific Department Store (Tàipíngyáng Bǎihuò)   Běijīng's newest department store stocks vast quantities of shoes and beauty products. The inevitable top-floor food court has excellent Japanese and Korean noodle stalls, while the basement supermarket stocks a good selection of chocolates, wine, and organic vegetables. The Starbucks on the first floor is said to be Běijīng's hippest. (Can a Starbucks be hip? You be the judge.) Gōngtǐ Běi Lù 2A, Cháoyáng Qū. ☎ 010/6539-3888. Daily 10:30am–10pm. Bus: 701 from Dōngsì Shí Tiáo metro stop (213) to Sān Lǐ Tún.

Parkson (Bǎishèng Gòuwù Zhōngxīn)   Specializing in expensive clothing and fashions for wealthy young locals, this department store is showing signs of wear. On the fifth floor is an excellent arts-and-crafts department, which complements an in-house gallery (p. 140). There's a clean and cheap food court on the sixth floor and a well-stocked supermarket in the basement. Fùxíng Mén Nèi Dàjiē 101, Xīchéng Qū. ☎ 010/6601-3377. Daily 9am–10pm. Metro: Fùxíng Mén (114/204, exit B).

DRUGSTORES

Watson's   Watson's is a large, Western-style drugstore, the only such store in Běijīng, with a wide range of imported beauty and health aids, from cosmetics to toothpaste, tampons to Tylenol. Two locations: Holiday Inn Lido, Cháoyáng Qū, ☎ 010/ 6436-7653, 9am–9pm; and Full Link Plaza, Cháoyáng Mén Wài Dàjiē 18, Cháoyáng Qū, ☎ 010/ 6588-2145, daily 10am–9pm. Metro: Cháoyáng Mén (212).

Wángfǔjǐng Drugstore   This convenient downtown emporium has a small selection of Western cosmetics and health aids, along with a large selection of traditional Chinese medicines. Wángfǔjǐng Dàjiē 267, Dōngchéng Qū. ☎ 010/6524-9932. Daily 9am–8pm. Metro: Wángfǔjǐng (118, exit A).

JEWELRY

Hóng Qiáo Shìchǎng (see section 2 of this chapter), also known as the Pearl Market, has dozens of jewelry stalls (mostly pearls and jade) on its third and fourth floors. Unless you're an expert, this is not the place to make large purchases.

Běijīng Gōngměi Dàshà   The third-floor stalls stock all varieties of jade, from green Khotanese nephrite to Burmese jadeite. They're terribly popular with Hong Kong visitors. Count on paying no more than a third of the marked price. Wángfǔjǐng Dàjiē 200, Dōngchéng Qū. © 010/6523-8747. Daily 9:30am–8pm. Metro: Wángfǔjǐng (118, exit A).

Shard Box Store (Shèndégé Gōngyìpǐn)   The wall of JCB, Amex, and Visa credit-card stickers on the front door are fair warning—you aren't among the first to discover this cute jewelry shop. Even former first lady Rosalyn Carter has preceded you here. The shard boxes—supposedly made from fragments of porcelain vessels smashed during the Cultural Revolution—make nice souvenirs. The jewelry is a mixture of colorful curiosities gathered from Mongolian and Tibetan regions, and pieces crafted in nearby workshops. You can also design your own jewelry. Rìtán Běi Lù 1 (continue east from northeast corner of Rìtán Gōngyuán), Cháoyáng Qū. © 010/6500-3712. Daily 8:30am–7:30pm. Metro: Yǒng'ān Lǐ (121, exit A).

Xīncāng Zhūbǎo   Jewelry Street (Zhūbǎo Yì Tiáo Jiē) is another traditional market cleaned up and forced indoors. But at least they left it in its original spot. This is the largest of more than 20 shops. The first floor stocks a full range of gemstones, wedding rings, and necklaces. Have a peek at the second floor, which stocks Western antiques—Swiss gramophones, American bibles, old telephones, and a suit of plate armor. There's even some fine French chinoiserie, which has come full circle. Yángròu Hútòng 2 (cross over and continue north; Jewelry St. is marked by an archway), Xīchéng Qū. © 010/6618-2888. Daily 10am–5pm. Bus: 808 from north of Xīdān metro stop (115, exit A) to Xīsì.

MALLS & SHOPPING PLAZAS

China's new generation of leaders would love nothing better than to wake up and find a more populous version of Singapore outside the gates of Zhōng Nán Hǎi. This isn't going to happen, but window-shopping in modern shopping malls is all the rage with Beijingers.

China World Trade Center Shopping Center (Zhōngguó Guójì Màoyì Zhōngxīn)   Usually simply called "Guómào," this three-level mall caters to foreign business travelers and expatriate families. The ground level of China World contains airline offices, American Express, a food court, and Běijīng's first (but now far from only) Starbucks. As well as the usual boutique clothing stores, there's CRC Supermarket (open daily 9am–9:30pm), which is crammed with imported edibles. A number of small Chinese arts-and-crafts gazebos line the main thoroughfare. Jiànguó Mén Wài Dàjiē 1, Cháoyáng Qū. © 010/6505-2288. Daily 10am–9:30pm. Metro: Guómào (122).

COFCO Plaza (Zhōngliáng Guǎngchǎng)   In this modern eight-floor mega-mall, you'll find branches of HSBC (open Mon–Fri 9am–12:30pm and 1:30–5pm), CITS, Baskin-Robbins, Starbucks, and McDonald's. Park 'N' Shop is in Basement One. Expensive clothing and furniture stores dominate most of the mall. An underground walkway connects this mall to the north side of Cháng'ān Jiē. Jiànguó Mén Nèi Dàjiē 8, Dōngchéng Qū. © 010/6526-6666. Daily 9am–9pm. Metro: Jiànguó Mén (120/211, exit C).

Full Link Plaza (Fēnglián Guǎngchǎng)   Opened in 1997, this spacious mall is a collection of chic foreign and local chain stores. In the basement is a

Park 'N Shop supermarket. The first floor boasts a Watson's Drug Store and a Nautica outlet; the second floor has Esprit and MacGregor. There's a Kenny Roger's Roasters Restaurant on the fourth floor, and Air France on the fifth floor. On the first floor is Běijīng's most lavish Starbucks, with a glass-walled meeting room. Cháoyáng Mén Wài Dàjiē 18, Cháoyáng Qū. ✆ 010/6215-5511. Daily 10am–9pm. Metro: Cháoyáng Mén (212, exit B).

Lufthansa Yǒuyì Shopping Center (Yānshā Yǒuyì Shāngchéng) Located on the east side of the Third Ring Road and connected to the Kempinski Hotel, the Lufthansa Center is the largest mall in northeast Běijīng. There's a range of upscale specialty shops, boutiques, restaurants, and arts-and-crafts outlets on the upper floors, and a well-hidden bookstore tucked away on the sixth floor (take the elevator). There's a currency exchange on the fifth floor, which you'll need if you plan on doing a lot of shopping at the overpriced supermarket and deli in the basement. Liàngmǎ Qiáo Lù 52, Cháoyáng Qū. ✆ 010/6435-4930. Daily 9am–10pm. Bus: 701 from Dōngsì Shí Tiáo metro stop (213) to Yānshā.

Oriental Plaza (Dōngfāng Xīn Tiāndì) Asia's largest shopping complex stretches from Wángfǔjǐng to Dōngdān. Supplanting the world's biggest McDonald's (razed in 1999), the plaza cost $2 billion to build and was backed by a Hong Kong billionaire referred to as "enigmatic" or "elusive." This huge two-story arcade is divided into five themed malls with silly names such as "Wonderful World." There's a Watson's drugstore; Sony ExploraScience museum for children; Schlotzsky's Deli; Danesi's Cafe; Be There or Be Square Cafe (p. 84); the Wángfǔjǐng Paleolithic Museum; and "Oriental Honey World," which disappointingly turns out to be a place to amuse children. The Oriental Harbour Plaza stands right in the middle of all the consumption. Dōng Cháng'ān Dàjiē 1, Dōngchéng Qū. ✆ 010-8518-6363. www.orientalplaza.com. Summer daily 9:30am–10:30pm; winter daily 9:30am–9:30pm. Metro: Wángfǔjǐng (118, exit A).

Sun Dong An Plaza (Xīn Dōng'ān Shìchǎng) Built in 1998, this huge mall surrounds twin atriums and is largely filled with designer clothing shops. Aside from the usual Western and Japanese food chains—Baskin-Robbins, Pizza Hut, McDonald's, KFC, Yoshinoya, UCC, Starbucks, and Délifrance—there's an excellent hotpot restaurant, Dōngláishùn, on the fifth floor. Chinese medicine outlets, tea shops, and "Old Běijīng Street" await gullible shoppers in the basement, which also holds a children's jungle gym. Bank of China has a branch on the first floor (open Mon–Fri 9am–noon and 1:30–5pm). Wángfǔjǐng Dàjiē 138, Dōngchéng Qū. ✆ 010/6527-6688. Mon–Thurs 9am–9pm; Sat–Sun 9am–10pm. Metro: Wángfǔjǐng (118, exit A).

MODERN ART

Many branches of traditional Chinese art have been on the wane since the Táng dynasty (618–907 A.D.). So rather than encourage the 5,000-year-old tradition of regurgitation, look for something different. It's a much better investment.

East Gallery (Yìsēn Huàláng) Although quality varies, the East Gallery is the best of the locally run modern art galleries. The backdrop is magnificent, as you clamber up the narrow stairwells of the Déshèng Mén arrow tower (p. 146). You can visit the Ancient Coin Exhibition Hall downstairs. Běi Èr Huán Lù, Déshèng Mén Jiànlóu (just east of the metro stop), Xīchéng Qū. ✆ 010/8201-4962. Daily 9am–5:30pm. Metro: Jīshuǐtán (218, exit A).

Red Gate Gallery (Hóng Mén Huàláng) Opened by the delightfully camp Brian Wallace in the early 1990s, Red Gate has regular exhibitions featuring the work of its dozen or so artists. The Dōngbiàn Mén watchtower (admission ¥10/ $1.25) provides an airy and atmospheric viewing space. Chóngwén Mén Dōng Dàjiē, Dōngbiàn Mén Jiǎolóu (10-min. walk south), Dōngchéng Qū. ⓒ 010/6525-1005. www.redgate-gallery.com. Daily 10am–5pm. Metro: Jiànguó Mén (120/211, exit C).

MUSIC

The second floor of the **Foreign Language Bookstore** (p. 170) boasts a wide range of Chinese music. There's Chinese opera, maddening cross-talk *(xiàng-sheng)*, bland mando-pop, and even a small alternative *(fēi zhǔliú)* music section featuring local bands such as Thin Man and Second Hand Rose. The alternative philosophy doesn't extend to the Western music section, which relies heavily on the talents of Richard Clayderman, Kenny G, and Boyzone.

Běijīng Yīnyuè Shūdiàn   At this store, located just to the east of the north end of the Wángfǔjǐng pedestrian mall, the top floor has a large range of sheet music at prices far cheaper than in the West. Composers' names are in Chinese, of course, but names are transliterated (Beethoven becomes Bèiduōfēn, Liszt is rendered as Lǐsītè), so you may be able to make yourself understood. If not, names are often written in English above the scores. Dōng'ān Mén Dàjiē 16. ⓒ 010/ 6525-4458. Daily 9am–7pm. Metro: Wángfǔjǐng (118, exit A).

Pǔluó Chàngpiān Chāoshì (Polo Records)   Despite numerous well-publi-cized and highly photogenic police crackdowns, pirated *(dàobǎn)* CDs are read-ily available in Běijīng. This shop, whose entrance is marked by a wall of black-and-white photographs, was among the first to stock their shelves with non-pirated *(zhèngbǎn)* CDs. Imported CDs are ¥148 ($18)—more than 10 times the price of a pirated CD—while local CDs start at ¥18 ($2.20). Remem-ber that it's tough enough being a musician in China without having to do it for free. Xīzhí Mén Nèi Dàjiē 26 (walk south to a large intersection and turn right; the store is across a footbridge on the south side), Xīchéng Qū. ⓒ 010/6618-3891. Daily 9:30am–6:30pm. Metro: Jīshuǐtán (218, exit C).

OUTDOOR EQUIPMENT

Sānfū Hùwài Yòngpǐn (Sanfo Outdoors) *(Value)*   The hiking bug came late to China, but this shop, which began life as an outdoor club at Peking Univer-sity, has a dedicated following of students and young professionals. Unlike the knockoffs for sale at Hóng Qiáo and elsewhere, Sanfo stocks only the genuine article, and products come with a warranty. They have their own line of sleep-ing bags, and they still organize weekend trips to the wilderness around Běijīng. There are branches in Jīn Zhī Qiáo Dàshà west of Guómào (ⓒ 010/6507-9298), and northwest of Peking University (ⓒ 010/6262-1004). Mǎdiàn Nán Cūn 4 Lóu 5. ⓒ 010/6201-5550. www.sanfo.com.cn. Daily 9am–8pm. Metro: Jīshuǐtán (218), then bus no. 919 to Běijiāo Shìchǎng.

3501 PLA Surplus Store (3501 Gōngchǎng)   The official disposal store of the world's largest army is a delightful mix of durable outdoor gear and kitsch Communist memorabilia. Where else will you find army greatcoats and Léi Fēng hats, sturdy compasses and binoculars, and watches commemorating the 50th anniversary of liberation? Dōng Sān Huán 23 (just south of Jīng Guǎng Zhōngxīn), Dōngchéng Qū. ⓒ 010/6585-9312. Daily 9am–5:30pm. Metro: Guómào (122, exit A).

SHOES

Nèi Lián Shēng Xiédiàn   Cloth-soled "thousand layer happy shoes" *(qiāncéng bùxié)*, loved by martial arts stars and aging Communist leaders alike, are hard to find. Cheaper plastic-soled shoes are taking their place. A workshop behind this shop, founded in 1853, still turns them out; these shoes are well stitched and very comfortable. There are also some gorgeous women's shoes, modeled on Qīng fashions. Fortunately, they are now available in larger sizes. Bargaining is fruitless. Dàzhàlán Jiē 34. © 010/6301-4863. Sun–Thurs 8:30am–8pm; Fri–Sat 8:30am–8:30pm. Metro: Qián Mén (208, exit C).

SILK, FABRIC & TAILORS
The third floor of **Sānlǐtún Yǎxiù Fúzhuāng Shìchǎng** (formerly the Kylin Plaza) is a fine place to look for a tailor (see section 2 of this chapter).

Běijīng Sīchóu Diàn (Běijīng Silk Store)   Tucked away in a narrow *hútòng* just west of and running parallel with Qián Mén Dàjiē, this bustling store is said to date from 1840. Prices for tailoring and raw materials are surprisingly reasonable. Zhūbǎo Shì 5 (just south of metro stop), Chóngwén Qū. © 010/6301-6658. Daily 9am–7:30pm. Metro: Qián Mén (208, exit C).

Dàxīn Fǎngzhī Gōngsī *Value*   It might not be as prestigious as other tailors, but with hand-tailored *qípáo* typically costing less than ¥200 ($25), it's impossible to argue with the price. Right next door to Yoshinoya Dairy Queen. Xīnjiēkǒu Nán Dàjiē 22 (walk south for 10 min.; the shop is on the left side, just beyond the main intersection), Xīchéng Qū. © 010/6618-7843. Daily 8:30am–8pm. Metro: Jīshuǐtán (218, exit C).

Ruìfúxiáng Chóubù Diàn   You'll find piles of gorgeous silk brocade at this store, in the trade for 110 years. They specialize in *qípáo* (¥500/$60 and up), which take 1 week to tailor, with a couple of fittings. If you're pushed for time, they can complete it in 2 days for an additional charge. They also have an outlet at Wángfǔjǐng Dàjiē 190 (© 010/6525-0764), just north of Gōngměi Dàshà. Aim to bargain 30% to 50% off the marked prices. Dàzhàlán Jiē 5, west off Qián Mén Dàjiē, Chóngwén Qū. © 010/6303-5313. Daily 9am–8pm. Metro: Qián Mén (208, exit C).

Yuánlóng Sīchóu Gǔfèn Yǒuxiàn Gōngsī (Yuánlóng Silk Co. Ltd)   The artisans of Yuánlóng suffered tough times during the Cultural Revolution, when foreign ties and bourgeois products were frowned upon. Now both are back in vogue, and the artisans are in the sights of most Western tour groups and dignitaries. They moved in 2001, and are now found in their original location, just northwest of Hóng Qiáo Shìchǎng. A huge range of silk fabric occupies the third floor; prices are clearly marked and surprisingly competitive. A *qípáo* or suit can be made in a couple of days, but it's best to allow at least a week. Exquisite (and expensive!) silk carpets from Hénán are sold on the first floor. Try not to visit at midday, when the third floor is overrun by tour groups. Tiān Tán Lù 55 (northeast side of Tiān Tán Gōngyuán), Chóngwén Qū. © 010/6702-2288. Daily 9am–6:30pm. Bus: 807 from Chóngwén Mén metro stop (209, exit B) to Hóng Qiáo.

SKATEWEAR
Yì SK8 *Kids*   With acres of empty concrete, the capital is a skateboarder's paradise. The skating park in Tiān'ān Mén Square is a distant memory, but the owners of this shop can steer you in the right direction. Decks and wheels are imported, but locally made skate fashions are reasonably priced and feature striking designs. Xīnjiēkǒu Běi Dàjiē 70 (south of the metro stop, on the east side opposite Xīnjiēkǒu Sān Tiáo), Xīchéng Qū. © 010/6618-3148. Daily 10am–9pm. Metro: Jīshuǐtán (218, exit C).

All the Tea in China

Mǎlián Dào, south of Xī Zhàn, might not sell all the tea in China, but with over a mile of shops hawking tea leaves and their paraphernalia, it feels like it. The chain stores are here, but most shops are run by the extended families of tea growers from Fújiàn and Zhèjiāng, and many rate this friendly street as the highlight of their visit. The four-story **Tea City (Chá Chéng** (✆ **010/6328-1177),** in the middle of the street on the west side, is a pleasant spot to start. The Běijīng outlet of **Měnghǎi Cháchǎng** (ext. 8165), run by an affable Huí (Muslim) gentleman, found at the south end of Tea City's first floor, stocks exquisite black tea. Oolong tea *(wūlóng chá)* is usually encountered in the West in a substandard and nasty form; don't miss the chance to taste the genuine article. Black tea *(hóng chá)* and Pǔ'ěr tea (sold in round briquettes, one of the few teas that improves with age) are usually sold by the same vendors. There is such a wide range of flavors—from the flowery *gāoshān* to the caffeine-laden *tiě guānyīn,* from the milky *jīnxuān* to the sweet aftertaste of *rénshēn* (ginseng)—that most shoppers find a brew to suit them. Try **Táiwān Tiānbǎoyáng Míngchá** (ext. 8177), on the west side of Tea City's first floor. Wherever you shop, remember that tasting tea does not mean that you're obliged to buy tea. Tea sets, in particular pottery, are the other big draw of Tea City. **Zǐyù Táofáng** (✆ **010/6327-5268),** on the east side of the second floor, sells exquisite pots and cups molded from Yíxīng clay. Bargain hunters should visit **Jīngmǐn Cháchéng,** an older wholesale market, further south on the same side of the street.

SUPERMARKETS

Běijīng's hotels often have lobby shops with overpriced snacks and bottled water, but for Western groceries you have a few options.

Carrefour (Jiālèfú Chāoshì)   This French supermarket chain is the most successful in Běijīng, with six outlets at last count. Stores near embassy areas, such as the Guózhǎn outlet in the northeast, stock the widest range of foreign goodies. The Guózhǎn store offers a delivery service for surrounding areas. Běi Sānhuán Dōng Lù Yī 6 (southwest of Sānyuán Qiáo), Dōngchéng Qū. ✆ **010/8460-1030.** Daily 8am–10pm.

Jenny Lou's (Tiānshùn Chāoshì)   A grocer popular with expats, Jenny Lou's carries excellent fresh fruits and vegetables, some imported. The cheese and bread selections in the attached deli are excellent. For orders over ¥100 ($12), they will deliver to your hotel. Rìtán Gōngyuán Běi Lù 4 (east of the northeast side of Rìtán Park), Cháoyáng Qū. ✆ **010/6586-0626.** Daily 8am–9pm. Metro: Yǒng'ān Lǐ (121).

TEA

If you're serious about tea, there's only one place to go—**Mǎlián Dào** (see the "All the Tea in China" box in this chapter). If you can't make the trek, try one of these shops.

Gēng Xiāng   With a 2002 survey finding that more than half of Běijīng's teas have traces of pesticides or heavy metals, organic teas are a sensible choice. The largest retailer of organic tea in Běijīng, Gēng Xiāng, survived the scandal with their reputation enhanced. Their green tea *(lǜ chá)* is among the best in China. Dì'ān Mén Wài Dàjiē 116 (south of Drum Tower), Xīchéng Qū. ℂ 010/6404-0846. Daily 8am–8pm. Metro: Gú Lóu Dàjiē (217).

Tiān Fú Jítuán (Ten Fu Tea)   Not quite the McDonald's of tea, but at last count there were 26 branches in Běijīng. This store is the largest. Their jasmine tea *(huā chá)* is excellent. Wángfǔjīng Dàjiē 176, Dōngchéng Qū. ℂ 010/6525-4722. Daily 8:30am–7:30pm. Metro: Wángfǔjīng (118, exit A).

9

Běijīng After Dark

by Josh Chin

If you measure a city's nightlife by the number of chances for debauchery it offers, then Běijīng has never held (and probably will never hold) a candle to such neon-lit Babylons as Shànghǎi and Hong Kong. If, instead, you measure nightlife by its diversity, the Chinese capital rivals any major city in Asia.

Such was not always the case. As recently as a decade ago, Běijīng's populace routinely tucked itself into bed under a blanket of Máo-inspired puritanism shortly after nightfall, leaving visitors with one of two tourist-approved options: Attend Běijīng opera and acrobatic performances in a sterile theater, or wander listlessly around the hotel in search of a drink to make sleep come faster.

Since then, the government has realized there is money to be made on both sides of the Earth's rotation. The resulting relaxation in nocturnal regulations, set against the backdrop of Běijīng residents' historical affinity for cultural diversions, has helped remake the city's nightlife. Opera and acrobatics are still available, but now in more interesting

venues, and to them have been added an impressive range of other worthwhile cultural events: teahouse theater, puppet shows, intimate traditional music concerts, live jazz, even the occasional subtitled film.

This diversity continues with Běijīng's drinking and dance establishments, of which there are scores. Although they don't quite match Shànghǎi's for style, they are generally cheaper and offer something for just about every mood. With the opening of a few modern dance clubs, the city's cheesy old discos are thankfully no longer the only dance option, although the latter can still be tremendously entertaining on the kitsch level. The same goes for karaoke, a favorite in China as it is in Japan. Foreign-Chinese interaction in bars hasn't progressed much beyond the sexual exploitation so rampant in the 1920s and 1930s, but this is by no means a necessary dynamic, and the traveler not afraid to bumble through language barriers can often make fruitful contact with local people over a bottle or two of beer.

1 Performing Arts

BĚIJĪNG OPERA

Běijīng opera (*jīngjù*) is described by some as the apogee of traditional Chinese culture and, at least according to one modest Chinese connoisseur, is "perhaps the most refined form of opera in the world." Many who have actually seen a performance might beg to differ with these claims, but few other Chinese artistic traditions can match it for sophistication and pure stylized spectacle.

The Běijīng tradition is young as Chinese opera styles go. Its origins are most commonly traced to 1790, when four opera troupes from Ānhuī Province arrived in Běijīng to perform for the Qīng court and decided to stay, eventually absorbing elements of a popular opera tradition from Húběi Province. Initially performed exclusively for the royal family, the new blended style eventually trickled out to the public and was well received as a more accessible alternative to the elegant but stuffy operas dominant at the time.

How it could have ever been considered accessible is mystifying to most foreign audiences. The typical performance is loud and long, with archaic dialogue sung on a screeching pentatonic scale, accompanied by a cacophony of gongs, cymbals, drums, clappers, and strings. This leaves most first-timers exhausted, but the exquisite costumes and martial arts–inspired movements ultimately make it worthwhile. Probably the opera's most distinctive feature is its elaborate system of face paints, with each color representing a character's disposition: red for loyalty, blue for bravery, black for honesty, and white for cruelty.

Communist authorities outlawed the "feudalistic" classics after 1949 and replaced them with the Eight Model Plays—a series of propaganda-style operas based on 20th-century events that focus heavily on class struggle. Many of these are still performed and are worth viewing if only to watch reactions from audience members, some of whom have seen these plays dozens of times and will loudly express their disgust when a mistake is made. But the older stories, allowed again after Máo's death, are more visually stunning. Among the most popular are *Farewell My Concubine,* made famous through Chén Kǎigē's film of the same name, and *Havoc in Heaven,* which follows the mischievous Monkey King character from the Chinese literary classic *Journey to the West.*

Several theaters now offer shortened programs more amenable to the foreign attention span, usually with English subtitles or plot summaries. Most people on tours are taken to the cinema-style **Líyuán Theater (Líyuán Jùchǎng)** inside the Qián Mén Hotel (nightly performances at 7:30pm; ¥30–¥200/$3–$25) or to one of several other modern venues. These are affordable but supremely boring. Your time and money are much better spent at one of the traditional theaters below.

Húguǎng Guild Hall (Húguǎng Huìguǎn Xìlóu)   This combination museum-theater, housed in a complex of traditional buildings with gray tile roofs and bright red gables, has a connection with Běijīng Opera dating back to 1830. To the right of the main entrance is a small museum filled with old opera robes and photos of famous performers (including the legendary Méi Lánfāng), probably interesting only to aficionados. On the left is the expertly restored theater, a riot of color with a beautifully adorned traditional stage, paper lanterns hung from the high ceilings, and gallery seating on all three sides. Subtitles are in Chinese only, but brochures contain brief plot explanations in English. Performances take place nightly at 7:30pm. Hǔfáng Lù 3 (at intersection with Luómǎshì Dàjiē; plaza out front contains colorful opera mask sculpture). ℂ 010/6351-8284. Tickets ¥100–¥380 ($12–$48). Metro: Hépíng Mén (207); walk south 10 min.

Teahouse of Prince Gōng's Mansion (Gōng Wáng Fǔ Cháguǎn)   Not a traditional opera venue, Prince Gōng's teahouse is nevertheless picturesque, with a rare bamboo motif on the exterior beams and columns and an intimate interior outfitted with polished wood tables and pleasing tea paraphernalia. This is opera for tourists, kept short and sweet, with a guided tour of the surrounding gardens included in the price (see Prince Gōng's Mansion, p. 142). There are several performances daily until 4:30pm. Liǔyīn Jiē 17. (Signposted in English at top of Qián Hǎi Xī Dàjiē [running north off Píng'ān Dàdào opposite north gate of Běi Hǎi Park]; turn left at sign and follow alley past large parking lot. Entrance marked with huge red lanterns.) ℂ 010/ 6616-8149. Tickets ¥60 ($8).

Zhèngyǐcí Xìlóu (Zhèngyǐcí Theater)   The 340-year-old Zhèngyǐcí is under constant threat of extinction but is the first choice for authentic Běijīng opera when it's open. A Míng dynasty temple converted into an opera theater in 1712, it fell to other uses after 1949 and was in danger of being torn down until a local businessman reopened it in 1995. Since then, funding problems and its position at the center of a large urban reconstruction project have limited the number of performances. The theater itself is similar to the Húguǎng Guild Hall, with the same high ceilings and gallery seating, but it has a decidedly more local feel. Perhaps most unique, the staff themselves are connoisseurs, more interested in opera than in collecting tourist dollars. Pray it survives. Performances are held most nights at 7:30pm (call to check). Qián Mén Xī Héyán Jiē 220 (walk south of the Hépíng Mén Quánjùdé, take 1st left). ℭ 010/8315-1650. Tickets ¥150–¥280 ($19–$35). Metro: Hépíng Mén (207).

ACROBATICS

China's acrobats are justifiably famous, and probably just a little bit insane. This was the only traditional Chinese art form to receive Máo's explicit approval (back flips, apparently, don't count as counterrevolution). While not culturally stimulating, the combination of plate spinning, hoop jumping, bodily contortion, and seemingly suicidal balancing acts make for slack-jawed entertainment of the highest order. Shànghǎi is the traditional home of acrobatics and boasts its best troupes, but the capital has done a fair job of transplanting the tradition.

The city's best acrobatics *(zájì)* venue is the **Wànshèng Jùchǎng** on the north side of Běi Wěi Lù just off Qián Mén Dàjiē (west side of the Temple of Heaven); performances are by the fairly famous Běijīng Acrobatics Troupe (ℭ **010/6303-7449**; nightly shows at 7:15pm; ¥100–¥150/$12–$19). The acrobats at the **Cháoyáng Jùchǎng** (Dōng Sān Huán Běi Lù 36; nightly shows at 7:15pm; ¥100–¥150/$12–$19) are slightly clumsier but the theater is more conveniently located, a short taxi ride from most of the city's better restaurants and close to the main bar district.

PUPPETS

Puppet shows *(mù'ǒu xì)* have been performed in China since the Hàn dynasty (206 B.C.–A.D. 220). The art form has diversified somewhat over the past two millennia, coming to include everything from the traditional hand puppets to string and shadow varieties. Plot lines are usually simple, and some hardly qualify as stories, but the manipulations are deft and the craftsmanship is exquisite. Most performances, including weekend matinees, are held at the **China Puppet Art Theater (Zhōngguó Mù'ǒu Jùyuàn),** in Ānhuá Xī Lǐ near the North Third Ring Road (ℭ **010/6424-3698**); tickets cost ¥20 to ¥25 ($2–$3).

OTHER VENUES

Běijīng hosts a growing number of international music and theater events every year, and its own increasingly respectable outfits—including the Běijīng Symphony Orchestra—give frequent performances. Among the most popular venues for this sort of thing is the **Běijīng Concert Hall (Běijīng Yīnyuè Tīng;** ℭ **010/6605-5812**), at Běi Xīnhuá Jiē in Liùbùkǒu (Xuānwǔ). The **Poly Theater (Bǎolì Dàshà Guójì Jùyuàn;** ℭ **010/6500-1188**, ext. 5127), in the Poly Plaza complex on the East Third Ring Road (northeast exit of Dōngsì Shí Tiáo metro station), also hosts many large-scale performances, including the occasional revolutionary ballet. For information on additional venues and the shows they're hosting, check one of the expatriot magazines.

2 Teahouse Theater

Traditional teahouse entertainment disappeared from Běijīng after 1949, but some semblance survives in a number of modern teahouses that have grown up with the tourism industry. Snippets of Běijīng opera, cross-talk (stand-up) comedy, acrobatics, traditional music, singing, and dancing flow across the stage as you sip tea and nibble snacks. If you don't have time to see these kinds of performances individually, the teahouse is an adequate solution. If you're looking for a quiet place to enjoy a cup of jasmine and maybe do some reading, look to one of the real teahouses listed later in this chapter.

Lǎo Shě's Teahouse (Lǎo Shě Cháguǎn)   This somewhat garishly decorated teahouse is named for one of the most famous novels by celebrated Chinese writer Lǎo Shě (see Lǎo Shě Jìniànguǎn [Former Residence of Lǎo Shě], p. 141). Performances change nightly but always include opera and acrobatics. It pays to buy the more expensive tickets, as views from the rear seats are frequently obscured. Nightly shows at 7:50pm. Qiánmén Xī Dàjiē 3 (west of Qián Mén on south side of the st.). © 010/6303-6830. Tickets ¥40–¥130 ($5–$16).

Tiānqiáo Happy Tea House (Tiānqiáo Lè Cháguǎn)   The Tiānqiáo puts on essentially the same show as Lǎo Shě's Teahouse, but it is larger and somewhat classier, with gallery seating framed in dark lacquered wood and a less eye-straining color scheme. They offer a roast duck dinner option (reservations required) for those who want to kill two birds in a single venue. Performances take place nightly at 8pm (arrive at 6:30pm for dinner). Běi Wěi Lù, just west of intersection with Qián Mén Dàjiē (west side of Temple of Heaven). © 010/6304-0617. Tickets ¥180 ($22), or ¥330 ($41) with dinner.

3 Cinemas

State limitations on freedom of expression and the profusion of black market DVDs have both taken their toll on China's film industry, but Běijīng has enough true film fanatics to support a handful of theaters. **Cherry Lane Movies** (© 010/6461-5318; ¥50/$6), run by a long-tenured and long-winded American expatriate, shows older and some new Chinese films with English subtitles on the weekends; films are listed at www.cherrylanemovies.com and are screened at the Hilton Hotel's Fountain Terrace, with a free beverage and reduced-priced food provided by the hotel. **Space for Imagination** (Hézi Kāfēiguǎn; Xī Wàng Zhuāng Xiǎoqū 5; © 010/6279-1280), a smallish cafe near the east gate of Tsinghua University (Qīnghuá Dàxué), offers free screenings of Chinese independent and experimental films and a few foreign films of the same nature. Finally, the **UME International Cineplex** (Huáxīng Guójì Yǐngchéng; Shuāngyúshù Xuéyuàn Nán Lù 44; © 010/6255-5566; ¥50–¥80/$6–$10), a full-scale theater just north of the Third Ring Road and southeast of Rénmín University, occasionally shows undubbed Hollywood films and Chinese blockbusters with English subtitles.

4 Live Music

Most of the bars on Sānlǐtún North Bar Street offer nightly live "music" performances by cover bands, usually of scant talent and almost invariably Filipino in origin. But there are several small venues, most of them in Cháoyáng, which host an increasingly varied lineup of musical acts. Performers range from traditional folk instrumentalists to jazz ensembles and rock outfits, and are usually

Rainbow Sexuality Under the Red Flag

Same-sex relationships between men have a history of acceptance in China dating as far back as the Zhou period (1100–256 B.C.). In official records of the Hàn dynasty (206 B.C.–A.D. 220), 10 emperors are described as openly bisexual and are listed with the names of their lovers. In the centuries following the Hàn, homosexuality was generally accepted among men, so long as it didn't interfere with their Confucian duty to marry and perpetuate the family name. Partly due to the influence of Western missionaries, homosexuality was outlawed by official decree in 1740, but Judeo-Christian notions of shame never fully took root in China and the practice persisted. Under the Communists, however, homosexuality came to be seen as disruptive of the social order, and persecution of gays was sanctioned during the Cultural Revolution.

The situation has improved over the past decade, but only a little. In 2002, the government rescinded its 1989 edict describing homosexuality as a psychological disorder, but laws still prohibit expat magazines from talking about gay bars (described instead as bars "for the alternative set"). The general populace tends to ignore the existence of gay relationships, a mental trick made easier by the fact that it's considered normal for men to be physically affectionate regardless of sexual orientation. As in ancient times, many gay men still marry and have children to satisfy their parents.

The only genuine gay bar in Běijīng is **Drag-on** (Lóng Bā; ✆ 010/6417-3493) on Xìngfú Cūn Zhōng Lù, in an alley northwest of the Neo Lounge (see section 6 of this chapter) near the Sānlǐtún drinking district. Foreigners and Chinese mix better here than anywhere else, by dint of necessity. The dance floor is among the city's liveliest, frequently commandeered by some truly stunning drag queens, and there is accommodation for the less flamboyant in a number of quieter booths near the door. There are other gay-leaning bars in Běijīng, but most are either overly cartoonish or downright seedy.

For lesbians, the scene is truly grim. There is almost no lesbian culture to speak of, and women perceived as homosexual are often subject to harassment. In the context of Chinese patriarchy, lesbianism has never received much attention. Outside a brief appearance in the Chinese classic *Dream of the Red Mansion,* it is invisible in literature, and the pressures of China's skewed gender ratio—an excess of boys brought on by age-old prejudices in response to the one-child policy—has made many single Chinese men resentful of any reduction in the pool of potential wives.

If there's a lesbian bar in Běijīng, it is **On/Off** (Shàng Xià Xiàn; ✆ 010/6415-7413 or 010/6415-8083), located 2 blocks west of Neo Lounge not far from Drag-on at Xìngfú Yī Cūn Zhōng Lù 5. The bar's name is a reference to its clientele: gay some nights, straight others. Entertainment of late has been mostly transgender and drag shows, which has driven off much of the female clientele, but it's still your best bet.

interesting, if not always good. (See Appendix A: "Běijīng in Depth" for more on the city's better bands.) Most venues are bars open nightly from around 5pm to 1 or 2am, although few offer live acts every night. There is usually a small cover charge on performance nights (¥5–¥40/$1–$5), depending on the number of acts and their prestige. *City Weekend, that's Beijing,* and www.Xianzai.com maintain somewhat accurate listings of what is playing where and when.

Běijīng CD Jazz Club (Běijīng CD Juéshì Jùlèbù)   A cozy club, modeled on the owner's favorite music venue in Europe, this is the best place to see jazz in Běijīng. Live performances take place on a small velvet-backed stage, under portraits of Coltrane and Davis, Wednesday through Sunday nights. If it's a special act, get there early: Views from the outer room are obscured. Dōng Sān Huán, south of the Agricultural Exhibition Center (Nóngzhǎn Guǎn) main gate (down small path behind trees that line sidewalk). ✆ 010/6506–8288. Cover ¥30 ($4).

Big Easy (Kuàilè Zhàn)   No longer Běijīng's top jazz venue (it lost that title to the Běijīng CD Jazz Club—see above), the superbly styled Big Easy is still the most atmospheric. The dark Bourbon Street interior is heavy on polished wood and brass, with a thick railing along the open second floor perfect for leaning on when there's a band on the stage downstairs. Nóngzhǎnguǎn Nán Lù (Cháoyáng Gōngyuán south gate). ✆ 010/6508-6776.

CD Café (CD Kāfēwū)   This is Běijīng's best venue for live music, especially of the just-above-underground variety. The space is nothing fancy but pleasant enough, with a large stage and nice balcony seating. Many of Běijīng's best bands play here with fair regularity, including some of the more talented punk outfits. Dōng Sān Huán, 50m (165 ft.) south of Agricultural Exhibition Center (Nóngzhǎn Guǎn). ✆ 010/6501-8877. Cover ¥30–¥50 ($4–$6).

Get Lucky Bar (Háoyùn Jiǔbā)   This odd, incredibly remote bar is an occasional venue for Běijīng's much-documented punk shows. It has a vague, inexplicable American West theme, with wagon wheels and rough wood walls, and there's a row of suspicious karaoke rooms in back. A Chinese version of heavy metal played on a five-note scale sometimes substitutes for punk, with the occasional drag show or two when music acts fall through. On south side of Běi Tùchéng Lù in Táiyáng Gōng area, several blocks east of the UIBE campus south gate (Dùiwài Jìngmào Dàxué Nán Mén). ✆ 010/6429-9109. Cover ¥10–¥30 ($1–$4).

River (Hé)   This strangely calm bar buried in the bacchanalian madness of South Bar Street is partly owned by the Wild Children (Yě Háizi), one of Běijīng's most respectable folk bands. It hosts frequent (and free) folk-rock performances, and the occasional open-mic night. West side of S. Bar St. (Dōngdàqiáo Xiéjiē). ✆ 010/6594-4714.

Sānwèi Bookstore (Sānwèi Shūwū)   The tiny Sānwèi has a well-worn teahouse upstairs that hosts intimate concerts on the weekends. Fridays it's jazz and Saturdays it's classical Chinese, usually with a minority twist. This is the city's finest venue for Chinese traditional music, if only because you sit close enough to really experience it. Tea and snacks are included in the price. Friday and Saturday performances take place at 8:30pm. Fùxīng Mén Nèi Dàjiē 60, opposite the Minorities Palace (Mínzú Gōng). ✆ 010/6601-3204. Cover ¥30 ($4).

Treelounge   SARS did little for most of Běijīng's nightspots, but it was the making of this stylish, relaxed club. While other venues ducked for cover behind surgical masks, Treelounge stayed open and had its pick of the live music scene. The bar would likely have succeeded even without SARS, though, thanks largely to its affable Kiwi owner, who rode into China on his bike in 2000 and has been Běijīng's favorite barman ever since. The eclectic lineup is strong on reggae, hip-hop, and electronica. There's a shady patio for the summer months, a cozy fire-place for winter, and delicious vegetarian fare year-round. East side of the East Third Ring Road (next to CD Cafe). ℰ 1351/101-0967. Cover varies for performances.

5 Clubs & Discos

The average Chinese will lump all dancing establishments into a single cate-gory—*tiàowǔdiàn* (dancing place), or, if they try it in English, "dee-si-ko." But while the distinction between a Běijīng disco and a Běijīng dance club is lost on most locals, it is readily apparent to any foreigner. Discos are typically old and cavernous, with exaggerated decor, horrible music, and a rich, wholly Chinese clientele whose clumsy attempts to imitate Western modes of style and dance will send shivers down your embarrassed spine. Clubs, by contrast, are newer, smaller, and more stylish, with a DJ-dominated atmosphere closer in feel to what you'd find in the United States or Europe. The club clientele is rich as well, but more diverse (featuring both Chinese and foreigners) and not quite as clueless.

Both discos and dance clubs charge high covers (anywhere from ¥50–¥150/ $6–$19). Both tend to get crowded on weekends around 10pm and empty around 3am, although a few clubs will host special parties that last until dawn. There is some activity on Thursday nights, but the rest of the week is slow. Dis-cos pre-date the days of the drinking district and hence are scattered randomly around the city. Clubs tend to be situated next to bars, in foreigner-heavy areas like Sānlǐtún and Cháoyáng Park.

Banana (Bānànà)   Banana is one of Běijīng's oldest and most popular discos. This new, larger location is a classic bit of 1990s Miami Beach postmodernism with fake palm trees and white Doric columns. The crowd is mostly local richies: black-clad men and skinny women who wear sunglasses at night. The sound sys-tem produces enough bass to loosen tooth fillings. Jiànguó Mén Wài Dàjiē 22 (in front of Scitech Hotel). ℰ 010/6528-3636. Cover ¥30 ($4).

The Club @ Sānlǐtún (Sānlǐtún Jùlèbù)   This is the slightly more lounge-like reincarnation of Vogue, the defunct dance club that once defined Běijīng nightlife. This new version has a small dance floor surrounded by semi-private clusters of low velvet couches, suffused throughout with dim red light. Local and foreign DJs spin mostly house and techno. Downstairs is the Viper Room, a sep-arate cigar and winebar. The upstairs level houses Citronelle, a stylish but oth-erwise bland and overpriced Vietnamese restaurant. Situated inside a pea-green building with Art Deco iron railing, the club is just down the street from Poacher's (see below). In an alley of Sānlǐtún N. Bar St. (30m/99 ft. west of a small ICBC branch). ℰ 010/6416-1077 or 010/6417-7791. Cover ¥30–¥50 ($4–$6).

Club FM (FM Jùlèbù)   Firenze is an upscale restaurant by day, but when night falls, it is transformed into this upscale drinks and dance venue known as FM. The techno-driven dance floor in the basement is usually packed on Friday nights. Upstairs is a sit-down area crowded with tables and couches, where funk and house are played loud enough to make conversation difficult. The decor is pleasantly fashionable, if unimaginative. Rìtán Gōngyuán S. Gate. ℰ 010/8562-2308. No cover.

The Den (Dūnhuáng)   The Den is Běijīng's longest-standing meat market and an institution among youthful travelers. There's a vague opium den theme

> ### Moments Karaoke: Down that Drink and Pop in Those Ear Plugs, Ma, It's Time to Sing
>
> No one knows why Asian cultures have embraced karaoke (pronounced "*kǎlā* okay" in Mandarin) with such red-faced gusto, or why so many foreigners adopt the enthusiasm once they're on Eastern soil. Maybe the food lacks some amino acid crucial to the brain's shame function. Or maybe it's just fun to get soused and pretend you have talent thousands of miles from anyone who cares. It doesn't really matter either way. Spend enough time in Bĕijīng and sooner or later you'll find yourself standing before a TV screen, beer and microphone in hand, with a crowd of drunkards insisting you sing to the Muzak version of a Beatles hit. Refuse and your Chinese host loses face; comply and you receive applause. Resistance is futile. Most karaoke venues in Bĕijīng are seedy and many are given over to less-than-legal side entertainment, so if you have any choice in the matter head to Party World, also known as the **Cash Box** (Qián Guì; ☎ **010/6588-3333;** open 24 hr.), the city's classiest and best-equipped do-it-yourself concert venue. Located southeast of the Full Link Plaza, at the corner of Cháowài Shìchǎng Jiē and Cháowài Nán Jiē, Cash Box boasts a hotel-like lobby, pleasantly decorated private rooms, and a wide selection of Western songs, some even released in the last decade. Prices range from ¥35 to ¥295 ($4–$37) per hour, depending on size of the room and night of the week. There's usually a line, so you'll have to give them your name early. You wouldn't want to embarrass yourself anywhere else.

downstairs, with low light and lots of quasi-ornate wood embellishments, but the main draw is the sweaty, no-frills dance floor upstairs, crowded until the wee hours. Music is mostly 1990s pop dance hits. There's an authentic Western brunch here, with eggs Benedict and bagels, from 9am to 1pm. Intersection of Gōngtǐ Dōng Lù 4A, next to the City Hotel (Chéngshì Bīnguǎn). ☎ 010/6592-6290. Cover ¥30 ($4).

6 Bars

Although most average Chinese still prefer to get drunk at dinner, the Western pub tradition has gained ground among younger locals, and the city boasts a large, ever-growing population of establishments devoted exclusively to alcohol.

Drinking in Bĕijīng occurs in one of several districts, each with its own atmosphere and social connotations. The city's oldest and still most popular drinking district is **Sānlǐtún,** located between the east second and third ring roads around the Workers' Stadium (Gōngrén Tǐyùchǎng). The area's name comes from Sānlǐtún Lù, a north-south strip of drinking establishments a long block east of the Workers' Stadium that at one time contained practically all of the city's bars. Now known as North Bar Street (Sānlǐtún Jiǔbā Jiē), it has been overshadowed by other clusters of bars on South Bar Street (also called Dōngdàqiáo Xiéjiē) a half block east of the City Hotel, in the Xìngfúcūn area north of the stadium, and scattered around the stadium itself. Bars here are rowdy and raunchy, and packed to overflowing on weekends. Similar watering holes surround the south and west gates of **Cháoyáng Gōngyuán** (park) to the east, an area the government has tried to promote as the new drinking district because it has fewer residential buildings. Bars and clubs in **Hǎidiàn,** the city's university district to the north-west, congregate around the gates of several universities and cater to a predictable crowd of local English majors and foreign students.

The fastest-growing spot for late-night drinking is the **Back Lakes (Shíchà Hǎi** or **Hòu Hǎi),** a previously serene spot with a few discreetly fashionable bars north of Běi Hǎi Park which now threatens to explode into a riot of hip. Neon has become a common sight, and several dance clubs are in the works, but for now this remains the finest place in the city for a quiet drink.

Běijīng bars generally open around 5 or 6pm and stay open until the last patrons leave or until the staff decides it wants to go home, usually by 2am on Friday and Saturday nights. Several of the Back Lakes bars double as cafes and open as early as 11am.

ClubFootball (Wànguó Qúnxīng Zúqiú) Běijīng has several sports bars, but ClubFootball is the only genuine specimen. TVs hang from every corner, tables are wobbly, whitewashed brick walls bear the appropriate mix of action stills and team banners, and there's foosball to one side. Grab a stool at the wood bar and note the crescent-moon dents left by overzealous bottle-wielding patrons. The emphasis is on soccer, with occasional rugby, baseball, and American football. Beer is cheap and the chili is fantastic. Chūnxiù Lù 10 (near Sānlǐtún; attached to the Red House). © 010/6417-0497.

The Hidden Tree (Yǐnbì de Shù) The name comes from a gnarled tree growing through the middle of the main room, but what makes this bar truly unique is its selection of Belgian beer: Trappist and abbey ales, lighter wild-fermented lambics, and several wheat (white) beers. The stock changes, but there's always bottled Chimay and draft Hoegaarden. Passable single-malts, cigars, and a pleasant but unpretentious brick and wood interior complete the picture. Halfway down S. Bar St. (Sānlǐtún), on left/east side (look for tree jutting from front of building). © 010/6509-3642.

Jazz-ya (Juéshì) At 8 years old, this hovel of a bar has to qualify for some sort of career achievement award. They've added a few new velvet couches (already scarred by cigarette burns) to spruce up the battered decor, but no one comes here for the setting. They come instead for the city's best Long Island iced tea (¥50/$6)—delicious, potent, and a tremendous bargain in early evening lubricants. Sānlǐtún Běi Jiē 18 (Sānlǐtún), down 1st alley on right after passing Public Space. © 010/6415-1227.

John Bull Pub (Zūnbó Yīngshì Jiǔbā) John Bull is one of the older bars in Běijīng and bills itself as the city's only real British-style pub. The heavy-wood decor and menu say pub, but the atmosphere doesn't, except when there's rugby on TV. The Guinness could be better, but the fish and chips are among the best in China. The Yorkshire pudding and bangers and mash are reasonable approximations. Guānghuá Lù 44, north of the diplomatic compound. © 010/6532-5905.

Lotus Bar (Liánhuā Jiǔbā) Set inside a narrow 70-year-old two-story house east of the Back Lakes, Lotus's small, artsy interior appeals to the city's shyer hipsters. The best reason to come is the pair of couches next to the upstairs window, with bird's-eye views of recently reconstructed Yāndài Xiéjiē, a quainter-than-quaint *hútòng* running east from the intersection of Hòu Hǎi and Qián Hǎi.

Pleasant outdoor seating on the next-door roof is available in summer. If the bar is too crowded, head across the street to Ŏu, a similarly decorated Thai restaurant under the same management. Yāndài Xiéjiē 29 (Back Lakes; in 1st hútòng on right walking south from Drum Tower; look for a circular window above a bamboo and glass doorway). ✆ 010/6407-7857.

Neo Lounge (Jiǔshíjiǔ Jiǔláng)   Owned by Henry Lǐ, the same Běijīng party czar who runs The Club (see section 5 of this chapter), this bar is superstylish minimalism for the deliberately tousled hair set. The chairs are velvet, the drinks are expensive, and there's a gigantic mirror behind the bar. DJs spin appropriately moody electronica and there is the occasional live band. This was Quentin Tarrantino's watering hole in 2002, during the filming of *Kill Bill.* Xìngfú Yī Cūn Zhōng Lù 99 (Sānlǐtún), west of Sānlǐtún N. Bar St. across Xīn Dōng Lù. ✆ 010/ 6416-1077.

No Name (Bái Fēng de nèi ge jiǔbā)   This is the hip little bar that started it all in the Back Lakes, and it's still unmatched for stoned artist cool. Decor changes seasonally, but it's always imaginatively mellow. The bar is next to and owned by the people behind Nuage (p. 86). They serve the best gin-and-tonic in town, inexplicably left off the menu. Qián Hǎi Dóng Yán (Back Lakes; east side of the Yíndìng Bridge). ✆ 010/6401-8541.

Pass-by Bar (Guòkè Jiǔbā)   Relocated in a restored courtyard house down a *hútòng* east of Qián Hǎi in 2002, Tibetan-themed Pass-by is more gathering place than nightspot, with an extensive English-language library, a useful message board, rotating photo exhibits on the walls, and a good mix of Chinese and foreign regulars. There's great Italian food by a chef stolen from Annie's (p. 93) and a separate nonsmoking section—almost unheard-of in a Běijīng bar. The courtyard is idyllic in summer with outdoor seating. Internet access is available (¥10/$1 per hr.). Nán Luógǔ Xiàng 108 (Back Lakes; alley is to left/west of a Muslim restaurant on the north side of Ping'an Dadao—walk north 150m/492 ft.). ✆ 010/8403-8004.

Poacher's Inn (Yǒuyì Qīngnián Jiǔdiàn)   Mayhem. People at this absurdly popular dive don't gyrate half naked on the tables as often as they used to, but it still gets plenty lewd on Friday and Saturday nights. This is the cheapest and busiest bar in Sānlǐtún, with some of the city's best people-watching. You'll have to get there before 10pm to nab a chair, but you won't sit for long anyway. Běi Sānlǐtún Nán (Sānlǐtún), west off Sānlǐtún N. Bar St. (Take left at the small Industrial and Commercial Bank of China branch on the west side of N. Bar St., then the 1st right.) ✆ 010/6417-2632.

Press Club Bar (Jìzhě Jùlèbù)   The nearby Beijing International Club, renowned in a previous era by as the meeting spot for foreign correspondents, inspired this upscale bar inside the St. Regis Hotel. The elegant space, with leather-bound tomes, marble fireplace, leather armchairs, and brocade sofas, seats just 55. Old prints and vintage photos of Běijīng pundits and reporters from days past line the long bar. The place closes at midnight. Jiànguómén Wài Dàjiē 21 (at rear of St. Regis's main building). ✆ 010/6460-6688.

Public Space (Bái Fángzi)   Another Henry Lǐ venture, this is the only establishment on the original bar street worth your time. No Filipino bands or hideous decor here. Just a dark, semi-stylish space, slightly overpriced drinks, and sidewalk seating from which to people-watch. Sānlǐtún Jiǔba Jiē 50 (Sānlǐtún). ✆ 010/6416-0759.

Rive Gauche (Zuǒ Àn)   A lot of the bars in the Back Lakes strive for style. This one just has it. Overstuffed couches separated by dark wood panels make for elegant lounging with far less than the usual clutter. Large windows in front provide clear views of the lake in a spot where few people wander. The menu has a full page of fortified coffees you'll definitely want to try. Prices are steep, but are worth it for the quiet atmosphere. Qiánhái Běi Yán 11 (Back Lakes). (From bottom of Qián Hǎi, walk 5 min. north along west side; bar is unmarked, in the front building of a courtyard house with tall wooden doors.) ℂ 010/6612-9300.

World of Suzie Wong (Sūxī Huáng) Named for the fictional Hong Kong hooker with a heart of gold, this is the see-and-be-seen venue for nouveau-riche Chinese and newly arrived expatriates. DJs so cool it hurts play music for head-bobbers in the main room, and there's a Míng-style canopy bed next to the bar where the exhibitionists sit. Get there early to stake out one of the row of semi-private alcoves to the side, luridly lit and luxuriously outfitted with plush couches covered in brocaded pillows. West gate of Cháoyáng Park (above Mirch Masala). ℂ 010/6593-6049.

7 Cafes & Other Drinks Spots

Just like the Manchurian hordes did 3½ centuries earlier, **Starbucks** swept into Běijīng in the 1990s and quickly conquered it. Branches are everywhere, including the China World complex, the Oriental Plaza, the Pacific Century Plaza near Sānlǐtún, and, yes, the inner court of the Forbidden City. By far the city's most popular coffee chain, it is particularly beloved of young local women in search of eligible expatriates. There are other options (see below) but, sadly, few offer a better brew.

Despite the coffee invasion, Běijīng is still ultimately tea territory, and many of the most pleasant sipping experiences are to be had in the small teahouses that lie scattered about the city.

Bella (Bèilā) This is a small chain of locally owned cafes, popular more for its proximity to Sānlǐtún than for its coffee. They produce decent baked goods and are a favorite gathering place for expatriate wives. All three branches are open from 9am to 9:30pm. Sānlǐtún Xī Wǔ (5) Jiē 1, northeast of the Spanish embassy (ℂ 010/8451-7489); Sānlǐtún N. Bar St., opposite the French School (ℂ 010/6417-3449); and next to the Yàxiù Market (ℂ 136/9113-6430).

Purple Vine Tea House (Zǐténg Lú Cháguǎn) This tiny teahouse next to the Forbidden City is one of the most peaceful in Běijīng, with private rooms separated by wood lattice screens and a small fountain in front that fills it with the sound of water. Order one of the more expensive oolong teas (¥200–¥400/ $25–$50) and you'll be treated to the Chinese version of a tea ceremony, less aesthetically pleasing than the Japanese version but with a better-tasting end product. The menu is in English. Open daily noon to 2am. Nán Cháng Jiē 1, at the intersection with Xī Huá Mén (just outside west gate of the Forbidden City). ℂ 010/6606-6614.

rbt (Xiānzōnglín) A ubiquitous drinks chain from Taiwan (via Hong Kong), rbt is Běijīng's best source for *zhēnzhū nǎichá* (pearl milk tea), a cloudy tea-based concoction with large tapioca balls, served in a variety of flavors. Exaggerated faux-forest interiors, with rope-swing chairs in the windows, underscore the oddity. The English menu features a small selection of good snacks. Branches are easily recognized by their bright green signs featuring a little white cartoon rabbit. Open daily from 9am to 1am. Convenient branch at Dōngdān Dàjiē 69 (just north of the Oriental Plaza). ℂ 010/6527-7896.

Sculpting in Time (Diāokè Shíguāng) This was once Běijīng's most famous film cafe, but it lost that niche to Space for Imagination (see section 3 of this chapter) when it was forced to move from its original location (at the east gate of Peking University). Now at the Běijīng Institute of Technology, it seldom shows films but is still popular with students, foreign and Chinese both. A second branch in the Western Hills (© 010/8529-0040), south of the main entrance to Fragrant Hills Park, has a pleasant remoteness and a large outdoor deck with views of the park. Both serve adequate coffee and Western snacks. Open daily from 9am to 1am. Wēigōngcūn Xī Kǒu 7 (Lìgōng Dà Nán Mén), just to left of the university's south gate. © 010/6894-6825.

The Teahouse of Family Fù (Chǎ Jiā Fù)   Located in a unique octagonal building on the south bank of Hòu Hǎi, the Fù family's teahouse is among the city's most charming, furnished throughout with a pleasantly haphazard assortment of Míng reproduction furniture. Owned by a former mechanics professor and run with help from his friendly English-speaking mother, it sometimes plays host to poetry readings, lectures, and classical Chinese music performances. Teas are reasonably priced (¥50–¥152/$6–$20 for pot with unlimited refills) and presented on a fan. Semi-private rooms branch off to all sides. Free snacks. Open from 11am to midnight. Hòu Hǎi Nán Àn, next to Kǒng Yǐjǐ. © 010/6616-0725.

10

The Great Wall & Other Side Trips from Běijīng

by Graeme Smith

The hills around Běijīng are dotted with fascinating sights, the foremost, of course, being the **Great Wall.** Many of the sights listed in this chapter can be seen in a single excursion, which can include other sights just on the outskirts of the city. Nearly all organized tours include a stop at the **Míng Tombs** on the way to the Great Wall at **Bā Dá Lǐng** and **Jūyōng Guān. Tánzhè Sì** and **Jiètái Sì** are readily combined as an agreeable day trip, and the intriguing **Tiányì Mù** (p. 143), a cemetery for eunuchs on the western outskirts of town, is on the road to the quiet courtyard houses of **Chuān Dǐ Xià.**

Surprisingly, the most enjoyable way to reach many of these sights is by public transportation. Although slower than an organized tour, public bus or train travel is flexible, doesn't drag you to dubious attractions, and costs a fraction of the overpriced tours offered by

hotels. If you're short on time, an option is to hire a taxi for the day (see section 2, "Getting Around" in chapter 3). An entertaining (if slightly rushed) choice is to join a Chinese bus tour. Air-conditioned buses for these tours leave when full early in the morning from various metro stations, and make stops at two or three sites. Your last resort should be hiring a car through your hotel or a tour agency for a ludicrous fee. There is no need to hire an English-speaking guide.

When heading out of town, avoid weekend mornings when traffic can be gridlocked. Attempting to return on Sunday afternoon is also frustrating. Even on weekdays, allow at least half a day, and usually a full day, to explore the sights listed in this chapter. Take a picnic and take your time. For some destinations, an overnight stay is recommended.

1 The Great Wall (Wànlǐ Chángchéng) ✦✦✦

Even after you dispense with the myths that it is a single continuous structure and that it can be seen from space (it can't, any more than a fishing line can be seen from the other side of a river), China's best-known attraction is still mind-boggling. The world's largest historical site is referred to in Mandarin as **Wànlǐ Chángchéng** ("10,000-Lǐ Long Wall" or simply "Very Long Wall"). The Great Wall begins at Shānhǎi Guān on the Bó Hǎi Sea and snakes west to a fort at Jiāyù Guān in the Gobi Desert. Its origins date back to the Warring States Period (453–221 B.C.), when rival kingdoms began building defensive walls to thwart each other's armies. The king of Qín, who eventually conquered the other states to become the first emperor of a unified China, engaged in large-scale wall building toward the end of his reign, although tales of 300,000 conscripted laborers are embellishments of subsequent dynasties. During the Hàn dynasty

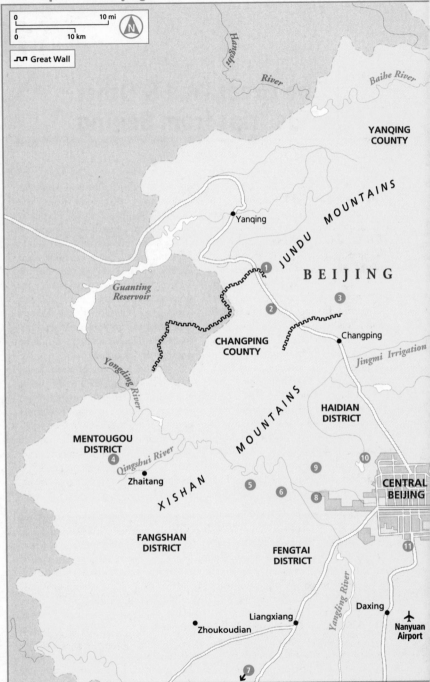

0   10 mi
0   10 km

⌐⌐ Great Wall

Hanshi River

Baihe River

YANQING
COUNTY

Yanqing

JUNDU MOUNTAINS

B E I J I N G

①

②

③

Guanting Reservoir

CHANGPING
COUNTY

Changping

Jingmi Irrigation

Yongding River

HAIDIAN
DISTRICT

MENTOUGOU
DISTRICT

④

Qingshui River

Zhaitang

⑨

⑩

CENTRAL
BEIJING

X I S H A N   M O U N T A I N S

⑤

⑥

⑧

⑪

FANGSHAN
DISTRICT

FENGTAI
DISTRICT

Yanqing River

Daxing

Zhoukoudian

Liangxiang

Nanyuan
Airport

⑦

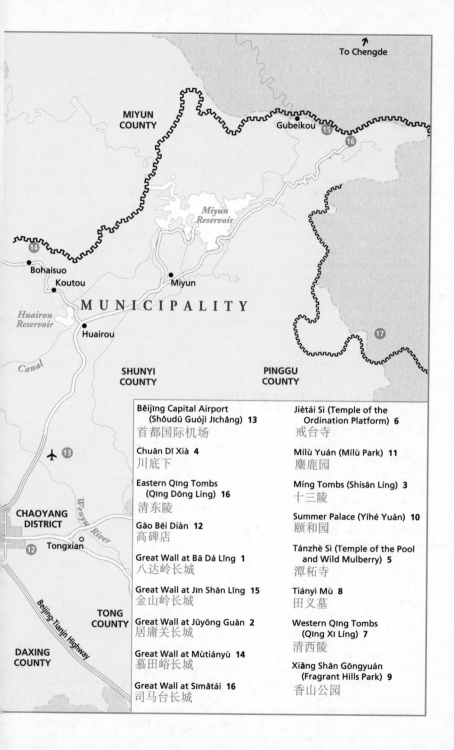

To Chengde

MIYUN
COUNTY

Gubeikou ⑮
⑯

*Miyun
Reservoir*

⑭
Bohaisuo
Koutou
Miyun

M U N I C I P A L I T Y

*Huairou
Reservoir*
Huairou

⑰

Canal

SHUNYI
COUNTY

PINGGU
COUNTY

✈ ⑬

CHAOYANG
DISTRICT

Wenyu River

⑫ Tongxian

TONG
COUNTY

Beijing-Tianjin Highway

DAXING
COUNTY

Běijīng Capital Airport
(Shǒudū Guójì Jīchǎng) **13**
首都国际机场

Chuān Dǐ Xià **4**
川底下

Eastern Qīng Tombs
(Qīng Dōng Líng) **16**
清东陵

Gāo Bēi Diàn **12**
高碑店

Great Wall at Bā Dá Lǐng **1**
八达岭长城

Great Wall at Jīn Shān Lǐng **15**
金山岭长城

Great Wall at Jūyōng Guān **2**
居庸关长城

Great Wall at Mùtiányù **14**
慕田峪长城

Great Wall at Sīmǎtái **16**
司马台长城

Jiètái Sì (Temple of the
Ordination Platform) **6**
戒台寺

Mílù Yuán (Mílù Park) **11**
麋鹿园

Míng Tombs (Shísān Líng) **3**
十三陵

Summer Palace (Yíhé Yuán) **10**
颐和园

Tánzhè Sì (Temple of the Pool
and Wild Mulberry) **5**
潭柘寺

Tiányì Mù **8**
田义墓

Western Qīng Tombs
(Qīng Xī Líng) **7**
清西陵

Xiāng Shān Gōngyuán
(Fragrant Hills Park) **9**
香山公园

(206 B.C.–220 A.D.), the Wall was extended west, and additions were made in completely different locations, according to the military needs of the day.

Although many tour guides will try to persuade you otherwise, the Míng Wall you see today is unrelated to the Qín Wall, which lay far to the north. The Míng even went to the trouble of calling their wall Biān Qiáng (Frontier Wall) to avoid comparisons with the tyrannical first emperor of China, Qín Shǐ Huángdì. The original Wall was built almost entirely from tamped earth, and often crumbled away within decades of being constructed. Talk of satellite mapping the current Wall is fanciful—for most of its length, the structure is barely visible from the ground. This, and the fact that there is no single "Great Wall," makes it impossible to pin down the Wall's precise length.

Those with an interest in exaggerating Chinese xenophobia portray Wall building as an essential part of the national psyche, but after the Hàn (206 B.C.–220 A.D.), few dynasties bothered with Wall construction, and relied mostly on trade, diplomacy, and the odd punitive expedition to keep the peace. Even during the inward-looking Míng dynasty, the Wall was viewed by many at court as an ancient version of the Star Wars missile-defense idea—absurdly expensive and successful only in antagonizing China's neighbors. With the Míng wracked by internal rebellion, the Qīng armies simply bribed the demoralized sentries. The Qīng left the Wall as a monument to folly, and while early Western visitors were impressed, it became a source of national pride only recently. Dr Sun Yat-sen was among the first to promote it as a symbol of national strength, an idea the communists adopted, including it in the National Anthem. The Wall's most easily visited sections are **Bā Dá Lǐng** and **Jūyōng Guān,** while **Mùtiányù, Jīn Shān Lǐng,** and the vertiginous **Sīmǎtái** require a full day's outing.

THE GREAT WALL AT BĀ DÁ LǏNG ✿✿
70km (43 miles) NW of Běijīng

The first section of the Great Wall opened to tourists, the portion at **Bā Dá Lǐng** remains the most popular. In 1957 it was fully restored to its original Míng appearance—although the reconstruction was sloppier than subsequent efforts at Mùtiányù and particularly Jīn Shān Lǐng and Sīmǎtái, where efforts were taken to preserve a sense of antiquity. A cable car was added at Bā Dá Lǐng in the 1980s, followed later by a museum, a Circle Vision Theater, several restaurants, a large number of souvenir stands, and a KFC. Criticized by Wall "purists" for this profusion of facilities and an unimaginative restoration, it is still one of the most dramatic sections of the Great Wall. Set in a steep, forested mountain range, Bā Dá Lǐng offers tremendous views and, for those willing to travel beyond the restored sections, worthwhile hiking.

> **Impressions**
> *After beholding China's wonder of the world, I would hesitate to cross the street to see Egypt's Pyramids.*
> —William Geil, *The Great Wall of China*, 1909

Construction of this section of the Great Wall began in 1368 and continued for over 200 years. Built of stone, the Wall averages 7.2m (24 ft.) in height, 6.3m (21 ft.) in width at its base, and 5.4m (18 ft.) in width at its top. The sides are covered in stone, the top in layers of brick. The interior is a mixture of soil and rubble, painstakingly tamped into place. In unrestored sections, where the masonry has crumbled away, you can spy the striations. Running the length of

---

> **Tips** Travelers with Disabilities
>
> Exploring the Great Wall is tough enough for people in good shape. For those with disabilities, the Wall is a nightmare. At Bā Dá Lǐng a cable car provides access, but there are still steps to negotiate up to the cable car, and steep steps up to the Wall. There are no elevators or wheelchair assists at any of the sections.

---

the Wall, gateway arches and watchtowers served as a highway through the mountains. (Five horses could ride abreast, drawing carriages.)

ESSENTIALS
VISITOR INFORMATION   The ticket office at Bā Dá Lǐng is open from 6:30am to 7pm. Admission is ¥45 ($6) in summer, ¥40 ($5) in winter. A round-trip ride on the cable car costs ¥50 ($6) per person.

GETTING THERE   The cheapest way to get to Bā Dá Lǐng is on the red-and-yellow striped (air-conditioned) **bus no. 919** (daily 6am–6pm, about every 30 min.; 1-hr. trip; ¥10/$1), which leaves from the east side of Déshèng Mén. A comfortable option is to take one of the air-conditioned city-sponsored **tourist (yóu) buses** (© 010/6779-7546): *Yóu* no. 1 leaves from the northeast side of Qián Mén (daily 6am–noon, every 20 min.; ¥50/$6), and *yóu* no. 2 leaves from Dōng Zhí Mén and the Běijīng Railway Station (daily 6:30–10am, every 30 min.; ¥50/$6); the price includes Jūyōng Guān (see below) and one of the Míng Tombs (usually Dìng Líng, p. 199). A round-trip **taxi** should cost less than ¥300 ($38). **Group tours** are typically combined with a trip to the Míng Tombs and cost around ¥400 ($50) per person.

THE GREAT WALL AT JŪYŌNG GUĀN
59km (37 miles) NW of Běijīng

The most conveniently accessed section of the Wall is also the most historically significant. Guarding one of the two crucial passes to Běijīng (the other is to the northeast, at Gǔ Běi Kǒu) and the vast North China Plain, **Jūyōng Guān (Dwelling in Harmony Pass)** was the site of pitched battles, involving Jurchen, Mongol and, more recently, Japanese invaders. There may have been fortifications here as early as the 6th century, before Běijīng existed. Climbing the steep section to the left offers marvelous views of Bā Dá Lǐng, snaking up the mountains to the north, and south toward Běijīng (in the event of a clear day). Restorations from 1993 to 1997 created over 4km (2½ miles) of wall, but railings mar the effect; there's little feeling of antiquity. All the construction must have eaten into the advertising budget, as crowds are thinner here than at Bā Dá Lǐng.

It's worth stopping at Jūyōng Guān to view the ancient and remarkable **Yún Tái (Cloud Platform)** ✰✰✰, which once stood astride the old road running northwest into Mongol territories. Dating from 1342, it was the base for three Tibetan-style stupas, which were toppled by an earthquake and replaced during the Míng dynasty by a Chinese-style Buddhist temple, also destroyed (by fire) during the early Qīng. The central tunnel is carved with elephants, Buddha figures demonstrating different *mudra* (hand positions), the four heavenly kings, and six different scripts. Facing north, the languages on the right-hand wall are Chinese, Xī Xià (the script of a vanished Tibetan race, decimated by Genghis

Tips On the Wild Wall

The sections of the Great Wall described in this chapter are all easy to reach and suitably stunning, but they represent only a part of what the Wall has to offer. Travelers with time and the inclination to explore beyond these are strongly encouraged to join a trip to the crumbling **"unofficial" sections of the Wall** that snake through more remote areas north of Běijīng. William Lindesay, a Briton who has been walking along and writing about the Great Wall since the mid-1980s, organizes excursions for the company **Wild Wall.** Joining one of his tours is the best way to learn about the Wall's construction and destruction, both by human and natural forces, from a knowledgeable source who cares a great deal more than most Chinese do about the Wall's preservation.

Wild Wall is based out of one of two modernized farmhouses, the first and more fully outfitted just north of Běijīng, and the second somewhat more primitive (but still comfortable) in Héběi. Wild Wall's most common weekend trips run 3 days (Fri–Sun) and cost $200 (prices are quoted in U.S. dollars), including guided hikes, accommodation in a farmhouse, and excellent home cooking (transportation to the farmhouse is an extra $65). Although a little pricey, these weekend trips are highly recommended and typically happen twice or three times a month. Day hikes are also available. More strenuous "Extreme Treks," which include camping along the Wall, usually run only twice a season. For details and booking information, see the website, **www.wildwall.com.**

Khan's armies during the 14th century), Uighur, and Mongolian. The top script is Sanskrit, with Tibetan below.

ESSENTIALS
VISITOR INFORMATION The ticket office at Jūyōng Guān (© **010/6977-0394**) is open daily from 8am to 4pm. Admission is ¥40 ($5) in summer, ¥35 ($4.40) in winter.

GETTING THERE For public transport information, see "Getting There" for Bā Dá Lǐng, above. A round-trip **taxi** should cost less than ¥200 ($25).

THE GREAT WALL AT MÙTIÁNYÙ
90km (56 miles) NE of Běijīng

The Great Wall at Bā Dá Lǐng proved so popular that authorities restored a second section of the Wall to the east in 1986. **Mùtiányù** is slightly less crowded than Bā Dá Lǐng, but it does have its own traffic jams in summer. Located in a heavily forested area, it's especially photogenic in rainy, misty weather. You can hop over a fence to see more tempting, unrestored sections, but those planning to survey the entire length of restored wall will find themselves with little energy remaining. As at Bā Dá Lǐng, there is a cable car to help those who need it.

ESSENTIALS
VISITOR INFORMATION The ticket office (© **010/6162-6873**) is open 24 hours. Admission is ¥35 ($4); the cable car costs ¥50 ($6) round-trip.

GETTING THERE   Mùtiányù is not as easy to reach as Bā Dá Lǐng. Most hotels can arrange **guided group tours** for around ¥250 ($31). The *yóu* **no. 6** combines a trip to Mùtiányù with visits to a temple and a lake; it leaves from the northeast side of the Xuānwǔ Mén (206) metro stop (Sat–Sun 6:30–8am, every 30 min.; ¥50/$6). The bus stops at Mùtiányù for about 3 hours. A **taxi** will cost between ¥200 and ¥400 ($25–$50).

THE GREAT WALL AT JĪN SHĀN LǏNG

130km (81 miles) NE of Běijīng, 90km (56 miles) SW of Chéngdé

Located in Héběi Province, this is the least visited and least spoiled of the Wall sections listed in this chapter. **Jīn Shān Lǐng** is 10km (6¼ miles) east of Gǔ Běi Kǒu (Old Northern Pass), through which Qīng royalty passed on the way to their summer retreat at Chéngdé (Jehol). The Wall here is in good condition, as it was a recent (after 1570) rebuild of an existing Míng wall, and construction was overseen by the outstanding general, Qī Jìguāng. The defensible pass, whose heart lies to the west at Gǔ Běi Kǒu, was 27km (17 miles), stretching all the way to Sīmǎtái in the east. Bricks are smaller, reflecting advances in wall-building technique. The Wall features unusual circular towers and elaborate defensive walls leading up to towers. Management dreams of tourist hordes—a cable car has been built, along with gradually rusting amusements—but the remoteness of the site makes large-scale tourism unlikely. The walk to **Sīmǎtái** (see below) is reason enough to visit.

ESSENTIALS
VISITOR INFORMATION   The ticket office (© **0314/883-8378**) is open 24 hours. Admission is ¥30 ($3.70).

GETTING THERE   Appealingly, Jīn Shān Lǐng can be reached by **train** from the Běijīng Běi Zhàn (North Railway Station), just north of the Xī Zhí Mén metro stop (201, exit A). A special tourist train for Gǔ Běi Kǒu, the L671 departs daily from mid-April to October at 7:25am (daily; 2½-hr. trip; ¥20/$2.50). The rest of the year, the slower L815, departing at 8am, will take you there (4-hr. trip; ¥10/$1.25). Returning trains depart at 3:05pm and 4:15pm, respectively. Walking down from the station, you can either find lodgings in the village of Gǔ Běi Kǒu Héxī Cūn, or take a minivan directly to the Wall (25-min. trip, ¥20/$2.50). From Xī Zhí Mén bus station, some **buses** to Chéngdé (daily 6am–5:30pm, about every 20 min.; 2½-hr. trip; ¥46/$5.75 for an Iveco or similar) also pass by the entrance, where you face either a 6km (4-mile) hike or haggling for a minivan (¥10/$1.25).

WHERE TO STAY   Standard rooms start at ¥140 ($17) in the dull but clean **Jīn Shān Lǐng Bīnguǎn,** to the right just inside the entrance. Staying at one of the simple courtyard houses in **Gǔ Běi Kǒu Héxī Cūn,** just below the railway station, is a cheaper and more appealing option; accommodations are usually ¥10 ($1.25) per person, and home-cooked meals are similarly priced.

THE GREAT WALL AT SĪMǍTÁI ★★

124km (77 miles) NE of Běijīng

Somewhat tamed after a series of deaths led to the closing of its most dangerous stretch, Sīmǎtái nevertheless remains one of the best options for those who want more of a challenge from the Great Wall. The most harrowing portion, steep and unrestored, is on the east (right) side of the Mìyún Reservoir. Several

---

Moments Jīn Shān Lǐng to Sīmǎtái

One of the all-time great Wall hikes extends east from Jīn Shān Lǐng to the Mìyún Reservoir. Roughly 10km (6¼ miles), the hike takes 4 hours at a leisurely pace. During summer, the watchtowers provide welcome shade, but the walk is best attempted in autumn when the sky is an intense cobalt blue and trees glow with golden and red hues. The middle part of the hike, as the postcard vendors fall away and the Wall begins to crumble, can be truly sublime. Do as the locals do and swap your entrance ticket with hikers walking in the other direction; otherwise you will be charged admission to both sites. A number of hotels provide transportation, including the Far East Youth Hostel (© 0138/0135-8094; most days 7:30am; ¥90/$11). Otherwise, take an air-conditioned bus from Xī Zhí Mén's long-distance bus station to Mìyún (daily 6am–4pm, every 30 min.; ¥15/$2), then hire a minivan *(miàndī)* to drop you off at Jīn Shān Lǐng and pick you up at Sīmǎtái for around ¥100 ($12)—withhold payment until after you're picked up.

---

gravel-strewn spots here require all four limbs to navigate. The endpoint is the **Wàngjīng Tǎ,** the 12th watchtower. Beyond this is the appropriately named **Tiān Qiáo (Heavenly Bridge),** a thin, tilted ridge where the Wall narrows to only a few feet—the section that is now off-limits. Despite the danger, Sīmǎtái can get rather crowded on weekends, especially since a cable car was installed, and souvenir vendors can be a nuisance. Those who speak Chinese would do well to pretend otherwise, or risk listening to hard-luck stories for their entire hike. The round-trip hike to Tiān Qiáo takes roughly 3 hours at a moderate pace. The section of Sīmǎtái west of the reservoir is initially better restored and connects to another section of the Great Wall, Jīn Shān Lǐng, in Héběi Province (see the box "Jīn Shān Lǐng to Sīmǎtái" above).

ESSENTIALS
VISITOR INFORMATION The ticket office, a 10-minute walk away in a small village south of the reservoir, is open 8am to 10pm in summer and 8am to 6pm in winter. Admission is ¥30 ($4). The cable car runs only from April to November; a round-trip ride to the no. 8 Tower costs ¥50 ($6), or ¥30 ($3.60) one-way.

Those walking west to Jīn Shān Lǐng will be charged ¥5 (60¢) to cross a bridge. It is possible to skirt around the left side of the reservoir via an aqueduct and a water-bottling factory, although you face shysters trying to convince you that the road is closed ("to protect the cultural relics") and that the only way to proceed is to pay ¥40 ($5) for a 1-minute boat ride.

GETTING THERE The best no-hassle option is to visit with one of the **Youth Hostelling International tours** (© 0138/0135-8094; ask for "Simon"); these typically leave the Far East Youth Hostel (p. 75) daily at 7:30am and cost ¥80 ($10) for simple transportation. The *yóu no.* 12 travels to Sīmǎtái from northeast of the Xuānwǔ Mén (206) metro stop (Apr to mid-Oct Sat–Sun 6:30–8:30am, every 30 min; ¥70/$9); you get about 3 hours at the site. A round-trip **taxi** ride should cost less than ¥400 ($50).

2 Míng Tombs (Shísān Líng)

48km (31 miles) NW of Běijīng

Of the 16 emperors who ruled China during the Míng dynasty (1368–1644), 13 are buried in a box canyon at the southern foot of Tiānshòu Shān (hence the Chinese name Shísān Líng, the 13 Tombs). The first emperor of the Míng, Hóngwǔ, is entombed in Xiào Líng, near Nánjīng. The location of the second emperor's tomb is uncertain, while the unfilial seventh emperor, who usurped the throne after his brother was taken by the Mongols, was buried near the Summer Palace among the graves of concubines. Despite these omissions, this is the most extensive burial complex of any Chinese dynasty. A red gate sealed off the valley, guards were posted, and no one, not even the emperor, could ride a horse on these grounds. The site was chosen by the Yǒnglè emperor, who also oversaw the construction of the Forbidden City. Protected from the bitter northern winds by a mountain range, the tombs are constructed in conventional fashion, with memorial halls at the front and burial chambers to the rear.

The entrance to the **Míng Tombs,** a long and celebrated **shén dào (spirit way)** is lined with statues of guardian animals and officials. Only three of the Míng Tombs—**Dìng Líng, Cháng Líng,** and **Zhāo Líng**—have been restored, and only one (Dìng Líng) has been fully excavated. Many of the buildings mirror Míng palaces found in the city. Because of this, the sight can be boring to people who've had their fill of imperial architecture. The Míng Tombs are at their most charming along the **shén dào** and on the grounds of **unrestored tombs** (free admission). In contrast, the restored tombs are dank, overcrowded, and uninspiring. The Míng Tombs are so unpopular with foreign tourists that they are often excluded from tour-group itineraries.

ESSENTIALS

GETTING THERE   The valley is just off the freeway that goes to Bā Dá Lǐng. Many **Chinese bus tours** to Bā Dá Lǐng also come here, visiting the spirit way and one of the tombs at blinding speed, but if you want time to explore some unrestored tombs (highly recommended), you'll have to make a separate trip. The most comfortable means of public transport is air-conditioned **bus no. 845** from the Chēgōng Zhuāng (202) metro stop (a 5-min. walk north of exit B) to Zhèngfǎ Dàxué in Chāngpíng (daily, about every 15 min.; 1½-hr. trip; ¥9/$1), then cross the street and take **bus no. 314** to the Nán Xīn Cūn stop (daily, about every 20 min.; 15-min. trip; ¥1/15¢), which is adjacent to the entrance to the spirit way. From there, you can continue north to either Dìng Líng Dàokǒu to visit Dìng Líng, a further 2km (1¼-mile) walk to the west, or on to the terminus at Cháng Líng. It is also possible to take the green-and-white *zhī* (express) version of **bus no. 919** to Zhèngfǎ Dàxué from Déshèng Mén (daily, about every 30 min.; 1-hr. trip; ¥9/$1). A **taxi** hired in Běijīng should cost less than ¥400 ($50).

EXPLORING THE AREA

The **spirit way (shén dào)** (admission Apr–Nov ¥30/$3.70, Dec–Mar ¥20/$2.50; daily 8am till dusk) is not to be missed. The main entrance to the valley is the **Dà Hóng Mén (Great Red Gate),** remarkably similar to gates found in the Forbidden City, beyond which is a pavilion housing China's largest memorial stele, and beyond that the spirit way. The path, slightly curved to fool evil spirits, is lined on either side with willows and remarkable **carved stone animals** and human figures, considered among the best in China. The statuary includes pairs of camels, lions, elephants, and mythical beasts, such as the *qílín,* a creature of immense virtue referred to as the "Chinese unicorn" even though it has two horns. The craftsmanship here is far superior to that of the Qīng Tombs (see below).

The largest and best preserved of the 13 tombs is 4km (2½ miles) ahead: **Cháng Líng** (admission ¥45/$5.60 summer, ¥30/$3.70 winter; daily 7am–4:30pm), the tomb of the Yǒnglè emperor (reign 1403–1424). The layout is identical to the tomb of the first Míng emperor in Nánjīng. It feels like the Forbidden City in miniature, and is perhaps disappointing if you've seen the palace already. Most striking is **Líng'ēn Diàn** 𝄐, an immense hall in which the interior columns and brackets have been left unpainted, creating an eye-catching contrast with the green ceiling panels. Slightly wider than the Hall of Supreme Harmony, Líng'ēn Diàn contains a three-tiered platform and building materials that are superior to those of the Forbidden City.

The 4,000-sq.-m (13,000-sq.-ft.) **Underground Palace** at **Dìng Líng** (admission ¥60/$7.50 summer; ¥40/$5 winter; 8:30am–5pm), rediscovered in 1956, was the burial place of the Wànlì emperor (reign 1572–1620), his wife, and his favorite concubine. Construction of the burial chamber commenced before the emperor was 20 years old, making him "the living ancestor" in the words of Ray Huang, author of an absorbing account of Wànlì's reign, *1587, A Year of No Significance.* The "palace" is a vast marble vault, buried 27m (88 ft.) underground and divided into five large chambers. It's all a bit disappointing. The corpses have been removed, their red coffins replaced with cheap replicas, and burial objects moved to aboveground display rooms. The original marble thrones are still there, though, now covered in a small fortune of *rénmínbì* notes tossed by Chinese visitors hoping to bribe the emperor's ghost to grant them good luck. Outside, behind the ticket office, is the new and quite respectable **Shísān Líng Bówùguǎn (Míng Tombs Museum),** with short biographies of all the entombed emperors; several reproduced artifacts; a detailed, wood reproduction of the Líng'ēn Diàn; and a 1954 photo of Máo reclining and reading a newspaper on a half-buried marble incense burner at Cháng Líng.

3 Eastern Qīng Tombs (Qīng Dōng Líng) 𝄐𝄐

125km (78 miles) E of Běijīng

The **Qīng Dōng Líng** have been open for more than 20 years but are still little visited despite offering considerably more to visitors than tombs of the Míng. Altogether 5 emperors, 15 empresses, 136 concubines, 3 princes, and 2 princesses are buried in 15 tombs here. The first to be buried was Shùnzhì—the first Qīng emperor to reign from Běijīng—in 1663, and the last was an imperial concubine in 1935. The tomb chambers of four imperial tombs, the **Xiào Líng** (the Shùnzhì emperor), **Jīng Líng** (Kāngxī), **Yù Líng** (Qiánlóng), and **Dìng Líng** (Xiánfēng), are open as well as the twin **Dìng Dōng Líng** tombs (Dowager Empress Cíxǐ and Empress Cí'ān). Others of interest include a group site for the Qiánlóng emperor's concubines.

ESSENTIALS

VISITOR INFORMATION The tombs are in Zūnhuà County, Héběi Province (daily 8am–5:30pm summer, 9am–4:30pm winter). The *tōng piào,* which offers access to all the tombs, costs ¥81 ($10).

GETTING THERE A special Qīng Dōng Líng *yóu* **bus** departs from northeast of the Xuānwǔ Mén (206) metro stop (summer only, daily 7:30am; 3-hr.

trip; ¥80/$10); this gives you about 3 hours at the site. If you want to explore at your own pace, you'll have to hire a cab or take a rickety local bus (daily 6:30am–4:30pm; 3½-hr. trip; ¥24/$3) to Zūnhuà from just east of the Dàwàng Lù (123) metro stop (exit C), then hire a *miàndī* (minivan) to take you the rest of the way (about ¥20/$3). An assortment of three-wheelers will offer to take you around the site with a first asking price of ¥10 ($1.25).

EXPLORING THE AREA

Although few others are as elaborate, the **Xiào Líng** was the first tomb on the site, and a model for others both here and at the Western Qīng Tombs. As here, usually an approach road or **spirit way** may have guardian figures, and the entrance to the tomb itself is usually preceded by a large stele pavilion and marble bridges over a stream. To the right, the buildings used for preparation of sacrifices are now usually the residences of the staff, and hung with washing. Inside the gate, halls to the left and right were for enrobing and other preparations, and now house exhibitions, as usually does each **Hall of Eminent Favor,** at the rear, where ceremonies in honor of the deceased took place. Behind, if open, a doorway allows access past a stone altar to a steep ramp leading to the base of the **Soul Tower.** Through a passageway beneath, stairs to either side lead to a walkway encircling the mound, giving views across the countryside. If the tomb chamber is open, a ramp from beneath the Soul Tower leads down to a series of chambers.

The twin **Dìng Dōng Líng** tombs have nearly identical exteriors, but Cíxǐ had hers rebuilt in 1895, 14 years after Cí'ān's death (in which she is suspected of having had a hand), using far more expensive materials. Everywhere there are reminders of the Forbidden City, such are the terrace-corner spouts carved as water-loving dragons *(chē)*. The interior has motifs strikingly painted in gold on dark wood, recalling the buildings where she spent her last years. There are walls of carved and gilded brick, and superbly fearsome wooden dragons writhe down the columns. After this, the other tombs seem gaudy.

The enclosure of the **Yù Fēi Yuán Qīn (Garden of Rest)** contains moss-covered tumuli for 35 of the Qiánlóng emperor's concubines. Another is buried in a proper tomb chamber, along with an empress whom Qiánlóng had grown to dislike.

The **Yù Líng** has the finest tomb chamber, a series of rooms separated by solid marble doors, with its walls and arched ceilings engraved with Buddha figures and more than 30,000 words of Tibetan scripture. The 3-ton doors themselves have reliefs of bodhisattvas (beings on the road to enlightenment) and the four protective kings usually found at temple entrances. This tomb would be worth the trip in its own right. The **Jīng Líng** is the tomb of Qiánlóng's grandfather, the Kāngxī emperor, and is surprisingly modest given that he was possibly the greatest emperor the Chinese ever had, but that's in keeping with what is known of his character. The spirit way leading to the tomb has an elegant five-arch bridge; the guardian figures are placed on an unusual curve quite close to the tomb itself, and are more decorated than those at earlier tombs.

4 Western Qīng Tombs (Qīng Xī Líng) ⓕ

140km (87 miles) SW of Běijīng

The Yōngzhèng emperor broke with tradition and ordered his tomb to be constructed here, away from his father (the Kāngxī emperor). His son, the Qiánlóng emperor, decided to be buried near his grandfather and that thereafter burials should alternate between the eastern (see above) and western sites, although this was not followed consistently. The first tomb, the **Tài Líng,** was completed in 1737, 2 years after the Yōngzhèng reign. The last imperial interment was in 1998, when the ashes of Aisin Gioro Henry Pǔyí, the last emperor, were moved to a commercial cemetery here. He and 2 consorts were added to 4 emperors, 4 empresses, 4 princes, 2 princesses, and 57 concubines. The site is rural, with the tombs overlapped by orchards and agriculture, and with chickens, goats, and the odd rabbit to be encountered.

The **Chāng Líng** (tomb of the Jiāqìng emperor) and **Chóng Líng** (tomb of the Guāngxù emperor) are also open, as well as the **Chāng Xī Líng** with the extraordinary sonic effects of its **Huíyīn Bì**—an echo wall where, as the only visitor, you can try out the special effects available only in theory at the Temple of Heaven (p. 126).

ESSENTIALS

VISITOR INFORMATION   The ticket office is open from 8am to 5pm; a *tōng piào* (good for access to all the tombs) costs ¥80 ($10) and is good for 2 days. There's no access by tourist bus—part of the appeal for most visitors.

GETTING THERE   Take a **bus** to Yìxiàn from the Lízé Qiáo long-distance bus station (daily 6:50am–5pm, every 15 min.; 3-hr. trip; ¥40/$5), then switch to a minivan *(miàndī)* for the 15km (9¼-mile) ride to the tombs (around ¥20/$3). Unless you make a very early start, you may want to spend the night at the modest **Qīng Xī Líng Bīnguǎn,** on the site itself (© 0312/471-0038; fax 0312/471-0012; ¥140/$17 standard room in new building), or at **Guìbīn Lóu,** on the main road passing the site (© 0312/471-0883; ¥188/$23 standard room). By **taxi** it's a reasonable day-trip down the Jialíngshí Freeway from the Southwest Third Ring Road to the turnoff for Gāo Bēi Diàn to the west, and beyond to Yì Xiàn. It's possible to visit **Marco Polo Bridge (Lú Gōu Qiáo)** on the way.

EXPLORING THE AREA

The **Dà Bēi Lóu,** a pavilion containing two vast stelae, is on the curved route to the **Tài Líng.** The general plan of the major tombs follows that of the eastern tombs and, in fact, the **Chāng Líng,** slightly to the west, is almost identical, brick for brick, to the Tài Líng, although the rear section with soul tower and tomb mound is not open. The Jiāqìng empress is buried just to the west on a far smaller scale in the **Chāng Xī Líng,** the tomb mound a brick drum. But the perfectly semicircular rear wall offers the whispering gallery effects found at some domed European cathedrals, and clapping while standing on various marked stones in the center of the site produces a variety of multiple echoes, while speech is amazingly amplified. The empress can't get much peace.

As if to reflect that the Qīng were already in decline, the Dàoguāng emperor's **Mù Líng** is much more modest than those of his predecessors, missing stele pavilion or spirit way, and largely unpainted. The tomb mound is also a modest brick-wall drum. The Guǎngxù emperor was the last to complete his reign (although his aunt, Cíxǐ, is again suspected of shortening it), and his **Chóng Líng,** which uses more modern materials than other tombs, wasn't completed until 1915, well after the last emperor's abdication.

Several other rather battered tombs are open, and more are being opened, including recently the **Tài Líng Fēi Yuán Qǐn,** a group of concubine tumuli, individually labeled with the years in which the concubines entered the Yōngzhèng emperor's service and their grades in the complex harem hierarchy.

The ashes of **Pǔyí** (properly known as the Xūantǒng emperor) lie buried on the eastern end of the site, up a slope behind a brand-new Qīng-style memorial arch *(páilou)*, and behind a shoddy, modern carved balustrade. Neighboring plots are available for the right price.

5 Tánzhè Sì & Jiètái Sì ✦

Tánzhè Sì 48km (30 miles) W of Běijīng; Jiètái Sì 35km (22 miles) W of Běijīng

Buried in the hills west of Běijīng, **Tánzhè Sì (Temple of the Pool and Wild Mulberry)** and **Jiètái Sì (Temple of the Ordination Platform)** are the tranquil kinds of Chinese temples visitors imagine before they actually come to China. These temples were unusual because they received imperial support (Qīng rulers preferred Tibetan Buddhism), and both have long been popular with local pilgrims. They were also loved by early Western residents, who rented out halls inside the temples.

ESSENTIALS

VISITOR INFORMATION   Admission to Tánzhè Sì (© **010/6086-2505**) is ¥35 ($4), and the ticket office is open from 8am to 5:30pm in summer and 8:30am to 4:30pm in winter. Admission to Jiètái Sì (© **010/6980-6611**) is ¥35 ($4), and the ticket office is open year-round from 8am to 6pm.

GETTING THERE   Both temples are easily accessible by taking **bus no. 931** from the Píngguǒ Yuán (103) metro stop to **Tánzhè Sì** (daily 7am–5:30pm, about every 30min.; 1-hr. trip; ¥2.50/40¢). At the far western end of Line 1 at the Píngguǒ Yuán metro stop (exit D), take a right and continue straight a few minutes to the bus station (be sure to take the plain red-and-beige, rather than the red-and-yellow *zhī* version of the bus). At Tánzhè Sì, the last stop on this line, hike up the stone path at the end of the parking lot. From there, take **bus no. 931** east 13km (8 miles) to **Jiètái Sì,** where you reach the site by walking uphill from the bus stop. On weekends, the *yóu* **no. 7** tourist bus runs from the northeast corner of Qián Mén (Sat–Sun 7am–8:30am, every 30 min.; ¥60/ $7.50), but it regrettably includes a stop at the garish Shíhuā Caves. Round-trip by **taxi** costs less than ¥300 ($37).

WHERE TO STAY   At both temples, basic but acceptable accommodations are available for those who want (or need) to spend more time in quietude.

EXPLORING THE AREA

Tánzhè Sì ✦✦, set in peaceful forested grounds, dates back to the Western Jìn dynasty (265–316), well before Běijīng was founded. In the main courtyard on the central axis is a pair of 30m (100-ft.) ginkgo trees, supposedly planted in the Táng dynasty (618–907), as well as several apricot trees, cypresses, peonies, and

---

Impressions

If you want to get some idea of the road to Chieh T'ai Ssu [Jiètái Sì], go to the British Museum and look at the Chinese paintings—above all at the "Earthly Paradise." But fill its air with a delicate scent, hardly more than a freshness, and yet more; and break its silence with the loud, sweet notes of hidden babblers among bare, wayside bushes, and with the tapping and scraping of the small feet of donkeys on steep cobbles.
—Ann Bridge, *Pekin Picnic,* 1932

purple jade orchids. The complex is extensive, and is said to have provided a model for the layout of the Forbidden City. Above and to the right of the main courtyard lies a rare **stupa yard** *(tǎ yuán)*, stone monuments built in different styles over a period of several centuries and housing the remains of eminent monks. The **Guānyīn Diàn,** at the top of the western axis, was favored by Princess Miào Yán, a daughter of Kublai Khan; she is said to have prayed so fervently here that she left footprints in one of the floor stones (now stored in a box to the left). The main object of interest to local visitors is the **stone fish** *(shí yú)* to the left and behind this hall. Rubbing the relevant part of the fish is said to cure the corresponding malady. Everyone seems to rub its stomach.

The **ordination platform** *(jiètái)* at **Jiètái Sì** ✿, China's largest, is a three-tiered structure with 113 statues of the God of Ordination placed in niches around the base; it's located in the **Jiè Tán Diàn (Hall of the Altar of Ordination)** in the far right (northwest) corner of the temple. It looks, as novelist Ann Bridge put it, "like a very high four-poster bed." Ceremonies conducted on this platform to commemorate the ascension of a devotee to full monkhood required permission from the emperor. Often referred to as the "Běidà [Peking University, nominally the best university in China] of Buddhism" for its ability to attract the most promising monastic scholars, along with temples in Quánzhōu and Hángzhōu, it has been the most significant site for the ordination of Buddhist monks for 900 years. Surrounding courtyards have ancient, twisted pines (as venerable as the temple itself) and fragrant peony gardens.

6 Chuān Dǐ Xià

100km (62 miles) W of Běijīng

Originally called **Cuàn Dǐ Xià (Under the Stove),** this tiny village of around a hundred souls is an ideal 2-day trip for those with a passion for Chinese vernacular architecture or those keen for a glimpse of life in rural China. Set in a narrow valley off the old trade route to Shānxī, Chuān Dǐ Xià boasts the best-preserved *sìhéyuàn* (courtyard houses) in the Běijīng region. Opened to tourism in 1997, more than 70 dwellings are said to be here.

The impressive dwellings were designed by scholar-officials from the Míng who fled to this remote village toward the end of the dynasty. There they lived out one of the most pervasive legends in Chinese literature, that of the Peach Sanctuary (Táohuā Yuán), where inhabitants live peacefully in a hidden rural Arcadia, preserving the superior traditions of an earlier era. Corn dangles from the eaves of the ancient dwellings, donkeys plow the fields, and the hills are alive with wildflowers. The village faces south, nestled on the north side of the valley.

ESSENTIALS

VISITOR INFORMATION The ticket office (© 010/6981-9090) is open from 9am to 4:30pm. Admission to the village costs ¥20 ($2.50).

GETTING THERE From the Píngguǒ Yuán (103) metro stop, turn right out of the southeast (D) exit and continue for a few minutes to the **bus no. 929 zhīxiàn stop** (the last sign) for the bus to Zhāitáng (daily 7am–5pm, every hour; 2½-hr. trip; ¥6/75¢). While traveling from the city, you'll leave behind the smokestacks of Shǒu Gāng (Capital Iron and Steel Works, Běijīng's no. 1 polluter). From Zhāitáng, **minivans** *(miàndī)* (¥10/$1.25) travel to Chuān Dǐ Xià. The last bus returns from Zhāitáng at 4:10pm. A *miàndī* from Píngguǒ Yuán costs ¥130 ($16) one-way. A **taxi** from Běijīng costs ¥400 ($50) round-trip.

WHERE TO STAY   For those staying overnight, most lodgings offer basic accommodations (no shower) for ¥15 ($1.80). The friendly and freshly renovated **Lǎo Mèng Kèzhàn,** no. 23 in the lower part of the village (© **010/6981-9788**), is recommended. Their restaurant, which adjoins the rather quiet main road, is an agreeable spot for alfresco dining.

EXPLORING THE AREA

The area is a magnet for artists, poets, and period-drama camera crews; many local tourists are mystified by the lack of karaoke bars, duck boats, and "hair-dressers" that any self-respecting resort should boast. One Beijinger asked in frustration, "Is there anything at all to do here?" A local, not much caring for his tone, deadpanned, "Absolutely nothing. You'd better go home." Wander through the narrow lanes, their walls still showing faded slogans from the 1966–76 Cultural Revolution, including LONG LIVE CHAIRMAN MÁO, WORKERS OF THE WORLD UNITE, and USE MÁO ZÉDŌNG THOUGHT TO ARM YOUR MINDS.

Beyond the village, the path continues to rise, passing an intriguing open-air grain mill before entering groves of peach trees. The next village, **Bǎiyù Cūn,** is around 6km (3¾ miles) to the northwest. The dwellings of this larger settlement are arranged in the more plebeian *píngfáng* (bungalow) style.

Appendix A: Běijīng in Depth

by Peter Neville-Hadley and Josh Chin

1 Běijīng Today

As the English literary eccentric Osbert Sitwell remarked during a visit to Běijīng in the 1930s, "Restoration is often the favourite weapon of Siva the Destroyer, and can achieve more in a few weeks than can whole centuries of decay."

Some vengeful deity certainly seems to walk the streets of China's capital today, and he carries a brush with which he daubs on doors and walls the character *chāi*—"demolish." Within weeks, entire city blocks of historic housing vanish as the result of his attentions, their occupants driven away with compensation inadequate to replace their lost homes. Gossip among foreign journalists has it that by the time of the Běijīng Olympics in 2008, only 20 or so of the ancient *hútòng* (alleyways) will be left, and these will have been carefully refashioned in a dismaying Disneyfication to make them more appealing to visitors.

Once the ancient buildings come down to be replaced by shiny shops, the *chāi* character seems to reappear. But one little brush stroke is missing from the new version in shop windows—a *diǎn*, the smallest of all strokes, and little more than a dot. This tiny difference is enough to change the character's sound to *zhé*, and its meaning to something more constructive. Preceded by a number, *zhé* represents the number of tenths of its original price for which merchandise is now on sale. *Qī zhé*, seven-tenths, would appear in Western shop windows as *30% off.*

Dateline

- 930–1122 A provincial town roughly on the site of modern Běijīng becomes the southern capital of the Khitan Mongol Liáo dynasty, thousands of kilometers from the ancient centers of early Hàn Chinese empires.
- 1122–1215 The city is taken over by the Jurchen Tartar Jīn dynasty, first as Southern Capital, then Central Capital, as its empire expands.
- 1267–1367 The Mongol Yuán dynasty, having conquered most of Asia and eastern Europe, rebuilds the city on the modern site as the capital Khanbalik; Dà Dū (Great Capital) in Mandarin; Cambulac in Marco Polo's account of the city.
- 1273–1292 Marco Polo, his father, and his uncle are supposedly in China, much of the time in Khanbalik. There's some doubt as to whether Polo ever visited China at all, but his account (or his ghostwriter's account) of the capital captures the imagination of European readers for several centuries afterward.
- 1368 The Míng dynasty, having driven out the Mongols, establishes its capital at Nánjīng. Dà Dū becomes Běipíng (The Pacified North).
- 1420 The Yǒnglè emperor, third of the Míng, returns the city to capital status, the better to repel attacks by the Mongols from the north. He becomes the first Chinese emperor to reign from Běijīng, and the first to give it that name: "Northern Capital." Míng dynasty Běijīng is overlaid on the Yuán foundations, and the Forbidden City and Temple of Heaven are constructed.

You may be impressed at first by all the shiny new buildings—but look more closely and you'll spot numerous incomplete projects and shuttered stores. And despite the supposedly explosive expansion of the Chinese economy, reported in unverifiable figures even the government doesn't believe, shops are *always* advertising sales.

Lazy Western journalism produces excitable reports of Cartier showrooms and shops with imported Italian designer baby clothes, and uncritically repeats impressive but unverifiable claims about growth. But the vast majority of the young and trendy are out in the suburbs buying fake versions or discovering real goods that somehow got separated from the rest of their consignment, going for a tenth of the price or less. In the temples to consumerism on the showcase shopping streets, you'll see that window-shoppers vastly outnumber those making purchases. In supermarkets, older people can be found puzzling over imported items whose prices they can't afford anyway. The reality is that however many glitzy new shopping malls open, the disposable income to support them is not there.

Even according to the inflated figures of the government's national statistics bureau, the monthly income of the average household in Běijīng is ¥1,174 ($145), of which ¥1,079 ($135) is disposable income. That's about $550 of disposable income per person per annum—well above the national average. But a cup of Starbucks coffee is still a luxury, and those seen sipping a latte are in no way typical of Běijīng.

THE POLITICAL LIFE OF BĚIJĪNG Sitting at the heart of power, Beijingers are supposedly the nation's most sensitive to subtle changes in the political winds, but these days there is ever-decreasing interest. Officials are almost universally

1549 Mongol horsemen fire a message-bearing arrow into a Chinese general's camp saying that they will attack Běijīng the following year. Despite this advance announcement, they duly make their way up to the city walls as promised. So much for the Great Wall.

1550 In response to Mongol attacks, a lower southern extension to the city wall is begun, eventually enclosing the commercial district, the important ceremonial sites of the Temple (Altar) of Heaven and Altar of Agriculture, and a broad swath of countryside (which remains free of buildings well into the 20th. century). The whole system of walls is clad in brick. Běijīng remains largely the same for the next 400 years, when casual destruction under the Republic turns into organized vandalism under the People's Republic.

1601–1610 After years of campaigning, Italian Jesuit Matteo Ricci finally receives permission to reside in Běijīng and stays until his death, founding an influential Jesuit presence that survives well into the Qīng dynasty.

1644–1911 As peasant rebels overrun the capital, the last Míng emperor is driven to suicide by hanging himself from a tree in what is now Jǐng Shān Park, behind the Forbidden City. Shortly afterward, the rebels are driven out by invading Manchu forces, whose Qīng dynasty transfers its capital from Manchuria to Běijīng, absorbing China into its own empire. Chinese are expelled from the northern section of the city, which becomes the home of Manchu military and courtiers. The southern section becomes the Chinese quarter of Běijīng.

1793–1794 George III's emissary to the Qiánlóng emperor visits China and passes through Běijīng, staying outside the city at a vast area of parks and palaces. His requests for increased trade and for a permanent trade representative in Běijīng are turned down in a patronizing letter written even before he arrives. China is about to discover that Great Britain, and not itself, is the superpower of the day.

continues

deemed corrupt, and the leadership's gyrations in trying to demonstrate that the capitalism red in tooth and claw to which it now subjects its citizens is actually socialism "with Chinese characteristics" make the supposedly heroic leaders increasingly ridiculous. This is a pensionless "socialism," with no job security, no free medicine or free schooling, massive and growing unemployment (at least double the official figures), and bribes necessary at every turn to get things done. To most young people who missed the vast political movements of the second half of the 20th century, the Communist Party is an irrelevance—something that merely gets in the way on the road to a better life.

You'll find no free discussion of such issues in the government-controlled press, of which it is sometimes joked that the only true piece of information is the date. Constant announcements that production is up, that the minorities are happy, and that standards of one kind or another have been improved are usually fair indications that the opposite it true. The more often and more stridently a claim is made, the more confidence there is in the opposite view.

Television and print media, under complete government control, are stuck in a time warp. Instructions to study the latest political "theory," such as ex-president Jiāng Zémín's recent dim-witted attempt to pass off the Party's U-turn to capitalism as a development of Marxism, is still headline news. It's hardly surprising that the best-selling publication in China is a magazine dealing with soccer, although Jiāng's *Three Represents* theory is probably in there, too, next to pictures of David Beckham.

Even five-star-hotel access to the BBC or other foreign news channels (forbidden to ordinary domestic viewers) may suddenly "break down" around important political anniversaries, June 4 in particular. Once the anniversary is

- 1858 The Second Opium War sees the Qīng and their Chinese subjects capitulating in the face of the superior military technology of "barbarians" (principally the British) for the second time in 16 years. Under the terms of the Treaty of Nánjīng, China is forced to permit the permanent residence of foreign diplomats and trade representatives in the capital.
- 1860 The Qīng imprison and murder foreign representatives sent for the treaty's ratification. British and French rescue forces occupy Běijīng and destroy a vast area of parks and palaces to the northwest, some of the remnants of which form the modern Summer Palace. The Chinese loot what little the foreigners leave and put most of the area back under the plow. Foreign powers begin to construct diplomatic legation buildings just inside the Tartar City's wall east of the Qián Mén.
- 1900 The Harmonious Fists, nicknamed the Boxers, a highly superstitious anti-foreign peasant movement, besieges the foreign residents of the Legation Quarter, with the initially covert and finally open assistance of imperial troops. The siege begins on the 19th of June and is only lifted, after extensive destruction and many deaths, by the forces of Eight Allied Powers (several European nations, Japanese, and Americans) on August 14. Boxers, imperial troops, Chinese, foreign survivors, and allied soldiers turn their attention to looting the city. Payments on a vast indemnity take the Qīng a further 39 years to pay in full, although the British and Americans use much of the income to help found Peking University and other institutions, and to pay for young Chinese to study overseas.
- 1911 The Qīng dynasty's downfall is brought about by an almost accidental revolution, and betrayal by Yuán Shìkǎi, the man the Qīng trust to crush it. Although it is quite within his power to do so, he negotiates with both sides and extracts an abdication agreement from the infant emperor's regent and an agreement from the rebels that he will become the first president of the new republic.

safely past, access is mysteriously restored. No view other than that sanctioned by the Party may be broadcast.

You'll find no free discussion of political issues online either, where an estimated 30,000 people are employed to monitor websites and chat rooms, and where postings critical of the government are swiftly deleted. Western media sites offering alternative viewpoints are usually blocked, and even common search engines such as Google go through blackout periods.

Privately you can say what you like, but publicly you'd better accept that "without the Communist Party there'd be no New China," as the slogan has it. Even if you are merely theoretically interested in the idea of transition to full democracy, you'd better not meet to discuss it in any organized way. A group of just four individuals who did so in 2003 received long jail sentences for their temerity.

The loudest political voices are those of Bĕijīng's taxi drivers, at least within the confines of their vehicles. Theirs are the easiest opinions to canvass, and they are quoted with embarrassing frequency in Western newspaper articles as spokesmen for the ordinary Beijinger. In 2002 the government issued specific instructions forbidding the taxi drivers to talk about politics to foreigners, but because they are never named in articles, this injunction has been ignored, and they continue in their Western-appointed role of Everyman.

"The Communist Party has done more damage to Bĕijīng than the Nationalists, the Japanese, or anyone else ever did," they say. "The Communist Party only cares about itself." And they are right in both cases.

In the months leading up to the Olympic committee's decision in 2002, every foreign passenger who could understand enough Mandarin had to listen to bitter complaints that in support of Bĕijīng's bid the drivers were being forced to learn 100 simple

1915 Yuán Shìkǎi revives annual ceremonies at the Temple of Heaven, and prepares to install himself as first emperor of a new dynasty, but widespread demonstrations and the fomenting of a new rebellion in the south lead him to cancel his plans. He dies the following year.

1917 In July a pro-monarchist warlord puts Pǔyí back on the throne, but he is driven out by another who drops three bombs on the Forbidden City, only one of which actually explodes on target. The imperial restoration lasts exactly 12 days.

1919 Students and citizens gather on May 4 in Tiān'ān Mén Square to protest the government's agreement that Chinese territory formerly under German control be handed to the Japanese.

1924 The "Articles Providing for the Favourable Treatment of the Great Ch'ing [Qīng] Emperor after his Abdication" provide for the emperor to continue to live in the Forbidden City pending an eventual move to the Summer Palace. But in November he is removed by a hostile warlord and put under house arrest, later escaping to the Legation Quarter with the help of his Scottish former tutor.

1928 Despite fighting among warlords, many of whom are only nominally loyal to the Republic, the Nationalist Party forces in the south declare Nánjīng the capital, and Bĕijīng reverts to the name of Bĕipíng. In the following years many ancient buildings are vandalized or covered in political slogans.

1933 With Japanese armies seemingly poised to occupy Bĕijīng, the most important pieces of the imperial collection of antiquities in the Forbidden City are packed into 19,557 crates and moved to Shànghǎi. They move again when the Japanese take Shànghǎi in 1937, and after an incredible journey around the country in the thick of civil war, 13,484 crates end up with the Nationalist government in Táiwān in 1949.

continues

English sentences. Examinations were pending. But as soon as Běijīng had won, the books and tapes they'd been forced to buy all quietly disappeared. Questions were greeted with laughter. "They've won the Games now. They're not bothered."

Under the emperors, Běijīng was a city of walls within walls, with the imperial family and courtiers living in secure private compounds. Under the new emperors, merely the locations have changed.

At the top end is the "New Forbidden City" of Zhōng Nán Hǎi, the former imperial playground west of the Forbidden City, now home to the Party's top brass. But it's not the only city of walls: Many other guarded compounds exist containing ramshackle six- to ten-story brick and concrete blocks of remarkable hideousness, housing the cadres (officials) of various government ministries, the staff of the water company and other public utilities, and their friends and relations. They have private shops and restaurants that once offered them much more than was available to ordinary people, but that now act more as memorials to the surly service that was the norm before a modest quantity of free enterprise was permitted. Despite the decrepit exteriors, the accommodations inside these compounds are far more spacious than those of the average citizen, and while many Běijīng residents still have to leave their houses to use malodorous public facilities, these enjoy inside lavatories and bathrooms.

A CONSUMER SOCIETY Until the 1980s it seemed that everyone was in uniform. The very rare young man wearing a pair of jeans might as well have been carrying a big banner saying "counterrevolutionary." Blue or green "Máo" suits (Zhōngshān fú) or uniforms provided by work units (employers) were the norm for both sexes.

■ 1935 Further mass demonstrations in Tiān'ān Mén Square in December decry the government's impotence in the face of Japanese advances. The crowds are hosed and clubbed, and there are mass arrests.

■ 1937 Japanese forces, long in occupation of Manchuria and patrolling far beyond what the treaty permits them, pretend to have come under attack near the Marco Polo Bridge, occupy Běijīng, and stay until the end of World War II ("The War Against Japanese Aggression" to the Chinese).

■ 1949 Máo Zédōng proclaims the creation of the People's Republic of China from atop the Tiān'ān Mén on October 1. A vast flood of refugees from the countryside takes over the courtyard houses commandeered from their owners, and those houses which once held a single family now house a dozen. Temples are turned into army barracks, storehouses, and light industrial units.

■ 1958–59 In a series of major projects to mark 10 years of Communist rule, the old ministries lining what will be Tiān'ān Mén Square and its surrounding walls are all flattened for the construction of the Great Hall of the People and the vast museums opposite. These and Běijīng Railway Station are built with substantial Soviet help, which shows in the design. The city walls, which have survived 400 years of iniquities, are pulled down by "volunteers" after work and school, to be replaced with a metro line and a ring road for an almost completely carless society. The stone from the walls goes to line a system of tunnels into which the entire city population can supposedly be evacuated in case of attack.

■ 1966–76 Across China the destruction of old things reaches its peak as bands of Red Guards, fanatically loyal to Máo, roam around fighting each other, pulling down ancient buildings, burning books, and smashing art. Even the tree from which the last Míng emperor supposedly hung himself is cut down. Intellectuals are bullied, imprisoned, tortured, and murdered, as is anyone with a history of

But as soon as she was permitted to do so, Miss Běijīng removed her peaked cap, shook down her tresses, and went wild. From the sighting of the first pair of high heels and the return of the skirt, it seemed only moments before hemlines shot up from calf to nearly waist level and stayed there. Overnight, colors went from khaki to clashing neons, simply because they could. Bus conductresses, now able to own more than just their uniforms, could be found selling tickets in spangled Lycra more suitable for the primitive discos that were starting to draw carefully monitored crowds.

Things have now settled down, but anything goes, including dresses diaph-anous enough to reveal rather more than a glimpse of stocking. The male, on the other hand, has mostly remained dowdy, and seems happy merely to have swapped one uniform for another. Typically jacketless, Mr. Běijīng wears a short-sleeve shirt with a collar but no tie, and gray slacks. He parades his status through his shoes, watch, and belt, with the buckle, mobile phone, and large bunch of keys all mounted at his waist.

The government would send tanks back into Tiān'ān Mén Square at a moment's notice to suppress dissent, but the genie of consumerism is permanently out of the bottle, and to stay in power by any means but brute force, the Communist Party must feed an insatiable desire not just for the bare necessities of life, but for disposable goods with designer logos. Fakes will do, of course, and fakes are what most buy in back-street markets, but that tiny portion of the population who can buy a Mercedes will certainly do so, and will thank the Party for the opportunity rather than complain that it has held them back for so many decades.

At the end of the 1980s foreign residents and visitors alike would still coo with delight at the sight of milk and

links to foreigners, however tenuous. Scores are settled by denunciation, and tens of millions die. The education system comes to a complete halt. Many antiquities impounded from their owners are simply sold to foreign dealers by weight to provide funds for the government, which later decries the supposed foreign theft of Chinese antiquities.

- 1976 The death of the relatively moderate leader Zhōu Ēnlái, who is credited with mitigating to a small degree some of the worst excesses of the Cultural Revolution, leads to over 100,000 demonstrating against the government in Tiān'ān Mén Square. The demonstrations are labeled counter-revolutionary, and hundreds are arrested. The death of Máo Zédōng, himself estimated to be responsible for about 38 million deaths, effectively brings the Cultural Revolution to an end. Blame for the Cultural Revolution is put on the "Gang of Four"—Máo's wife and three other hardline officials, who are arrested. The 450-year-old Dà Míng Mén in the center of Tiān'ān Mén Square is pulled down to make way for Máo's mausoleum. Leaders put their backing behind Dèng Xiǎopíng, who returns from disgrace to take power and launch a program of openness and economic reform. His own toleration for public criticism also turns out to be zero, however.

- 1989 The death of the relatively moderate but disgraced official Hú Yàobāng causes public displays of mourning in Tiān'ān Mén Square, which turn into a mass occupation of the square protesting government corruption. Its hands initially tied by the presence on a state visit of the Soviet Union's Mikhail Gorbachev, the Party sends in the tanks live on TV on the night of June 4. Estimates of the number of deaths vary wildly, but the number is thought to run to several hundred unarmed students and their supporters.

continues

butter in the Friendship Stores, which only accepted hard-currency vouchers and which Chinese were not even permitted to enter. Now most Western fashion labels have Běijīng outlets, as do interior design companies, supermarkets, fast-food chains, and luxury-car suppliers. Numerous foreign companies sucked in by the myth of high-speed growth are making a loss or making a far from respectable return on their investment. But they comfort each other in their far-sightedness, and wait for the economic miracle repeatedly promised in the press.

EVERY MAN FOR HIMSELF

Milk may be found in every Běijīng convenience store now, but the milk of human kindness remains rather harder to find.

"What's the difference between your country and mine?" is a fairly popular question from taxi drivers, and one that leaves the Mandarin-speaking foreign visitor floundering as to where to begin: An independent judiciary? Rule of law? Freedom to have as many children as you like? Freedom to live where you like? Freedom to go overseas without asking permission? Freedom of the press?

■ 1999 The 50th anniversary of the founding of the People's Republic is the subject of vast, carefully stage-managed celebrations in the center of Běijīng, whose face-lift for the television cameras is said to have cost the Běijīng municipal authorities alone around US$14 billion, which includes removing all billboards advertising foreign brands, massive repainting and reconstruction along Cháng'ān Jiē, and the repaving of the whole of Tiān'ān Mén Square in granite. One hundred thousand handpicked supporters "spontaneously" shout slogans that have been carefully written down for them. It's the world's largest pantomime.

■ 2001 Běijīng is awarded the 2008 Summer Olympics, and as a result the destruction and complete redevelopment of the city accelerates, to the immense personal profit of the developers. That some are related to the top members of the administration is common knowledge.

Once, tired from a long flight, I was asked this question as we passed a crowd gathering around a bloody collision between a car and a cyclist, and I glumly answered, "When we see an accident, we run to help. When you see an accident, you run to look."

The driver nodded in agreement. "Yes," he said, "that's right. But there are *so many* of us." He drove on without stopping.

Beijingers expect to be cheated both by their rulers and by each other. They complain bitterly, but they have no hesitation in cheating others when they can wangle a university place for an academically unsuccessful child because of a favor owed, when they can get access to rail tickets at peak periods because an uncle works at the station, or when they barter their own access to some privilege for something else they want. When they need something, their first question is not "Where do I line up?" but "Who do I know?" The Chinese expression *xiān lái, xiān chī,* means "first to come, first to eat." This seems to suggest not the idea of forming a fair lineup, but the necessity of barging to the front.

Complaints about government corruption and the privileges reserved for cadres are not usually based on a general moral principle, but on not getting a slice of the pie. Sympathy for others tends to extend no further than immediate family members, close friends, and those with whom the Chinese have *guānxi*—people who owe them or to whom they owe favors. Everyone else is just in the way and is often simply pushed out of it, as you will discover when you try to board a bus, line up to buy a ticket, or stand at any junction and observe the driving.

Běijīng may only represent Běijīng, but Beijingers, like everyone else in China, think themselves superior to Chinese from everywhere else. Finding themselves in difficulties away from home, they will appeal to other Beijingers for help. Faced with problems when overseas, they'll appeal for solidarity to any-one of Chinese descent—"We're Chinese: We should help each other." Back in Běijīng they'll use "country girl" as a term of abuse, and they are quite convinced that the several million migrant workers who now illegally call the capital home are responsible for the rise in crime. But they'll complain loudly when street food stalls vanish, smaller restaurants close, and garbage services slow to a halt because those who do the menial labor they themselves despise have been tem-porarily driven out of town for some Party celebration or committee meeting.

ROUND EYES & YELLOW HAIR   Foreigners are not relatives and do not understand *guānxi*. To some Beijingers they are figures of fun. To the few directly involved in commercial relationships with foreigners, they are strikingly naive and their extraordinarily deep pockets are to be dipped into as much as possible (the more apparently sweet-natured your tour guide, the more careful you should be). Foreigners have an amazing tendency to smile and give away extra money even after being thoroughly fleeced. To stallholders, shopkeepers, and representatives of the tourism industry, they are therefore thoroughly welcome—in any society where most transactions involve bargaining, the ignorant outsider always will be. Shanghainese, Cantonese, and other outsiders will be taken for a ride when possible, but foreigners can be taken much more easily, and much further.

While central Běijīng is fairly used to the sight of enormous people with big round eyes and yellow or red hair, many Chinese visitors to Běijīng are catching their first sight of the rare and exotic foreign species. Most foreigners restrict themselves to the bigger attractions, the hotel complexes, the joint-venture office towers, and the bar areas, so even a foreigner entering an ordinary department store elsewhere in the city can still have a traffic-stopping effect.

"*Lǎo wài*," (Foreigner) the Chinese will observe without lowering their voices. They'll nudge each other and point you out, "Look! *Lǎo wài*." And sometimes they'll shout at you, "*Lǎo wài!*," with complete indifference to any offense taken.

The presence of everything foreign from McDonald's to Mercedes doesn't indicate the presence of a larger world picture, but rather an increasingly long checklist of which possessions indicate a degree of Westernization. Heaven, according to one recently popular Běijīng joke, is a German house, a Japanese wife, and an American salary. Heaven's only Chinese element is the cook. Yet at the same time, it is taken as axiomatic that Chinese culture is superior.

The West is a place to live neither for democratic ideals nor to avoid the one-child policy (which anyone with cash or the right *guānxi* can get around), but largely for the chance to earn more money and gain a higher standard of living.

You'll likely pass through Běijīng completely unaware of all these undercur-rents. Běijīng will open up just enough for you to pass through and close up again behind you, and you'll leave no more trace, in Pearl Buck's memorable phrase, "than a finger drawn through water."

2 Religion

Freedom to practice religion is enshrined in the Chinese constitution. In reality, of course, this right is subject to frequent and occasionally violent suspension—during times of political upheaval like the Cultural Revolution (1966–76) or, as in the case of Tibetan Buddhism and the banned spiritual movement Fǎlún

Gōng, when specific groups are thought to pose a threat to Communist rule. Despite this, China has maintained what must rank among the world's most varied collection of religious traditions, encompassing not only native belief systems—Confucianism and Daoism—but Buddhism, Islam, and several strains of Christianity as well.

Those on tours of Chinese temples, churches, and mosques in the 1980s and early 1990s were wise to exercise a robust skepticism. The monks and nuns you encountered were invariably a specially selected bunch, likely to bombard foreigners with tales of how wonderfully supportive the government was. And the prettiest and best-restored temples were often barely more than showpieces, where it seemed incense was burned only to cover the sour smell of an Epcot-style cultural commodification.

But as faith in Communism wanes (to the point where some Chinese use the greeting *tóngzhì,* or comrade, with thinly veiled sarcasm), religious buildings are slowly recovering their vitality as places of genuine worship, sources of guidance in the moral vacuum of a new market-driven society.

Maps of pre-Communist Běijīng show an astoundingly large number of religious structures, from the grandest of glazed-tile complexes in the city's imperial quarter to hundreds of tiny shrines nestled in the maze of *hútòng.* Most were destroyed or converted to other uses immediately following the Communist victory in 1949 and during the Cultural Revolution. Several dozen more have been bulldozed as part of modern reconstruction efforts, and all but the most prestigious will probably disappear in the future.

China has always been a secular state, but as in European capitals prior to the 20th century, the line between religion and government in Míng- and Qīng-era Běijīng was usually blurred. The most direct example is the **Lama Temple (Yōnghé Gōng),** an immense imperial residence-turned-temple that houses a ritual urn used during the reign of the Qīng Qiánlóng emperor to determine reincarnations of the Dalai Lama, leader of the dominant Buddhist sect in distant Tibet.

The tradition continues today, with Communist leaders playing a controversial role in selecting the most recent Panchen Lama (2nd from the top in the Tibetan Buddhist hierarchy) and threatening to do the same after the death of the current Dalai Lama, the exiled Tenzin Gyatso.

CONFUCIANISM

The moral philosophy said to have originated with Kǒngzǐ—a 5th-century-B.C. figure also known as Kǒng Fūzǐ (Latinized to "Confucius" by Jesuit supporters enthusiastic about his "family values")—is not really a religion or even a well-defined thought system. Indeed, there is no word in Chinese for Confucianism but only *rú,* a rather vague term that connotes scholarship and refinement. The ideas about proper conduct and government as remembered by Kǒngzǐ's disciples in works like the *Lúnyǔ (Analects)* have nevertheless exerted more influence on China than either Buddhism or Daoism and have proven more resilient than anything written by Marx or Máo.

The *Analects* offer pithy observations on dozens of topics ("Don't use a cannon to kill a mosquito," "The noble person is not a tool," and so on), but the three most important concepts are filial piety, proper execution of ritual, and humanity toward others. Confucius has little trust in Heaven or nature. The ultimate concern is with tangible human relationships: those of the son with the father, the subject with the emperor, and friends with each other. These relationships are rigidly defined, and acknowledgement of them is the highest virtue. Chinese rulers recognized early on that this philosophy was perfectly suited to governing their vast empire. Mastery of Confucian classics, proven through a series of increasingly difficult Imperial Examinations, was a prerequisite for all government officials up until the very end of 19th century.

Confucian ideas were officially thrown on the trash heap of "feudal thought" after the Communists took over, but visitors to Běijīng need only go as far as a restaurant to realize how little this has meant. At any large table, diners will take seats according to their relationship with the host, toasts will be carried out with ritual precision, and forms of address will vary depending on who is speaking to whom. The Imperial Examinations, too, have been resurrected in the recently revived nationwide College Entrance Exam, success in which is considered vital to any young person's future. Some students even study for the exam at **Guózǐjiàn** (the old Imperial College) in northeastern Běijīng while their parents burn incense for them next door at the **Kǒng Miào,** the second largest Confucian temple after the one in Confucius's hometown of Qūfū in Shāndōng Province.

Although even the most modern Chinese display an attachment to family and ritual, cynical observers note that the emphasis on humanity seems to have disappeared. It is debatable, however, whether this was ever as forceful an idea in China as Confucius wanted it to be.

DAOISM

China's only native-born religion, Daoism (Taoism) began, like Confucianism, as a philosophical response to the chaos and bloodshed prevalent in China during the Warring States period (403–221 BC). It later split into several schools, certain of which absorbed elements of folk religion and concentrated on alchemy and other practices it was hoped would lead to immortality. With its emphasis on change and general distrust of authority, Daoism was the antithesis of Confucianism and remained largely on the fringes of Chinese civil society, more at home in the mountains than in the cities.

The oldest Daoist texts are the esoteric *Dào Dé Jīng* (or *Tao Te Ching,* "Classic of the Way and Virtue") and the *Zhuāngzǐ,* a prose book sometimes compared in its sly playfulness with the work of Nietzsche. Both deal with the Way *(Dào),* a broad philosophical concept also mentioned by Confucius but described in a wholly different manner. In the *Dào Dé Jīng,* ostensibly written by a quasi-mythical figure named Laǒzǐ, the Way is more gestured at than defined, as in the famous opening line: "The way that can be spoken of/Is not the constant way."

The *Zhuāngzǐ* elaborates, but doesn't necessarily illuminate: "Saying is not blowing breath, saying says something; the only trouble is that what it says is never fixed. Do we really say something? Or have we never said anything? . . . Wherever we walk how can the Way be absent?"

The Daoists' dismissal of language, their habit of asking absurd questions, and their frequent self-contradictions are attempts to shake readers free of reason, which is said to obscure an understanding of the Way because it seeks to impose a rigid framework on a universe that is constantly changing.

Despite the *Dào Dé Jīng's* remarkable global popularity as a deep source of mystical truths, one scholar, D. C. Lau, makes a convincing case that the book is best understood as a simple survival manual, its support for strength-in-supplication designed to help powerless Chinese avoid having their heads cut off at a time when such brutality was not at all uncommon.

Daoists today make up a tiny portion of the population (less than 1%, according to some estimates), and most reside far from Běijīng. There has been a revival of interest in the more philosophical side of Daoism in recent years, but this is largely invisible, and visitors who've read the *Tao of Pooh* and *Te of Piglet* are often disappointed by what they find at the few remaining active temples. Daoist complexes like Běijīng's immense **Báiyún Guàn** are garish and loud, reflecting the religious branch's fondness for magic potions and spells, with little of the contemplative feel most Westerners expect.

BUDDHISM

Buddhism traveled from India through Central Asia and along the Silk Routes to China sometime in the 1st century and began to flourish after a crisis of confidence in Confucianism caused by the fall of the Later Hàn dynasty (A.D. 25–220). But it would never achieve the same dominance as Confucianism, in large part because of the Buddhists' insistence that they exist beyond the power of the state, the monks' rejection of traditional family relationships, and the populace's xenophobic wariness of a foreign philosophy. Buddhism did become sufficiently pervasive during the Táng dynasty (618–907) to merit its own department in the government, but a neo-Confucian backlash under the succeeding Sòng dynasty (960–1279) saw it lose influence again. Although it never fully recovered the power it held under the Táng, Buddhism continued to have wide popular appeal and is still China's most prevalent organized religion.

All Buddhists believe human suffering can be stopped by eliminating desire. But where the older Buddhism of India was a sparse atheistic tradition concerned with little more than the individual's achievement of Nirvana (enlightened detachment from desire), Buddhism in China gradually absorbed elements of Daoism and local folk religion to become an incredibly complex belief system with various gods and demons, an intricately conceived heaven, several hells, and dozens of boddhisattvas (beings who have attained enlightenment but delay entry into Nirvana out of a desire to help others overcome suffering).

Among the various schools that eventually developed, the most popular was the Pure Land School, a faith-based tradition not unlike Christianity that believed the simple evocation of the name of Amitabha Buddha would result in the devotee's being reborn in the western paradise (the Pure Land), from which it would be easier to attain enlightenment. This tradition is still so popular in China that visitors will hear chants of Āmítuófó (the Mandarin transliteration of Amitabha) at several temples throughout Běijīng. A more revolutionary development was achieved by the Chán school (better known by its Japanese name, Zen), which held that even laypeople could achieve instantaneous enlightenment through a simplified but incredibly intense form of meditation.

Buddhist temples in Běijīng often contain large images of Mílefó (Maitreya, the Future Buddha) depicted in both Chinese (fat and jolly) and Tibetan (thinner and more somber) guises, and of Guānyīn (Avalokitesvara, the Boddhisattva of Compassion), a lithe woman in the Chinese style and a multi-armed, multi-headed man in the Tibetan. The Manchu rulers of China's final dynasty, the Qīng (1644–1911), tried to maintain cultural ties with several ethnic groups on the fringes of the Chinese empire, which explains the unusual prevalence of Tibetan Buddhist architecture in Běijīng. Most noticeable are the two *dagobas* (Tibetan-style stupas), towering white structures like upside-down ice cream cones, at **Běi Hǎi Gōngyuán** and **Bái Tǎ Sì.**

ISLAM & CHRISTIANITY

Islam entered China through Central Asia in the 7th century, staying mostly in the northwestern corner of the empire, in what is now the Xīnjiāng Autonomous Region. It was introduced to more central regions through the occasional eastward migration of Xīnjiāng's Uighur people, and through the arrival of Arab trading vessels in southeastern ports like Quánzhōu during the Sòng dynasty (960–1270), but it failed to catch on with Hàn Chinese the way Buddhism did. Those Hàn who did convert are now lumped into a separate ethnic group, the Huí. Běijīng's Huí and Uighur populations don't mix as much as their shared religious beliefs might lead you to expect, the former dominating southeastern Běijīng around the **Niú Jiē Mosque** and the latter kept mostly in a series of constantly shifting ghettos. A visit to the mosque on Niú Jiē reveals Chinese Islam to be pretty much the same as Islam anywhere else; the glazed-tile roofs and basic layout resemble those of Buddhist or Daoist temples, but the main hall faces west (toward Mecca) rather than south, women and men pray separately, and there are absolutely no idols anywhere.

The first Christian missionary push to make much headway in China came in the 17th century, when Jesuits, led by Italian Matteo Ricci, sought to convert the country by first converting the imperial court. Ricci and his cohorts wowed the Qīng rulers with their knowledge of science, art, and architecture (see Jonathan Spence's excellent *The Memory Palace of Matteo Ricci* for more about this) but ultimately failed to make Catholics of the Manchus. Subsequent missionaries, both Catholic and Protestant, continued the war on Chinese superstition and met with some success, but they were also seen as a nuisance. Christianity was linked with both major popular uprisings in the Qīng period—the Tàipíng Rebellion, led by a man named Hóng Xiùquán, who claimed to be Jesus's younger brother; and the Boxer Rebellion, a violent reaction to the aggressive tactics of missionaries in northern China which led to the siege of Běijīng's Legation Quarter.

Běijīng is particularly leery of Catholics, many of whom refused to join Protestants in pledging first allegiance to the state after 1949 and instead remained loyal to the Pope. Missionaries, it goes without saying, are not allowed in China anymore, but many sneak in as English teachers (a favorite tactic of the Mormons in particular). There are separate churches in Běijīng for foreigners, off-limits to Chinese, although foreigners are allowed to attend Chinese services. The Gothic-style church built in 1904 on the site of Ricci's house still stands near the Xuānwǔ Mén metro stop, and replicas of the Jesuits' bronze astronomical devices can be seen at the Ancient Observatory northeast of the main railway station.

Outside of monks and nuns, few Chinese people limit their devotion to a single tradition, instead choosing elements from each as they suit their particular circumstances. "Every Chinese," a popular saying goes, "is a Confucian when things are going well, a Daoist when things are going badly, and a Buddhist just before they die." But even this is a relatively rigid formulation—a Chinese person will often cross religious boundaries in the space of a single day if he thinks his problems merit the effort.

This pragmatic approach to beliefs allows not just individuals but also groups to create new religious systems with bits stolen from older traditions. Despite the government insistence that it is a cult, the Fǎlún Gōng's combination of Buddhism with *qìgōng* exercises and Daoist-like claims to impossible physical feats is very much in keeping with the Chinese tradition of religious collage. Unfortunately, its success has put Chinese leaders in mind of another tradition— the violent overthrow of dynasties by popular religious movements.

Despite the rise in religious participation, most visitors to Běijīng still complain of a made-for-tourists feel in most of the city's temples. Given the tidal wave of foreigners' cash that flows into places like the **Lama Temple**, this will probably never change, or at least not in Běijīng proper. For those willing to make the trip, however, the seldom-visited areas just outside Běijīng are home to several temples, such as **Tánzhè Sì** and **Jiètái Sì,** where tourism plays a secondary role to genuine religious practice. It is in places like these that you're most likely to witness the reawakening of China's older belief systems.

3 Film & Music

FILM

It is a perpetual source of frustration for Chinese filmmakers that foreign audiences are so easily duped. The most internationally successful films about China—Ang Lee's *Crouching Tiger, Hidden Dragon,* Zhāng Yìmóu's *Raise the Red Lantern,* Bernardo Bertolucci's *The Last Emperor*—wallow in marketable clichés. The China presented by these films exists almost solely in the simplified past tense, a mélange of incense, bound feet, and silk brocade designed to appeal to foreign notions of the country as unfathomably brutal and beautiful with an interminably long history.

Up until the late 1990s, much of the blame for this belonged to the government, which allowed the export of only those movies unlikely to provoke criticism of the present state of things, regardless of what they said about the past. Recently, however, films that deal with modern China, complex and often comic stories about everything from politics to relationships to harebrained attempts at money-making, have found their way to foreign viewers.

Běijīng sits at the center of the Chinese film world and serves as the setting for most of the best films now being produced in China. Many of these cannot be seen even in Běijīng itself except at small screenings unlikely to attract the attention of state censors. But those with access to a decent video rental shop will find a few.

Even Blockbuster carries copies of *Shower* (*Xǐzǎo,* 1999), Zhāng Yáng's at times sappy but ultimately enjoyable story of a Běijīng bathhouse owner and his two sons (one of them retarded) struggling to maintain a sense of family despite pressures of modernization. The film's depiction of a doomed *hútòng* neighborhood and the comic old characters who inhabit it won smatterings of praise in limited U.S. release and criticism from the Chinese authorities, who claimed it was anti-progress. *Big Shot's Funeral* (*Dà Wàn,* 2001), with bald-headed Everyman Gê Yōu as the camera operator who plans a ludicrously elaborate funeral for a famous American director (an uninspired Donald Sutherland) after the latter slips into a coma while filming in Běijīng, is a typical Chinese comedy that made it to U.S. theaters on Sutherland's star power but which falls flat most of the time. The far superior *Beijing Bicycle* (*Shíqī Suì de Dānchē,* 2000), a remake of the Italian classic *The Bicycle Thief,* is an unflinching examination of class differences that follows the efforts of a freshly arrived peasant to retrieve his stolen bicycle from the spoiled rich kid who has bought it on the black market.

Among the earlier generation of films, two that deal specifically with Běijīng were big hits at Cannes, and you should have no trouble finding them. *Farewell My Concubine* (*Bà Wáng Bié Jī,* 1993), directed by Chén Kǎigē and starring the talented Gǒng Lì, is a long bit of lushness about a pair of Běijīng opera stars more dramatic in their alleged rivalry over a woman than they are on stage. Zhāng Yìmóu's unrelenting primer on modern Chinese history, *To Live* (*Huózhe,* 1994), also with Gǒng Lì, traces the unbelievable tragedies of a single Běijīng family as it bumbles through the upheavals of 20th-century China, from the civil war through the Great Leap Forward and Cultural Revolution and into the post-Máo reform period.

Only specialty shops are likely to carry *In the Heat of the Sun* (*Yángguāng Cànlàn de Rìzi,* 1995), a smart and deceptively nostalgic coming-of-age film about a pack of mischievous boys left to their own devices in Cultural Revolution–era Běijīng. Penned with help from celebrity rebel writer Wáng Shuò, it was one of the first pictures to break free of the ponderous melodrama that dominated Chinese cinema through most of the 1990s. Another hard-to-find movie that marks a fresh departure from the standard fare is French New Wave—styled *Chicken Poets* (*Xiàng Jīmáo Yíyàng Fēi,* 2002), the story of a poet who loses the ability to write, moves to Běijīng to aid a friend in a scheme to sell black chicken eggs, and then discovers a black-market "how to" CD-ROM on poetry that makes him a literary giant.

MUSIC

The vapid, factory-produced syrup of **Mandopop** (think Celine Dion by way of Britney Spears sung in Mandarin) blares out of barber shops and retail stores in Běijīng, as elsewhere in China. But like Washington, D.C. and London, China's capital is ultimately a rock 'n' roll town.

Godfather of Chinese rock **Cuī Jiàn,** somewhat of joke now as he clings to fading fame, got his start here in the early 1980s. A decade later, Chinese-American Kaiser Kuo, front man for the no-longer-existent headbanger outfit **Tang Dynasty (Táng Cháo),** helped kick off a pretentious and fairly derivative heavy metal scene. But it wasn't until a shipment of Nirvana CDs found its way into local record shops in the late 1990s that Běijīng finally developed a genuine musical voice.

Like the Velvet Underground did in the U.S. 20 years earlier, Nirvana's *Nevermind* inspired nearly every Chinese kid who heard it to pick up a guitar and start a band. Investigations into Kurt Cobain's roots led to punk, which made its first major appearance in Běijīng in late 1997 at the Scream Club, a sweaty dive in the battered Wǔdàokǒu neighborhood. It was a natural response to Běijīng's swaths of urban decay and post-Tiān'ān Mén political disillusionment, and American pop culture magazines as big as *Details* quickly tapped the snarling, mohawked youth—most better at posing with their instruments than actually playing them—as easy symbols of China's new lost generation.

Běijīng's punks were probably never as concerned with political protest as they were made out to be, and are even less so now as they enjoy the fruits of small-scale fame (punks are among the few Chinese men able to attract Western women). But they continue to draw relatively large foreign audiences, and a handful have actually begun to produce music worthy of all the attention. The vulgar but talented **Brain Failure (Nǎo Zhuó)** and ska-influenced **Reflector (Fǎnguāng Jìng)**—both born at the now-defunct Scream Club—have each recorded listenable songs (available through www.scream-records.net) and evolved beyond just spitting beer in their live shows (though you can still expect the occasional shower). Also on Scream Records, the all-girl pop punk group **Hang on the Box (Guà Zài Guìzi Shang),** with two albums available at www.hangonthebox.com, sings in charmingly accented English and was cool enough to play the South by Southwest festival in Austin, Texas, in 2003.

Chinese musicians wanting to produce significant popular music suffer from the same dreadful self-consciousness of working in a foreign idiom as do artists in other imported media. Some try desperately (and without much success) to create "rock with Chinese characteristics," while others opt to simply lay Chinese lyrics over melodies lifted, sometimes note for note, from Western CDs. Even the most creative of efforts will sound suspiciously derivative, and those that don't usually appeal only to Mandarin-speaking foreigners who delight primarily in their ability to understand the lyrics.

Běijīng Band 2001, a CD sampler of 10 bands at the artier end of the rock spectrum, compiled by former resident and music producer Matthew Corbin Clark, offers some measure of hope. Easily obtainable at home via the website www.beijingband.com, the compilation offers everything from echoes of *Talking Heads '77* and early *Sparks* to glam-rock guitar excess, neo-folk, and the jarringly dissonant, most of it taking itself extremely seriously and technically very able, if not always strictly enjoyable.

Second Hand Rose (Èrshǒu Méiguī) is featured on the compilation, but they sound much better on their own eponymous full-length CD (available only in Běijīng), an excellent effort that stitches together Chili Peppers guitar, folk instrumentals, and sardonic *èrrénzhuàn* opera–influenced lyrics ("I'm a name brand cigarette/I've been stuffed in the mouth of a poor man") into one of the very few uniquely Chinese sounds you'd actually want to hear. The band's live performances, built around the raised-eyebrow theatricality of cross-dressing singer Liáng Lóng, are among the most entertaining musical experiences not just in China, but anywhere. They play semi-frequent shows at Běijīng's CD Cafe.

Folk rockers **Wild Children (Yê Háizi),** also on the compilation, have their roots in the pared-down musical traditions of northwestern China, and play pleasantly repetitive chant-heavy acoustic songs likely to appeal more to the World Music set than to Dylan devotees. They appear regularly at River (Hé), Běijīng's live folk venue, of which they are part-owners. Information on the band's own recordings and its history, along with MP3s and videos, can be found at www.wildchildren.net.

For information on when and where the above bands might be playing, check music listings in either *City Weekend* or *that's Beijing,* both available free in hotels, bars, and cafes where foreigners gather. Online, subscribe to the Xianzai Beijing newsletter at www.xianzai.com.

4 The Běijīng Menu

One of the best things about any visit to China is the food, at least for the independent traveler. Tour groups are often treated to a relentless series of cheap, bland dishes designed to cause no complaints and to keep the costs down for the Chinese operator, so do everything you can to escape and order some of the specialties we've described for you in chapter 5. Here they are again, in alphabetical order and with characters you can show to the waitress.

Widely available dishes and snacks are grouped in the first list; you can order most of them in any mainstream or *jiācháng cài* ("homestyle") restaurant. Some dishes recommended in this guidebook's reviews of individual restaurants are commonly available enough to be on this first list. Note that some of the specialty dishes in the second list are only available in the restaurants reviewed, or in restaurants offering a particular region's cuisine.

Supplement these lists with the bilingual menu from your local Chinese restaurant at home. The characters will not be quite the same as those used in Běijīng (more similar to those used in Hong Kong and Macau), but they will be understood. Don't expect the dishes to be the same, however. Expect them to be *better.*

Any mainstream non-specialty restaurant can and will make any common Chinese dish, whether it's on the menu or not. But don't expect Běijīng cooks to manage the subtler flavors of Cantonese cooking, for instance, unless the restaurant advertises itself as a southern-food specialist.

Outside the big hotels and expat cafe-bar ghettos, few restaurants have English menus. If, near your five-star hotel, you see restaurants with signs saying

ENGLISH MENU, there's a fair chance you are going to be cheated with higher prices, and you should eat elsewhere (unless it's an obvious backpacker hangout).

Dishes often arrive in haphazard order, but menus generally open with *liáng cài* (cold dishes). Except in top-class Sino-foreign joint-venture restaurants, you are strongly advised to avoid these for hygiene reasons. The restaurant's specialties also come early in the menu, often easily recognized by the facts that they have significantly higher prices and that if you dither, the waitress will recommend them, saying, "I hear this one's good." Waitresses always recommend ¥180 ($23) dishes, never ¥18 ($2.25) ones. Some of these dishes may occasionally be made from creatures you would regard as pets or zoo creatures (or best in the wild), and parts of them you may consider inedible or odd, like swallow saliva (the main ingredient of bird's nest soup, a rather bland and uninteresting Cantonese delicacy).

Main dishes come next; various meats and fish are followed by vegetables and *dòufu* (tofu). Drinks come at the end. You'll rarely find desserts outside of restaurants that largely cater to foreigners. A few orange slices may appear, but it's best to forgo them.

Soup is usually eaten last. Outside Guăngdōng Province, Hong Kong, and Macau, rice also usually arrives toward the end; if you want it with your meal, you must ask (point to the characters for rice, below, when the first dish arrives).

There is no tipping. Tea, chopsticks, and napkins should be free (although if a wrapped packet of tissues arrives you may pay a small fee), service charges do not exist outside of major hotels, and there are no cover charges or taxes. If you are asked what tea you would like, know that you are going to receive something above average and will be charged for it. Be careful—some varieties cost more than the meal itself.

Most Chinese food is not designed to be eaten solo, but if you do find yourself on your own, ask for small portions *(xiăo pán, 小盘)*, usually about 70% of the size of a full dish and about 70% of the price. This allows you to sample the menu properly without too much waste.

WIDELY AVAILABLE DISHES & SNACKS

PINYIN	ENGLISH	CHINESE
bābǎo zhōu	rice porridge with nuts and berries	八宝粥
bāozi	stuffed steamed buns	包子
bīngqílín	ice cream	冰淇淋
chǎo fàn	fried rice	炒饭
chǎo miàn	fried noodles	炒面
cōng bào niúròu	quick-fried beef and onions	葱爆牛肉
diǎnxin	dim sum (snacks)	点心
dìsān xiān	braised eggplant with potatoes and spicy green peppers	第三鲜
gānbiān sìjìdòu	sautéed string beans	干煸四季豆
gōngbǎo jīdīng	spicy diced chicken with cashews	宫爆鸡丁
guōtiē	fried dumplings/ potstickers	锅贴
hóngshāo fǔzhú	braised tofu	红烧腐竹

PINYIN	ENGLISH	CHINESE
hóngshāo huángyú	braised yellow fish	红烧黄鱼
huíguō ròu	twice-cooked pork	回锅肉
huǒguō	hotpot	火锅
jiānbǐng	large crepe folded around fried dough with plum and hot sauces	煎饼
jiǎozi	dumplings/Chinese ravioli	饺子
jīngjiàng ròu sī	shredded pork in soya sauce	京酱肉丝
mápó dòufu	spicy tofu with chopped meat	麻婆豆腐
miàntiáo	noodles	面条
mǐfàn	rice	米饭
mù xū ròu	sliced pork with fungus (mushu pork)	木须肉
niúròu miàn	beef noodles	牛肉面
ròu chuàn	kebabs/kabobs	肉串
sānxiān	"three flavors" (usually prawn, mushroom, pork)	三鲜
shuǐjiǎo	boiled dumplings	水饺
suānlà báicài	hot and sour cabbage	酸辣白菜
suānlà tāng	hot and sour soup	酸辣汤
sù miàn	vegetarian noodles	素面
sù shíjǐn	mixed vegetables	素什锦
tángcù lǐji	sweet-and-sour pork tenderloin	糖醋里脊
tǔdòu dùn niú ròu	stewed beef and potato	土豆炖牛肉
xiàn bǐng	pork- or vegetable-stuffed fried pancake	馅饼
xīhóngshì chǎo jīdàn	tomatoes with eggs	西红柿炒鸡蛋
yáng ròu chuān	barbecued lamb skewers with ground cumin and chili powder	洋肉串
yóutiáo	fried salty donut	油条
yúxiāng qiézi	eggplant in garlic sauce	鱼香茄子
yúxiāng ròu sī	shredded pork in garlic sauce	鱼香肉丝
zhēngjiǎo	steamed dumplings	蒸饺
zhōu	rice porridge	粥

SPECIALTY DISHES (FROM BĚIJĪNG & ELSEWHERE) RECOMMENDED IN RESTAURANT REVIEWS

PINYIN	ENGLISH	CHINESE
bōluó fàn	pineapple rice	菠萝饭
cùngū shāo	deep-fried pork with medicinal herbs	寸骨烧
dà pán jī	diced chicken and noodles in tomato sauce	大盘鸡
dāndān miàn	noodles in spicy broth	但但面
Dōngběi fēngwèi dàpái	northeast-style braised ribs	东北风味大排

PINYIN	ENGLISH	CHINESE
Dōngpō ròu	braised fatty pork in small clay pot	东坡肉
é'gān juǎn	goose liver rolls with hoisin sauce	鹅肝卷
gǒubùlǐ bāozi	pork-stuffed bread dumplings	狗不里包子
guōbā yóuyú	squid with crispy fried rice	锅巴鱿鱼
jiàngshāo qiézi	braised eggplant	酱烧茄子
jīngjiàng ròusī	shredded pork with green onion rolled in tofu skin	京酱肉丝
jīnpái tiáoliào	"gold label" sesame sauce (for Mongolian hotpot)	金牌调料
jīròu sèlā	deep-fried chicken pieces with herb dipping sauce	鸡肉色拉
kǎo yáng ròu	roast mutton	烤羊肉
làbā cù	garlic-infused vinegar	腊八醋
láncài ròusōng sìjīdòu	green beans and salty vegetable in lettuce leaf	榄菜肉松四季豆
láncài sìjīdòu	green beans stir-fried with salty vegetable	榄菜四季豆
lǎogānmā shāojī	spicy diced chicken with bamboo and ginger	老干妈烧鸡
làròu dòuyá juǎnbǐng	spicy bacon and bean sprouts in pancakes	腊肉豆芽卷饼
làwèi huájī bǎozǎi fàn	chicken and sweet sausage on rice in clay pot	腊味滑鸡煲仔饭
málà lóngxiā	spicy crayfish	麻辣龙虾
mǐlà luófēiyú	diced deep-fried fish with garlic and hot peppers	米辣罗非鱼
mìzhì zhǐbāo lúyú	paper-wrapped perch and onions on sizzling iron plate	秘制纸包鲈鱼
nóngjiā xiǎochǎo	soybeans, green onion, Chinese chives, and green pepper in a clay pot	农家小炒
qiáo miàn māo ěrduo	"cat's ear" buckwheat pasta with chopped meat	荞面猫耳朵
ròudīng báicài xiànbǐng	meat cabbage pie	肉丁白菜馅饼
shānyào húlu	red bean rolls with mountain herbs	山药葫芦
shēngjiān bāozi	pork-stuffed fried bread dumplings	生煎包子
shǒubā fàn	Uighur-style rice with raisins and mutton	手扒饭
shuǐzhǔ yú	boiled grass carp in spicy broth with numbing peppercorns	水煮鱼

PINYIN	ENGLISH	CHINESE
suànxiāng jīchì	garlic paper-wrapped chicken wings	蒜香鸡翅
tiānfú shāokǎo yángtuǐ	roasted leg of mutton with cumin and chili powder	天福烧烤羊腿
tiěbǎn hēijiāo yuánpái	fake pork patties on a sizzling plate with pepper sauce	铁板黑椒圆排
tǔdòu qiú	deep-fried potato balls with chili sauce	土豆球
xiāngcǎo cuìlà yú	whole fried fish with hot peppers and lemon grass	香草脆辣鱼
xiǎolóng bāozi	pork-stuffed steamed bread dumplings	小笼包子
xièsānxiān shuǐjiǎo	boiled crab dumplings with shrimp and mushrooms	蟹三鲜水饺
yáng ròu chuàn	spicy mutton skewers with cumin	羊肉串
yángyóu mádòufu	mashed soybean with lamb oil	洋油麻豆腐
yánjúxiā	shrimp skewers in rock salt	盐局虾
yì bǎ zhuā	fried wheat cakes	一把抓
yóutiáo niúròu	sliced beef with fried dough in savory sauce	油条牛肉
zhāngchá yā	crispy smoked duck with plum sauce	樟茶鸭
zhá qiéhé	pork-stuffed deep-fried eggplant	炸茄合
zhǐbāo lúyú	paper-wrapped perch in sweet sauce	纸包鲈鱼
zhūròu báicài bāozi	steamed bun stuffed with pork and cabbage	猪肉白菜包子
zhútǒng jī	chicken soup in bamboo vessel	竹筒鸡
zhútǒng zhūròu	steamed pork with coriander	竹筒猪肉
zuìxiā	live shrimp in wine	醉虾

Appendix B:
The Chinese Language

by Peter Neville-Hadley

Chinese is not as difficult a language to learn as it may first appear to be—at least not once you've decided what kind of Chinese to learn. There are six major languages called Chinese. Speakers of each are unintelligible to each other, and there are, in addition, a host of dialects. The Chinese you are likely to hear spoken in your local Chinatown or Chinese restaurant, or used by your friends of Chinese descent when they speak to their parents, is more than likely to be Cantonese, which is the version of Chinese used in Hong Kong and in much of southern China. But the official national language of China is **Mandarin** (**Pǔtōnghuà**—"common speech"), sometimes called Modern Standard Chinese, and viewed in mainland China as the language of administration, of the classics, and of the educated. While throughout much of mainland China people speak their own local flavor of Chinese for everyday communication, they've all been educated in Mandarin which, in general terms, is the language of Běijīng and the north. Mandarin is less well known in Hong Kong and Macau, but it is also spoken in Táiwān and Singapore, and among growing communities of recent immigrants to North America and Europe.

Chinese grammar is considerably more straightforward than those of English or other European languages, even Spanish or Italian. There are no genders, so there is no need to remember long lists of endings for adjectives and to make them agree, with variations according to case. There are no equivalents for the definite and indefinite articles ("the," "a," "an"), so there is no need to make those agree either. Singular and plural nouns are the same. Best of all, verbs cannot be declined. The verb "to be" is *shì*. The same sound also covers "am," "are," "is," "was," "will be," and so on, since there are also no tenses. Instead of past, present, and future, Chinese is more concerned with whether an action is continuing or has been completed, and with the order in which events take place. To make matters of time clear, Chinese depends on simple expressions such as "yesterday," "before," "originally," "next year," and the like. "Tomorrow I go New York," is clear enough, as is "Yesterday I go New York." It's a little more complicated than these brief notes can suggest, but not much.

There are a few sounds in Mandarin that are not used in English (see the rough pronunciation guide below), but the main difficulty for foreigners lies in tones. Most sounds in Mandarin begin with a consonant and end in a vowel (or -n, or -ng), which leaves the language with very few distinct noises compared to English. Originally, one sound equaled one idea and one word. Even now, each of these monosyllables is represented by a single character, but often words have been made by putting two characters together, sometimes both with the same meaning, thus reinforcing one another. The solution to this phonetic poverty is to multiply the available sounds by making them tonal—speaking them at different pitches, thereby giving them different meanings. *Mā* spoken on a high level tone (1st tone) offers a set of possible meanings different from those of *má* spoken with a rising tone (2nd tone), *mǎ* with a dipping then rising tone (3rd tone), or *mà* with an abruptly falling tone (4th tone). There's also a different meaning for the neutral, toneless *ma*.

In the average sentence, context is your friend (there are not many occasions in which the 3rd-tone *mǎ* or "horse" might be mistaken for the 4th-tone *mà* or "grasshopper," for instance), but without tone, there is essentially no meaning. The novice best sing his or her Mandarin very clearly, as Chinese children do— a chanted sing-song can be heard emerging from the windows of primary schools across China. With experience, the student learns to give particular emphasis to the tones on words essential to a sentence's meaning, and to treat the others more lightly. Sadly, most books using modern Romanized Chinese, called *Hànyǔ pīnyīn* ("Hàn language spell-the-sounds"), do not mark the tones, nor do these appear on **pīnyīn** signs in China. But in this book, the authors, most of whom speak Mandarin, have added tones to every Mandarin expression, so you can have a go at saying them for yourself. Where tones do not appear, that's usually because the name of a person or place is already familiar to many readers in an older form of Romanized Chinese such as Wade-Giles or Post Office (in which Běijīng was written misleadingly as Peking); or because it is better known in Cantonese: Sun Yat-sen, or Canton, for instance.

Cantonese has *eight* tones plus the neutral, but its grammatical structure is largely the same, as is that of all versions of Chinese. Even Chinese people who can barely understand each other's speech can at least write to each other, since written forms are similar. Mainland China, with the aim of increasing literacy (or perhaps of distancing the supposedly now thoroughly modern and socialist population from its Confucian heritage), instituted a ham-fisted simplification program in the 1950s, which reduced some characters originally taking 14 strokes of the brush, for instance, to as few as three strokes. Hong Kong, separated from the mainland and under British control until 1997, went its own way, kept the original full-form characters, and invented lots of new ones, too. Nevertheless, many characters remain the same, and some of the simplified forms are merely familiar shorthands for the full-form ones. But however many different meanings for each tone of *ma* there may be, for each meaning there's a different character. This makes the written form a far more successful communication medium than the spoken one, which leads to misunderstandings even between native speakers, who can often be seen sketching characters on their palms during conversation to confirm which one is meant.

The thought of learning 3,000 to 5,000 individual characters (at least 2,500 are needed to read a newspaper) also daunts many beginners. But look carefully at the ones below, and you'll notice many common elements. In fact, a rather limited number of smaller shapes are combined in different ways, much as we combine letters to make words. Admittedly, the characters only offer general hints as to their pronunciation, and that's often misleading—the system is not a phonetic one, so each new Mandarin word has to be learned as both a sound and a shape (or a group of them). But soon it's the similarities among the characters, not their differences, which begin to bother the student. English, a far more subtle language with a far larger vocabulary, and with so many pointless inconsistencies and exceptions to what are laughingly called its rules, is much more of a struggle for the Chinese than Mandarin should be for us.

But no knowledge of the language is needed to get around China, and it's almost of assistance that Chinese take it for granted that outlandish foreigners (that's you and me unless of Chinese descent) can speak not a word (poor things) and must use whatever other limited means we have to communicate—

this book and a phrase book, for instance. For help with navigation to sights, simply point to the characters in this book's map keys. When leaving your hotel, take one of its cards with you, and show it to the taxi driver when you want to return. In section 2, below, is a limited list of useful words and phrases that is best supplemented with a proper phrase book. If you have a Mandarin-speaking friend from the north (Cantonese speakers who know Mandarin as a 2nd language tend to have fairly heavy accents), ask him or her to pronounce the greetings and words of thanks from the list below, so you can repeat after him and practice. While you are as much likely to be laughed *at* as *with* in China, such efforts are always appreciated.

1 A Guide to Pīnyīn Pronunciation

Letters in pīnyīn mostly have the values any English speaker would expect, with the following exceptions:

c *ts* as in bi*ts*

q *ch* as in *ch*in, but much harder and more forward, made with tongue and teeth

r has no true equivalent in English, but the *r* of *r*eed is close, although the tip of the tongue should be near the top of the mouth, and the teeth together

x also has no true equivalent, but is nearest to the *sh* of *sh*eep, although the tongue should be parallel to the roof of the mouth and the teeth together

zh is a soft j, like the *dge* in ju*dge*

The vowels are pronounced roughly as follows:

a as in f*a*ther

e as in *e*rr (*leng* is pronounced as English "lung")

i is pronounced *ee* after most consonants, but after c, ch, r, s, sh, z, and zh is a buzz at the front of the mouth behind closed teeth

o as in s*o*ng

u as in t*oo*

ü is the purer, lips-pursed u of French t*u* and German *ü*. Confusingly, **u** after j, x, q, and y is always ü, but in these cases the accent over "ü" does not appear.

ai sounds like *eye*

ao as in *ou*ch

ei as in h*ay*

ia as in *ya*k

ian sounds like *yen*

iang sounds like *yang*

iu sounds like *you*

ou as in t*oe*

ua as in gu*a*va

ui sounds like *way*

uo sounds like *or,* but is more abrupt

Note that when two or more third-tone "ˇ" sounds follow one another, they should all, except the last, be pronounced as second-tone "´."

2 Mandarin Bare Essentials

GREETINGS & INTRODUCTIONS

ENGLISH	PINYIN	CHINESE
Hello	Nǐ hǎo	你好
How are you?	Nǐ hǎo ma?	你好吗？
Fine. And you?	Wǒ hěn hǎo. Nǐ ne?	我很好你呢？
I'm not too well/things aren't going well	Bù hǎo	不好
What is your name? (very polite)	Nín guì xìng?	您贵姓
My (family) name is . . .	Wǒ xìng . . .	我姓。。。
I'm known as (family, then given name)	Wǒ jiào . . .	我叫。。。
I'm [American]	Wǒ shì [Měiguó] rén	我是美国人
[Australian]	[Àodàlìyà]	澳大利亚
[British]	[Yīngguó]	英国
[Canadian]	[Jiānádà]	加拿大
[Irish]	[Àiěrlán]	爱尔兰
[New Zealander]	[Xīnxīlán]	新西兰
I'm from [America]	Wǒ shì cóng [Měiguó] lái de	我是从美国来的
Excuse me/I'm sorry	Duìbùqǐ	对不起
I don't understand	Wǒ tīng bù dǒng	我听不懂
Thank you	Xièxie nǐ	谢谢你
Correct (yes)	Duì	对
Not correct	Bú duì	不对
No, I don't want	Wǒ bú yào	我不要
Not acceptable	Bù xíng	不行

BASIC QUESTIONS & PROBLEMS

ENGLISH	PINYIN	CHINESE
Excuse me/I'd like to ask	Qǐng wènyíxià	请问一下
Where is . . . ?	. . . zài nǎr?	。。。在哪儿？
How much is . . . ?	. . . duōshǎo qián?	。。。多少钱？
. . . this one?	Zhèi/Zhè ge . . .	这个。。。
. . . that one?	Nèi/Nà ge . . .	那个。。。
Do you have . . . ?	Nǐ yǒu méi yǒu	你有没有。。。？
What time does/is . . . ?	. . . jǐ diǎn?	。。。几点？
What time is it now?	Xiànzài jǐ diǎn?	现在几点？
When is . . . ?	. . . shénme shíhou?	。。。什么时候？
Why?	Wèishénme?	为什么？
Who?	Shéi?	谁？
Is that okay?	Xíng bù xíng?	行不行？
I'm feeling ill	Wǒ shēng bìng le	我生病了

TRAVEL

ENGLISH	PINYIN	CHINESE
luxury (bus, hotel rooms)	háohuá	豪华
high speed (buses, expressways)	gāosù	高速
air-conditioned	kōngtiáo	空调

NUMBERS

Note that more complicated forms of numbers are often used on official documents and receipts to prevent fraud—see how easily one can be changed to two, three, or even ten. Familiar Arabic numerals appear on bank notes, most signs, taxi meters, and other places. Be particularly careful with *four* and *ten,* which sound very alike in many regions—hold up fingers to make sure. Note, too, that *yī,* meaning "one," tends to change its tone all the time depending on what it precedes. Don't worry about this—once you've started talking about money, almost any kind of squeak for "one" will do. Finally note that "two" alters when being used with expressions of quantity.

ENGLISH	PINYIN	CHINESE
zero	líng	零
one	yī	一
two	èr	二
two (of them)	liǎng ge	两个
three	sān	三
four	sì	四
five	wǔ	五
six	liù	六
seven	qī	七
eight	bā	八
nine	jiǔ	九
10	shí	十
11	shí yī	十一
12	shí èr	十二
21	èr shí yī	二十一
22	èr shí èr	二十二
51	wǔ shí yī	五十一
100	yì bǎi	一百
101	yì bǎi líng yī	一百零一
110	yì bǎi yī (shí)	一百一（十）
111	yì bǎi yī shí yī	一百一十一
1,000	yì qiān	一千
1,500	yì qiān wǔ (bǎi)	一千五百
5,678	wǔ qiān liù bǎi qī shí bāi	五千六百七十八
10,000	yí wàn	一万

MONEY

The word *yuán* (¥) is rarely spoken, nor is *jiǎo,* the written form for ¹/₁₀ of a *yuán,* equivalent to 10 *fēn* (there are 100 *fēn* in a *yuán*). Instead, the Chinese speak of "pieces of money," *kuài qián,* usually abbreviated just to *kuài,* and they speak of *máo* for ¹/₁₀ of a *kuài. Fēn* have been overtaken by inflation and are almost useless. Often all zeros after the last whole number are simply omitted, along with *kuài qián,* which is taken as read, especially in direct reply to the question *duōshǎo qián*—"How much?"

ENGLISH	PINYIN	CHINESE
¥1	yí kuài qián	一块钱
¥2	liǎng kuài qián	两块钱
¥0.30	sān máo qián	三毛钱

ENGLISH	PINYIN	CHINESE
¥5.05	wǔ kuài líng wǔ fēn	五块零五分
¥5.50	wǔ kuài wǔ	五块五
¥550	wǔ bǎi wǔ shí kuài	五百五十块
¥5,500	wǔ qiān wǔ bǎi kuài	五千五百块
Small change	língqián	零钱

BANKING & SHOPPING

ENGLISH	PINYIN	CHINESE
I want to change money (foreign exchange)	Wǒ xiǎng huàn qián	我想换钱
credit card	Xìnyòng kǎ	信用卡
traveler's check	lǔxíng zhīpiào	旅行支票
department store	bǎihuò shāngdiàn	百货商店
	gòuwù zhōngxīn	购物中心
convenience store	xiǎomàibù	小卖部
market	shìchǎng	市场
May I have a look?	Wǒ Kànyíxia, hǎo ma?	我看一下，好吗？
I want to buy . . .	Wǒ xiǎng mǎi . . .	我想买。。。
How many do you want?	Nǐ yào jǐ ge?	你要几个？
Two of them	liǎng ge	两个
Three of them	sān ge	三个
1 kilo (2.2 lb.)	yì gōngjīn	一公斤
Half a kilo	yì jīn	一斤
	or bàn gōngjīn	公斤
1 meter (3¼ ft.)	yì mǐ	一米
Too expensive!	Tài guì le!	太贵了
Do you have change?	Yǒu língqián ma?	有零钱吗

TIME

ENGLISH	PINYIN	CHINESE
morning	shàngwǔ	上午
afternoon	xiàwǔ	下午
evening	wǎnshang	晚上
8:20am	shàngwǔ bā diǎn èr shí fēn	上午八点二十分
9:30am	shàngwǔ jiǔ diǎn bàn	上午九点半
noon	zhōngwǔ	中午
4:15pm	xiàwǔ sì diǎn yí kè	下午四点一刻
midnight	wǔ yè	午夜
1 hour	yí ge xiǎoshí	一个小时
8 hours	bā ge xiǎoshí	八个小时
today	jīntiān	今天
yesterday	zuótiān	昨天
tomorrow	míngtiān	明天
Monday	Xīngqī yī	星期一
Tuesday	Xīngqī èr	星期二
Wednesday	Xīngqī sān	星期三
Thursday	Xīngqī sì	星期四
Friday	Xīngqī wǔ	星期五
Saturday	Xīngqī liù	星期六
Sunday	Xīngqī tiān	星期天

TRANSPORT

ENGLISH	PINYIN	CHINESE
I want to go to . . .	Wǒ xiǎng qù . . .	我想去。。。
plane	fēijī	飞机
train	huǒchē	火车
bus	gōnggòng qìchē	公共汽车
long-distance bus	chángtú qìchē	长途汽车
taxi	chūzū chē	出租车
airport	fēijīchǎng	飞机场
stop or station (bus or train)	zhàn	站
(plane/train/bus) ticket	piào	票

NAVIGATION

ENGLISH	PINYIN	CHINESE
North	Běi	北
South	Nán	南
East	Dōng	东
West	Xī	西
Turn left	zuǒ guǎi	左拐
Turn right	yòu guǎi	右拐
Go straight on	yìzhí zǒu	一直走
crossroads	shízì lùkǒu	十字路口
10 kilometers	shí gōnglǐ	十公里
I'm lost	Wǒ diū le	我丢了

HOTEL

ENGLISH	PINYIN	CHINESE
How many days?	Zhù jǐ tiān?	住几天？
standard room (twin or double with private bathroom)	biāozhǔn jiān	标准间
passport	hùzhào	护照
deposit	yājīn	押金
I want to check out	Wǒ tuì fáng	我退房

RESTAURANT

ENGLISH	PINYIN	CHINESE
How many people?	Jǐ wèi?	几位
waiter/waitress	fúwùyuán	服务员
menu	càidān	菜单
I'm vegetarian	Wǒ shì chī sù de	我是吃素的
Do you have . . . ?	Yǒu méi yǒu . . . ?	有没有。。。？
Please bring a portion of . . .	Qǐng lái yí fènr . . .	请来一份儿。。。
beer	píjiǔ	啤酒
mineral water	kuàngquán shuǐ	矿泉水
Bill, please	jiézhàng	结帐

SIGNS

Here's a list of common signs and notices to help you identify what you are looking for, from restaurants to condiments, and to help you choose the right door
at the public toilets. These are the simplified characters in everyday use in
China, but note that it's increasingly fashionable for larger businesses and for
those with a long history to use more complicated traditional characters, so not
all may match what's below. Also, very old restaurants and temples across China
tend to write their signs from right to left.

ENGLISH	PINYIN	CHINESE
hotel	bīnguǎn	宾馆
	dàjiǔdiàn	大酒店
	jiǔdiàn	酒店
	fàndiàn	饭店
restaurant	fànguǎn	饭馆
	jiǔdiàn	酒店
	jiǔjiā	酒家
vinegar	cù	醋
soya sauce	Jiàngyóu	酱油
bar	jiǔbā	酒吧
Internet bar	wǎngbā	网吧
cafe	kāfēiguǎn	咖啡馆
teahouse	cháguǎn	茶馆
department store	bǎihuò shāngdiàn	百货商店
	gòuwù zhōngxīn	购物中心
market	shìchǎng	市场
bookstore	shūdiàn	书店
police (Public Security Bureau)	gōng'ānjú	公安局
Bank of China	Zhōngguó Yínháng	中国银行
public telephone	gōngyòng diànhuà	公用电话
public toilet	gōngyòng cèsuǒ	公用厕所
male	nán	男
female	nǚ	女
entrance	rùkǒu	入口
exit	chūkǒu	出口
bus stop/station	qìchē zhàn	汽车站
long-distance bus station	chángtú qìchē zhàn	长途汽车站
luxury	háohuá	豪华
using highway	gāosù	高速
railway station	huǒchē zhàn	火车站
hard seat	yìng zuò	硬座
soft seat	ruǎn zuò	软座
hard sleeper	yìng wò	硬卧
soft sleeper	ruǎn wò	软卧
metro/subway station	dìtiě zhàn	地铁站
airport	fēijīchǎng	飞机场

ENGLISH	PINYIN	CHINESE
dock/wharf	mǎtóu	码头
passenger terminal (bus, boat, and so on)	kèyùn zhàn	客运站
up/get on	shàng	上
down/get off	xià	下
ticket hall	shòupiào tīng	售票厅
ticket office	shòupiào chù	售票处
left-luggage office	xíngli jìcún chù	行李寄存处
temple	sì	寺
	miào	庙
museum	bówùguǎn	博物馆
memorial hall	jìniànguǎn	纪念馆
park	gōngyuán	公园
hospital	yīyuàn	医院
clinic	zhěnsuǒ	诊所
pharmacy	yàofáng/yàodiàn	药房/药店
travel agency	lǚxíngshè	旅行社

Index

See also Accommodations and Restaurant indexes, below.

ACCOMMODATIONS